Adaptive Security and Cyber Assurance for Risk-Based Decision Making

Tyson T. Brooks
Syracuse University, USA

A volume in the Advances in Systems Analysis,
Software Engineering, and High Performance
Computing (ASASEHPC) Book Series

Published in the United States of America by
IGI Global
Engineering Science Reference (an imprint of IGI Global)
701 E. Chocolate Avenue
Hershey PA, USA 17033
Tel: 717-533-8845
Fax: 717-533-8661
E-mail: cust@igi-global.com
Web site: http://www.igi-global.com

Library of Congress Cataloging-in-Publication Data

Names: Brooks, Tyson T., author.
Title: Adaptive security and cyber assurance for risk-based decision making
    / by Tyson T. Brooks.
Description: Hershey, PA : Engineering Science Reference, [2023] | Includes
    bibliographical references and index. | Summary: "This book explores
    adaptive security techniques through CyberAssurance for risk-based
    decision making in the context of software-based systems and discusses
    ways to achieve it. It identifies a discipline termed CyberAssurance,
    which considers the interactions of assurance-enhancing technology,
    system architecture, and the development life cycle. It looks at
    trust-enhancing technology in some detail, articulating a strategy based
    on three main prongs: building software that behaves securely
    (high-confidence design techniques), executing software in a protected
    environment (containment), and monitoring software execution for
    malicious behavior (detection). Applying these three prongs in
    combination in the proper architectural and life cycle contexts provides
    the best risk strategy methods for increasing our trust in
    software-based for Internet of Things (IoT), Cloud, and Edge systems"--
    Provided by publisher.
Identifiers: LCCN 2022041695 (print) | LCCN 2022041696 (ebook) | ISBN
    9781668477663 (h/c) | ISBN 9781668477670 (s/c) | ISBN 9781668477687
    (eISBN)
Subjects: LCSH: Computer networks--Security measures. | Management
    information systems--Security measures. | Computer crimes--Risk
    assessment. | Adaptive computing systems.
Classification: LCC TK5105.59 .B77 2023 (print) | LCC TK5105.59 (ebook) |
    DDC 005.8--dc23/eng/20221115
LC record available at https://lccn.loc.gov/2022041695
LC ebook record available at https://lccn.loc.gov/2022041696

This book is published in the IGI Global book series Advances in Systems Analysis, Software Engineering, and High Performance Computing (ASASEHPC) (ISSN: 2327-3453; eISSN: 2327-3461)

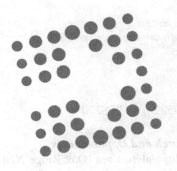

Advances in Systems Analysis, Software Engineering, and High Performance Computing (ASASEHPC) Book Series

Vijayan Sugumaran
Oakland University, USA

ISSN:2327-3453
EISSN:2327-3461

MISSION

The theory and practice of computing applications and distributed systems has emerged as one of the key areas of research driving innovations in business, engineering, and science. The fields of software engineering, systems analysis, and high performance computing offer a wide range of applications and solutions in solving computational problems for any modern organization.

The **Advances in Systems Analysis, Software Engineering, and High Performance Computing (ASASEHPC) Book Series** brings together research in the areas of distributed computing, systems and software engineering, high performance computing, and service science. This collection of publications is useful for academics, researchers, and practitioners seeking the latest practices and knowledge in this field.

COVERAGE

- Distributed Cloud Computing
- Computer Graphics
- Parallel Architectures
- Computer System Analysis
- Metadata and Semantic Web
- Human-Computer Interaction
- Performance Modelling
- Software Engineering
- Enterprise Information Systems
- Storage Systems

IGI Global is currently accepting manuscripts for publication within this series. To submit a proposal for a volume in this series, please contact our Acquisition Editors at acquisitions@igi-global.com or visit: https://www.igi-global.com/publish/.

Titles in this Series

For a list of additional titles in this series, please visit:
https://www.igi-global.com/book-series/advances-systems-analysis-software-engineering/73689

Quantum Computing and Quantum Cryptography in Future Computers
Bhawana Rudra (National Institute of Technology, Karnataka, India)
Engineering Science Reference • ©2023 • 300pp • H/C (ISBN: 9781799895220) • US $270.00

Developing Linear Algebra Codes on Modern Processors Emerging Research and Opportunities
Sandra Catalán Pallarés (Universidad Complutense de Madrid, Spain) Pedro Valero-Lara (Oak Ridge National Laboratory, USA) Leonel Antonio Toledo Díaz (Barcelona Supercomputing Center, Spain) and Rocío Carratalá Sáez (Universidad de Valladolid, Spain)
Engineering Science Reference • ©2023 • 266pp • H/C (ISBN: 9781799870821) • US $215.00

New Approaches to Data Analytics and Internet of Things Through Digital Twin
P. Karthikeyan (National Chung Cheng University, Chiayi, Taiwan) Polinpapilinho F. Katina (University of South Carolina Upstate, USA) and S.P. Anandaraj (Presidency University, India)
Engineering Science Reference • ©2023 • 307pp • H/C (ISBN: 9781668457221) • US $270.00

Futuristic Trends for Sustainable Development and Sustainable Ecosystems
Fernando Ortiz-Rodriguez (Tamaulipas Autonomous University, Mexico) Sanju Tiwari (Tamaulipas Autonomous University, Mexico) Sailesh Iyer (Rai University, India) and José Melchor Medina-Quintero (Tamaulipas Autonomous University, Mexico)
Engineering Science Reference • ©2022 • 320pp • H/C (ISBN: 9781668442258) • US $270.00

Emerging Technologies for Innovation Management in the Software Industry
Varun Gupta (Universidad de Alcalá, Madrid, Spain) and Chetna Gupta (Jaypee Institute of Information Technology, Noida, India)
Engineering Science Reference • ©2022 • 282pp • H/C (ISBN: 9781799890591) • US $270.00

Technology Road Mapping for Quantum Computing and Engineering
Brojo Kishore Mishra (GIET University, India)
Engineering Science Reference • ©2022 • 243pp • H/C (ISBN: 9781799891833) • US $250.00

Designing User Interfaces With a Data Science Approach
Abhijit Narayanrao Banubakode (MET Institute of Computer Science, India) Ganesh Dattatray Bhutkar (Vishwakarma Institute of Technology, India) Yohannes Kurniawan (Bina Nusantara University, Indonesia) and Chhaya Santosh Gosavi (MKSSS's Cummins College of Engineering, India)
Engineering Science Reference • ©2022 • 325pp • H/C (ISBN: 9781799891215) • US $270.00

701 East Chocolate Avenue, Hershey, PA 17033, USA
Tel: 717-533-8845 x100 • Fax: 717-533-8661
E-Mail: cust@igi-global.com • www.igi-global.com

I would first like to give honor to my Lord and Savior Jesus Christ whom all my blessing and strength come from in my life. To my parents, my dad [the late] F. Burrell Brooks and my mom, W. Michelle Brooks for all their love, encouragement, and guidance over my life. An extra special thanks to the loves of my life - my wife Lisa and children, Tyson Jr., and Taylor, for always supporting and loving me in whatever initiative 'keeps me in the basement on the computer'. In addition, I would like to thank all my other family members and professional colleagues for all the continued support, love, and prayers in all my professional endeavors.

Table of Contents

Preface

OVERVIEW

Risk management of security operations should allow management to balance the operational and economic costs of protective measures and mitigations strategies to achieve gains in capabilities by protecting an organization's network and its data. A risk-based approach to secure networking ensures improved corporate governance and transparency of decision-making through managing risks that threaten the ongoing sustainability of the overall security architecture. To formulate improved and more informed risk management decisions, the discipline of "risk-based decision analysis" to capture data that is relevant to risk management decisions and to interpret the meaning of that data for the decision-makers, with respect to those decisions, is pertinent.

A risk management decision analysis approach provides a more accurate approximation of the consequence, likelihood, impact, and overall risk and uses both qualitative and quantitative methodologies to yield more accurate analysis, if the availability and quality of the inputs are appropriate. Using a risk management decision analysis process that is faithful to the "observations" as described by the input data, sound in its transformation of input data to analytical results and provides a straightforward interpretation of those results in a format that helps decision-makers gain meaningful insights; with respect to the risk management decisions that will be facing an organizations network.

All decision making within an organizations' security architecture, whatever the level of importance and significance, involves the explicit consideration of risks and the application of risk management to some appropriate degree. For security risk management to be successfully integrated into the fabric of security operations, defensive cyber operations (DCO) capabilities areas and zones, it must become a fundamental aspect of how the networks routinely operate. Since risk management is the process of identifying risk, assessing risk, and taking steps to reduce risk to an acceptable level, the management of the network ought to include a foundation for effective risk management, containing the practical guidance necessary for assessing and mitigating potential risks.

Risk can be defined as the probabilistic measurement of the likelihood that an adversary threat will initiate an attack (e.g., physical and/or cyber) with an estimate of the impact (e.g., harm) based on intent, capability and targeting. Through a future uncertain event or condition, risk, if materialized, results in an outcome contributing towards a negative impact that can be expected to result in harmful consequences against operations, individuals, systems, etc. which can be measured through a level of uncertainty (Walley, 1996). Risks to networks and devices has to take into consideration the probabilities of the likelihood of a given adversary threat-source exercising particular potential vulnerabilities through some form of attack and the resulting negative impact(s) of those adverse events. The level of impact is governed by the potential operational impacts and in turn produces a relative value for the criticality and sensitivity of the network system components and data.

Probabilistic risk determinations provide a more comprehensive enterprise-wide concept that encompasses a better-reasoned understanding of the nature of uncertainty that the network will face. Standard risk assessment decision analysis techniques call for the development of a probabilistic value that an attack will be attempted [e.g., $p(attempt)$], the likelihood of success [e.g., $p(success|attempt)$] and adversary's probability of success [e.g., $p(success)$] leading to an expected value of harm [e.g., $v(harm)$]. A probability is a function of time and resources (e.g., skills, technology, money, and manpower). Probability of attempt, p(attempt), involves the likelihood of a payoff, the likelihood of harm to the adversary, and the resources expended. The probability of attempt includes a psychological aspect that attempts to estimate the adversary's perception of our ability to detect their attack, our ability to attribute their attack, and our ability to retaliate. The probability of success, $p(success)$, identifies the probability of an adversary successfully completing the attack; while the probability of success given attempt, $p(success|attempt)$, measures the likelihood that an attack will succeed using available time and resources. The expected value of harm, v(harm), determines the value to the adversary of the harm caused by related consequences to the loss of confidentiality, integrity, or availability characteristics of data.

These probabilistic determinations require subject matter experts (SME) assistance in understanding the capabilities and behaviors of our adversaries and it is recommended that this data is elicited directly (e.g., SMEs estimates, customer input, preference functions from decision-makers, etc.) by consulting with SME attack analysts, adversary analysts, mitigation analysts and/or information assurance/network defense security experts. An improved understanding of the nature of risk facilitates more informed decision-making, increases the ability to exploit opportunities and minimizes the harm against the network.

Risks are inherent in all decisions and efforts of an organizations operational network. Therefore, understanding risk is an essential element of successful security operations decision-making. Probabilistic risk determinations identified for risk management decision analysis is viewed as central to the network management processes; such that risks will be considered in terms of properly identifying the effects of uncertainty on security operations objectives. The governance structure and process are based on supporting the management of risk and effective risk management is regarded by senior managers as essential for the achievement of the overall organizational objectives.

Cybersecurity is fond of bragging that, "as far as we know, no adversary has ever exploited communications because of a failure in our risk management processes". Clever design and finely honed risk assurance techniques, which allow us to guarantee the ability of our security equipment to perform as expected have historically enabled us to produce products, which our customers can trust. Over the years we have optimized and codified our assurance methodology to catch even minute flaws in a system design. Constant change, however, in both technology and in the environment in which we must do business have inexorably eroded the foundations on which we built trust in the past. Today's Information Assurance (IA) systems consist increasingly of software components, performing functions of varying degrees of criticality, coming to us from diverse sources and development settings. We find ourselves forced to rely on technology we do not trust.

The target audience for this book is for those currently working in the cybersecurity and risk management fields looking to explore adaptive security techniques through CyberAssurance for risk-based decision making in the context of software-based systems and discusses ways to achieve it. It identifies a discipline termed CyberAssurance, which considers the interactions of assurance-enhancing technology, system architecture, and the development life cycle. It looks at trust-enhancing technology in some detail, articulating a strategy based on three main prongs: building software that behaves securely (high-confidence design techniques), executing software in a protected environment (containment), and monitoring software execution for malicious behavior (detection). Applying these three prongs in combination in the proper architectural and life cycle contexts provides the best risk strategy methods for increasing our trust in software-based for Internet of Things (IoT), Cloud, and Edge systems.

The mission of cyber defenders is as monumental as it is unprecedented: protect vital systems from millions of ongoing attacks while simultaneously fortifying those systems against future 5/6G IoT un-realized threats. Adding to the complexity are demands from industry leaders to deepen the nation's connectedness to a vast online world where national boundaries often are left unguarded, bystanders become unwitting accomplices, and adversaries hide behind everything from popular software to social networks. The pressing imperative to react quickly to these constant attacks makes it difficult to find the time and resources needed to build capabilities focused on anticipating future threats before they result in costly systems damage or information leakage.

ATTACKER APAPTATION FOR DEFENSIVE MEASURES

Cyber-professionals recognize that some defensive measures could exacerbate cyber-defense challenges by motivating attackers to adapt — unintentionally inspiring attackers to develop more potent and resil-ient capabilities. This book focuses on the role cyber-assurance for decision-making plays in spurring cyber-attack modifications, especially with respect to IoT/Cloud/Edge computing systems. While the need to react to today's attacks will likely persist indefinitely, this book aims to begin helping organiza-tions with its wealth of tacit knowledge, deep expertise, and sophisticated capabilities into establishing more anticipative defensive postures. The stakes could not be higher: developing a structured lens for constructing smarter, more anticipative defensive strategies could be the difference between more ef-fectively influencing the opportunity space for tomorrow's would-be attackers and remaining locked in a cyber "arms race" that plays to the advantage of nimble, decentralized adversaries.

Recognizing the complexity of the cyber-attack space and the need for a coordinated defensive strat-egy, this book aims to provide the leaders with an analytic decision-making lens for understanding and surfacing defensive patterns against software-based cyber-attacks. First, this book identifies the concept of CyberAssurance for assessing systemic influencers shaping cyber-attacks — the enablers, constraints, and actors that collectively make up the attack ecosystem. Next, it identifies a structured approach to understanding attacker motivations in order to identify attacker operational priorities —where attackers are most likely to adapt in response to defensive measures.

Together, these frameworks for understanding the cyber-attack ecosystem and attacker motivations contributed to the development of the R2FS framework. This framework is organized into four categories, each analyzed according to the following structure:

1. **Recognition**- the identification of a cyber-attack being performed leading to the fortification of smart devices before gaining access to IoT networks and systems.
2. **Fortification** - to apply automatic embedded network protection techniques in smart devices for protecting IoT devices and networks during a cyber-attack.
3. **Reestablishment** - a means to return the devices to its operational condition after a cyber-attack through remapping to a different network route from the attack.
4. **Survivability** - the capability of an entity to continue its mission even in the presence of cyber-attacks, internal failures, or accidents.

Going forward, organizations could use this taxonomy in its efforts to systematize its knowledge of attacker adaptation in response to defensive measures, e.g., by building computational, rule-based models designed to anticipate the kinds of adaptation outlined in this book. Armed with a shared analytic lens for understanding attacker adaptation, analysts and researchers will be better equipped to anticipate and prepare for attacker adaptation. Ultimately, this preparedness can lead to quicker and more effective responses to cyber threats, as well as a heightened ability to shape the cyber-attack arena through intentional and future-oriented defensive strategies.

ORGANIZATION OF THE BOOK

The book is organized into ten chapters. A brief description of each of the chapters follows:

Chapter 1 identifies the concept of cyber-assurance as a means of internet of things smart devices and networks providing the opportunity of automatically securing themselves against security threats. This chapter looks at this concept as a means to provide embedded security within these IoT devices to allow these new networks to operate correctly even when subjected to a cyber-attack.

Chapter 2 reviews the importance of risk management as an informal reference guide to information security personnel involved in making risk management decisions. This chapter provides introductory information on basic risk and risk management concepts as it applies to information systems. It also provides a useful common reference in supporting the remaining chapters in this book.

Chapter 3 provides information on the three major elements of risk (vulnerability, threat, and mission impact) and how threat information is often the most elusive to obtain. This chapter provides a basic, introduction and reference to general threats to information systems and serves as a starting point for analysts to better understand the threats aligned against their critical information infrastructures.

Chapter 4 discusses impact of value function variability in value-focused models to compare different alternatives in terms of their overall value for achieving a top-level objective. This chapter discusses two additional sources of variability that can also significantly influence the final decision accuracy pertaining to building a software-based system and provides a methodology for estimating and reducing the magnitude of these effects on the final decision for building the system.

Chapter 5 addresses swing weight development for computing platforms using a swing weight technique for determining weighting factors indirectly through systematic comparison of attributes against the one deemed to be the most important. This chapter presents a new procedure to elicit from a decision-maker information regarding additive value weights and uses the maximum entropy methodology to demonstrate how to construct a set of additive value weights based solely on the elicited information.

Chapter 6 presents utility curves for decision-making for computing platforms for constructing a best probability model, based only upon the information revealed by observations and using the maximum entropy method. This chapter develops two types of utility curves, each based on a one of two no-preference rules and the types of utility functions encountered in trade-off design.

Chapter 7 provides attack adaptation patterns for defensive operations by the creation of a framework to better understanding the opportunity space for attackers and affect how attacks evolve over time. The chapter looks at an ecosystem framework, which informs the attack adaptation taxonomy and factors into an attacker's decision to pursue a particular adaptation strategy when confronted with disruptive defensive measures.

Chapter 8 analyses intelligence modeling for cyber-physical systems. The chapter looks at Internet of Things network information flows pertaining to cyber-physical systems platforms in achieving the integration of various security controls. This chapter also introduces a new model for cyber-attack defense modeling required to address cyber-physical attacks.

Chapter 9 presents probability elicitation and an examination for large Bayesian networks to either aid decision-making or provide a descriptive model of behavior. This chapter discusses Bayesian networks and how they describe and visualize in a compact graphical form the probabilistic relationships between variables of interest.

Chapter 10 concludes with modeling parameters and techniques for risk modeling. The chapter discusses attack/defense modeling parameters, Cyber-Assurance metrics, and Cyber-Assurance for risk-based decision-making.

Tyson Brooks
Syracuse University, USA

Acknowledgment

The author would like to acknowledge the assistance of the faculty at the Syracuse University School of Information Studies (iSchool) and the College of Engineering and Computer Science. Without their support, this book would not have become a reality. The author would like to acknowledge the valuable contributions of the reviewers regarding the improvement of quality, coherence, and content presentation of chapters.

Chapter 1
Cyber–Assurance

ABSTRACT

Assurance is a measure of confidence in a system based upon a composition of its trust, correctness, integrity, security, and reliability. Cyber-assurance is defined as a means of internet of things (IoT) smart devices and networks providing the opportunity of automatically securing themselves against security threats; the concept of cyber-assurance must provide embedded security within these IoT devices to allow these new networks to operate correctly even when subjected to a cyber-attack. Assurance is the evidence, which convinces us that an above-defined property holds. Techniques such as testing, disciplined development, formal methods, and others to build up evidence for each of these desired properties. This chapter defines trust as confidence based on the available evidentiary mechanisms that the software that will behave reliably and correctly while maintaining the integrity and security of itself and the system in which it is embedded. An assurance strategy is a plan for how to provide the evidence that a system merits our trust.

INTRODUCTION

The internet of things (IoT) refers to the network or networks encompassing the use of standard Internet Protocol (IP) technologies to connect people, processes, and things to enable new cyber-physical systems (Brooks, 2020). Whereas previously, the Internet has generally been understood as comprising a network of computers, the adoption of mobile, embedded sensors and other technologies is expanding this definition to include people and objects outfitted or embedded with smart sensors (Brooks, 2017). As this trend grows over time with improved technology and less expensive hardware, the number of connected "objects" will trend toward all-encompassing devices, sensors, instrumentation, mobile and fixed assets and people. Cyber-assurance, the justified confidence that networked systems are adequately secure to meet operational needs under a cyber-attack, is required for IoT devices and networks (Brooks & Park, 2016).

Reactions to the cyber-assurance dilemma range across the spectrum from denial-refusal to use software components for high-assurance applications, to defeatism-abdication of quality control of any kind because it all seems too hard (Brooks, 2017). While the former is merely unrealistic, the latter is irresponsible.

DOI: 10.4018/978-1-6684-7766-3.ch001

Edge-based systems for the IoT are here; it now falls to us to develop a cyber-assurance methodology to enable us to use them safely (Brooks, 2017). Fail-safe design, redundancy, tamper-detection were all once new ideas that, once embraced, radically changed both evaluation and development. A mature assurance model for Edge-based systems will require both new tools and new practices (Cao et al., 2020).

Edge computing constitutes a new concept in the computing landscape as the technology brings the service and utilities of cloud computing closer to the end user and is characterized by fast processing and quick application response time (Wang et al., 2020). Edge computing refers to locating applications – and the general-purpose compute, storage and associated switching and control functions needed to run them – relatively close to end users and/or IoT endpoints (Want et al., 2020). This greatly benefits applications performance and associated quality of experience (QoE) and it can also improve efficiency and thus the economics depending on the nature of the specific application. Edge computing is also important for localization of data and efficient data processing. Industry and Government regulations may require localization of data for security and privacy reasons. Certain application scenarios may pose restrictions on the use of excessive transport bandwidth or may require transport to external sites to be scheduled by time-of-day, requiring local storage or caching of information. Additionally, there may need to be local processing of information to reduce the volume of traffic over transport resources.

As the cyber mission has evolved to encompass the availability, integrity, authentication, confidentiality and non-repudiation requirements of information systems, a solution set has arisen to accomplish that mission which relies on elements of protection, detection and response. Our software trust strategy must be similarly multidimensional. While prevention is clearly the best cure, in practice, achieving the desired level of trust in a system containing software will require active components, mainly containment and detection, to compensate for what can't engineered into protection (Weyns, 2020).

So how can we trust software...? Very carefully! Every aspect of the software life cycle must be considered against an adversary threat model to determine what opportunities for attacker and defender exist. In this chapter, we will examine the life cycle and point out risks and mitigation strategies. We will suggest a model of the architecture design space, based on three axes corresponding to our technology prongs, i.e., assured development techniques, containment and monitoring. We will look at a specific example and see how it exploits those prongs to build a trusted IoT system containing some untrusted components. Finally, we'll offer some recommendations for implementation, now and in the future. It seems clear that, even with a small investment, cybersecurity can take advantage now of already available, cost-effective technologies and processes to achieve higher degrees of trust in current developments while continuing research to address more problematic gaps.

Assurance is a measure of our confidence in a system based upon a composition of its trust, correctness, integrity, security and reliability. Cyber-Assurance is defined as a means of IoT smart devices and networks providing the opportunity of automatically securing themselves against security threats; the concept of cyber-assurance must provide embedded security within these IoT devices to allow these new networks to operate correctly even when subjected to a cyber-attack (Brooks, 2020). First let's state some definitions to use in defining assurance in the context of the Edge environment.

· If our computers could talk to us about how well they were performing they might say, "I compute correctly," to indicate that their programming delivers the intended functionality, i.e., what it was specified and designed to do. We define correctness to be the property that the software works as specified when executed.

- If computer were to say, "I compute with integrity," it would mean that its software has not been modified and thus will continue to do as intended. Integrity can be defined as the property that no undetected or unauthorized modification of the software has occurred.
- If the computer could say, "I compute securely," it would mean that it does not do "wrong things" with the resources entrusted to it. Traditionally these bad behaviors fall into three categories: unauthorized modification, unauthorized disclosure and denial of service. We define security to be the property that the software does only what it is supposed to and neither permits unauthorized actions nor prevents authorized actions.
- When our computer states, "I compute reliably," it means that most of the time it will execute accurately. We therefore define reliability to be the probability that the software will run as required without failure for a given period.

Given this definition of trust, for any development we must determine both the appropriate amount of trust needed to satisfy our requirements and the appropriate means for assessing its presence. The Common Criteria[1], with its protection profiles, security targets and evaluation assessment levels (EAL), provides one roadmap to follow in choosing and building secure software products. Rating Maintenance Phase (RAMP), Trusted Product Evaluation Program (TPEP) and other programs have also attempted to gauge the trustworthiness of software[2]. Criteria-based techniques, however, give us a sense of trust based on a single snapshot in time and may not reflect the operational environment in which the software exists. We must do more than just measure the evidence emerging from our software development techniques. We must also practice diligence in assessing and maintaining assurances through detection and containment techniques applied during operation of our system. With this combination of assurances and diligence, software can be used more safely in security systems.

Trust, of course, does not have to be all or nothing, it merely must be sufficient. We can practice cyber-assurance engineering and analyze our applications to determine how much trust to strive for in each component. Security-critical and integrity-critical software should be developed to be highly trusted; those applications that do not affect the secure behavior of the system need not be developed to as high a standard of trust (Weyns, 2020). That said, even with careful analysis, it may not be easy to determine a priori whether and which software will have a security impact. As part of the assurance-engineering phase, therefore, containment and detection mechanisms must be designed into the architecture to mitigate any residual risk, which can't be eliminated through high-confidence design and development.

While not impossible, achieving trust is not an easy task. The developer, the evaluator, the user and the defender/attacker will each define adequate trust according to his subjective frame of reference. Security engineers must balance conflicting goals of assurance, functionality, ease of use, cost and time to delivery (Wu et al. 2016). A goal of this chapter is to broaden the knowledge of the tools and techniques, which are available to those performing this task.

WHY IS THE EDGE HARD TO ASSURE?

Edge computing (EC), also known as Mobile Edge Computing, based IoT is a rapidly developing paradigm to providing geographically distributed computing and storage resources to smart devices and applications at the edge of the network (Li et al., 2018). By allowing high-volume data generated by a massive amount of networked smart devices (e.g., mobile devices, self-driving cars and fitness trackers)

Figure 1. The typical structure of an Edge Computing topology

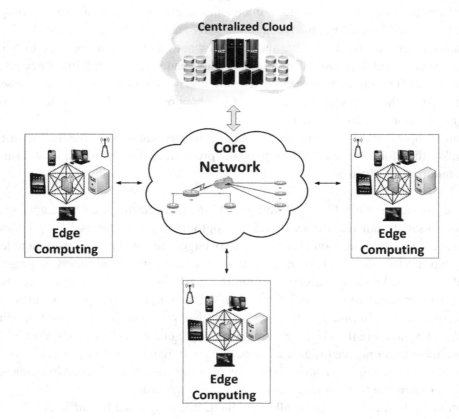

in modern IoT systems to be processed at the edge, it promises to greatly reduce the network stress on the core networks of mobile service providers (Li et al., 2018). Acting as the first line of defense for high-volume IoT data, EC infrastructures allow performing computationally intensive data processing tasks such as data filtering, as well as persistence of raw data at the edge and, at times, transmit significantly lesser amounts of data at lower frequencies to the cloud environments for further analytics (Tran, et al., 2017). This data accumulated at the edge of the network inherently creates a distributed topology of data silos across different EC environments (see Figure 1).

In modern IoT systems, machine learning (ML) based predictive analytics becomes popular to solve challenging problems and uncover new patterns for people and enterprises alike. However, as to the use of EC in modern IoT systems, the distributedness of data sources it introduces and complex communication topologies with which these EC environments are linked to each other make existing predictive analytics strategies obsolete in such a context (Hu et al., 2015). For example, most traditional ML strategies designed for existing cloud-based IoT systems demand the data to be accumulated centrally (Abeysekara, et al., 2019). This undisputedly defies the goals of EC as it causes significant stress on the core mobile networks due to the data generated in large volumes by the IoT devices. This calls for efficient and scalable ML strategies that not only fit into a distributed setting, but also can perform atop high-volume data (Abeysekara, et al., 2019).

In addition, most ML strategies proposed for IoT systems assume that the data generated by sensor service providers and consumers across the entire network can be represented by a single distribution. As a result, they often hypothesize that a single global prediction model can represent the characteristics of the underlying application domain (e.g., a global trust prediction model used by self-driving cars to predict trustworthiness of all IoT services). This one-size always- fits-all approach based on independent and identically distributed (IID) assumptions of the data is often restrictive in EC-based IoT systems (Abeysekara, et al., 2019). For instance, the heterogeneity of sensor service providers and consumers taking part in transactions can potentially result in datasets with distinct characteristics (i.e., non-IID) in different EC-environments (Abeysekara, et al., 2019). Hence, there is an apparent need for strategies that allow training high-quality decentralized local models that fit into the nature and structure of each distributed datasets accumulated across different EC environments. Furthermore, some EC environments can accumulate data from sensor service providers and consumers with similar configurations and characteristics, thereby producing similarly poised prediction models that may not necessary be trusted.

Thomas Edison encouraged us not to give up when searching for solutions because even 'when we think that we have exhausted all possibilities, we really haven't'[3]. In the context of software this admonition can be rephrased as "When you think you have exhaustively removed all possibilities for error, remember this, you haven't." To trust software, we need to know that it works, that it does not do anything other than what it was developed to do, that it has not been changed and that its environment protects it from undue influences.

Any assurance strategy for Edge-based systems must have to change or compensate for:

· Shoddy design and documentation practices. Software developers do not routinely maintain a disciplined development process. Errors, whether accidental or intentional, may be introduced that might not be discovered until it is too late.
· Monolithic and overly complex software systems, which exceed the capabilities of current analysis and testing techniques to evaluate. Even simple software routines can be difficult to test; developers often rely on vastly inadequate techniques to verify correct behavior of large systems. Complexity creates serious challenges in foreseeing the interactions of large numbers of components.
· Uncontrolled changes during the development life cycle. Software's greatest advantage - its ability to be easily modified whether in development or in the field - also gives rise to its greatest weakness. Since it can be changed so easily, opportunities exist throughout its life cycle to replace crucial pieces of software with corrupted or untrustworthy code.
· The complex environment (e.g., hardware and operating system [OS]) required to host software. For example, the Windows 10 operating system, for example, includes millions of lines of code, which contain many known and unknown bugs. An untrustworthy computing environment can undermine hard-won trust in the application software.
· Poor choices in implementation. Determining the trust of systems composed of components of varying trust levels is an active area of research. Trusted components can be used poorly and result in weak systems; untrusted components may be used judiciously to good effect. Analysis of the system and good implementation are key. Nonetheless, not only do we increasingly rely on systems constructed from numerous components, but also often, those systems are both dynamic and distributed. These characteristics can dramatically increase the complexity of the trust equation.

Design flaws affect our ability to trust software in several ways (Tsui et al., 2022). Clearly, mistakes degrade system correctness, integrity and reliability, but, less obviously, they also provide opportunities, which an adversary can exploit to cause insecure or untrustworthy behavior. Inadequate protection during construction, delivery, storage and operation may allow opportunities for sabotage and subsequent loss of trust (Tsui et al., 2022. Deliberate acts of sabotage are not, however, necessary if the software contains flaws, which permit security breaches. Regardless of the way flaws may be introduced, they serve to undermine our trust in the software.

The shortcomings highlighted above are not insurmountable and they should certainly not be summoned up as an argument for abandoning trust technology altogether. Tackling them will require both technologically- and policy-based tools. Fortunately, many improvements are available now, which can bolster our confidence in Edge-based systems. Let us begin our discussion of remedies by exploring the sorts of technology in our solution set. With that background, we can examine the software life cycle and identify opportunities to mitigate the vulnerabilities inherent in it.

DEALING WITH ASSURANCE IN COMPLEX IOT SYSTEMS

Cyber-Assurance engineering is system engineering with a twist. We can think of it as the analysis, which must be performed and the architecture that will thereby be developed to achieve the level of trust we desire. The trust engineer must shape the design of the system with a cyber-assurance strategy in mind, parceling out functionality and controlling component interaction astutely, to minimize risks in both its execution and its development. High-confidence design, containment and monitoring comprise the three technological prongs of our approach to cyber-assurance engineering.

High-confidence design methods remain our greatest hope in building future systems and should be applied where possible in today's sensitive applications. While, in the past, systems may have been simple enough to support a build and evaluate model, it is increasingly difficult to verify the correctness of today's IoT systems after the fact. High-confidence design methods are to assurance as prevention is to health. Following the wisdom that some diseases are preventable but incurable, they seek to build in correctness from the beginning.

Another problem more commonly encountered in developing systems for sensitive IoT applications today than in the past is that the values of the commercial marketplace often drive choices with a significant impact on assurance. Cost, schedule, vendor profitability, interoperability—we can probably think of dozens of constraints, which dilute our control over system development. As we attempt to deliver increased functionality and availability at lower cost, even the most sensitive applications may contain mostly commercial off-the-shelf (COTS) components of unknown trustworthiness. In this situation, it could be wisest to rebuild self-contained, critical components using high-confidence design techniques while using alternative trust-building approaches to increase our confidence in the system.

Our second prong evolves from an old computer security doctrine called least privilege. This commonsense design approach decomposes a task into elementary sub-tasks and then grants to each sub-task only the minimum capabilities necessary for it to do its job (Tsui et al., 2022). Many software exploits take advantage of using excessive privilege, so enforcement of least privilege can be a powerful deterrent. This approach depends, of course, upon our ability to isolate and contain the behavior of each sub-task. To continue our medical metaphor, containment is a sort of virtual quarantine; it allows us to limit the damage, which unintended or harmful actions can have on our system.

Monitoring, diagnosing malicious activities in our system, if you will, is a third technique, which can help us build trust. Cybersecurity organizations have used various forms of monitoring for decades in the design of cryptographic equipment. Duplication and checking, for example, is a standard technique for verifying the correct continued operation of critical hardware functions. Other common forms of monitoring in cryptographic systems include check words and known-answer tests. Present-day forms of monitoring developed to help detect unusual or suspicious behavior in computer systems include such techniques as anomaly detection and profiling. As a secondary line of defense, monitoring has a long history of contributing to our trust in critical systems.

High-Confidence Architecture

As most security professionals know, the application of verification and validation techniques after the fact is both prohibitively expensive and generally inconclusive. We must conclude that, if post hoc analysis cannot be relied upon, trust must be built into software from the outset. We will gain assurance using high-confidence design techniques, which provide an appropriate starting point for developing trusted systems.

From the perspective of assured system design the core of the software problem is that we attempt to build systems whose complexity exceeds our intellectual ability to understand it. Cyber organizations Specware and Programmatica tool development projects, along with other system development environments such as B-Method, Eiffel, CafeOBJ, Esterel and Maude, attempt to correct this imbalance through a software development approach called correct by construction (Bordis et al. 2022). Correct-by-construction techniques attempt to reason about the specification of a problem and then automate the construction of a solution based upon that specification (Runge et al. 2022). They seek to balance traditional software engineering approaches for complex systems with the mathematical formalisms needed to verify security properties across entire systems. Since these techniques must be both mathematically precise and highly usable in practice, they must be intelligent tools with knowledge of the semantics of the problem domain and of the target programming language. By decreasing human involvement in writing actual code, they should function to ensure that the software behaves as intended, to make software easier and faster to produce, to increase the quality of the finished product and to enable software to adapt to changing requirements and environments. These techniques will help software engineers to achieve trusted designs during the early part of the development life cycle and to reduce the burdensome cost of certifying the security of complex information systems.

In addition to correct-by-construction techniques, we are also pursuing techniques intended to improve the efficacy of software testing during development. Several techniques originally developed for formal verification, Java program verification, for one, hold promise for improving current testing practice. Formal verification techniques are most useful when specific expert knowledge can be applied with high pay-off potential. One such area is in the analysis of reactive and concurrent systems, where testing is problematic because it is difficult to predict and exercise all possible system interactions. In concurrent systems many processes occur in parallel in an unpredictable and overlapping fashion, while in reactive systems processes maintain an ongoing and complex relationship with their environment. Model checking appears a promising approach in the analysis of concurrent programs. This mathematically based technique analyzes the behavior of complex algorithms by representing the paths a process can take as transitions of a set of finite state machines. Examination of the state transition system of the machines quickly reveals undesired or unexpected behavior. With its extremely efficient search procedures, model checking can scale to handle systems with more than 10120 reachable states. Model checkers can thus be used to augment testing in cases where the complexity of the software logic would overwhelm traditional approaches. Other tools available to improve software testing include SPARK examiner, SPADE Simplifier, Spin, SteP, ESC/Java and Verisoft.

The usability of current high-confidence techniques is a legitimate concern, which hinders their widespread adoption. General-purpose languages have no syntax with which to specify the behaviors of interest to us, nor to enforce or enable desired properties (for example turning fault tolerance mode on and off). Current technologies often require that desired behavior be tediously and repeatedly built into each application domain and into each application. Consequently, the software development and software assurance processes are often conducted as separate and even conflicting activities. The creation of an integrated combination of logically precise, automated mechanisms that focus on the elimination of sources of error and on the early detection and correction of errors that arise is in great demand. In response to these needs, we have research underway to identify ways in which high-confidence techniques can be integrated into standard software life cycle tools and practices. One example of this approach is the incorporation of security-relevant knowledge into design tool environments and methodologies so that the resulting products can benefit from this information as they are developed. To address the usability issue, we have embarked on research to reduce the need for manual and labor-intensive analysis through improved automated deduction and to improve ease-of-use via domain-specific implementations of high-confidence techniques.

For example, High-confidence Cryptographic Service Providers (HCCSP) could exemplify our emphasis on refining tools through experimentation and engineering—attacking realistic problems to demonstrate the efficiency and effectiveness of our technology and, in the process, producing software reference implementations using high-confidence design techniques (Ma, 2022). The methodologies that could emerge from a HCCSP would enable cryptographic experts to construct and configure high-confidence cryptographic software without needing to possess a deep understanding of the underlying assurance technologies. By developing a methodology for producing high-grade cryptographic services in a repeatable, high-confidence manner, HCCSP would make available reusable, high-confidence reference implementations of numerous cryptographic services including signing and verifying, digest and hash generation and encryption and decryption functions. Specific HCCSP deliverables, for instance, a Cryptol cryptographic programming language, could address cryptographic interoperability requirements.

CONTAINMENT

Since it is unlikely that we can build IoT systems whose components are 100 percent trustworthy, it is only prudent to try to limit the impact of improper software behavior, whether malicious or not. Toward this end, a robust computing environment, which can contain the ill effects of errant code, is desirable. Operating system security kernels, type enforcement, mandatory access controls, trusted paths, virtual machines and other techniques should be considered in our arsenal of containment technology.

Containment as a security technique is not new; castle and prison designers have practiced the basics of this approach for hundreds of years. The fundamental idea is simple - create a space where the arbitrary actions of your adversary have little or no effect on your important activities. Medieval castle designers chose to construct a small, safe, self-sufficient space wherein critical functions, such as government, could take place protected from the outside world — the same design approach used in many modern

Communication security (COMSEC) devices. Today's prison designers take the opposite tack, using the secure space instead to confine and limit the resources of dangerous individuals so that they cannot affect the world outside the space. This latter design approach is used in many general-purpose secure computing situations (e.g., JAVA sandbox). Both approaches build barriers between the trusted and the untrusted and both require essentially the same design tradeoffs.

All effective containment approaches depend upon complete isolation. Somewhere within our Edge-based system we must find some trusted mechanism which can enforce the separation of components (Cao et al., 2020). Luckily, we do not have to gain trust in all the underlying software, only a small layer near the hardware (e.g., an operating system security kernel). Alternatively, we can use separate hardware for trusted and untrusted operations and depend upon our ability to gain trust in the relatively simple hardware interfaces that implement the separation we desire (e.g., air gaps or NRL's data pump, which implements a one-way data transfer path) (Kang et al.,1997).

Strictly speaking, containment works best when absolute separation is the desired result. In most real-world situations, controlled movement among the "separate" domains is what is desired. This additional requirement significantly complicates matters because it adds ambiguity (i.e., keep things separate except when they need to come together). Further, it introduces the additional problem of having to check all data movement between domains to prevent either pollution of the trusted space or unauthorized removal of valuables from it. In these situations, firewalls, guards and operating system protection measures can help. All these techniques, however, are limited by our ability to clearly articulate the rules of movement and to check for and detect contraband. If we can focus on very small, well-defined domains (fine-grained protection), stating the rules clearly becomes simpler and the contraband checks will be more likely to be effective.

The primary challenge in designing containment mechanisms comes in balancing granularity of protection against ease of use and cost. Fine-grained controls are better at preventing collusion and limiting damage, but they tend to have a greater impact on performance and are more complicated to set up and maintain. Coarse granularity protection shifts more responsibility for trust to the entities, which we wish to isolate, but because there are many fewer access decisions, the controls are more efficient and easier to set up and maintain.

Cyber Organizations research on the containment problem has examined how to build flexible controls, which can support movement between domains and provide appropriate contraband checks, all at an acceptable cost. Research work in high-speed firewall technology (e.g., SONET Network Interface Unit and ATM firewall) as well as ongoing research in secure operating systems (e.g., Security-enhanced Linux) and secure distributed computing provide the system security designer with many useful building blocks (Tsui, 2022). In situations where it is desirable or necessary to execute suspicious software, virtual machine technology can provide a "sandboxed" environment capable of constraining aberrant behavior. With the use of one-way data pumps, to move data into the sandbox and sanitizing filters, to export data from the sandbox, we have a way to gain trust in a system, which includes untrusted components. Cyber Organizations BoxTop implements the ideas just described and is successfully used to process data and execute software programs whose pedigree precludes their direct introduction into operational systems. While research continues to add to this set of tools, existing containment technologies, when combined in appropriate architectures with the other trust approaches outlined in this chapter, can enhance the trust of systems containing untrusted software. Such systems should pose a significantly greater challenge to our adversaries than would otherwise be the case.

MONITORING

No truly robust security solution should depend solely upon using prevention or containment techniques. Well-engineered solutions will usually include some detection component to sound the alarm in case the protective walls are breached. Currently there are two primary approaches to detecting malicious code. The first is to examine the code for malicious content and the second is to study the code's behavior. Neither of these strategies is foolproof, the drawbacks of the former have been discussed earlier and the infeasibility of exhaustively testing complex software presents an obstacle to the latter, which should explain our emphasis on high-confidence design and containment techniques. There is value in recognizing a problem as quickly as possible when it occurs and there are some tools at our disposal.

Some limited types of code analysis technology are presently available and improved technology is under development. Current tools generally rely on a catalog of known patterns to detect malicious code, as for example, virus scanners. Techniques under development include identifying common practices of malicious code writers to produce a more robust tool and comparing the structure of suspect code to benign similar applications (e.g., compare a new web browser with a known version of Chrome). Since these techniques depend upon programmer behavior patterns rather than on attributes of the program itself, the effectiveness of the techniques is reduced if they are made public. An attacker could adapt his techniques to avoid detection, although probably at some performance, space, or stealth penalty.

High-quality checksums represent a technique, which can be useful in detecting post-production code modification attacks. Checksums, i.e., calculated values, which capture the state of a computer file at a given point in time, are simple, readily available and effective. They can provide a trusted signature to be stored and verified against as needed to ensure the continued integrity of software. A checksum-based approach relies upon our having had confidence in the code at some point in time (for example, just prior to shipment), the availability of a high-confidence signature checker and the ability to protect the checksum itself from adversary modification.

If errors in or modifications to software cannot be caught before deployment, measures which can detect an attack in progress are the next best thing. Some tools have been demonstrated to be quite effective and efficient at monitoring and detecting apparent malicious behavior as it happens (Wardle, 2022; Chysi, 2022). These types of tools depend upon our ability to characterize intended system behavior, either by specifying normal behavior or by identifying normal behavior through observation. Once a baseline for normalcy is established, subsequent observations which deviate from what is expected can be flagged for further investigation. This technique can be quite effective for simple, single-purpose programs (e.g., daemons, simple servers, etc.), although the specification or training efforts can be difficult. Since behavior profiling methods require constant monitoring if they are to be kept up to date, employing them incurs a small but unavoidable performance penalty. It is not uncommon for detection and containment techniques to require similar technical mechanisms. Frequently, the only difference between containment and detection is whether to allow an access or merely to log it in some manner.

STRATEGIES FOR ACHIEVING VARYING DEGREES OF TRUST

So, how does one gain trust in IoT Edge-based systems? Ideally, as much as possible of the software in the system would be carefully designed and implemented using processes that minimize error and prevent subversion. To bridge the assurance gap formed when we cannot apply high-confidence design techniques to gain the necessary assurance, we will compensate with clever application of containment and monitoring techniques: containment to limit the damage that untrusted software might cause and monitoring to inform us as the damage occurs. It should be remembered that these techniques are not some sort of magic whitewash which can be applied by unskilled laborers to cover over problems caused by shoddy development practices. Rather, they must be viewed as complementary techniques chosen and applied by the skilled artisans whom we call trust engineers.

The three complementary trust techniques discussed so far - assurance, containment and monitoring — need to be used together to achieve the levels of trust required in a system. Up to this point we have examined the techniques separately but said little about how they would work together operationally. A natural question arises regarding what portions of the trust space are acceptable for any given system. Does it make sense to have highly assured software running in an environment with little containment and with no monitoring? Why take the risk? Can we use software for which we have no evidence of trustworthiness? With strict containment and for non-security related functions, perhaps. Unfortunately, there is no cookbook to consult in making these decisions. With an understanding of where our system falls in the trust cube and the wisdom and experience we have obtained in designing traditional systems, we can make judgments about where we need to be. We can then determine a strategy to move the system to safer regions using improved assurance, stricter containment and heightened monitoring.

ASSURANCE ENGINEERING EXAMPLE – SECURE REMOTE ACCESS

To illustrate the application of assurance engineering to system architecture, let us consider a specific generic example. Users in the commercial sector alike share the desire for secure remote access. A typical application might see a laptop computer used as the platform to allow access to and protect data communicated to and from remote locations across unprotected IoT channels and to secure data on local storage devices when the machine is shut down. For reasons of functionality and of cost, commodity software and hardware could be the components of choice for such a system.

A commodity solution to the remote access problem would likely employ an Intel Pentium-based laptop computer with a Microsoft Windows 10 operating system (OS). This approach could provide communications encryption using Window's IPSec capability and storage encryption using the native Encrypting File System (EFS). Functionally, the requirements for secure remote access would be met; however, our ability to obtain a high degree of trust in this solution would not be as certain. Achieving trust in our all-commercial solution is quite problematic. The requirement to satisfy the user's expectations for look and feel through commercial off-the-shelf (COTS) software directly conflicts with our need for assurance that the system will indeed provide the needed security. Even if we trust EFS and IPSec to do their jobs properly, especially questionable is the ability of our all-COTS system to protect itself from malicious elements, such as viruses, in the environment in which it will be deployed.

In the end, responsibility for the integrity of the application ultimately falls to the OS. OSs are intended to provide controlled access to all system resources, thereby assuring that data is not communicated, modified, or destroyed without proper authorization. An OS should also ensure that critical security functionality, such as encryption, cannot be bypassed or caused to operate incorrectly. It should provide this protection even in the presence of computer viruses or other malicious code. Unfortunately, commodity operating systems do not now have the robustness to provide the protection we require for our remote access solution. Today's computer-literate user is very aware of the vulnerability of his Windows-based computing environment to the email viruses, web viruses, etc., which commonly afflict commodity software. We must therefore seek another way to gain the trust we require.

As the first step in our assurance engineering of this solution, we need to cordon off the security-critical functions (i.e., communications encryption and media encryption) from the user's untrustworthy operating environment (i.e., Windows 10 OS). Our plan will be to use the containment prong of our methodology to isolate and protect the security functions from any malicious activity in the user environment. In the past, we ensured the integrity of security functions by implementing them in hardware, so that they could not be corrupted by untrusted software and by constructing the architecture of the system to prevent them from being bypassed. While separate hardware for security is certainly possible, it has drawbacks, including high cost, inflexibility and inconvenience (e.g., size, weight, power, etc.) which make it undesirable for our remote access solution.

As an alternative isolation approach, we propose the use of a Virtual Machine Monitor (VMM). By creating multiple abstract representations of the host computer processor hardware, a VMM effectively gives us discrete machines within the machine. Type II VMMs, those which operate in conjunction with an underlying operating system, have recently become commercially available for Intel x86-based computers and provide several isolation/containment capabilities which are useful for a remote access solution: 1.) We can implement our communications security function in a special purpose virtual machine whose only task is IPSec encryption. The small size and limited functionality of this VM will simplify validation. The fact that this VM will not be used to run any user applications software will protect it from subversion by common virus infections and other malicious code. 2.) This IPSec VM can be connected serially with the end-user VM and the isolation properties of the VMM can prevent the encryption function from being bypassed. 3.) The Host OS can provide another layer of protection to our architecture using its access control mechanisms. With an appropriate security policy, such as is available from the Security Enhanced Linux OS, we can enforce the hardware configuration of the virtual machines and their in-line network connectivity in the face of operator errors and even some flaws in the VMM.

By using a virtual machine architecture, we have obtained the following trust-enhancing characteristics:

- The end user VM can run any appropriate commercial or open-source software.
- Communications encryption is isolated in a small, special-purpose VM
- The end-user environment software cannot affect the encryption VM
- The encryption VM does not run any (potentially malicious) user software
- The encryption VM function cannot be bypassed

Next, consider the protection required for data at rest – media encryption. Since a Type II VMM is used, disk I/O performed in a VM is intercepted and performed by the Host OS. In addition to isolating VM's from each other, the VMM also isolates each VM from the Host OS. We can take advantage of this isolation by performing disk encryption within the Host OS transparent to all the VM's. In order to protect the integrity of the Host OS, no user applications software (e.g., mail, web browser, news, etc.) is allowed to run on it; furthermore, the Host OS can be configured so that it has no addressable networking TCP/IP stack and so is effectively invisible to network attackers.

Once again, the use of a Type II VMM has allowed us to obtain additional trust-enhancing characteristics, including:

- Host OS disk encryption is invisible to every VM
- Host OS disk encryption cannot be affected or bypassed by malicious VMs
- Host OS integrity is enhanced by eliminating execution of user software
- Host OS integrity is enhanced by making it invisible from the network.

With our remote access architecture fortified by separation mechanisms, we can turn our attention to another prong of our assurance engineering methodology – high-confidence design. The approach we have selected requires the following assurances:

- The VMM/Host OS combination must guarantee isolation among VMs and Host OS. The IPSec VM must perform encryption properly
- The Host OS must guarantee that the IPSec encryption cannot be bypassed. The Host OS must perform media encryption properly

While obtaining these assurances is a challenge, it is a substantially smaller one than that posed by our only commercial solution. In the latter case, it would be necessary to perform the verification of a large, complex, monolithic system composed of a commercial OS and all the applications software. Compounding the problem, we would also need assurance that any future applications software and OS upgrades would remain secure—a potentially unbounded task! Using our compartmentalized approach, only the end-user environment is subject to frequent change or upgrade and those changes do not require re-evaluation of other system components. The approaches we choose for providing the needed guarantees may vary from formal methods-based design/development to rigorous analysis and red-teaming attack. Various high-confidence design techniques may be selectively applied according to the specific property requiring assurance. As an example, the correct operation of the VMM depends critically upon the correct translation of a small set of privileged processor instructions. The nature of the translation operation lends itself to formal design and verification techniques. Insisting on this degree of design rigor might well be appropriate during this time.

Having applied the design and containment prongs of our assurance engineering methodology, we can turn our attention to the monitoring prong to see how it can be used to increase trust. One form of monitoring which has grown rapidly in popularity is the personal firewall. A firewall can monitor traffic flowing into and out of the remote access workstation. If we observe unexpected addressees or data formats, the firewall can discard the traffic, alert the user, or take some other appropriate action. We can exploit the capabilities of the VMM architecture to locate our firewall within the shelter of its own dedicated virtual machine, adding a simple and effective protective measure. We can also use the Host OS to monitor system activity relating to virtual hard drives and virtual I/O devices. By monitoring write activity to critical files of any of the virtual machines, we could detect anomalous and possibly malicious, activity. For example, a virus executing in the end-user virtual machine could be detected and thwarted if it attempted to destroy critical system files. Additional development work would be required to provide this new capability, but it could be provided if warranted. Finally, to add some measure of failure protection to the system, a simple plug-in card could be added to provide a "watch dog" function. With this example we conclude the discussion of assurance engineering in system architecture design. It is now time to think about it in the context of system development.

Cyber-Assurance Engineering the Lifecycle

Somewhere within the software life cycle— analysis, design, coding, testing, deployment and operation, lie all our opportunities for obtaining the assurance we seek. Each individual stage of the cycle poses unique problems, some technological, some practical, which we can address with the proper combination of process, people and technology measures. The secure remote access example above focuses on the outer stages, i.e., design and operation, probably the most clearly visible phases of the cycle. In what follows we'll look more closely at the inner stages as well and examine some of the openings we have for inserting trust-enhancing practices.

As our willingness to accept software of diverse provenance grows, the probability of deliberate sabotage becomes ever greater as well. The insider threat exists in all phases of the life cycle of software and it remains particularly difficult to eliminate. An insider with access to a system during any part of its development could introduce faults and undocumented features. Insider threat mitigation should include process and doctrine measures that emphasize individual accountability and increase the insider's risk of being discovered. Checks and balances should be implemented which increase the need for the insider to collude with others to be successful and/or infiltrate multiple development phases, thereby increasing his risk of discovery. As we examine the life cycle, we should consider the damage a malicious adversary can do, but we should not fail to remember that if software continues to be produced with unintentional faults, insiders are not necessary to breach system defenses. Our analysis will therefore treat the vulnerabilities stemming from both deliberate and inadvertent practices.

The following Table 1 summarizes the life-cycle phases we'll discuss below:

Table 1. Edge Life Cycle Revisited

Software Phase	Definition	Examples: Unintended shortcomings; adversary behavior	Example Mitigation Strategies
Analysis & Design	From Initial Idea to Design Specifications	Incomplete requirements or design leading to unintended behavior; subtly alter system specifications to create a flaw	· Construct adversary threat model · Trust Engineer up front · Lay groundwork for configuration control Intelligent design tools · Design quality analysis
Code	From the Initial Prototypes to Code	Implementation errors; insert code into dead code areas.	· Defensive programming · Automated code generation · Programming best practices · Traceability of code to specs · Accountability management
Test	From Integration & Test to Final Build	Failure to run sufficient Test cases; modify test procedures to ignore the effects or presence of the malicious software	· Specification-based testing · Logic analysis · Behavior analysis · Finite-state analysis · Diagnosis
Deployment	From packaging to installing on site	Incorrect installation settings for given environment; replace software en route to destination and use.	· Acceptance Testing Signature techniques Tamper protection · Controlled compilation
Operation	From Initial Delivery to Final Destruction and Replacement	Bypassing security to expedite; operational work; alter and access code in place through electronic connectivity; infiltrate during routine maintenance.	· Containment and Detection · Tight Configuration Control · Maintenance integrity strategy

ANALYSIS PHASE

Experience has shown the near impossibility of retrofitting security after a system development is completed: Obviously, a mature architectural framework may not accommodate security afterthoughts; more subtly, late design changes generally result in poor documentation and will decrease the correspondence between requirements and implementation, undermining our trust in the system. Most fundamental for this section of the paper, however, is the recognition that life-cycle attacks occur during the development of a system and that that is when they must be addressed. Before one begins to design any information security system, therefore, one must consider and preferably document what sets of threats the system is expected to encounter and counter. This threat analysis should explore both adversary intent and adversary opportunity. A thoughtful threat analysis will yield the framework for assessing and maintaining trust through the various stages of the life cycle. Once the threat model is defined, the trust engineer can put into practice the ideas discussed earlier in the paper: defining which elements of the system are security-critical and require rigorous design and development, deciding how to build containment and detection elements into the system to add defensive layers, scoping out the logistics of development and shaping the environment to make it difficult for an adversary to mount life-cycle attacks.

DESIGN AND CODE

Recall from our earlier definition of trust that we seek sufficient evidence for the correctness, integrity, security and reliability of our software. The software engineering community at large shares our interests in correctness and reliability and we can profit from the tools those interests have generated. While not irrelevant to the outside, security and integrity are our concerns. Fortunately, it turns out that many tools and practices developed with correctness or maintainability in mind can help build confidence in the security and integrity of our software as well. Getting greatest value from those techniques requires that we lay some groundwork early in the design of our system.

Attacks on the early stages of the life cycle involve corrupting the specifications to include malicious functionality and introducing code, which is not in compliance with the specs. These are the actions of people, so one strategy to prevent such attacks is to get the humans out of the equation. In fact, tools exist to automate several aspects of the design and coding phases of the life cycle (Tsui et al., 2022). Requirements capture and traceability tools enable developers to state the desired functionality of the system in constrained terms. Specification tools can take the formal requirements, which emerge from that process and provide input for code-generation tools. If this sort of design methodology is followed, humans have much less opportunity to inject themselves into the process. A second means of deterring the malicious insider comes through increasing accountability. If formal requirements capture has been done, tools exist which can analyze the relationship between specifications and software modules. Such an analysis could help find code with no specified purpose, for instance. The design phase is also the time to implement a framework for configuration management. Configuration management tools keep track of the system as it evolves, generating an audit trail linking changes to specific people. Design reviews, peer critiques, structured walkthroughs—all subject the system plan to increase and valuable scrutiny.

It is desirable and quite possible to get some idea of how the system will behave before any coding takes place. Quality analysis tools, as for example, McCabe Associates' Battlemap[4] and Intellect[5], can characterize the complexity of the design, identify inefficiencies and redundancies and provide insight into expected performance. When the development paradigm does not allow us to write programmers out of the story, it is still possible to gain some assurance by implementing practices, which heighten accuracy, clarity and integrity. Defensive programming tools, which enforce good coding style, can help catch common mistakes like buffer overflows and uninitialized variables. Reusing code wherever possible makes the debugger's job that much simpler. In some cases, we may be able to complement our attempts to increase accuracy with techniques, which compensate for its absence. One such approach is fault-tolerant design—logic devised to detect unexpected/unacceptable outcomes caused by faults and then re-direct processing through backup logic.

Clarity in coding generally leads to greater accuracy, but significantly, for our special interests, it also lightens the evaluator's burden. Industry standard best practices such as structured programming, object-oriented design and modularity make it more difficult to hide malicious routines. Less complex software will also be easier to analyze and test. In addition to using the accountability tools which configuration management provides, we can consider building into the code at this time detection and containment defenses of integrity, which will not be invoked until the system is operating. Proof-carrying code (PCC), code which carries along with-it verifiable assertions about its functionality, can be useful when integrity needs to be checked on the fly, such as for mobile code (Necula, 1997). Another real-time verifier is the execution monitor, a technique for assessing whether code is behaving as expected by watching the order in which instructions fire. If we must use untrusted code of unknown robustness, we can probably help it withstand some attacks by wrapping it in a trusted software filter to shield it from malicious input (the castle keep model of our containment prong).

TESTING

Typically, the difficulty of making trust decisions increases when available evidence is not recorded during development. However, some of the assurance, which emerges from the design and coding phase lies in intangibles like clarity, there, is hard evidence to be gathered as well. Metrics on complexity, records of who has touched the software and when, a map of the correspondence between requirements and code, are examples of evidence, which could be required of developers. Another important and often overlooked deliverable, which should follow from the design and coding phase, is documentation of testing requirements. The testing phase can bolster our sense of confidence in the system only if we feel we have covered the unknowns well. Some of the design tools described in the section above possess mechanisms to allow us to capture that sense of what it will be important to test and using them can help us generate good test plans.

There are two main categories of testing: Static testing methods focus on the code itself, while dynamic testing affords insight into the way the software behaves within its operational environment. Today's static analyzers can process some 10,000 lines of code per minute, reporting on modularity, cyclomatic complexity and areas of dead or lightly used code, inter alia. A dynamic tester attempts to exercise software through the tasks and situations it will likely encounter. Using such a tool requires the creation of a profile, which captures the desired scenarios and temporal parameters. An example of this dynamic approach would be the practice known in reliability testing as operational profile testing. In this procedure, software is treated as a black box and failure data gathered by running enough operational tests to estimate the software's reliability and to assign a quantitative degree of confidence to that estimate.

Clearly, we are in the most favorable situation when development is under our control and we have requirements, specifications, documentation and source code to match up against the software we are testing. In that situation, we can take advantage of automated testing tools to match those artifacts against behavior. Unfortunately, there are times when code is dropped on our doorstep. In that case we can amass some assurance through diagnostic testing—by running the software in a heavily instrumented sandbox and watching its behavior, for instance, or by analysis using dynamic reverse engineering techniques. If we have a good relationship with the vendor we can study and red team the source code until we are, satisfied we have done everything possible and then place the code in virtual escrow.

While we cannot anticipate all the possibilities that lead to insecure behavior, testing goes, a long way toward providing evidence needed to trust software. Testing artifacts should be configuration-controlled along with other software development evidence for later use in making trust decisions. Standard practice should require this kind of data for GOTS. In addition, the Common Criteria should be used to enforce these requirements more generally, especially for software intended for the higher EAL levels. Process has a big impact on the effectiveness of testing. Test plans need to be written, followed and test results should be reported and maintained as part of the overall process.

DEPLOYMENT PHASE

Deploying software to production environments requires the safe delivery of the software to operational sites, the controlled installation of the software and verification that the software is ready for use. The opportunities for subversion in delivery are the stuff of which spy novels are made; to thwart them we need the means to ensure that the software we so laboriously analyzed in the previous phases is the software which gets installed. Methods of making tampering evident include protective packaging, digital signature techniques and digital watermarking. Protective packaging helps to deter interference during shipping and storage when an adversary might attempt to swap our version of the software for his. Digital signatures and digital watermarking are both ways of enabling the software to carry evidence of its authenticity, evidence which can persist even after the software has been installed. Briefly, the digital signature is akin to a checksum on the software, but it is protected and authenticated through cryptography.

As with a checksum, any changes to the software will cause the digital signature to become invalid. Further, recomputing the signature and binding it to the software requires an authorized key. Digital watermarking falls within the more general field of steganography, i.e., hiding information. Here some sequence of bits is buried within the software in a way only known to the legitimate developer/customer. A watermark reinforces integrity in two ways: only genuine software will contain it and unauthorized changes to the software may destroy it. Last, if we are very worried about the possibility of a malicious insider in the software house itself, we may choose to compile the software ourselves following extensive analysis of the source code.

Not all vulnerabilities in this phase derive from malicious intent, of course. After installation, maintaining our trust in software requires that users and administrators be trained regarding proper operation and handling. Automated tools to identify mistakes in the installation of software are available and should be used.

OPERATION PHASE

Operation is the culmination of our assurance engineering exercise, when we will see whether the safeguards, we have built into the system can handle the threats the system encounters, but it is also the beginning of a long period of vigilance and maintenance for which a plan is essential. The discovery of anomalies and the installation of new versions (where version means a group of error fixes and/or additional functionality) continue through the life of the system. During operation the detection components built into the system will begin to sense the errors and attacks for which they were intended. Seamless functionality will require a well-conceived strategy for responding to these events.

The inevitable, deliberate changes made to the system over its lifetime provide ongoing opportunities for insecure behavior to be introduced, either intentionally (subverting the source/delivery of the product or directly influencing the maintainer) or unintentionally (unforeseen interactions with the rest of the software product or system). This maintenance portion of the software lifecycle has been reported in the past to consume 50% of the resources of software during its existence, but unfortunately, it is most often treated as a secondary life-cycle activity, from its planning and funding to the execution of necessary activities (Farroha & Farroha, 2014).

While during development, it might have been possible to require that a new evaluation of the entire system accompany any changes, once the system is in operation such a strategy becomes impractical. Evaluation in the maintenance context will more often consist of an attempt to pinpoint the impact of changes to the system.

Programs such as the Common Criteria and the UK's Certificate Maintenance Scheme (CMS) have wrestled with how to preserve the integrity of a software product in the maintenance phase (Matheu-Garcia et al. 2019). From their experiences we can abstract a few dos and don'ts:

1. Step 1: Do plan for software security maintenance by creating an integrated logistic support plan at program inception—consider that the experts who developed the system will rarely be available for or interested in menial maintenance chores; documentation, such as that emerging from a mature development process, is essential.
2. Step 2: Don't let the fox in the henhouse—a failing of CMS was a lack of independence between maintainers and certifiers, with one single entity, the vendor, responsible for maintenance re-engineering and security evaluation.
3. Step 3: Wherever possible, reuse certified software, evaluation techniques, documentation, tools, etc.

Beyond the accidental errors addressed by the above, maintenance activity also provides a particularly attractive setting for a malicious adversary. Long periods of trouble-free operation tend to lower the guard of system caretakers. To facilitate updates, it is not unusual for system security controls to be deactivated and unknown and unvetted personnel to be brought on site to perform specialized functions. Procedures and doctrine should heighten awareness of such threats and dictate how and when to permit maintenance to occur. Appropriate version and configuration controls should also exist so that the system can be rolled back to a previous secure state if necessary.

THE IDEAL TRUSTED EDGE

What might the ideal trusted Edge look like to us? First, cleared people in a secure environment would have built it. Secondly, a mature repeatable, documented software engineering process would have been used, to include:

- A requirements specifications and analysis phase based on something like protection profiles accomplished using mathematics and formal modeling for completeness and correctness where appropriate.
  Simple, modular and fault-tolerant designs. Designs modeled and analyzed with respect to trust requirements (security policy, etc.).
- Automated code development used and code proven correct. Reused software wherever possible
- Statistically significant testing completed verifying specified functionality, including developer and independent tester-based test scenarios.
- Operational testing done as well.
- System level integration testing completed demonstrating reliability targets met.
- The user would have accepted the software after a demonstration assuring him of proper functionality, reliability and robustness.

Third, a mature, qualified, independent evaluation would have approved the software based on the best NIAP capability augmented with a thorough C group style security evaluation[6]. Available to the evaluators would be:

- Processes, software products and technologies used.
- Metrics on functional correctness, completeness, reliability and quality.
- Evidence from all development activities to be used in the trust decision as well as for writing the doctrine for using this software.

Last, the ideal trusted software would be maintained in a trusted software lifecycle support system made up of good people, process and technology.

WHAT DOES TRUST COST?

To consider the cost implications of improving trust, one must first consider the implications of ignoring it. The Pentium floating point bug, for example, not only cost Intel multiple millions of dollars in recalls and retooling, but also did inestimable damage to their reputation (Russinoff, 2022). Pentium market share plummeted as other chip manufacturers quickly exploited consumer misgivings to sell their wares. As a result of the Intel experience, all major chip manufacturers now employ experts in model checking to improve their chip verification and validation capabilities.

We must also consider how we can better walk our talk. We take seriously the crucial role our systems play in supporting the warfighter's mission. Increased cost of trust versus potential loss of lives? Certainly, a sobering tradeoff. Interestingly our counterparts have already embarked on a course to bring their software engineering capabilities to CMM level 3. This decision reflects a determination that, in the end, the value of assurance justifies the up-front impact to schedule and dollars.

RECOMMENDATIONS

Cyber-Assurance can increase its trust in Edge-based systems with today's technology. We recommend the following courses of action:

·   Develop a threat model and an assurance strategy for each development.
·   Require evidence and due diligence on the part of software developers. When we don't control development carefully consider life cycle and architectural risk mitigation strategies.
·   Shoot for at least Capability Maturity Model (CMM) level 2 or 3 software engineering maturity in system developments. One wonders why we continue to operate at CMM level 1 when industry best practice is CMM 4. Other industries (medical, avionics and aerospace) use CMM level 5 processes successfully based on the economics of their businesses.
·   Develop a new functional security requirements specification (FSRS) that meets the needs of today defined in terms of the common criteria language.
·   Be willing to make the short-term investments associated with adopting the unfamiliar technology discussed in this paper to gain the long-term value inherent in moving to better processes, tools and people.

Technology can provide the silver bullet only if the developing organizational environment and infrastructure are mature enough to take maximum advantage of it. To be consistently successful the organization must define its goals and implement them through universally accepted system engineering practices. We must move away from our typical process, which often involves non-repeatable heroic efforts, towards a repeatable, measurable and well-managed process. Until management can characterize the behavior of such a project, the corporation will not recognize success.

CONCLUSION

The techniques and technology discussed in this paper provide a strong foundation for the construction of an assurance methodology for Edge-based systems, but significant hard problems remain to be solved. Further research on how we can better use high-confidence design, containment and monitoring to achieve our trust goals is still needed. We list here some of the remaining gaps:

·   Complex software of unknown IoT origin (improve tools)
·   We need to develop tools and techniques for assessing the trustworthiness of IoT software. Even though we cannot solve the general problem of assessing arbitrary software (theoretically impossible), we can better use the intelligence we have to make reasonable assessments within the constraints in which we must operate. When using these smart tools in conjunction with the output of high confidence development tools and processes the assessment tasks should be tractable.

- Containment tools require complex settings (Knowledgeable tools for supporting containment) Here we need to develop intelligent tools to help the customer cope with complex security policy issues. For example, security-enhanced Linux offers the user unprecedented granularity in controlling access to system resources. We would like to give those users the ability to implement a specific policy without having to become operating system experts.
- Develop security component composition capabilities (Analyzing defense in depth). We talk a lot about defense in depth, but we don't really know how to assess the overall trustworthiness of systems comprising components with varying degrees of associated assurance. In addition, we need to develop techniques for assessing the residual risk when we combine high-confidence design, containment and monitoring techniques in concert.

As the foregoing sections have shown, we can begin reaping the benefits of assurance engineering and our three technology prongs today. High-confidence design techniques are no longer found only in university labs. Many have emerged as practical, commercial tools (e.g., Bell Lab's Spin, Mercury Interactive's Xrunner & WinRunner, Cadence System's Formal Check and Prover Technology's Prover Plug-in) and are in use by numerous industry leaders (e.g., Intel, Lucent Technologies, IBM, AMD). A large industry in host-based and network-based intrusion detection products has also developed over the past several years in response to the lack of effective assurance and containment mechanisms in commercially available systems. Process, which reflects management's commitment to developing trusted Edge-based systems, is an enabler for all the other techniques. The system engineering apparatus must support the assurance-engineering ethos. Without this commitment consistent success in achieving trust is impossible.

REFERENCES

Abeysekara, P., Dong, H., & Qin, A. K. (2019, July). Machine learning-driven trust prediction for mec-based iot services. In *2019 IEEE International Conference on Web Services (ICWS)* (pp. 188-192). IEEE. 10.1109/ICWS.2019.00040

Bordis, T., Runge, T., Schultz, D., & Schaefer, I. (2022). Family-based and product-based development of correct-by-construction software product lines. *Journal of Computer Languages*, 101119.

Brooks, T. (2020). An internet control device embedded sensor agent. *International Journal of Internet of Things and Cyber-Assurance*, *1*(3-4), 267–290. doi:10.1504/IJITCA.2020.112534

Brooks, T. T. (Ed.). (2017). *Cyber-assurance for the Internet of Things*. John Wiley & Sons.

Brooks, T. T., & Park, J. (2016). *Cyber-Assurance Through Embedded Security for the Internet of Things*. John Wiley & Sons. *Ltd*, 2, 101–127.

Cao, K., Liu, Y., Meng, G., & Sun, Q. (2020). An overview on edge computing research. *IEEE Access: Practical Innovations, Open Solutions*, 8, 85714–85728. doi:10.1109/ACCESS.2020.2991734

Chysi, A., Nikolopoulos, S. D., & Polenakis, I. (2022). Detection and classification of malicious software utilizing Max-Flows between system-call groups. Journal of Computer Virology and Hacking Techniques, 1-27.

Farroha, B. S., & Farroha, D. L. (2014, October). *A framework for managing mission needs, compliance, and trust in the DevOps environment. In 2014 IEEE Military Communications Conference.* IEEE.

Hu, Y. C., Patel, M., Sabella, D., Sprecher, N., & Young, V. (2015). Mobile edge computing—A key technology towards 5G. *ETSI white paper, 11*(11), 1-16.

Kang, M. H., Moore, A. P., & Moskowitz, I. S. (1997, August). Design and assurance strategy for the NRL pump. In *Proceedings 1997 High-Assurance Engineering Workshop* (pp. 64-71). IEEE. 10.1109/HASE.1997.648040

Li, H., Ota, K., & Dong, M. (2018). Learning IoT in edge: Deep learning for the Internet of Things with edge computing. *IEEE Network, 32*(1), 96–101. doi:10.1109/MNET.2018.1700202

Ma, Q. (2022, February). Design of High-Confidence Embedded Operating System based on Artificial Intelligence and Smart Chips. In *2022 Second International Conference on Artificial Intelligence and Smart Energy (ICAIS) (pp.* 58-62). IEEE. 10.1109/ICAIS53314.2022.9742917

Matheu-García, S. N., Hernández-Ramos, J. L., Skarmeta, A. F., & Baldini, G. (2019). Risk-based automated assessment and testing for the cybersecurity certification and labelling of IoT devices. *Computer Standards & Interfaces, 62,* 64–83. doi:10.1016/j.csi.2018.08.003

Necula, G. C. (1997, January). Proof-carrying code. In *Proceedings of the 24th ACM SIGPLAN-SIGACT symposium on Principles of programming languages* (pp. 106-119).

Runge, T., Potanin, A., Thüm, T., & Schaefer, I. (2022). Traits for Correct-by-Construction Programming. *arXiv preprint arXiv:*2204.05644.

Russinoff, D. M. (2022). *Formal Verification of Floating-Point Hardware Design.* Springer. doi, 10, 978-3.

Tran, T. X., Hajisami, A., Pandey, P., & Pompili, D. (2017). Collaborative mobile edge computing in 5G networks: New paradigms, scenarios, and challenges. *IEEE Communications Magazine, 55*(4), 54–61. doi:10.1109/MCOM.2017.1600863

Tsui, F., Karam, O., & Bernal, B. (2022). *Essentials of software engineering.* Jones & Bartlett Learning.

Wang, X., Wang, J., Xu, Y., Chen, J., Jia, L., Liu, X., & Yang, Y. (2020). Dynamic spectrum anti-jamming communications: Challenges and opportunities. *IEEE Communications Magazine, 58*(2), 79–85. doi:10.1109/MCOM.001.1900530

Wardle, P. (2022). *The Art of Mac Malware: The Guide to Analyzing Malicious Software.* No Starch Press.

Weyns, D. (2020). *An Introduction to Self-adaptive Systems: A Contemporary Software Engineering Perspective.* John Wiley & Sons.

Wu, C. H. J., & Irwin, J. D. (2016). *Introduction to computer networks and cybersecurity.* CRC Press. doi:10.1201/9781466572140

ENDNOTES

1 The Common Criteria. https://www.commoncriteriaportal.org/

2 Trusted Product Evaluation Program. https://uh.edu/tech/cisre/resources/ia-resources/_files/Rain bowSeries/tpepprocedures.htm

3 goodreads.com. https://www.goodreads.com/quotes/97717-when-you-have-exhausted-all-possibilities-remember-this---you

4 McCabe Software. http://www.mccabe.com/

5 Intellect. https://www.intellect.com/

6 National Information Assurance Partnership. https://www.niap-ccevs.org/Ref/Evals.cfm

Chapter 2
Risk Management:
Is It Needed?

ABSTRACT

This chapter is intended as an informal reference guide to information security personnel involved in making risk management decisions for computing systems and for those personnel that support those risk management decisions through design, analysis, policy development, or implementation. The scope of the chapter is introductory information on basic risk and risk management concepts as it applies to information systems (i.e. - the combination of hardware, software, operating systems, personnel, policy, physical location and the supporting operations, maintenance, and logistics that provide the information services necessary to support operational missions). It is not a comprehensive treatment of the subject; however, information and cyber security professionals will hopefully find this a useful common reference in supporting the remaining chapters in this book and when asked to participate in critical risk management decisions.

INTRODUCTION

Within computing environments, risk management has become a widely used phrase to describe how we determine a suitable level of investment in security (Hopkin, 2018). Often risk management has been characterized as the antithesis of risk avoidance – the investment of whatever resources is necessary to eliminate any risk. Risk avoidance is really just one style of risk management. Total risk acceptance can be viewed as the opposite style of risk management to risk avoidance. Both deal with strategies for managing the various elements of risk to fit within an acceptable range along a continuous spectrum of risk. Likewise, both provide an approach for dealing with the fundamental risk management decision . . . "How best do I invest my constrained, available resources among a variety of alternative options to best accomplish my assigned mission in a potentially hostile environment?"

Sometimes this investment decision is portrayed as a contest between investment in functionality or security (Boranbayev et al., 2022). They are treated as if functionality and security are independent of one another and measured against different requirements (Boranbayev et al., 2022). This is a poor

DOI: 10.4018/978-1-6684-7766-3.ch002

portrayal of the risk management decision since most computing systems are required to be operational in varying degrees of a hostile environment. Within a hostile environment, it is often the investment in security measures that allow there to be any functionality at all. A better portrayal of the risk management question would be the determination of the proper balance of the costs and benefits derived from any system feature (functional or security) to the success of the mission in the operational environment. How much functionality or how much security is in a system is NOT the ultimate measure. Operational mission success is the fundamental yardstick of any risk management decision.

Because of its widespread application within various industries, this chapter provides a basic reference guide to fundamental concepts of risk management. This chapter will introduce the concepts of:

- What is Risk and Risk Management?
- The Cyclical Risk Management Process
- Risk Analysis
- Types of Risk Analysis
- Risk Acceptance Strategies
- The Risk Management Infrastructure
- Roles and Responsibilities – The Risk Team

IS RISK MANAGEMENT NEEDED?

To understand the purpose and role of Risk Management, we must first understand the notion of risk. Sometimes risk is referred to as the harm that can occur as the result of different actions. At other times we use that term to mean the likelihood of a harmful event happening. Risk is sometimes used to mean the characteristics of a system that are being exploited or even used to mean the source of a hostile action. At times we even try to define risk in terms of a specific mathematical function. Risk and risk management are many things to many people. In practice, we do not have a common understanding of risk nor a common approach to risk management.

So, what is Risk? At its most fundamental level:

Risk is the combined note of the Harm caused by specific events and the Likelihood that Harm will happen

And what is Risk Management?

Risk management is the analysis of alternative courses of action and the selection and implementation of that course of action, which in a potentially hostile environment best supports an organization's operational objectives.

And what are Risk Management Decisions?

Risk management decisions deter the proper balance between the costs and benefits of functionality and security from among the available alternatives, which best satisfies the operational objectives in the face of a potentially hostile environment.

These basic concepts become more and more complex as we try to provide more rigorous definitions to what is meant by HARM, LIKELIHOOD and how those notions are COMBINED to form the notion of RISK, however, to establish a common approach to addressing risk, we need to develop a common:

1. Understanding of the separate notions of *harm* and *likelihood*,
2. Understanding of how to combine those separate notions into a *single notion of risk*
3. Understanding of the *concern* we place on that risk
4. Understanding of what *acceptable* and *unacceptable* risk is.
5. Approach toward *comparing* and *contrasting the risks (harm and likelihood)* of various courses of action and characterizing the costs and benefits of each.

BASIC INTUITIVE RISK EXAMPLE

As individuals making decisions that affect only our own personal lives, we have an intuitive understanding of these risk concepts without the need of formal definitions or complex analyses.

For example:

We intuitively understand that the destruction caused by an asteroid hitting the earth can be devastating to not only our way of life, but also to our fundamental existence. We also intuitively understand that this event is unlikely to occur in our individual lifetime. As we internalize the harm and the likelihood of that event occurring, we each have our own value system for understanding our individual level of concern for that combined state of harm and likelihood.

What we do about that state of risk is dependent upon:

1. Our personal abhorrence to (or fear of) the harm that may result.
2. Our ability to influence either the likelihood or the harm caused by the event.
3. Our willingness to invest in influencing either the likelihood or the harm.

We are left with the following choices in this case:

1. Accept the risk and not worry about it.
2. Accept the risk but continue to worry about it.
3. Legislate the events from happening.
4. Invest in various sets of countermeasures to change the likelihood or harm

Our selection will be based upon our own individual concern for the risk of this event, the costs and benefits of each of the alternatives and resources available.

An outline of an intuitive risk management decision for this situation might be as follows:

OPERATIONAL OBJECTIVE: Live a long and prosperous life.
EVENT: A large asteroid hitting the Earth.
HARM: Destruction of the earth, our way of life and our individual lives!
LIKELIHOOD: Most likely won't happen in our lives.
RISK: Really small chance of something really bad happening.
CONCERN: Compared with other risks, there are probably many other things that have a greater chance of harming our lives than this.
ACCEPTABLE RISK: This is below an intuitive threshold of concern. Wouldn't invest much, if anything, even if something could be done about this.
ALTERNATIVES:
  1. *Do Nothing* - Accept the risk and not worry about it.
  2. *Worry* - Accept the risk but continue to worry about it.
  3. *Outlaw Asteroid Hits* - Establish a policy prohibiting asteroid hits.
  4. *Flail at the Night* - Invest in various sets of countermeasures to try to change the likelihood or harm.
COST/BENEFIT:
  1. *Do Nothing* - No current or future costs. Will not waste time or energy on something that probably can't be influenced anyway. Does nothing about harm or likelihood. Would be unprepared if the event occurs.
  2. *Worry* - No current or future direct expenditures but it wastes time and energy on something that probably can't be influenced anyway. Does nothing about harm or likelihood. Would be unprepared if the event occurs.
  3. *Outlaw Asteroid Hits* - No current direct expenditures. May require future expenditure to enforce the established policy. Enforcement is probably futile with current technology. Since it is unenforceable, any expenditure would be wasteful at this time. When and if the policy is enforceable, establishing the policy may prove to be beneficial. Currently this would waste time, energy and resources on something that probably can't be influenced anyway.
  4. *Flail at the Night* - Would expend current and long-term maintenance resources. Would invest in countermeasures that cannot really do anything about the harm or likelihood. Wastes time, energy and resources on something that probably can't be influenced anyway.
DECISION/SELECTION: *Choose Alternative 1. The "Do Nothing" option*. - By choosing this option the risk is being "accepted" although this state of affairs may not be desirable or meet a desired standard of "acceptability". It is simply the best of the available alternatives at this time.
DECISION RATIONALE: Alternatives 2, 3 and 4 expend resources or energy on an impossible attempt to either reduce the likelihood of an asteroid striking the earth or the consequences once it does strike. There is virtually nothing that can be done that can affect the risk of this event. Since it is a futile attempt to develop countermeasures or prohibit the harmful acts and because the event is so improbable, the decision is to not expend resources on an event we cannot control and influence.

As an augmentation of this option, we may want to establish a requirement or goal of being able to choose a more proactive response and may invest in a certain level of research and development to establish new options to be considered at future time. These future options may provide the capability of meeting a more desired state of affairs.

THE CYCLICAL RISK MANAGEMENT PROCESS

Within organizations, risk decisions are being made every day. Certainly, system accreditors, information security risk officers and designated approving authorities (DAAs) have the responsibility of making formal risk decisions that affect the operational effectiveness of supported missions. But risk decisions are more than just the formal "approval to operate" decisions. Risk decisions are made throughout the life cycle of the system at many operational levels. System Administrators deciding to upgrade an application or operating system to a newer version are making risk decisions. Development engineers making design trade-off decisions are making risk decisions. Even users deciding whether to open a file from an e-mail attachment or floppy disk are making risk decisions. Risk decisions that affect the operational readiness of a system are made every day, at all levels of responsibility. Some individuals make formal, conscious decisions, while others unknowingly make informal risk decision. Whether formal or informal, conscious or unknowing, each risk decision follows the same general risk management process. How well that process is followed and accomplished determines the quality of risk management employed.

The risk management process is a defined set of activities that lead to efficient and effective actions that acceptably control the risks (Boranbayev et al. 2022). The risk management process is cyclical in nature. It needs to be able to adjust and respond to changes in the system design and configuration, changes in the operating environment and changes to the supported mission – those elements that cause a resulting change in risk. As these parameters change over time, it is necessary to periodically revisit our understanding of the risks incurred operating within the current and projected environment and determine if a change in protection approach (technology, procedures, personnel) is warranted. These decisions concerning changes and their ultimate implementation are the focus of the process. To accomplish this requires the iterative application of the phases of risk management: Definition, Analysis, Development, Decision and Implementation. The specific phases of a risk management process can be diagramed in a risk management cycle as depicted in Figure. 1. - Basic Risk Management Process. The six phases of the risk management process/cycle are further defined below:

1. *Definition- Derive Security Policy and Requirements* – This phase focuses on deriving the security requirements or security policy from the operational need for the system to provide vital supporting operational functions and services in a potentially hostile environment.
2. *Analysis – Analyze Current Risk Posture* – This phase focuses on gaining insight into the risks that are being incurred or will be incurred based upon the operational usage of the system, the design and the hostile operating environment. This phase includes the supporting vulnerability/ attack analysis, threat analysis and mission impact analysis. These are then synthesized to provide analytical insights to the pressing operational, budgetary and risk questions pertinent to the decision-maker.
3. *Development – Identify and Characterize Alternation Courses of Action* – This phase focuses on developing sets of possible courses of action along with their relative costs and benefits. These options can include the "no change" option, the "shut down" option and various combinations of technical, procedural and personnel changes to the system to mitigate potential attacks or reduce

the operational impact of successful attacks. In limited circumstances, reducing the threat imposed by a hostile operating environment may be another available option.

4. ***Decision – Make Informed Mission Focused Decisions*** - This phase focuses on deciding between the various courses of action. This is a crucial element in the risk management process. The whole analysis processes up to this point is geared toward providing the decision-maker (individual or board of individuals) with the best information and insights on the various courses of actions available to them. The decision-maker needs to a) possess the authority to accept risk for the operational mission, b) understand the issues and information that is being presented concerning the alternative courses of action, c) be willing and able to make a decision concerning the proper balance between functionality and security that will most effectively support the operational mission in the potentially hostile operating environment and d) have the authority to direct that the approved course of action be implemented. The information presented to the decision maker needs to be developed with the goal of answering the critical questions of the decision maker, providing information that reflects objective analysis, testing the assumptions of the analysis and those of the decision maker and communicating insights in a form and format that is useful to the decision maker. The resulting decisions then must be documented, promulgated and turned into active means of implementation.

5. ***Implementation – Implement Decisions and Maintain System Effectiveness*** – Just as important as making informed decisions with the requisite authority is the effective implementation of the decided course of action and the maintenance of the integrity and effectiveness of the applied countermeasures. Without effective implementation of the decisions and controlled configuration management, the risk decisions are rendered moot with little to no effect on reducing the incurred risk.

Repeat – Revisit Risk Decisions as the Situation Changes – When the system changes, the environment changes, or the mission changes, the resulting risk posture has also changed. Therefore, any change requires a new cycle through the risk management process to determine whether or not the applied safeguards are still providing adequate security to support the overarching operational mission.

Risk Analysis

Risk analysis is that portion of the risk management process that collects and analyzes risk related data for the broader purpose of providing decision-makers information on the benefits and costs of alternative courses of action with respect to executing the assigned mission in a hostile environment (Hubbard, 2020). Traditionally within organization, they have followed an approach of "find a vulnerability – fix a vulnerability". This assumes that any vulnerability discovered can lead to such a devastating impact that we have no alternative but to invest immediate resources to eliminate it. Unfortunately, there are usually insufficient resources to pursue this approach. The limited, available resources need to be more efficiently expended against the vulnerabilities and attacks that will be most harmful to the mission. These are difficult decisions and require effective analysis to provide sound decision information and recommendations.

In Figure 2, Risk Decision Flow, diagrams a basic synthesis of information that culminates in the presentation of the costs and benefits of various alternative courses of actions for a decision. This is an expansion of the first four steps of the Risk Management Process leading to a risk management decision. The basic steps in a risk analysis are:

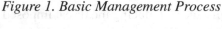

Figure 1. Basic Management Process

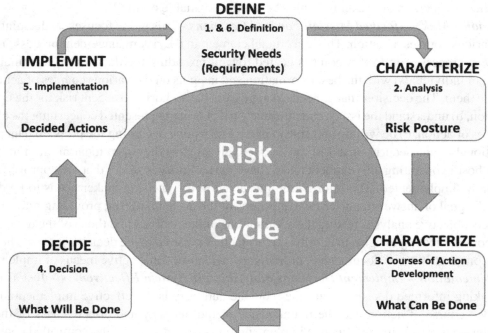

- **Foundation Research and Incident Analysis** - This is the basic foundation information collection activity of 1) discovering basic vulnerabilities to systems, technologies and applications; 2) collecting information about the culture, attitudes, preferences, capabilities and activities of various known and potential adversaries; and 3) conducting analyses of reported incidents to derive meanings and understanding from specific incidents and diagnosing broader trends from statistical analyses of composite incidents.
- **Basic Area Specific Analyses** - These are the traditional independent analyses that provide additional insights and meanings to the basic body of collected information. Each analysis typically results in a single-focus viewpoint and recommendations of 1) Vulnerabilities of a System; 2) Threats to a System; 3) Operational Impact to a Mission of loss of Information or Capability; or 4) Countermeasures. The typical approach to developing these analyses is to assign them to specialty organizations to produce a specialty focus report. These separate reports are then forwarded to the decision-makers and used as the basis for their risk decisions. Using these separate reports as the decision information, forces the decision-maker to internally synthesize the results of these separate reports.
- **Synthesized Risk Analysis** - A growing trend within organization is to take the separate area-specific analyses and conduct a synthesized focus analysis that combines and relates elements of the specialty-area analyses to address and answer specific issues necessary for making effective risk decisions. This approach applies additional analytical resources to synthesize and apply the vulnerability, threat, mission impact and countermeasure information to the specific situation.

Usually multi-discipline teams (e.g., risk team) are brought together with the express purpose of digesting, analyzing and interpreting the information to better assist the decision-makers in conducting this synthesis. The four steps of this synthesized risk analysis are:

1. ***Step1: Compare and Contrast Available Attacks*** - This type of analysis groups individual vulnerabilities into mission attack scenarios and then compares and contrasts these various scenarios based on: a) The immediate objective of the attack (i.e. defeat confidentiality, integrity, or availability); b) The ultimate impact on an operational mission; c) The costs and resources needed by an adversary in mounting the attack; d) The risks incurred by an adversary through possible detection, attribution and retaliation; and e) the likelihood of the attack being successful given satisfactory resources.

2. ***Step 2: Develop Theory of Adversarial Behavior*** - This analysis looks at the menu of attacks developed in the previous step from the perspective of various adversaries, or adversary groups, to determine which set of attacks they would more likely invest in during various phases of a conflict or competition. This helps to place the previously analyzed attacks in an adversary perspective by relating the attacks to a) Adversary Objectives, Intentions and Motives; b) Adversary Capabilities; c) Adversary Resources; d) Adversary tolerance for Risk; and e) Adversary preferences for attacks.

3. ***Step 3: Develop Theory of Mission Impact*** - This analysis takes the previous two analyses a step further by looking at what the ultimate operational impact might be, given that attacks of various types by various adversaries are successful. This step tries to put into an operational perspective the harm that can result from a successful attack. This resultant harm takes into account our capability of detecting and blocking the attacks, our ability to continue effective operations in the face of successful attacks and our ability to recover and reconstitute within an operationally acceptable period of time.

4. ***Step 4: Compare and Contrast Available Courses of Action*** - This analysis provides insights into how various countermeasure response actions improve or degrade the current risk posture and at what costs. It attempts to provide decision-makers with objective, costs and benefits of various proposed courses of actions. The alternatives considered can include 1) The "Do Nothing" alternative; 2) "Close all Vulnerabilities" alternative; and 3) Various differing sets of countermeasure and system changes (technical, procedural, or personnel). Costs can include budgetary costs, personnel costs and operational capability costs.

Figure 2. Risk Decision Flow

BASIC RISK DECISION FLOW

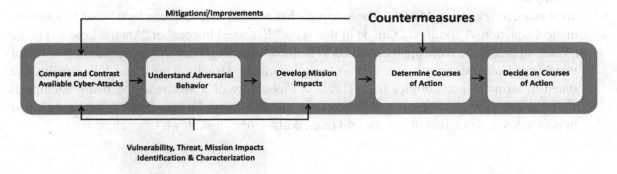

5.   ***Step 5: Decide on Course of Action*** - This is ultimately the responsibility of the decision author-ity. Each decision authority needs to be clear on the decisions that are being put before them, the relative cost and benefits of the various alternatives, possess the capability of understanding and appropriately weighing the results of analyses and be able to apply appropriate mission critical parameters to make difficult trade-off risk decisions.

TYPES OF RISK ANALYSES

Just as there is not a single approach to forecasting weather or the direction of the stock market, there is not a single approach to performing risk analyses. The form, approach and techniques used are dependent upon a variety of factors such as:

- The type, timeliness and granularity of the information desired to make risk decisions.
- The type, quality and availability of data to conduct the analysis.
- The appropriateness and availability of analytical techniques to provide insights to decisions.
- The experience and analytical skills of personnel available to perform analyses.
- The validity of the assumptions of the analytical technique.
- The risk decision strategy.
- The preferences of the Decision-Maker.

The types of analyses can range from a narrative dialog with "experts" to a highly complex computer simulation. Regardless of the approach chosen, there is no magic approach that can measure all risk. All of these approaches are models and descriptions of reality. However, regardless of the sophistication of the technique, they can never actually measure or define risk. Ultimately, the actual risk estimate rests in the reasoned judgement of the authorized decision-maker. The best that these models can ever do is to provide reasoned insights to assist decision-makers make a more informed decision.

The array of tools and techniques available to assist analysts in deriving insights into current and projected risks fall into several broad classes:

- **Quantitative** - These analytical tools and techniques treat the likelihood and impact parameters of risk as measurable quantities. They use mathematical, probabilistic and statistical techniques to derive insights into the relationships between threats, vulnerabilities, impacts and risk under varying conditions. These approaches rely heavily on a solid foundation of data and well-defined assumptions.
- *Mathematical Formula Model* – These approaches assume that Risk can be defined as a mathe-matical equation. A common example of this is the "Expected Impact" or "Annual Loss Exposure (ALE)" approach. In these approaches risk is defined as the mathematical combination of a Threat variable, a Vulnerability variable and an Impact Variable. Usually, Threat and Vulnerability are stated in terms of probabilities (i.e., Threat = Probability of a hostile action being attempted; Vulnerability = Probability of a hostile action being successful given that it is attempted) and Impact measured in terms of a value unit (e.g., dollars, lives lost, down time, etc.).

- *Stochastic Model* - These mathematical models take into account a range of uncertainty in the variables through use of probability distributions on variables. Monte Carlo simulations are a form of this type of model.

- **Qualitative** - These are tools and techniques that are used to capture and describe subjective impressions of Threat, Vulnerabilities and Impact under various conditions and use those to describe the risks. The rules of combination of the parameters usually are much more informal than quantitative approaches and rely heavily on experience, intuition and personal value judgements.

- **Expert Opinion Estimates** - These are approaches that derive estimates and value judgements from a set of individuals with an "expert" knowledge of specific areas (e.g., Threat, Vulnerability, Design, Mission Impact, or Risk) and experience in applying that knowledge to help decision-makers gain greater insight into Risks under various conditions. Dialog and discussion are often a major component of this approach with the assumption that "experts" discussing how all the elements work together to produce risk, can collectively agree upon a reasonable estimate for the risks. "Risk Juries" are an example of this "collective wisdom" approach. There are other "expert opinion" techniques that can be employed to help derive estimates on input parameters such as "Delphi" techniques. Although the data derived from expert opinions is subjective, there are techniques available to improve the quality of the captured estimates (Seaver et al. 1978). In many instances, "expert subjective estimates" are the only available source of data (Seaver et al. 1978). These estimates may be captured in a variety of formats:

  - **Situational Descriptions/Narrative** - In this approach, the elements of risk are simply described, allowing the decision maker to internally process and place value upon the various factors.
  - **Subjective Units of Measures** - In this approach the narrative subjective estimates are mapped to a set of common labels or symbols that form a common shorthand language for comparing, contrasting, combining and describing the estimates for the input values and the resulting risk. "High, Medium and Low", "Red, Yellow, Green" are both examples of this form of estimate representation. "Risk Planes" are a representation technique where "juries" are asked to portray various attacks on a graph with axes of undefined units of measure. The Vertical Axis portrays the group estimate for the relative *Impact* of a successful attack and the Horizontal Axis portrays the group estimate for the relative *Likelihood* of a successful attack.
  - **Quantitative Units of Measures** - In this approach the subjective estimates are described as if they were measurable quantities using quantitative units of measure. Subjective estimates on probabilities or value of impact (dollars, lives lost, down time etc.) are typical examples. Often this technique is used to augment quantitative approaches when firm data is unavailable.

- **Combination** - A risk analyst need not be constrained to pick only one type of analysis and may actually encourage the use and combination of several techniques to aid in deriving insight from the available data. For example, an analysis may use expert opinion to derive estimates and possibly uncertainty ranges, for input to a quantitative model. The analysis may then proceed as if it were a quantitative analysis. Then the results of that quantitative analysis may again be provided to a panel of experts to formulate their collective estimates based on their individual knowledge and experience as well as the results of the quantitative analysis. A challenge for any combined approach is to understand the subjective basis for the quantitative analysis and not portray it as a purely objective, quantitative analysis.

Risk Acceptance Strategies

Regardless of what analytical approach is used to capture, derive and relate insights to a risk decision, a fundamental question decision-makers are faced with is, "What is an acceptable level of risk?"

Unfortunately, risk usually can't be managed independently from other operational aspects of the system. Incorporating features and countermeasures that make a system more "secure" and thereby allowing it to continue to function in the face of a hostile attack, can also negatively impact such operational features as functionality, bandwidth, interoperability, availability and convenience. It also can increase the financial, personnel and operational costs of the system. Considering these dependencies between functionality, security and costs, the decision to be addressed is not simply the independent questions of "how much security" or "how much functionality" is needed to support the mission. Nevertheless, is a balancing of the benefits derived from additional functionality (i.e., able to more efficiently and effectively accomplish the mission) and the benefits derived from additional security (i.e., able to continue to operate in a hostile environment) vs. the costs of additional functionality (i.e., financial, personnel, increased risk) and the costs of additional security (i.e., financial, personnel, decreased functionality).

With this broader understanding of the fundamental risk decision, the answer to "What is an acceptable risk?" becomes the desired risk goal, but the risk decision is to choose the available alternative that best satisfies both the risk goal and the operational goal/ Hopefully at least one of the alternative combinations of functionality and security satisfies both goals. Often, none of the alternatives satisfy both goals and the decision-maker is faced with the selection of the best, sub-optimal alternative. This is the challenge that is faced by risk decision-makers . . . how much to invest in security to assure operational support in a hostile environment?

Three basic approaches to decision criteria are 1) a measurement/standards-based approach; 2) a characteristic enumeration-based approach; or 3) an analysis and reasoned judgement ("Case Law") approach. In many applications, these three approaches are used in a manner that treats "how much security is needed" as a question independent of operational concerns. The first two (Measurement and Enumeration) usually approach the security issue independently from operational concerns (although with thought, the operational aspects can also be factored into these approaches). The third approach (Reasoned Judgement) often builds upon and incorporates the first two approaches, where they are applicable, but also augments them with a human judgement to select the best alternative from the available alternatives. These three approaches to "acceptability" are described below:

- *Measurement/Standards Based* - In this approach Risk is assumed to be a measurable quantity and that some threshold of acceptability (standard) is established. The decision approach is to "measure" the risks of any situation and compare it to the standard. The Measurement/Standards Based approach to acceptability requires:
  A. Risk to be Measurable with a Common Unit of Measure
  B. Agreed upon Levels of Acceptability (Standards)
- *Characteristic Enumeration* - In this approach the "standard" is a checklist of desired or undesirable design features or operational characteristics. The "measurement" is determining whether or not those characteristics are present. The decision approach is to determine whether or not the sys-

tem "complies" with the enumerated characteristics list. Usually in this approach, "compliance" is assumed to be equivalent to "acceptable" (e.g., If you can demonstrate the system design and operation is compliant with all enumerated characteristics then the system is deemed acceptable for operation). The Characteristic Enumeration Based approach to acceptability requires:

A.   Enumeration of all desired or undesired traits for each situation.

B.   Evaluation to provide "assurance of compliance" with the enumerated traits.

- *Analysis and Reasoned Judgement (or "Case Law")* - In this approach the "standard" becomes the reasoned judgement of the authorized decision-maker(s) on the appropriate application of policy, precedence, logic and reason to specific situations. The "measurement" is the informed analysis and insights presented to the decision-maker. The decision approach is to provide decision-makers with evidence of a level of risk management that effectively and efficiently accomplishes all the supported missions operating within hostile operating environments. This evidence may include evidence of "compliance" with measurement standards or enumerated characteristic lists, previous decisions concerning similar systems in similar operating environments, as well as tests, studies and reasoned arguments. Reasoned Judgement is what is relied upon when measurement and compliance are, by themselves, not adequate to effectively manage the situational specific or dynamic aspects of risks. The Analysis and Reasoned Judgement ("Case Law") based approach to acceptability has the following characteristics:

  A.   A *Case Law Approach* is rooted in established policies and requirements *[Compliance]*.

  B.   A *Case Law Approach* uses previous specific application decisions to provide additional definition and guidance to related situations. *[Precedence]*.

  C.   A *Case Law Approach* gives the responsibility to authorized, accountable individuals for appropriate application of policies and precedence for determining a situation specific "level of acceptability". (Local Designated Approving Authority [DAA] for decisions that affect the local interests. Community DAA for decisions that affect community interests) *[Reasoned Judgement]*.

  D.   A *Case Law Approach* is flexible and dynamic enough to respond to a changing environment.

  E.   A *Case Law Approach* is dependent upon:

- Access to established policies, requirements and previous decisions along with their rationale.
- Analysis of the specific application by developers to appropriately apply policies, requirements and precedence to specific situations.
- Independent review to advise Decision-Makers of appropriate application of guidance and direction.
- Trained, Informed, Authoritative Decision Makers
- Recording and Posting of Decisions and Rationale
- Periodic Review and Updating of Policies and Guidance, to assure they apply to the current environment and correspond to current views of acceptability.

THE RISK MANAGEMENT INFRASTRUCTURE

The risk management decisions that are made and implemented through the risk management process are often difficult trade-off decisions that ultimately affect the overarching operational effectiveness of the supported mission. For the process to be effectively implemented, there needs to be a supporting risk management infrastructure. Twelve Pillars of this infrastructure are listed below. Without effective attention to these pillars, the risk management process can devolve into a set of chaotic and unassociated activities leading to uninformed, arbitrary decisions.

1. SOUND FOUNDATION CONCEPTS - Risk Management Theory and Practice Research
    ◦   At the core of effective risk management is an underlying theory about the elements of risk, major contributing factors to those elements, their definitions and relationships to each other and the concept of risk. In addition, there needs to be an understanding of ways we can and cannot influence the overall risk posture. This is the theoretical foundation that the application and practice of Risk Management is built upon. Those foundation concepts and their application need to be solidly studied and understood in order for their implementation to yield effective results.
2. EFFECTIVE TRAINING - Risk Management/Assessment Awareness, Education and Training
    ◦   Broad education of the decision-makers, system users, system administrators, security personnel, developers and analysts on the theory and practice of Risk Management is essential. There must be a common understanding of the concepts of risk management to be able to discuss, improve and implement a common, consistent, community approach to mitigating risk. Consequently, there needs to be a sound awareness, education and training in risk management before there can be significant improvement in the risk management decisions that are made.
3. ACTIVE SENIOR-MANAGEMENT INVOLVEMENT & SUPPORT - Community Agreement, Endorsement and Active Senior Management Support for Implementing Sound Risk Management
    ◦   The ultimate success in making quality risk management decisions is dependent upon active senior-management engagement, involvement and support. This involvement and support is needed not only for making quality decisions, but also for follow-through implementation of those decisions and for fundamental investment in the supporting infrastructure (i.e., requirements definition, data collection, design and development, analysis, dialog and discussion and enforcement.)
4. SOUND FOUNDATION INFORMATION/DATA - Active Collection, Analysis, Sharing and Synthesis of Mission Support, Configuration, Information Flow, Threat, Vulnerability, Mission Impact, Incident, Countermeasure and Risk Information.
    ◦   To develop secure, mission-supportive solutions and to make sound risk management decisions, sound system focused foundation information and data is essential. It is essential to understand 1) how the system supports overall operational mission effectiveness, 2) how a system is actually designed and/or deployed, 3) how information is intended to flow through the system, 4) vulnerabilities to the system and how adversaries may exploit them to effect the overall operational mission, 4) historical information about known incidents to helps to expose potential trends and 5) countermeasure characterization information to help provide an objective cost-benefit analysis. Sound attention to collecting and making available this foundation information can lead to the development of better and more operationally appropriate solutions and ultimately lead to better informed and more effective risk management decisions.

5. SECURE, MISSION-SUPPORTIVE SOLUTIONS - Providing a set of properly defined, characterized, developed, available and affordable solutions that provide a sufficient blend of functional and defensive characteristics to support the overarching mission within a hostile operating environment.

    ◦   Another essential element to effective risk management is available, sound and effective risk mitigation techniques that are affordable to incorporate and that contain an appropriate level of security commensurate with supporting operational objectives in its hostile environment. The solutions must balance the functional and defensive aspects of supporting the overarching mission. These solutions must address the broad spectrum of possible solutions that include varying degrees of a) Policy changes, b) Procedural changes, c) Configuration changes, d) Technology changes (hardware and/or software), e) Training changes, f) Personnel changes, g) Process changes. They must also be affordable and usable in their projected operating environments.

6. SUPPORTIVE TOOLS & TECHNIQUES - Development, continued improvement and sound application of tools and models to assist in providing risk insights to decision-makers.

    ◦   Designing information systems, analyzing those information systems, understanding the impact of sets of vulnerabilities and determining the costs and benefits of proposed sets of countermeasures, is complex and deals with a myriad of potential influencing elements and data. To better provide both sound design solutions and exploitation analysis insights to support sound risk management decisions, a variety of user-friendly tools and techniques need to be developed, made available and supported, to assist the wide variety of personnel asked to perform various risk management functions.

7. SOUND INSIGHTS FROM ANALYSIS - Provision of sound risk analysis results to support local and community risk decisions.

    ◦   The focus of any risk analysis needs to be to provide insights to help decision-makers make informed risk management decisions. The analyses should be geared to address the most critical cost and benefit information needed by decision makers to determine between various proposed courses of actions, with respect to the identified vulnerabilities, that if exploited can lead to unacceptable mission degradation, in a hostile operational environment. These analytical insights are the essential elements that differentiate informed decision making from arbitrary decision-making.

8. SOUND, INFORMED, AUTHORATATIVE DECISION MAKING - Development, Improvement and Sound Management of Decision-Making Bodies, their processes, their decision criteria and the promulgation of their decisions.

    ◦   Even given the best information, designs and analysis insights, sound risk management cannot be accomplished unless there is a clearly identified entity or entities, with 1) the responsibility, authority and information resources necessary to make accountable decisions and 2) the authority to hold others accountable for the implementation of those decisions. The definition and execution of that authority must be clear. The approval process and required information to make those decisions must be clear. The accountability for both the decisions and the implementation must be clear. And the fact that operations cannot occur without the decision-maker's explicit approval must also be clear. This responsibility demands that those exercising that level of decision-making authority must be clearly qualified to make the decisions. To aid in consistent decision-making, it is helpful to clearly articulate decision criteria that are pertinent across various ranges of decisions. These decisions in and of themselves form the basis for accountable actions and guidance to the developers of solutions and the operational community. Because of this influence of "precedence", these decisions need to be documented and made available for review and use by the broader community.

9. COORDINATED ACTION IMPLEMENTATION - Active Dialog, Agreement and Coordinated Implementation of Approved Risk Mitigation

    ○   Making sound, informed decisions is only the first part of risk management. Providing the resources, coordination and accountability for implementing those decisions is a fundamental necessity. It is essential that there is an accountable implementation phase of risk management.

10. SOUND DIRECTION & GUIDANCE - Development, continued Improvement, promulgation and sound application of community agreed upon policy, guidance and examples.

    ○   Information Systems, along with their security countermeasures, are extremely time consuming and costly to develop. Therefore, it is more effective to establish community agreed upon policy, guidance and examples based upon "lessons learned" that help to prevent the costly recurrence of flaws or solutions already deemed "unacceptable". This guidance needs to be derived from the decisions that are made by the decision makers, supported and/or changed by those decision makers and made available to the designers of solutions, supporting analysts and those ultimately responsible for operating and maintaining the integrity of the system.

11. ENFORCED CONFIGURATION MANAGEMENT - Establishment, review and reinforcement of procedures to assure sound configuration management.

    ○   In complex systems, the ultimate impact of even minor changes is difficult to determine and control. Authority to operate was granted by the decision-makers based on specific design configurations, rules and limitations related to a specific operating environment. Changes in the system or environment need to be documented, reviewed and approved to assure that unexpected additional unacceptable risk to both the local missions and potentially the operations of the connected community is not introduced through those changes. Policies, procedures and aperiodic validation of configuration are essential in maintaining the integrity and validity of the approved system and to prevent the initially approved configuration from being reduced to a chaotic configuration.

12. RAPID EMERGENCY RESPONSE - Rapid Detection and Identification of Emergency Situations; Rapid Alerting of effected Operations; Rapid Development, Promulgation and Implementation of Interim Measures of Mitigation; and an Active "Follow-through" Utilization of Established Risk Management Processes to discuss, develop and implement a sound, informed and effective long-term response to this and related situations.

    ○   Emergencies will arise that cannot be effectively dealt with through the normal timelines of a risk management process. An active, rapid, authoritative, emergency response system is essential for dealing with those immediate situations. This includes rapid detection, diagnosis, notification, interim response and recovery. Just as important as getting an interim response in place is the activation of the normal risk management process to determine, in a less emotionally charged environment, the most effective long-term response.

ROLES AND RESPONSIBILITIES - THE RISK TEAM

For an effective risk management process to occur, the efforts of individuals performing several distinct roles must be synthesized to provide focused and relevant information to support critical operational decisions. (See Figure 2. - Risk Decision Flow Diagram) It is not enough for the distinct roles to operate just within their defined areas of expertise and responsibility. It is essential that the assembled expertise collectively work toward providing the best risk information to the decision-makers! The role of the risk analyst is to facilitate the collective synthesis of mission impact, vulnerability, threat and countermeasure information into useful and relevant information for making those operational cost/benefit decisions. There are times when the risk analyst performs only this synthesis role with the support of a designated risk team. There are other times when, depending on the available resources and time sensitivity, the risk analyst takes on several, or at times all, of the roles required to make the process work.

In general, the types of roles necessary to support an effective risk management process include:

1. **Authorized Decision-Maker / Accreditor** – This role is vested with the authority to make binding decisions. This role can be filled either by an individual or a board. The decisions are both security oriented (determining how much security is adequate) as well as operational (determining what restraints on functionality are acceptable to gain greater assurance of other functions within a potentially hostile environment). Usually those filling these roles are formally designated (such as Designated Approving Authorities, DAA) and are involved in formal acceptance decisions at various points in a system's development. Those filling this role establish the requirement for a risk analysis, its resource constraints and its schedule, assists in establishing a qualified Risk Team, provides guidance and direction throughout the course of the risk analysis, listen to the presented information concerning the risks of operating and not operating, weighs this information against established acceptance criteria and their own operational values and make decisions on the most acceptable course of action. This course of action may be to approve operation of the system as is, postpone the decision until some set of actions occur, conditionally approve the system but require some set of additional actions, or disapprove operation.
2. **Risk Analyst** – This role is a facilitation and analysis role. The risk analyst is responsible for helping the Authorized Decision-Maker determine the issues that are most important to be studied to make a well-informed decision. The risk analyst is also responsible for developing a plan for the collection and analysis of information to provide relevant insights into those critical issues and for establishing a qualified Risk Team. The risk analyst then facilitates the execution of the analysis plan (usually with the active participation of analysts from specialized disciplines as part of a Risk Team). Once the analysis begins to derive insights and results, the risk analyst helps to portray and interpret the analysis results to the decision makers(s) in a way that most effectively conveys those insights.
3. **Operational Mission Representative** – This role is a representative and information source role. It is essential that vulnerabilities, threats and the costs and benefits of proposed countermeasures be place in the context of their support or harm to the operational mission. The individuals serving this role are ideally full members of the risk analysis team. They help assure that the operational perspective is fully integrated into the analysis and recommendations. Those filling this role help to assure the necessary operational contacts, requirements and judgements are applied throughout

the analysis. They also serve as an information conduit to the operational personnel, keeping them informed of trade-off decisions and representing the operational view in those trade-off discussions.

4. **System Configuration Engineer / System Administrator** – This role is a representative and information role that provides critical information on the exact current configuration, design and operation of the system and how well the system will function under various operational conditions and countermeasure strategies.

5. **Countermeasure Design Engineer / Analyst** – Those filling this role are responsible for identifying and characterizing the costs and benefits of several alternative countermeasure sets or "courses of action". They are usually full members of the risk analysis team working along-side the risk analysts, operational representatives, vulnerability analysts and threat analysts to determine how best to characterize the decision options.

6. **Vulnerability Analyst / Attack Analyst / System Evaluator** – Those filling this role are responsible for identifying individual vulnerabilities in a system, portraying them in the context of potential attack paths against the operation of the supported mission and characterizing them in terms of operations disrupted, costs to mount and risks incurred by the adversary in mounting. They are usually full members of the risk analysis team working along-side the risk analysts, the operational representatives, threat analysts and countermeasure analysts to determine how best to characterize the vulnerabilities and attacks.

7. **Threat Analyst** – Those filling this role are responsible for researching and applying current and projected knowledge of adversaries, their intentions, resources, capabilities, motivations, tolerance for risk and attack preferences to assist the risk analysis team in developing a theory on how adversaries would most likely choose which attacks to mount through various phases of conflict to achieve various objectives. They are usually full members of the risk analysis team working alongside the risk analysts, the operational representatives, vulnerability analysts and countermeasure analysts to determine how best to relate malicious intents and capabilities to their potential effect on operations.

8. **Implementation Engineer / Action Officer / Program Manager** – These are individuals responsible for the development and implementation of a functional capability that operates within an acceptable operational risk tolerance. They are often those with the responsibility for developing solutions to stated operational requirements and have the responsibility of implementing the course of action decided by the Decision Maker. Those charged with this responsibility interact frequently with the risk analysis team providing information on the proposed design and operation of the operational solution and gaining insights on potential ways to improve the design and reduce the risks. Usually, the more active the interaction and dialog between those in this role and the risk analysis team the more effective the solution in satisfying the operational requirement in the face of a hostile environment.

CONCLUSION

Making sound risk management decisions regarding information that is vital to the effective accomplishment of an organization's business/mission activities is becoming more and more important as our operations become more and more dependent upon the availability, integrity and confidentiality of critical sets of information. To make better and more informed risk management decisions, the discipline of "risk management decision analysis" must evolve to capture data that is relevant to the risk management decision and to interpret the meaning of that data for the decision-makers with respect to the risk management decisions they must make. There are many issues and challenges associated with developing a sound risk management decision analysis process that is faithful to the observations as described by the input data. Furthermore, it must be sound in its transformation of input data to analytical results and an honest interpretation of those results in a form and format that helps decision-makers gain meaningful insights with respect to the risk management decision they are faced with.

REFERENCES

Boranbayev, S., Amrenov, A., Nurusheva, A., Boranbayev, A., & Goranin, N. (2022, March). Methods and Techniques of Information Security Risk Management During Assessment of Information Systems. In *Future of Information and Communication Conference* (pp. 787-797). Springer, Cham. 10.1007/978-3-030-98015-3_53

Hopkin, P. (2018). *Fundamentals of risk management: understanding, evaluating and implementing effective risk management*. Kogan Page Publishers.

Hubbard, D. W. (2020). *The failure of risk management: Why it's broken and how to fix it*. John Wiley & Sons. doi:10.1002/9781119521914

Seaver, D. A., Von Winterfeldt, D., & Edwards, W. (1978). Eliciting subjective probability distributions on continuous variables. *Organizational Behavior and Human Performance*, *21*(3), 379–391. doi:10.1016/0030-5073(78)90061-2

Chapter 3
Threat as an Essential Element of Risk Management

ABSTRACT

Distributing critical and time-sensitive information to leaders and other essential decision authorities is an operational imperative and challenge for every organization. In short, the actual risks being incurred are not well understood. Of the three major elements of risk (vulnerability, threat, mission impact), threat information is often the most elusive to obtain. The purpose of this chapter is to provide a basic introduction and reference to general threats on information systems. This chapter will serve as a starting point for analysts to better understand the threats aligned against their critical information infrastructures and ultimately allow them to determine an appropriate level of investment more effectively in information systems security countermeasures.

INTRODUCTION: THE CHANGING NATURE OF THREAT

A threat is the potential for circumstances in which some agent might take some action, which could cause some event, having a consequence that could result in an impact--often-harmful (Huskaj et al., 2020). The "agent" is referred to as a threat agent and the "action," or attack is the set of steps taken to bring about the event. For the purposes of this chapter threat agents are divided into three general categories:

- **Adversarial**: Individuals, groups, organizations and nation states with the intent, motivation, capabilities, resources and the attack methods to exploit the vulnerabilities of an information system to further their objectives. This category includes malicious hackers, often referred to as "crackers." Another important dimension to adversarial threat is the willingness of the adversary to risk detection, attribution and retaliation.
- **Non-adversarial**: Individuals, groups, organizations and, in some circumstances, nation states that have no objectives, motivations, or intentions to cause harm to a system. This category includes authorized user errors and recreational hackers. Although there is no intention to cause

DOI: 10.4018/978-1-6684-7766-3.ch003

harm, they have the capability of doing the wrong thing at the wrong time and causing a level of harm that sometimes surpasses that of an adversary with intent to harm.

- **Natural and Technological Disasters**: This category includes weather phenomenon such as tornadoes and floods, as well as technological disasters such as toxic spills and power or telephone outages.

Non-adversarial and natural and technological disasters "agents" are random events that can be anticipated by analyzing historical data of occurrences. However, adversarial threat agents are complex and require the analysis of information that is often hard to come by. Important information needed to evaluate adversarial agents include their capabilities, motivations, intentions and willingness to incur the risk of discovery or retaliation. While none of the three categories can be ignored in an analysis of threats, this chapter will focus primarily on the adversarial threat.

INCREASING DEPENDENCE OF INFORMATION SYSTEMS

As an example, our nation's defense has long depended on maintaining an armed force equal to or greater than that of any potential adversary. The ability to deploy the force was dependent on a relatively structured command and control (C2) system based, for the most part, on dedicated information systems. In general, if an adversary intended to defeat us on the battlefield they had to equal or better our armed capability–to overwhelm either our military force directly or its command-and-control ability.

Command and control remain critical to effective national defense operations; however, today's C2 systems are highly dependent on complex distributed and highly automated networks and systems with open architectures. Distributed/automated functions are no longer fully under the control of commanders. Further, the nature of distributed systems and their associated vulnerabilities are often not understood by commanders or personnel under their command but are known to an increasing set of malicious individuals and groups. Today, access to defense information systems, exploitation tools and the ability/lack of ability to detect exploitation are all factors placing C2 systems at ever increasing risks. This reliance on information systems has extended into the private sector as well. Information technology has evolved from a repository and conduit for information, to become the controlling factor in virtually every aspect of the nation's activities—in peace and war. Until relatively recently, the major security issue of information technology was the protection of information from unauthorized disclosure. This major category of security issues has been termed Confidentiality (or loss of confidentiality).

However, information technology has become the means by which processes are accomplished, more and more by eliminating human intervention and replacing the human element with automated decisions, direction and action. In addition, complex searches, retrievals and analyses of information, unfathomable just ten years ago are now ready for command at the click of a mouse. The result is an unprecedented dependence on our information systems to be always accurate and available, as well as capable of protecting the confidentiality of the information. This introduces the remaining two security issues that have become concerns equal to confidentiality. These two issues are, integrity, or accuracy of information and programs and freedom from corruption and availability, or the uninterrupted use of information, programs and systems. Considered together, confidentiality, integrity and availability are termed security services.

INCREASING SOPHISTICATION OF ATTACKS AND EASE OF USE

Attacks on information systems and those who mount them, continue to demonstrate an increasing understanding of network structures, operating systems, hardware and software, protocols and the rapidly advancing technologies (Huskaj et al., 2020). Sophisticated intruders analyze the source code for network operating systems and other network application programs, such as email programs, to identify vulnerabilities. Intruders are increasingly targeting network infrastructures and software, including routers and firewalls, with new and increasingly complex attack tools and methods. Computer network attack tools developed by the more sophisticated intruders have become not only more effective, but easier to use, often requiring only minimal knowledge of networks and computer systems. These tools are widely available over the Internet and on "hacker" bulletin boards, providing individuals with limited or virtually no technical skills the ability to break into systems.

In addition to the increase in the availability of powerful, easy to use tools, today the risk of being caught is relatively low and attacks are often not detected. Since attacks can be launched from almost anywhere in the world, smart attackers often disguise their locations by launching the attack from a third-party machine.

The rapid proliferation of automated information systems, the increased availability of sophisticated tools and the lack of sufficiently developed and deployed effective protections make information systems increasingly lucrative targets for adversaries. This can be especially true since successful attacks can have widespread effects due to the large number of people and organizations that depend on the systems for the conduct of daily, often critical, operations. In addition, there is a wide variety of information, including business and economic information, government and national defense data and law enforcement information, stored and processed on today's information systems. Because, unlike past military operations, it does not take a large organization with extensive resources to devise and mount computer network attacks, attacks by individuals or small groups can allow them to effectively challenge, or counter, the capabilities of a larger, more powerful nation such as the United States.

THREAT AS AN ESSENTIAL ELEMENT OF RISK MANAGEMENT

Risk is defined as "a combination of the likelihood that a threat will occur, the likelihood that a threat occurrence will result in an adverse impact and the severity of the resulting impact," (Hopkin, 2018). Risk Assessment is defined as the "Process of analyzing threats to and vulnerabilities of, an information technology (IT) system and the potential impact that the loss of information or capabilities of a system" (Hopkin, 2018). From these definitions, the components of risk and their interrelationships can be depicted as shown in Figure 1.

In Figure 1, a threat may be viewed as an actual or potential event, caused by a threat agent, which exploits a vulnerability in an information system, with a resulting adverse impact on mission success or the involved asset, e.g., the physical assets of the information system. A threat event may be caused by an adversary--an individual, group, or nation state that has the intent, motivation and capability to cause harm--or human act (non-adversarial), or natural or technological disaster.

When one of the risk components is absent there is no apparent risk. However, it is impossible to be certain that all of the threats, vulnerabilities and mission impacts have been completely and accurately identified and defined. This means that the precise dimensions of risk at any given time will never be

Figure 1. Interrelationships of Risk

defined with 100% certainty. The central area of Figure 2, where all three elements overlap, represents the potential risk, i.e., where the threats, vulnerabilities and mission impacts are present. However, because of the imprecise nature of risk analysis, risk may exist outside this area and must be considered when making risk management decisions.

Risk management as a process concerned with the identification, measurement, control and minimization of security risks in information technology (IT) systems to a level commensurate with the value of the assets protected (Boranbayev et al., 2022). Effective risk management is a structured decision-making process, based on finding and implementing the most cost-effective security measures providing the greatest assurance of mission success. Figure 1 above depicts this risk management decision process. The process requires the analysis of the system and its environment to characterize how a system could be attacked; who or what threatens an attack; what impact a successful attack would have on the successful accomplishment of an organization's mission; and measures needed to thwart or mitigate an attack to enable decisions on the most effective use of resources to achieve the needed level of protection.

The Mission is the reason for an organization's existence and information systems exist to support the mission. Thus, the risk decision process begins with a determination of the organization's mission and functions; determining how critical the information system is to mission success, i.e., impact of loss or compromise of the system; and defining the need for security services in support of mission success. Analysts should consult the appropriate policy and guidance documents to determine the terminology appropriate to their organization. Regardless of the terminology, the importance of evaluating mission impact during the risk management process cannot be overemphasized. Threat, as defined earlier, is any circumstance or event with the potential to cause harm to a system. As shown in Figure 1, the characterization of threat is an integral and essential part of managing risk.

A vulnerability is a system characteristic (including hardware, software, physical, personnel, or cryptographic security issues) that could be exploited by an adversary or affected by a natural or unintentional man-made event to harm the system. An Attack is a sequenced set of activities that exploit specific vulnerabilities leading to the defeat of one or more desired security services. The characterization of vulnerabilities provides an understanding of what types of attacks could successfully defeat a system security service. Threat analysis is inextricably linked to vulnerability analysis in the risk management process. The vulnerability analysis characterizes what attacks could exploit a vulnerability and the threat analysis provides an understanding of which attacks are most likely to be attempted and by whom.

Once an understanding of the threats to and vulnerabilities of, a system, is achieved, a risk analysis is conducted to characterize and prioritize the risks against the impact on the success of the mission. Risk mitigation planning surfaces potential courses of action to eliminate or reduce risk by changing the threat environment. This is done by identifying measures that affect the adversary's potential for action or eliminate or reduce those vulnerabilities that the adversary could exploit. The probability of attack success given an attempt and the impact the successful attack will have on the mission are weighed against the cost of countermeasures and a management decision is made outlining a cost-effective course of action to decrease the risks to the system.

Risk is often viewed from two perspectives—community risk and local risk (Hubbard, 2020). Community risk assessments focus on the networked environment and the relationships between the available data, the known threats and the known and unknown vulnerabilities. However, networked environments are based on shared resources and open exchanges of data and services. This means that individual programs and organizations, once they are connected to a larger network become part of a community consisting of all systems using the same information infrastructure. The implication for system security personnel is that whatever risks are accepted by an information system belonging to individual programs or organization, are also imposed on the entire community, or more simply stated, risk accepted by one is shared by all. Thus, to maintain a secure network, local risk assessments by the individual programs and organization must be completed before seeking connection to other networks.

As illustrated in Figure 1, the analysis of threat is an essential element in the conduct of a risk assessment. It is possible to apply countermeasures to a vulnerability, or weakness, in an information system without systematically analyzing threat. However, the results will depend a great deal on luck and just how good the analyst has been when arbitrarily selecting vulnerabilities that will actually be used by an attacker. This document will provide an analytic structure that facilitates the identification of the most likely attacks and the attacks with the most serious adverse impact. This is done by examining the value of the target information system, the impact on mission and other valued resources that might result if the system were attacked, how that attack might come about and who the probable attacker(s) are performing these attacks.

THREAT AS HOSTILE INFORMATION OPERATIONS

The threat to U.S. information systems can be best viewed today in the context of hostile Information Operations (IO). By understanding the basic concepts of IO, the threat analyst can better understand the full scope of the "threat" posed to U.S. systems.

According to Joint Pub 3-13, Joint Doctrine for Information Operations, information operations are "actions taken to affect adversary information and information systems while defending one's own information and information systems" (Staff, 1998). Joint Chiefs of Staff (1998) further divides information operations into defensive and offensive, defined as follows:

"**Offensive information operations.** *The integrated use of assigned and supporting capabilities and activities, mutually supported by intelligence, to affect adversary decision-makers to achieve or promote* *specific objectives. These capabilities and activities include, but are not limited to, operations security, military deception, psychological operations, electronic warfare, physical attack and/or destruction, special information operations and could include computer network attack."*

Offensive IO are the tools and methodologies used by U.S. adversaries to attack U.S. systems to achieve their goals or to negatively impact the missions and goals of U.S. organizations.

*"***Defensive information operations.** *The integration and coordination of policies and procedures, operations, personnel and technology to protect and defend information and information systems. Defensive information operations are conducted through information assurance, physical security, operations security, counter-deception, counter-psychological operations, counterintelligence, electronic warfare and special information operations. Defensive information operations ensure timely, accurate and relevant information access while denying adversaries the opportunity to exploit friendly information and information systems for their own purposes."*

Defensive IO are those measures in response to the hostile IO threats to reduce or eliminate the potential for adverse impacts on U.S. systems as the result of adversary IO attacks. Rapid changes in information and communications technology are reshaping the world around us. Traditional notions about national security, economics and culture are giving way to new international models. Global, instantaneous communications systems are changing organizational structures and reducing timelines needed for carrying out activities. Offensive IO can mount in several ways to impact the success of an organization's mission (Huskaj et al., 2020). Because of the increased interconnectivity between organizations on a global scale, interdependent information and information systems are quickly replacing independent systems. This increase provides many benefits to organizations; however, such interdependence poses serious security threats. Because of this increased interdependence, an organization or system's security is reduced to that of the weakest component in the network, i.e., risk accepted by one is shared by all.

Attacks on information and information systems could have devastating effects on individuals, organizations and operations. Information operation attacks could be used to destroy an organization's operational integrity, manipulate, or destroy information within databases, deceive an organization's leadership, influence the decision-making process and restrict or deny vital services upon which mission success depends. In many cases, the adverse consequences of hostile IO could extend beyond individual organizations and affect entire regions or nations. Joint Chiefs of Staff (1998) outlines seven assigned and supporting IO capabilities and activities:

1. Operations Security
2. Deception
3. Psychological Operations
4. Electronic Warfare
5. Physical Attack/Destruction
6. Special Information Operations
7. Computer Network Attacks

These seven activities are not independent of one another and are often integrated into concerted attacks. There are several ways that these IO activities can be grouped, but this listing provides a convenient way to view aspects of hostile IO.

OPERATIONS SECURITY (OPSEC)

OPSEC is a process of identifying critical information and subsequently analyzing friendly actions attendant to military operations and other activities to:

1. Identify those actions that can be observed by adversary intelligence systems.
2. Determine indicators hostile intelligence systems might obtain that could be interpreted or pieced together to derive critical information in time to be useful to adversaries.
3. Select and execute measures that eliminate or reduce to an acceptable level the vulnerabilities of friendly actions to adversary exploitation.

Successful IO depends on OPSEC procedures and methodologies to ensure secrecy and surprise in the planning and execution of any attack.

DECEPTION

Deception is defined as measures designed to mislead the enemy by manipulation, distortion, or falsification of evidence to induce him to react in a manner prejudicial to his interests (Huskaj et al., 2020). There are three primary means of accomplishing deception: physical, technical and administrative. Physical means include the use of military or commercial operations, reconnaissance, training activities, dummy equipment and misleading activities. Technical means include the use of radiation, alteration, absorption, or reflection of energy; the emission or suppression of chemical or biological odors; and the emission or suppression of nuclear particles. Administrative means consist of methods, resources and techniques that convey or deny oral, pictorial, documentary, or other physical evidence to a foreign power. Deception operations represent a threat similar to Psychological Operations (PSYOPS), in that they also target the decision-making process. However, unlike PSYOPS, where an adversary is persuaded to behave in a manner that is emotionally charged or irrational, deception seeks to convince adversaries that certain choices are rational and based on the available data.

PSYCHOLOGICAL OPERATIONS (PSYOPS)

PSYOPS are operations planned to convey selected information and indicators to foreign audiences in order to influence their emotions, motives, objective reasoning and ultimately the behavior of governments, organizations, groups and individuals. Such actions pose a threat to organizations and nations because, if successfully conducted, they manipulate the decision-making process. Such manipulation could have adverse consequences by affecting the leadership, either as a whole or by targeting individual members within the group. Additionally, it may interfere with many other functions within an organization by altering perceptions regarding how information should be handled or interpreted and, thus, disturbing information flows.

ELECTRONIC WARFARE

Electronic warfare is any military action involving the use of electromagnetic and directed energy to control the electromagnetic spectrum or to attack an enemy. These actions pose significant risks to information, information systems, electronic- and energy-based sensors, electronic and computer-controlled systems and communications.

PHYSICAL ATTACK/DESTRUCTION

Destruction consists of physically destroying adversarial tactical and strategic assets, including personnel, facilities and equipment. The destruction of critical nodes of infrastructure and communications systems can disable or degrade the operation of necessary services and prevent organizations from completing their objectives and operations. Destruction poses a significant threat to nations and, to a lesser extent, private organizations because of its costly nature. Destroyed targets are costly to replace and the lack of their operation may result in failures at other vital points in operations. Destruction has traditionally been the primary means of warfare; however, other groups, such as criminals and terrorists, have adopted this method. Because of the widespread use of destruction, no organization is free from this threat.

COMPUTER NETWORK ATTACKS (CNA)

CNA are operations to disrupt, deny, degrade, or destroy information resident in computers and computer networks, or the computers and networks themselves (Huskaj et al., 2020). Equally important, CNA operations can be used to acquire the information stored or processed on a system for intelligence collection purposes. In this case, it is to the attacker's benefit not to corrupt or damage the information, but to have the owner continue to update and maintain the information without knowing that an attacker is reading it. CNA presents a serious threat to U.S. government and industry, threatening valuable information in and services provided by, computer systems. Furthermore, given the networked nature of the United States and to a larger extent the world, CNA operations can be conducted from almost any point on the globe, attacking targets located at almost any other point on the globe with almost total anonymity. The primary focus of this document is on CNA.

TARGETS OF INFORMATION OPERATIONS

Targets of information operations can be divided into three general categories:

1. Critical Infrastructures
2. Information and Data
3. Analytical Results and Decision Making

Each target category can be attacked by a variety of means and different levels of sophistication are required for the attacks to be successful.

CRITICAL INFRASTRUCTIONES

The information infrastructure interconnects every major public service infrastructure, making each of them nationally—and even globally—accessible to users. For example, The *Critical Foundations: Protecting America's Infrastructures, the Report of the President's Commission on Critical Infrastructure Protection*[1], report produced by the Presidential Commission on Critical Infrastructure Protection, grouped America's critical infrastructures into five categories: energy, telecommunications, physical distribution, banking and finance and vital human services. U.S. dependence on these critical infrastructures makes their predictable and reliable operations a matter of national security. However, because they are owned and operated primarily by the private sector, their security is the shared responsibility of government and private industry.

ENERGY

The single most important infrastructure to the United States and its industries is its electrical production and distribution system. The complex system currently in place represents the backbone of the nation, for without electricity, telecommunications, banking and finance, transportation and other vital services would not function. Consequently, the efficient and dependable production and distribution of electrical power is a vital national asset. When analyzing threats to information systems, the potential threats to supporting energy systems should also be evaluated since, without electricity, telecommunications and computer networks cannot function.

TELECOMMUNICATIONS

The U.S. telecommunications infrastructure refers to the nation's capacity to transmit information and communications over the Public Switched Network (PSN) and the Internet. This infrastructure is rapidly becoming the most important infrastructure to the national economy, national security and society as a whole. The infrastructure consists of numerous fiber-optic, copper and other cables that transmit information; satellite networks and their ground receiving stations; relays, routers, loops and other nodes on the national and global network; and computers used by individuals, businesses, academic institutions, military organizations and the government. Recent changes in the telecommunications, computer and broadcast industries are creating new technologies, access points and vulnerabilities that may threaten individual users, regional users and entire systems. Potential physical and cyber threats may target individual nodes within a network and create a chain reaction of failures and loss of service.

PHYSICAL DISTRIBUTION

The physical distribution networks consist of transportation and oil and gas infrastructures. The vast, interconnected network of highways, railroads, ports and inland waterways, pipelines, airports and airways facilitate the efficient movement of goods and people, including military equipment and personnel. Damage to these infrastructures would have a devastating effect on the economy, defense community and individual lives as goods would be unable to move and vital services could not be provided. Attacks on the physical distribution infrastructures may be conducted using a variety of methods, both physical and cyber and can severely affect an organization's ability to meet critical mission requirements.

BANKING AND FINANCE

The U.S. banking and finance infrastructures are critical to the economic well-being of the nation, including military payments for the procurement of critical resources and the payment of military personnel salaries. These infrastructures are considered relatively secure from physical threats due to sophisticated security procedures including redundancy, authentication, data storage and back-up procedures. While electronic or cyber-attacks have occurred, they have targeted individual holdings and are generally not considered a major threat to the entire system.

VITAL HUMAN SERVICES

Executive Order 13010[2] defined vital human service infrastructures to consist of the water treatment and supply system, emergency services and government services. Unlike other infrastructures, these systems are highly localized and do not form a national infrastructure. Nevertheless, disruptions to their reliable operation can significantly impact national security, the United States government and the private sector. Each of the vital human service infrastructures faces a different set of vulnerabilities. The nation's water supply system faces threats from chemical and biological toxins and weaknesses in its distribution and pumping system. Electronically controlled pumps and doors could be tampered with, such as causing a break in the pipes and valves that are responsible for distribution, thus resulting in a loss of service.

Emergency services, which consist of fire and ambulance services, are vulnerable to weaknesses in their command-and-control mechanisms. Because most of the command-and-control systems for emergency services rely on the PSN, failures in the telecommunications system may restrict or deny emergency services. In addition, jamming and other interference techniques may be used to disrupt or overwhelm the system.

Government human services are provided by such organizations as the Social Security Administration, the Centers for Disease Control, the National Weather Service, the Immigration and Naturalization Service and state welfare systems. As these organizations, become increasingly dependent on information technologies, such as electronic databases, remote access and the Internet, their potential for exploitation increases. Cyber-attacks to these systems may threaten the organization's ability to complete their missions, ultimately affecting the continuity of the U.S. government.

INFORMATION AND DATA

Information and data within information systems are prime targets of information operations. Such operations attempt to gain information or degrade, destroy, or otherwise manipulate data or communications in order to achieve objectives. In the past, information was vulnerable while it was being transmitted from one point to another; but upon receipt, it would be kept on paper, or in some form that was more difficult to access. Today, information is stored electronically and can be accessed instantaneously, making it vulnerable both in transit and when stored.

As organizations continue to expand the use of interconnected worldwide, automated information systems, including the Internet, more opportunities are available for computer intrusions. In the case of the Internet, computer intruders continue to take advantage of many of the same system vulnerabilities that they have for years since system administrators and security personnel have failed to institute security countermeasures necessary to protect their systems.

ANALYTICAL RESULTS AND DECISION MAKING

A third target set for information operations and information warfare is the analytical centers and decision-making processes of an organization. In such cases, the existing information infrastructure is not harmed, and data is not destroyed or manipulated once it is collected by an organization. Various methods of propaganda and misinformation are used to manipulate the thought or analysis processes of the targeted organization. While such strategies are not new, the proliferation of access points has dramatically increased with the spread of information technology. The Internet, Direct Broadcast Satellites (DBS), short-wave radio, wireless communications and other communications media represent the proliferation of low-cost, highly accessible communications technologies on a global scale. The United States and foreign competitors have equal access to U.S. open-source information; in fact, they have equal input into those resources as well. Their ability to place data into the system may steer analysis, or decision-making, along paths that otherwise would have been ignored or avoided. The objective of this type of attack is to either take the decision maker out of the process or to reduce the decision maker's ability to make correct decisions.

New technologies also provide propagandists and disinformers with very powerful tools. The U.S. movie industry has shown how powerful and convincing synthetic images can be and how commercially available technologies can be used to generate them. Historically, written material and radio have been used to create convincing synthetic events. Today's visual media can be manipulated to create powerful and realistic effects. In addition, the proliferation of global Internet access has opened a whole new realm for employing propaganda and deceptive information. The use of these new technologies in misinformation and deception operations can influence analytical results and the decision-making process when, in fact, the information conveyed is false, distorted, or taken out of context.

ANALYZING THE THREAT

An increasing dependence on information systems and a corresponding increase in the ability of adversaries to carry out malicious acts against these systems, demands that we strengthen our defenses. Before attempting to develop defensive countermeasures, a great deal must be learned about the mission to be performed, the mission's dependence on information systems and the adversary's potential involvement. The first step is to define the mission to be performed, followed by the steps listed below.

1.   **Step 1**: Identify the mission and determine mission reliance on the information system
2.   **Step 2**: Determine security services needed for the IS to be effective
3.   **Step 3**: Identify potential adversaries
4.   **Step 4**: Determine adversary intentions
5.   **Step 5**: Determine potential IO strategy of adversaries to support their intentions
6.   **Step 6**: Identify potential attack scenarios
7.   **Step 7**: Identify adversary characteristics and other factors affecting potential attacks
8.   **Step 8**: Match potential attacks with adversary characteristics and other factors

IDENTIFY THE MISSION AND MISSION RELIANCE ON THE INFORMATION SYSTEM

Whether short- or long-term, what is the organization's mission? This needs to be a concise statement. Information systems exist to support accomplishing the mission, so it must be determined just how much mission success relies on the correct and timely performance of the information system as displayed in Figure 2.

The assumption is that an IS will first be designed to provide the required performance without adversary interference. To determine what security services are needed, it is necessary to link mission-reliance to provision of necessary security services. These services are expressed as providing Confidentiality, Integrity and Availability and are also shown in Figure 2.

Figure 2. Analyzing the Threat - Mission

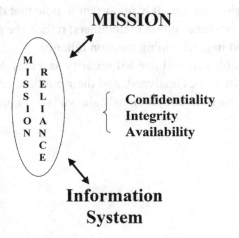

Analyzing the Threat

One way to determine necessary security services is to ask a series of mission-related questions about each security service. The following list illustrates some of the basic questions to be asked.

CONFIDENTIALITY

- ° Does the information residing on the IS have value to an adversary should they be able to obtain it in time to act on it?
- ° What are the greatest consequences that can reasonably be expected to occur if the security service of Confidentiality is breached?

≅ Within one minute after transmission/reception?

≅ Within one hour, one day, or one week?

- ° What exactly is the delineating point that Confidentiality can be breached without impact to the mission?
- ° What if Confidentiality is breached for 1%, 25%, 50%, or 75% of the traffic stored, processed, or transmitted on the system?

INTEGRITY

- ° How much does mission-success depend upon the accuracy or completeness of the information and programs on the system?
- ° What are the greatest consequences that can reasonably be expected to occur if the security service of Integrity is breached?
- ° What if Integrity is breached for classification; content; originator; recipient, or randomly?

AVAILABILITY

- ° How much does mission-success depend upon the continued availability of the information (files and databases) and the information system itself (ability to create, process, store, retrieve and transmit information)?
- ° What are the greatest consequences that can reasonably be expected to occur if information on the system were unavailable for some period of time?
- ° What if the period of time that the system is unavailable were one minute; five or 15 minutes; 24 hours, or permanently unavailable?
- ° What alternatives are available to continue operations when the system is disabled?

The above questions are only suggestive. The questions actually asked should result in an exhaustive description of the required security services. It is important to note that these types of questions are not asked of systems administrators or other system maintainers; rather, the person responsible for mission success must be directly involved in determining mission reliance.

Once mission-reliance is established and needed security services determined, potential adversaries can be identified, their characteristics analyzed, and their possible actions determined. This can be viewed in an expansion of the flow diagram previously shown (see Figure 3).

Figure 3. Analyzing the Threat - Adversary

Analyzing the Threat

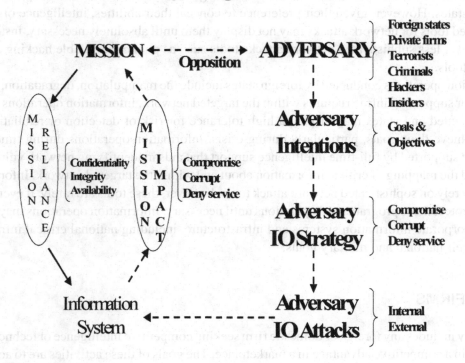

IDENTIFY POTENTIAL ADVERSARIES

The listed adversaries are grouped by category. Note that all adversaries are shown to be in opposition to various activities of the U.S. This conflict could come from historical opposition to the United States or allied grouping or could come from opposition to our objective (mission), or both.

FOREIGN STATES

This category includes any foreign country or Foreign Intelligence Services (FIS) of that country. Foreign states and their intelligence services may engage in intelligence and information operations to defeat the Confidentiality, Integrity and Availability of networked systems. Intelligence operations generally attack the Confidentiality of information within networks and their occurrence is quite frequent. Information operations attack the Integrity and Availability of data and network services and can be used to achieve many types of national and military objectives for the state.

The involvement of foreign states can be expected to encompass as many of the major interests of such entities, including economic, political, military, technology, etc., as the situation warrants. Many states are adapting their intelligence collection organizations and exploitation capabilities to incorporate

CNA along with already established HUMINT, IMINT, COMINT, SIGINT and OSINT capabilities. Intelligence operations generally have a low tolerance for risk. Sponsors are more likely to concentrate on avoiding detection, at the potential risk of revealing weaknesses in their target's security system and potential retaliation. State sponsored FIS activities are generally well funded and supported by their sponsoring states. However, given their preference to conceal their abilities, intelligence organizations with advanced tools for network attacks may not display them until absolutely necessary, instead relying on adequate yet less sophisticated network attacks tools such as publicly available hacking and system penetration tools.

Information operations conducted by foreign states include the manipulation, degradation, or destruction of data or supporting infrastructures within the targeted network. Information operations are heavily objective oriented and states may display a high tolerance for risk of detection or retaliation in their efforts to achieve their goals, particularly during crisis. Information operations during times of crisis are generally supported by full-time intelligence support that aids in identifying network vulnerabilities, structure and the mapping of critical information about and within the targeted network. Information operations may rely on sophisticated network attack tools; however, these tools are rarely, if ever, displayed in order to protect these programs and operations until necessary. Information operations may also target public and corporate information systems and infrastructure, including national critical infrastructures to achieve their national and military goals.

PRIVATE FIRMS

This category includes any foreign or domestic firm seeking competitive intelligence or technology information to gain a competitive advantage in a marketplace. The goals of these activities are to acquire trade secrets, proprietary information, marketing strategies, pricing data, negotiation strategies, technological research and development, etc. Often the technology information sought is considered "dual use" since it has both commercial and defense application potential. Because of the dual use nature of information, these firms may target both Government and Government contractor sites to obtain the information sought. These firms may also seek to discredit, delay, or disrupt, their competitors by tampering with data or perceptions about or from within the targeted company. In many countries, both friendly and hostile, private firms work in cooperation with that country's intelligence services.

TERRORISTS

This category includes both foreign and domestic organizations that engage in terrorist activities to further their goals. Terrorist organizations may be associated with a foreign state, a FIS, or criminal element, or may be just acting in a highly irrational way to gain, visibility and publicity for specific issues or to influence social, political, or military behavior amongst a targeted audience. Terrorist groups may engage in IO to achieve their operational goals. Terrorist groups have benefited from the evolution of communications and information technology, as they have embraced cellular and encryption technology to frustrate law enforcement personnel and have used the Internet to distribute propaganda regarding their organizations and objectives. It is likely that terrorist groups may engage in attacks against DoD and other systems vital to the United States military for many reasons. While expert opinion does not believe that attacks against information systems will supplant more violent terrorist actions, IO attacks may be used as adjuncts in an effort to maximize the impact of violent operations by complicating emergency responses and coordinated reactions to attacks. In addition, attacks on networks may disable certain physical security measures that may also increase the impact of violent attacks. After attacks occur, terrorists may attack systems in order to gather intelligence about planned responses or retaliation operations and potentially attempt to disrupt military responses to their acts of aggression.

CRIMINALS

This category includes individuals or organized criminal groups and may be either foreign or domestic. Organized crime is composed of the various national and international crime syndicates, drug cartels and well-organized gang activities. The primary objective of criminals is to realize financial profits and establishing control over markets. As with many national intelligence organizations, these groups are well funded and are quite experienced using information systems to their advantage. They regularly use the financial infrastructure to launder money. Their primary operational concern is avoiding interdiction, detection and apprehension. The backbone of successful criminal operations is intelligence collection and exploitation. As United States military and law enforcement operations continue to engage in mutually supporting operations, criminals have considerable interest in penetrating the DoD systems to collect intelligence about operations, policy, tactics, etc. Criminals generally have a low tolerance to the risk of discovery because the success of their operations depends upon their inability to be detected and apprehended.

HACKERS/CRACKERS

This category of adversary does not always fit into the "opposition" classification. The recreational hacker is one who visits a system just because it is there or because it poses a challenge to the hacker's knowledge and skills. The danger posed by recreational hackers is that the system may be harmed unintentionally. This is particularly true for the less sophisticated hackers, often referred to as "script kiddies," who use readily available tools developed by others. For example, recreational hackers often engage in a form of random selection for attacking a system, choosing *.mil* and *.gov* URLs as targets. Another method is to "surf" the Internet until they find an interesting location based on attention-getting characteristics such as an interesting Webpages or found through keyword or phrase searches. At the other end of the spectrum is the "cracker," who is a person with the capability to penetrate an information system for malicious purposes. The mainstream media routinely refer to both hackers and crackers as "hackers." Both hackers and crackers could be working, wittingly or unwittingly, for another category of adversary such as a foreign state or terrorist organization. Some recent foreign hacker activity suggests that many hackers/ crackers have some level of operational plan and may operate in concert with other hackers in mounting coordinated attacks. For example, a study of malware submitted to Virus Total shows cybercriminals and other threat actors are deploying a variety of abuse-of-trust approaches to spread malware and to dodge traditional defenses, often exploiting the implicit trust between a reputable software supplier and the use[3].

Hackers conduct attacks on systems for a variety of reasons. Some hackers attack information systems simply for the challenge of penetrating an important system based on the value of the information within the network. Others attack information systems for the purpose of revealing vulnerabilities and weaknesses in popular software applications and hardware. Finally, some hackers may attack information systems out a sense of financial or personal gain, effectively using their skills to steal money, or otherwise valuable data, which they can either sell or use to blackmail their victims. However, hackers often achieve access levels giving them the ability to attack the Integrity and Availability of the network, their personal motivations often prevent them from doing so.

Therefore, those hackers who penetrate a system simply because they are able to, pose a threat to the Confidentiality of computing systems, but generally do not seriously threaten the other security services. They tend to tamper only with the files they need to hide their presence into the system, such as entry logs and password files. This group is likely to attack computing networks because it makes an attractive target to these hackers. The fact that it is important to the United States military and intelligence community makes it an attractive target to hackers who are looking to feel important. Accessing networks that are considered important or regarded as difficult to penetrate satisfies the egos of these hackers who determine their targets based on the degree of difficulty involved in penetration.

However, some hackers may attack the other two security services if certain political conditions are met, as demonstrated by the attacks on India's nuclear weapons programs following their testing of a device. Hackers are prone to attacking systems that they believe to somehow threaten, or support activities, that threaten the public good. If the United States military engages in activities that hackers believe to threaten the "public good," the number of attacks against computing networks from this group can be expected to increase.

Hackers may also attack the computing systems out of a sense of public good. These hackers generally believe that revealing vulnerabilities and weaknesses in systems is acting on behalf of the public good. These hackers regularly test popular hardware and software applications looking for vulnerabilities. They routinely publicize their findings through trade magazines, Internet postings, conferences and other means. Hackers have been known to reveal weaknesses and flaws in e-mail software, web-browsers, operating systems, etc. Even if not directly attacking computing systems, these hackers may reveal and publicize vulnerabilities and weaknesses that directly affect the systems and software used by organizations. These hackers could potentially defeat any or all of the security services, however, risk is assumed to be low, as their primary interests lie in product testing and evaluation as opposed to malicious actions.

INSIDERS

This category poses the greatest threat to information systems since insiders are authorized users who perform unauthorized activities. Insiders may be acting on their own or in collusion with an individual or group that doesn't have authorized access on their own, including a FIS. Hostile insiders are often self-motivated and have some level of authorized physical or administrative access. Insiders are particularly difficult to prepare for and to defend against. Unlike external threats, insiders do not need to penetrate a system by defeating security services, but rather, are given access to the total system or portions therein. Even the most compartmented organizations must extend enough trust to employees and personnel to perform the duties for which they are assigned; therefore, some degree of access is usually available for exploitation. Furthermore, insiders possess the ability to defeat all the security services and would most likely place themselves in a position where the attack is not attributable to them. While the number of individuals within the DoD community that might potentially attack DoD systems is generally considered extremely low, the potential impact caused by an attack from this source could be massive. Adversarial insiders may engage in attacks for their own financial gain or have been recruited by adversary intelligence services. Others may be disgruntled employees. In addition, attacks from non-adversarial insiders may be the results of misuse, accidents, or other unintentional sources of harm such as the accidental insertion of malicious code from a downloaded or corrupted file.

DETERMINE ADVERSARY INTENTIONS

Intent is a combination of adversary goals and objectives, influenced by the adversary's technical and human resources, dollar costs, time (e.g., time in which to act), tolerance for risk (e.g., the risk of getting caught and the consequences) and motivation. Making a determination of likely intent is made more difficult by the fact that none of the above listed variables are constant. Rather, they are constantly changing and not always visible.

The first step in determining adversary probable intent is often a simple matter of viewing friendly goals and objectives and then constructing a list of all that oppose or are somehow in conflict with them, i.e., opposing intentions. However, with the United States a recognized world leader, its adversaries seem to multiply with each demonstration of that leadership. Sometimes neither adversaries nor their likely intent(s) are obvious. This would be especially true of the nontraditional adversaries such as terrorists and friendly foreign states that are also economic competitors.

Once probable intent is determined, it will be possible to predict, with some degree of certainty/uncertainty, the adversaries' IO strategy and later to identify potential attack scenarios that may be used to carry out that strategy. An IO strategy may be described as the tactics an adversary will employ against information system assets of another in order to further accomplishing their own goals and objectives. An IO strategy is the scheme and is carried out by attacks that will be discussed later.

DETERMINING ADVERSARY IO STRATEGY TO SUPPORT INTENT

IO strategies and their action element (i.e., attacks) will be targeted against the security services that will further the adversary's goals and objectives. This follows the flow shown in Figure 6. Possible adversary IO strategies are:

- C- To breach Confidentiality
- I - To corrupt Integrity
- A -To deny Availability

The matrix in Table 1 has been annotated with typical IO strategies that might be expected to support the listed intents. This is essential information for the analyst. Otherwise, he or she would have to consider all IO strategies as being equally threatening. There is no claim that the entries are complete or appropriate for each situation. It is up the threat analyst to construct a table of adversaries, intentions and potential IO strategies for each situation.

Table 1. IO Strategies in Support of Adversary Intent

INTENT	ADVERSARIES					
	Foreign State	Private Firm	Terrorists	Criminals	Hacker*	Insider*
Military Superiority	C-I-A					C-I-A
Economics Superiority	C					C
Political Unrest	C-I		C-I-A			C-I-A
Economic Espionage	C					C
Industrial Espionage	C	C				C
Disruption Financial Institutions	I-A		I-A		I-A	I-A
Physical Destruction	I-A		I-A			I-A
Theft	C	C	C	C-I	C	C
Malicious Activity	C-I-A		I-A		C-I-A	C-I-A

*Recall that hackers and insiders can be working alone or for/with another category of adversary

An adversary's use of IO strategies may change over time as the situation changes. For example, in time of peace a foreign country seeking military superiority might be primarily concerned with compromising information to learn of another's technology, contingency plans, capabilities and vulnerabilities. In time of crisis or armed conflict the same country's priorities might shift to corrupting the integrity of opposing information systems and/or denying their use to opposing forces. This view is compatible with the previous discussion that tied an adversary's goals and objectives to IO strategy. As the situation shifts (e.g., peace to war), so do the IO strategies that will support the new intent.

At this time, it can be said that potential adversaries have been identified along with their predicted goals and objectives and the IO strategies that they might use to further their overall goals and objectives. With this insight, threat analysts can focus their effort on attacks that carry out the identified IO strategies. Instead of jumping directly into attacks it is more realistic to do exactly what the adversary does--and that is gather facts, decide on a course of action and plan the attack. This effort can be termed pre-attack activities. The general steps of computer network attacks will be discussed in the next section.

COMPUTER NETWORK ATTACKS

An Attack Taxonomy

As defined earlier, an attack is a sequenced set of activities that exploit specific vulnerabilities leading to the defeat of one or more desired security services. A simple taxonomy can be used to help gain an appreciation of the total scope of a CNA attack. This taxonomy will also assist in understanding the importance of analyzing computer network attacks as part of threat analysis. From an operational viewpoint, attackers attempt to achieve objectives through a sequence of activities. These activities can be described as formulating an IO strategy, acquiring tools to execute the strategy, exploiting a system vulnerability to gain access and executing one or more processes designed to breach one or more security services. The taxonomy of this process can be depicted as follows:

Figure 4. CNA Taxonomy

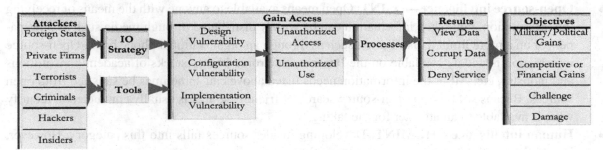

CNA Taxonomy

The entire CNA process must be analyzed as thoroughly as possible to achieve a useful characterization of the threat. Most of the elements of this taxonomy are discussed throughout the body of this chapter.

Pre-Attack Activities

A military force commander would seek information about an opponent before attacking and then meticulously, time permitting, plan the strategy and tactics to be used in the attack. The same is true of an information systems attacker. Although hackers might use a random method for selecting targets, sophisticated attackers normally use a structured approach to plan and execute an attack. This is especially true of the foreign intelligence services of country states. Understanding typical pre-attack activities can result in the early detection of a potential attack and by taking countermeasures can defeat the attack in its early stages.

Typical pre-attack activities include gathering information about the systems to be attacked, devising an attack plan and preparing for the attacks. As it happens, if we gather information about our own system just as we expect the adversary will do, we will be in a position to plan countermeasures for potential attacks, just as they will be in a position to undertake the attacks. The side that has done their homework the best will be in a better position to win the battle.

GATHERING INFORMATION

What does the adversary need to know about the target system? Typically, the attacker wants to know such information as the operating system and version, vulnerability patches that have/have not been applied, what services are running and on what ports, what network connections exist to the system, manufacturers' names and models of hardware (including peripherals such as printers), names of systems and network administrators, IP addresses, passwords and much more. In the following discussion, information gathering is explained in traditional INT or intelligence activity terms.

- **Open-source intelligence—OSINT**: Open means available to anyone with the means of receiving the information. Published information can be widely distributed through media such as newspapers or on a more limited distribution such as through an organizational phone book. Open-source information is widely available on the Internet, electronic library stacks of academic institutions and industry, etc. All of the information needs listed above can sometimes be satisfied from open sources. Because of this, an open-source search of friendly source is usually conducted to identify what is available to an attacker for the taking.
- **Human intelligence—HUMINT**: Developing insider sources falls into this category. However, in addition to the compromised employee/Service member, significant information can be obtained from unsuspecting employees, spouses, friends, etc. The method used in this case is social engineering, the art of extracting information by knowing human behavior. It is more difficult and riskier to obtain a password by attacking a system than it is by obtaining an employee's identification number (typically assigned to each employee in the commercial sector), phoning the systems administrator and asking for a password reset because the password was forgotten.
- **Signals intelligence—SIGINT**: Attempts might be made to intercept transmissions to determine the types and volume of communications, IP addresses of correspondents, message/email formats, encryption employed, etc.

The other categories of intelligence are Imagery (IMINT) and Measurement (MASINT) intelligence. These, however, would have limited use for systems attacks, although photographs of a facility (IMINT) might be useful for a physical attack on a facility.

One form of gathering information about a system is to make logical contact with it and, using various tools, ask the system questions about itself. Some of these activities might include: scanning to detect known vulnerabilities in the operating systems, hardware, or systems configuration, using custom scripts or programs such as SATAN[4]; probing to look for open services (such as ftp or telnet) to find potential access points, operating system(s) connections, etc.; pinging to map the network with all of it components. Less sophisticated adversaries, or ones with a high-risk tolerance of discovery, might scan a wide range of ports and/or systems on the target network, while adversaries with very low tolerance of discovery will selectively probe the potential target.

PLANNING AND PREPARATION

After a successful information gathering effort, the next step is to plan the attack strategy and gather attack resources such as tools. The selected attack strategy will reflect the adversary characteristics already discussed (available resources, risk tolerance, situation, etc.). The tools will be off the shelf (or Internet), customized off the shelf, or internally developed. If the port analysis detected ports with running services, then attack scripts need to be written or obtained from the Internet or other hacker sources. Depending on the software of the target system, stealth packages would be obtained (e.g., root-kit, mendax, daemonkit, etc.). If sniffers are to be used to obtain passwords, they may be obtained from Internet or hacker sources. The incident and vulnerability advisories of computer emergency response organizations (CERTs) are studied for known vulnerabilities and hacker sites consulted to obtain scripts to take advantage of them. A test run may be considered, perhaps against a test bed or a system that is similar to the target system, but not associated with it (to avoid tipping off the target).

POTENTIAL ATTACK SCENARIOS

Examining potential attack scenarios provides the threat analyst with an insight into the types of attacks that an adversary might consider using, given the adversary's capabilities for executing the scenario. The first look at possible attack scenarios is done without regard to potential adversaries. What is important now is identifying the technical potential for an attack. Later, when adversary characteristics and other factors are considered, a determination may be made as to whether a specific adversary will attempt a specific attack.

So how does an adversary identify potential targets? Through the various information gathering methods described previously. While state sponsored adversaries will generally have more, sophisticated resources available for conducting SIGINT, HUMINT and OSINT to identify potential targets, these types of activities can be found across the spectrum of potential adversaries. For example, a foreign state might use its FIS to mount a HUMINT effort and place a spy within the target organization, while a hacker might use social engineering via telephone to obtain essentially the same information. For scenarios where the access to target is remote, the passive intelligence gathering activities will often be followed up by active reconnaissance, such as port scanning the target. After collecting as much information about a potential target as possible, the adversary needs a tool that exploits a vulnerability of the target. Depending on the type of adversary and urgency of the attack, choice of vulnerability and/ or tool involves a variety of factors; however, one of the most important of which is the knowledge of the existence of a vulnerability.

Information about vulnerabilities and attacks is widespread. The practice of security through obscurity or attempting to limit the number of people that had knowledge of vulnerabilities, has given way to one of full public disclosure of vulnerabilities. Full disclosure is a double-edged sword, one that gives security administrators the knowledge to fix vulnerabilities in their systems before vendors can issue patches, but it also makes the knowledge available to those with malicious intent. Because of the wide dissemination of vulnerability information, the potential attacker community continues to grow rapidly. In addition to several emergency response team sites, such as the Cybersecurity & Infrastructure Security Agency Emergency Services Sector (ESS)[5] and the Carnegie Mellon Computer Emergency Response Team (CERT)[6], there are thousands of news groups, mailing lists and countless other web sites that contain this vulnerability information. The easy access to this information raises the apparent technical sophistication of an adversary. Certainly, the hackers that discover a particular vulnerability are technically astute, as we can assume the state sponsored adversaries are, but the availability of tools that implement sophisticated exploits can make it difficult to discern the actual technical sophistication of an adversary.

Discovery of new vulnerabilities varies from accidental to organized methodical approaches. One organized approach is in the Linux community where a line-by-line review of security relevant code is conducted by defensive security practitioners (but malicious individuals can obtain this information as well). This approach is not feasible for other platforms though, as the source code is not available (and vendors are not willing to dedicate the resources necessary to do the review themselves), so in those cases experimentation with the product is necessary. For particularly expensive products, this can, but does not necessarily restrict the pool of vulnerability researchers to those that are well funded and can purchase a system to experiment with. Certainly, the phone phreaking community is proof that purchasing a system is not necessary to discovering vulnerabilities in a system. Not many individuals, or even state-sponsored organizations for that matter, have the resources to purchase a telephone central office switch. In these cases, all it takes is the willingness to experiment with someone else's system and the inherent risk of discovery.

Given that an adversary has a target in mind and one or more applicable techniques, some sort of cost-benefit analysis has to be made whether to actually carry out the attack or not. For the average hacker, the existence of the target and technique can be sufficient, but at the other end of the spectrum, a state sponsored organization will have a much more complex decision-making process.

ATTACK PATHS

Up to now we have addressed IO strategies. Underlying those strategies are the actual steps necessary to exploit a set of vulnerabilities, leading to an adversary's desired consequences. The attack paths lead to an adversary's desired objective, i.e., defeat of a security service. The attack path begins with the first step toward accomplishing the objective. For example, an attack on confidentiality might begin with collecting information and reconnoitering the target system (i.e., pre-attack activities), then gaining access to the network. Several options might be available for gaining system access such as obtaining a valid user ID and password or hijacking an existing authorized session. Once access to the system has been obtained, the next step might be to obtain system privileges, followed by all the steps that lead to placing the "stolen" information or data in the hands of the adversary. Potential attack paths will be determined by the IO strategy that the adversary has selected and the tools that are available to the adversary, modified by adversary characteristics and other factors.

IDENTIFY ADVERSARY CHARACTERISTICS AND OTHER FACTORS AFFECTING POTENTIAL ATTACKS

An actual attack attempted by an adversary is dependent upon several factors. In this section we discuss those listed below:

1. The availability of the attack
2. The ability of the adversary to use the attack
3. The willingness of the adversary to execute the attack
4. The considerations of time

THE AVAILABILITY OF THE ATTACK

Is the attack well known and assumed to be available to the adversary? In the not-too-distant past, knowledge of computer security vulnerabilities was confined to the relatively small communities of security practitioners and sophisticated attackers. The rapid growth of the Internet has facilitated the exchange of this information, making it available to individual hackers, foreign intelligence services and anyone else with an interest in attacking the systems of others. Each day there are thousands of hackers attempting to penetrate information systems of the military, government, educational, commercial and individuals. When a vulnerability is found, it is often publicly disclosed, including the software steps necessary to exploit the vulnerability. There are news groups, mailing lists and countless web sites that contain this vulnerability information. Such easy access to information raises the technical capability of an adversary.

Another factor is the ability of sophisticated intruders to develop their own attack tools. It is difficult to determine exactly what has been developed and by whom, unless the tools have been detected during an actual attack or intelligence sources have been able to provide information that such development has been undertaken.

ABILITY TO USE THE ATTACK

It is one thing for an attack scenario or path to be known and quite another to have the capability to carry out the attack. Hackers that grab a tool from somewhere and blindly uses it are referred to as "script-kiddies," i.e., are able to recognize and download attack scripts written by others and made public. However, script-kiddie level hackers might be expected to randomly use a script in such a manner that would result in an unsuccessful attack. Although unsuccessful, such a random attack might inadvertently cause damage to the target system. A more sophisticated adversary would be expected to develop their own tools, but also take the tools harvested from publicly available sources and improve them or adapt them to suit their needs.

Another aspect of an attack is access. Each attack assumes a level of access as the attack's starting point. Some tools are designed to penetrate a system's perimeter. Other tools first require access to the target system before they can be used. Often tools are only effective against a specific version or configuration of an operating system or system's configuration. The greatest difference in access is between someone with authorized access to a system, e.g., an insider and one without authorized access. The insider with knowledge of attack tools and the skills to use them is, of course, potentially the most significant threat.

WILLINGNESS TO USE THE ATTACK

In this instance, willingness to execute an attack is based on the combination of several adversary characteristics:

- **Technical resources** - Do they have appropriate programs, tools and equipment?
- **Human resources** - Do they have the knowledge to use capabilities and skills to execute successful attacks?

- **Money resources** - Are adequate money resources available to develop and execute the attack? Some attacks might be undertaken with simple hardware and software resources and a connection to the Internet. Other resources might have to be bought at significant expense, e.g., a hacker for hire or the compromise of an insider with system's access.
- **Risk tolerance** - Are they willing to risk retribution for an attack? Is there a fear of being detected or a fear of the attack being attributed to them? Would executing an attack compromise the attack's future use?
- **Motivation** - Does the adversary have the persistence is pursuing their objectives? Motivation has the potential of being overridden by a low tolerance of risk or creating a fearless fanatic willing to attempt any attack.

CONSIDERATIONS OF TIME

The assessment of risk involves the analysis of facts and assumptions. However, these change over time and sometimes make a good analysis invalid. Some of the elements that can be affected by time include:

- **Resources** - Technical, human and money resources of an adversary can change overnight. In one case an adversary may be able to enhance these resources resulting in a dramatic increase in capabilities and attack skills. On the other hand, access might change as an insider's employment (human resource) is terminated or an Internet connection (technical resource) discontinued.
- **Perishability of a vulnerability** - The target system may undergo changes that eliminate a vulnerability, e.g., the normal upgrade of system software or the addition of technical or procedural security. Further, if an attack is to exploit a known vulnerability, there is a good chance that within a time a patch will be developed to overcome it. All of these changes will have the effect of making an attack unsuccessful.
- **The political, social and economic environment** - Changes in the environment can affect many facets of an attack. The adversary's intent will be affected should the situation transition from a peacetime to crisis to wartime. Also affected includes: the adversary's willingness to employ certain attack tools; accept a higher level of risk; expend human, technical, land, or money resources; etc. The changing situation could be less than peace to war, such as an economic or political change in the world, region or state. A sudden change in one country's dominance in the marketplace could have information operations ramifications.
- **The value of information** - While information itself does not change, without intervention, its value can. Information needed by us may be of no value if delayed or not received. Information in the hands of an adversary today might allow them to obtain their objectives (usually at the expense of our own objective) but be worthless to them tomorrow.
- **Historical Perspective** - Examining historical data concerning attacks can provide some insight into the likelihood that an adversary will mount an attack, especially if the adversary's capability and intent are adjudged to be high. Historical data can be obtained from intelligence organizations, law enforcement agencies and several computer incident response centers. For example, from 2016 through 2020, between 12 and 25 zero-day attacks were identified each year, about 21 per year on average; 80% of all successful data breaches in 2019 directly resulted from zero-day attacks; it's estimated that 42% of all attacks in 2021 were zero-day attacks[7]. The ripple effect

of these incidents, however, affected tens of thousands of sites and hosts. A detailed analysis of reported incidents could provide information concerning the perpetrator(s) of the incidents and help the threat analyst determine adversarial patterns and possible attack techniques that may be used. Historical data clearly has some value in analyzing past trends, but it must be kept in mind that it only provides information on what has been detected and reported and does not necessarily provide an accurate view of what would be attempted in the future.

MATCH POTENTIAL ATTACKS WITH ADVERSARY CHARACTERISTICS AND OTHER FACTORS

At this point the necessary information has been gathered to compare and contrast potential attacks to identify those attacks that will most probably be used in a given situation by a specific adversary. Knowing one's own system, its vulnerabilities and strengths and adversary goals, strategies and characteristics provides the basis for knowing the extent of the threat. Refer back to Figure 1 to view all of the factors that are to be considered so that the risk analyst may identify the possible action of the adversary. What the adversary most likely intends to do (IO strategy) leads the analyst to a set of attacks that will accomplish those objectives. Each adversary is then analyzed using a set of standard characteristics to estimate the attacks most likely to be used by each.

The impact of the selected attacks is then assessed for risk potential. The analyst will have to interpret, project and extrapolate the collected data so that it has meaning in the context of the target system, the adversary, the mission, etc. The data will have to be massaged and will require insights that can only be made by individuals that collectively have experience and knowledge in all of the areas, e.g., mission (operations), threat, vulnerabilities and attacks. Putting it all together will require informed judgement based on data that is often ill-defined and subject to change. The process is both art and science. It is assumed that attackers will use any means of penetration and will tend to first use the attacks that match their characteristics. Further, if an attack path is denied, an adversary will select an alternate path leading to the desired objective. Several attacks might be employed simultaneously, perhaps by independent sources.

To select the anticipated attacks the problem must be viewed from the adversary's point of view, not the view of the analyst. The task is difficult with no guarantee that the final analysis will correctly predict the future action of the adversary. One thing is certain; the more factual information that is available to and properly interpreted by the analyst, the better the chance of predicting adversary behavior.

SUMMARY

This chapter has provided a basic, unclassified introduction and reference to general threat to information systems. The old ways of analyzing threat pitted the might of armed forces against one another. Adversaries were considered creditable threats only if they possessed a sizeable, militarily advanced, armed force. However, the pervasiveness and magnitude of technological change have made the threat of hostile information operations a major factor in the arsenal of a potential adversary. Further, these changes have altered the characteristics of potential adversaries. Individuals as well as nation states have the potential to annoy, if not totally disrupt, a nation's critical infrastructures. Today's threat can be expected to come from almost anyone.

Threat, vulnerability and mission or assets are the ingredients of risk management. All risk components must be present to result in a risk. Without threat, a vulnerability cannot be exploited; and an exploited vulnerability without a mission or other asset to harm is of no risk. This document has addressed only the threat portion of the risk management process.

It is generally recognized that threat is difficult to analyze. This is because the data needed for analysis is often complex, hard to come by and, constantly changing. The data needed for a threat analysis requires an in-depth understanding of the adversary, their goals, objectives and characteristics and an appreciation of the situation and the dynamics of time. The results of a threat analysis need to be considered along with vulnerability/attack analysis and impact analysis in order to assess risk. This coordinated analysis of risk, using all of the risk components, can only be accomplished by actively involving threat, vulnerability and impact analysts, as well as those responsible for mission success–the planners and operators–into the process of deriving insights into the ways our critical information systems will be attacked and developing cost-effective ways to provide the requisite response to those attacks.

REFERENCES

Boranbayev, S., Amrenov, A., Nurusheva, A., Boranbayev, A., & Goranin, N. (2022, March). Methods and Techniques of Information Security Risk Management During Assessment of Information Systems. In *Future of Information and Communication Conference* (pp. 787-797). Springer, Cham. 10.1007/978-3-030-98015-3_53

Hopkin, P. (2018). *Fundamentals of risk management: understanding, evaluating and implementing effective risk management*. Kogan Page Publishers.

Hubbard, D. W. (2020). *The failure of risk management: Why it's broken and how to fix it*. John Wiley & Sons. doi:10.1002/9781119521914

Huskaj, G., Iftimie, I. A., & Wilson, R. L. (2020, June). Designing attack infrastructure for offensive cyberspace operations. In *European Conference on Information Warfare and Security*, ECCWS (pp. 473-482).

Staff, U. J. (1998). *Joint doctrine for information operations* [Joint publication 3-13]. Department of Defense.

ENDNOTES

1   https://www.hsdl.org/?abstract&did=986.

2   https://www.hsdl.org/?abstract&did=1613

3   https://www.darkreading.com/vulnerabilities-threats/virustot al-threat-actors-mimic-legitimate-apps-use-stolen-certs-to-s pread-malware.

4   https://networkencyclopedia.com/security-administrator-tool-for-analyzing-networks-satan/

5   https://www.cisa.gov/emergency-services-sector

6   https://www.sei.cmu.edu/about/divisions/cert/

7   https://purplesec.us/resources/cyber-security-statistics/

Chapter 4
Impact of Function Variability in Value–Focused Models

ABSTRACT

Value focused models (VFMs) are often used to compare different alternatives in terms of their overall value for achieving a top-level objective. Since VFMs are developed by subject matter experts (SMEs), they are inherently subjective. The impact of this subjectivity on the decision process is typically evaluated by performing a sensitivity analysis on the VFM weights generated by the SMEs. This chapter discusses two additional sources of variability that can also significantly impact the final decision accuracy pertaining to building a software-based system. A methodology is also provided for estimating and reducing the magnitude of these effects on the final decision for building the system.

INTRODUCTION

A common problem in an analysis of alternatives (AoA) is how to compare different alternatives in terms of their ability to achieve a top-level objective when the performance of the alternatives themselves is characterized by several heterogeneous attributes such as timeliness, accuracy, flexibility, etc. Value focused thinking (VFT) is a widely used method in decision theory that allows such comparisons to be made (Dell'Ovo & Oppio, 2018). The basic concept behind VFT is to decompose the top-level objective into a set of sub-objectives that are essential for achieving that top-level objective (Dell'Ovo & Oppio, 2018). These sub-objectives are then further decomposed into their own essential sub-objectives and this process continues until a level with measurable attributes like timeliness or accuracy is reached. The sub-objectives are then weighted based on their relative importance to one another.

This process produces a weighted hierarchical tree, or value focused model (VFM), that represents the top-level objective in terms of the important measurable performance attributes for achieving that objective (Belton & Stewart, 2002). The sub-objectives at the lowest level are often called value functions (VFs) and convert the measurable performance attributes into dimensionless values, typically taken to lie in the range between 0 and 1 (Belton & Stewart, 2002). These value functions and the weights in the

DOI: 10.4018/978-1-6684-7766-3.ch004

VFM then allow an alternative with heterogeneous attributes to be described by a single overall value between 0 and 1 that represents how well that alternative supports achieving the top-level objective.

VFMs are generally created with the assistance of subject matter experts (SMEs), who develop the tree, the weights and the value functions based on their own experience and understanding of the problem area (Keeney, 1992). As a result, VFMs are inherently subjective and the calculated overall value for an alternative is better considered as a variable whose actual value depends on the SME decisions about the important sub-objectives to be included in the tree, the value of the weights assigned to the sub-objectives, the character of the value functions at the bottom level of the tree and the accuracy of the performance estimates for the different alternatives (Keeney, 1992). This sensitivity of the calculated overall value to the parameters in the VFM is well recognized and a standard technique in using VFMs for decision support is to conduct a sensitivity analysis by varying the weights assigned to the tree. However, as discussed above, these weights represent only one source of variability in the top-level overall value.

This chapter extends this sensitivity analysis to include two additional sources of variability that have not been generally addressed in the past: (1) mismatches between the developers of a VFM and the users/customers of the final system selected for acquisition and (2) variability in the value functions themselves. A mismatch between VFM developers and the users/customers can potentially lead to one of several possible decision errors: selecting a system that is considered inadequate by the customers/users, rejecting a system that would be considered satisfactory by the customers/users, or acquiring a more expensive system than considered necessary by the customers/users. Variability in the value functions themselves can also increase the variability of the overall value calculated for an alternative, potentially reducing the statistical confidence that there is a significant difference in value between two alternative systems (Parnell et al. 2013). Furthermore, this chapter describes the types of conditions that can lead to a mismatch between the VFM developers, and the system users and it provides a methodology for calculating the impact of value function variability on the overall value of an alternative. Recommendations are also provided for how to reduce the impacts of both sources of variability on the decision process.

TYPES OF VALUE FUNCTIONS THAT CA BE IN A VFM

Figure 1 shows a notional bottom level of a VFM and illustrates that there are three types of value functions that may be used. Typical value functions can be a continuous curve, as shown on the left side of Figure 1, that converts a specific performance level, x_o, of a proposed system to a value, $v_o = p(x_o)$, from 0 to 1 (note: value ranges from 0 to 10 or 0 to 100 are also occasionally used). The horizontal x-axis varies from a minimum acceptable performance level, x_{min}, where the system is perceived as having no value for that attribute, to a maximum performance value, x_{max}, where additional performance adds no additional perceived value to the user or decision maker.

A value function can also be a discrete set of features, with each member of the set given a specific value, as shown in the center of Figure 1. These different features can be either discrete, stand-alone features or cumulative features, where feature B includes feature A as well, feature C includes feature B as well, etc. In the extreme case, a value function can be based on a single feature and its presence or absence determines whether the value is 1 or 0, respectively, as shown on the right side of Figure 1. Figure 1 also shows that weights are developed for each sub-level of each branch of the VFM independently and each set of weights is normalized to 1.

Figure 1. Example Value Functions

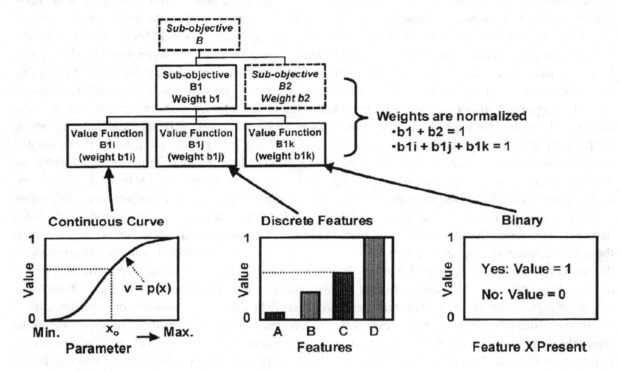

Development of Value Functions

Value functions that accurately reflect the SMEs' judgments are clearly essential to properly convert the performance of heterogeneous attributes to a common value scale and accurately compare alternatives. VFs are typically generated by groups of SMEs to ensure a general acceptance of the final VFM by the community, but consequently, the group can have differences of opinion about several important characteristics of a value function (Keeney, 1992).

For a continuous curve value function, one area where there may be differing views is on the appropriate range of interest for a performance attribute. This type of difference can often be resolved by taking the range from the smallest minimum to the largest maximum value of interest to the group. Another area where there may be differences of opinion is on the actual value assigned by the group for a specific performance level within that range. Because of differences in the experience and concerns of the SMEs, a group of SMEs will generally provide a range of values for a given level of performance. This range of values can be significant; it is not uncommon for a group of SMEs to provide value estimates ranging from 0.4 to 0.6, or wider, for the same performance level. This variability in value is typically widest at the center of the performance scale and usually decreases significantly at either end where the value approaches either 0 or 1. As a result, there is not really a well-defined, single-valued curve, but rather a distribution of values over some range.

For the discrete features type of value curve, the same two issues arise. There may be differences of opinion on which features should be included, as well as what value should be assigned to a particular feature. Differences of opinion over which features belong can usually be resolved by including the entire set of features identified by the SMEs as important. However, the difference of opinion about values means that a feature does not map to a single, well-defined value, but again is represented by a distribution of values over some range.

For the binary value function in Figure 1, neither of these issues typically occurs. The feature is simply accepted as important and given a value of 1 or 0 depending on its presence or absence. Consequently, the remaining of this technical note will focus on only the continuous and discrete features value functions.

The usual method for building these two types of value functions with a group of SMEs is to attempt to achieve a consensus within the group for a single value for a particular performance level or feature. Such a consensus can usually be achieved easily with most groups of SMEs and it makes the evaluation of alternatives with VFMs much easier. A common approach is to take the average of the different values proposed by the SMEs, possibly eliminating outliers from the averaging process and the group will frequently accept this average as a representative value. Nonetheless, this approach for developing a consensus obscures the fact that value functions are still statistical distributions based on a range of subjective views and not single-valued functions. A different group of SMEs might easily generate a different consensus value for that same performance level or feature, leading to a different evaluation of the various alternatives.

IMPACT OF MISMATCHES BETWEEN SME DEVELOPERS AND SYSTEMS USERS ON DECISION MAKING

As discussed above, developing value curves with a group of SMEs typically produces value curves that are better viewed as statistical distributions than as a well-defined single-valued curve. In addition to this variability, the actual shape of the value curve, or value distribution, can be quite different depending on the subjective views of the SMEs generating the value curve. In some cases, SMEs see the initial gains in performance as providing the most value, with decreasing increments of value for subsequent performance improvements. The result is a convex value curve, labeled "Decreasing returns to scale" in Figure 2. In other cases, SMEs may see little value in the initial performance gains, resulting in the

Figure 2. Types of Value Curves

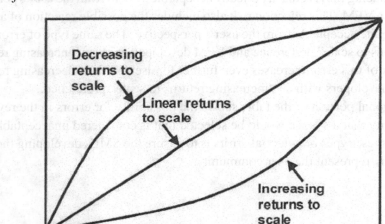

concave curve labeled "Increasing returns to scale." In other cases, SMEs may see equal increments in performance giving equal increases in value, producing the curve labeled "Linear returns to scale."

For simplicity, the statistical variability of the value curves is ignored in this figure and the curves shown can be considered as the mean value of the individual SME values. However, the figure does suggest one possible cause for the distribution in values about some mean value may be that the group of SMEs includes a mixture of SMEs who have very different views of how they value increases in performance over the performance range of interest.

This basic shape of the value curves can impact decision-making when there is a mismatch between the value-performance attitudes of the SMEs developing the VFM and the ultimate users of the system that is selected. Table 1 shows the possible combinations and the potential impact on the decision process. When the SMEs developing the value functions are matched to the ultimate system users in terms of their views about returns to scale, it is likely the alternatives selected based on the value functions will also be viewed as the correct ones by the system users.

Table 1. Impact of Value Preferences on the Decision Process

		Decreasing returns to scale	Linear Returns to scale	Increasing returns to scale
Users Value Preference	Decreasing returns to scale	Correct Decision	Risk of rejecting an acceptable system	Increased risk of rejecting an acceptable system
	Linear returns to scale	Risk of accepting a poor system	Correct Decision	Risk of rejecting an acceptable system
	Increasing returns to scale	Increased risk of accepting a poor system	Risk of accepting a poor system	Correct Decision

On the other hand, users with a preference for "decreasing returns to scale" would typically give more value to a system than would be reflected in the VFs developed by SMEs with a preference for "linear returns to scale", introducing the risk that a perfectly acceptable system from the user's perspective might be rejected using such a VFM. This rejection risk also includes the possible rejection of a less expensive system that would be quite acceptable from the user's perspective. The same type of error occurs for users with a "linear returns to scale" preference and VFM developers with an "increasing returns to scale" preference and the risk of this error increases even further for users with a "decreasing returns to scale" preference and VFM developers with an "increasing returns to scale" preference.

The lower left diagonal portion of the table shows the possibility for errors in the reverse direction, leading to the possibility that a system would be selected that is considered unacceptable by the users. The best way to avoid these types of potential errors is to ensure the SMEs developing the VFM and VF curves and values really represent the user community.

IMPACT OF VALUE CURVE DISTRIBUTIONS ON DECISION MAKING

Value curves are often shown in books and papers on as a single continuous, well-defined line, as indicated earlier in Figures 1 and 2. However, because value curves represent the subjective opinions of SMEs about the value of a particular level of system performance, there is often a distribution of values for the same level of system performance and the value curve is better considered as the mean value of a statistical distribution of values.

Similarly, the performance level of a particular system may be a well-defined value Xm or it may also be some distribution of performance about this mean value. Such performance distributions may be produced by two possible factors. The first factor is that performance estimates are often based on the SME's opinions and just as the case for value, there is also variability in how the different SMEs expect the system to perform. The second factor is that performance of the system is often affected by several random variables, such as environmental variability and the distribution shows the real range of system performance that can be expected in use. Which factor dominates may affect the decision process and different approaches may be needed to reduce this variability. Reducing the first factor may require better performance estimates while reducing the second factor may require design changes.

There are four possible cases of interest, as shown in Table 2. Each of these cases will be discussed in detail below.

Table 2. Value Curve Function and System Performance Variability Cases

System Performance	Single Value Curve	Value Curve Distribution
Single Value	A	B
Value Distribution	C	D

Case A: No Variability

Case A occurs when there is a single, well-defined curve for the VF and the system performance also has a single value, X_o. This case is the V easiest to address and, as shown in Figure 3, represents the situation often seen in papers and textbooks on VFT. The performance level, X, $V_o = p(x_o)$ varies from some minimum amount to some maximum amount and maps to a single point on the value axis through the curve for the value equation, $v = p(x)$. For discrete value functions, like those shown in Figure 1, a particular feature set just maps to a single value.

Case B: Value Curve Distribution and Single Value System Performance

Case B where the value curve function has some distribution while the system performance is a single value is the next easiest case to address. This case is best addressed by first deriving the general equation that describes how system performance maps to value. This general equation is identified here as equation (1):

Figure 3. Case A: No Variability

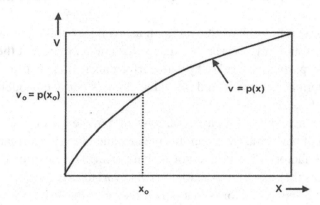

$$g(v) = \int\limits_{x\min}^{x\max} f(v,x)h(x)dx \tag{1}$$

In equation (1), h(x) represents the system performance distribution and g(v) represents the resulting value distribution. The term f(v,x) represents the value curve probability density function (pdf); the exact definition of f(v,x) is somewhat complex, dependent on how values are elicited from the SMEs. The product h(x)dx represents the probability that a system performance will lie in the range between x and (x+dx), while the product g(v)dv represents the probability that a system will have a value lying in the range between v and (v-I-dv). For case B, equation (1) reduces to the simpler equation (A6), reproduced here as equation (2):

$$g(v) = f(v, xo) \tag{2}$$

Figure 4 shows a simple example where the value curve pdf is uniformly distributed over a vertical value range, which has width H in the vertical direction. Because of the vertical normalization, the value curve distribution is simply the constant value 1/H in this range. As Figure 4 and equation (2) clearly show, the value curve pdf is simply mapped directly onto the v-axis; g(v) has the same value 1/H and the vertical value range along the v-axis depends on the slope of the value curve pdf at the point $x = x_0$. For discrete value functions like those shown in Figure 1, a particular feature set gets mapped onto a range of values.

The impact of case B for the decision maker is that broad value curve pdfs spread a well-defined system performance level, x_0, into a much broader range of values along the v-axis. As this spreading becomes broader and broader, the g(v) curves for two different alternatives, say x_0 and x, may begin to overlap, reducing the statistical confidence that the two alternatives are significantly different in their value.

Case C: Single Value Curve and System Performance Distribution

Case C occurs where the value curve is a single, well-defined curve and the system performance has some distribution. This case is considerably more complex than case B and the equation for g(v), is

Figure 4. Case B: Value Curve Function Variability
(Uniform Value Curve Function Distribution)

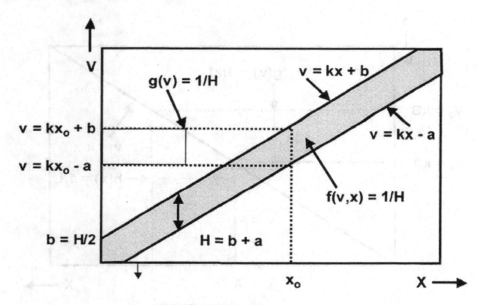

identified here as equation (3). In equation (3), $p^{-1}(x)$ is the inverse function which shows how to apply the equation in the special cases where the slope, $p'(x)$, is zero over some range, the inverse function has multiple values or the slope changes discontinuously at specific values of x.

$$g(v) = \int_{a\min}^{x\max} f(v,x)h(x)dx = \frac{h(x)}{p'(x)} @ x = p^{-1}(v)$$

$$\text{where } p'(x) = \frac{dp(x)}{dx} @ x = p^{-1}(v)$$

(3)

Figure 5 shows a simple example where a "linear returns to scale" value curve with constant slope k and a uniform system performance distribution are assumed. This performance distribution is mapped into a uniform value distribution along the v-axis with the magnitude of g(v) scaling inversely with both the performance distribution width, L and value curve slope, k. The slope, k and the range of system performance values determine the vertical range of values along the v-axis.

For value curves with a variable slope, the picture becomes even more complex, as shown in Figure 6. The inverse dependence of *g(v)* on the slope of the value curve now produces a nonlinear transformation, with *g(v)* values increasing in low slope regions and decreasing in high slope regions. For non-uniform performance distributions, even more complex shapes for the *g(v)* distributions may result.

Again, the implications for the decision maker are the same. As the performance distributions become wider and wider, the ability of the decision maker to discriminate between two alternatives as having a statistically significant difference in values decreases.

Figure 5. Case C: System Performance Variability
(Risk Neutral Value Curve)

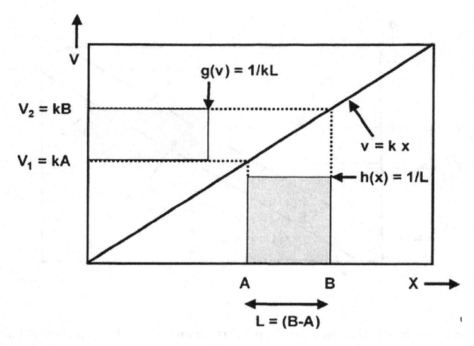

Figure 6. Case C: System Performance Variability
(Variable Value Curve)

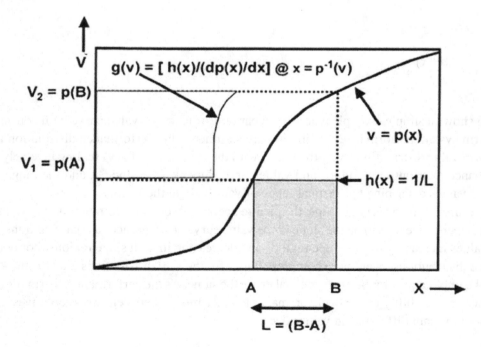

Case D: Value Curve Distribution and System Performance Distribution

Case D occurs when both the system performance and the value curves have distributions and is the most complex case since the impact on the g(v) distribution depends on the relative magnitudes of the two distributions. Equation (1) is the appropriate equation to solve for this case and Figure 7 shows a typical result when both the value curve and the system performance have uniform distributions.

Figure 7. Case D: System Performance and Value Curve Function Variability (Uniform Distributions)

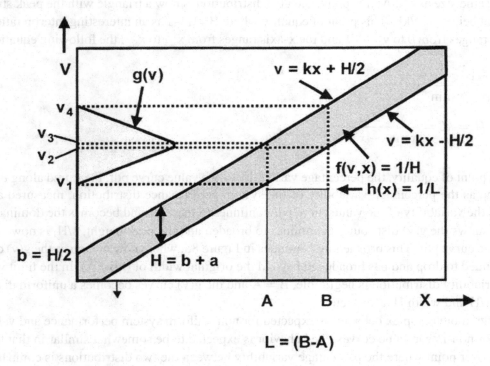

Figure 8. (a) H<kL; H≈0, (b) H<kL; H≈kL

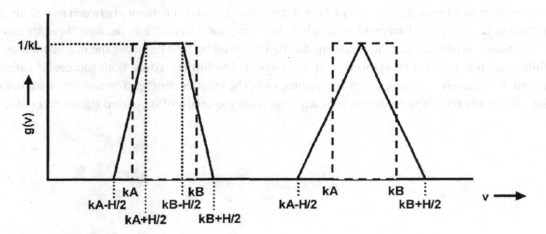

However, the behavior of g(v) can be better understood from the series of Figures 8a to 8d which show how g(v) changes from the case where the system performance pdf dominates to the case where the value curve distribution dominantes.

In Figure 11, if there is well-defined value curve (i.e., H = 0), the resulting g(v) distribution is basically Case C for a uniform system distribution over the performance range from x = A to x = B. For a constant slope value curve, g(v) is simply the rectangular box ranging from v = kA to kB with height 1/KL. As the value curve begins to change from a single well-defined curve to a pdf of width H, but while H is still small, the sides of the g(v) distribution begin to spread out and the peak begins to narrow, but still maintains the same amplitude. In Figure 8b, the value curve pdf has continued to widen until H is about the same size as kL. At this point, the g(v) distribution is now a triangle with the peak still having the original height of 1/kL. This point of equality where H=1(1- has an interesting interpretation. Since the v-axis ranges from 0 to v_{max} = 1 and the x-axis ranges from x_{min} to x_{max}, the following equation holds:

$$k = \frac{1}{x\max - x\min}$$

$$\frac{H}{v\max} = H = kL = \frac{L}{x\max - x\min}$$

(4)

At this point of equality, the percentage variability of the value curve pdf, measured along the v-axis, is the same as the percentage variability of the system performance distribution, measured along the x-axis. As the variability of the value curve pdf continues to increase and becomes the dominant factor, Figure 8c shows the g(v) distribution continues to broaden and the peak height, 1/H, is now controlled by the value curve pdf. This broadening continues in Figure 8d, where now the top of the g(v) curve has now continued to drop and has broadened beyond the original width of (kB-kA). In the limit where the system variability distribution is negligible, B = A and the g(v) curves becomes a uniform distribution of height 1/H and width H as expected.

Although more complex behavior is expected for non-uniform system performance and value curve pdfs and for non-linear value curves, the behavior is expected to be somewhat similar in that there will be a cross-over point where the percentage variability between the two distributions is comparable and away from that cross-over point, one or the other of the two distributions will dominate the g(v) value distribution. There is the usual implication for the decision maker that as the performance distributions become broader and broader, the ability of the decision maker to discriminate between two alternatives as having a statistically significant difference in values decreases. In addition, because there are now two sources for-this variability, decision making can be improved by first reducing the dominant source of variability down to near the cross-over point, then working to further reduce both sources of variability in tandem. Conversely, working to further reduce only the smaller source of variability may not offer any significant improvement in decision-making capability in terms of increased statistical confidence.

DERIVATION OF THE GENERAL EQUATION FOR MAPPING SYSTEM PERFORMANCE TO VALUE

Case A identified in the main paper is the only case where system performance maps to a single point on the value axis in a value function. In all other cases, system performance will map to some distribution of values along the vertical axis and an equation is needed that describes the shape of that value distribution.

Assume many SMEs have been assembled and they are asked for the value each of them would ascribe to a certain level of system performance, x_o. If we divide the value axis from 0 to 1 into many small bins, with each bin having a width dv and count the number of SME responses that fell into each bin, the resulting set of values provided by the SMEs can be described as a pdf function $f(v, x_o)$ that describes the fraction of SMEs who responded that the value fell in the bin between v and (v+dv), where v lies in the range 0 Lc v S 1. If we repeat this request to the SMEs for all possible values of x in the range of interest, we will generate a two-dimensional probability density function (pdf) for value: f(v,x) for 0 v S 1, x_{min} x x_{max}

The way values are elicited, asking for each SME to state the value they would assign for each performance level, x_o, means that this pdf is vertically normalized; specifically:

$$\int_0^1 f(v, xo)dv = 1 \text{ for } xmin \leq xo \leq xmax \tag{5}$$

Now let us also divide the performance axis into many small bins, with each bin having a width dx and assume that we have a proposed system whose performance can be described by a probability distribution function $h(x)$, where the quantity $h(x)dx$ represents the probability that the performance level falls in the bin between x and (x+dx). Because the proposed system must have some performance level, this distribution is horizontally normalized; specifically:

$$\int_{xmin}^{xmax} h(x)dx = 1 \tag{6}$$

Now what is required is the probability distribution function for value, $g(v)$, where the product $g(v)$ dv represents the probability that a particular system will map to a value between v and (v + dv). The product $g(v)dv$ is given by the equation:

$$g(v)dv = \int_{xmin}^{xmax} f(v, x)h(x)dxdv \tag{7}$$

In this equation, $f(v,x)dv$ represents the probability that the value falls in the bin from v to (v+dv) under the condition that system performance falls in the bin between x and (x+dx) while $h(x)dx$ represents the probability that the system performance does indeed fall in this bin between x and (x+dx). Integrating the product of these two probabilities over all possible values of x gives the value of $g(v)dv$. Canceling the term `clv' on both sides of the equation gives the result:

$$g(v) = \int\limits_{x\min}^{x\max} f(x,v)h(x)dx \tag{8}$$

Equation 8 represents the general solution for g(v) that would be used for Case D. However, it can be simplified for Cases B and C. Case B is the easiest special case to derive.

Case B Special Case

In Case B, the system performance is not represented by a distribution and has only the single value x_0. Equation 8 can be converted to this special case by replacing the distribution *h(x)* with the Dirac Delta function *δ(x)*, where:

$\delta(\text{x})=0$ for x $\mathnormal{1}^x o$

$$\int\limits_{-\infty}^{+\infty} \delta(x)dx = 1 \tag{9}$$

With this substitution, Equation 8 becomes:

$$g(v) = f(x,vo) \tag{10}$$

Case B then simply maps the vertical distribution of the value function at xo onto the value axis as g(v).

Figure 9. Dirac Delta Function Integration

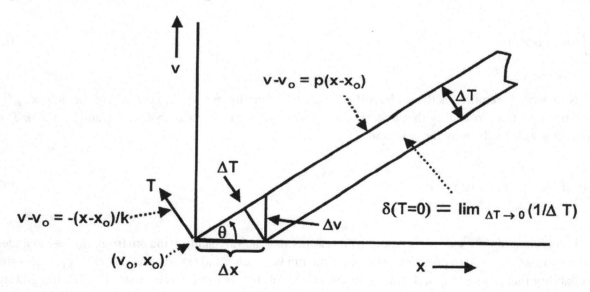

Case C Special Case

Case C is somewhat more complicated because the value curve is now represented by a line through (v, x) space. This case is best handled by representing the value curve initially as a thin, uniform, curving band and then letting the width of that band go to 0. Let the edge of this band follow the equation for the curved value line, $v = p(x)$ and consider a point (v_o, x_0) where $v_o = p(x_0)$. For simplicity, let us reset the origin at (v_o, x_o), as shown in Figure 9. Let us also temporarily assume the value curve is monotonic so the value v_o occurs only once, at $x = x_o$. This monotonic assumption will be relaxed at the end of the derivation.

The shaded band with width AT inclined at an angle 0 to the horizontal x-axis at the new origin represents the well-defined value curve. This inclination at the origin of angle 0 corresponds to a slope $k = Av/Ax = dp(x)/dx = \tan(0)$. As AT approaches 0 in the limit, this band becomes an infinitesimally thin line that can be represented by a Dirac Delta function $6(T=0)$ whose height equals $1/AT$ as AT approaches 0. The line T perpendicular to this band has a slope equal to $-1/k$ at the new origin. These limits ensure the integral of $6(T)$ along the line T equals 1, as shown by equation 11.

$$\int_{-\infty}^{+\infty} \frac{1}{\Delta T} dt = \int_{0}^{\Delta T} \frac{1}{\Delta T} dt = 1 \Rightarrow \lim \Delta T \to 0 \quad \frac{1}{\Delta T} = \delta(T = 0) \tag{11}$$

However, what is required is an expression for a vertically normalized probability $pdff(v,x)$ at the origin (v_o, x_o) as the width of this band narrows to a line. The appropriate distribution can be determined from the following vertical integration, where the scaling factor c is included to ensure vertical normalization:

$$\int_{-\infty}^{+\infty} \frac{1}{\Delta T} dt = \int_{0}^{\Delta T} \frac{1}{\Delta T} dt = 1 \Rightarrow \lim \Delta T \to 0 \quad \frac{1}{\Delta t} = \delta(T = 0) \tag{12}$$

Equations 11 and 12 show $c = cos(0)$ and since $T = 0$ along the T-axis only when $v = v_0$:

$f(v,xo)=0$ for $v{\neq}vo$

$$f(vo, xo) = \frac{\cos \theta}{\Delta T} \to \cos \theta \delta(T) \ as \ \Delta T \to 0 \tag{13}$$

If we now integrate along the x-axis through the origin, we now get:

$$\int_{0}^{\Delta x} f(vo, x)dx = \int_{0}^{\Delta x} \frac{\cos \theta}{\Delta T} = \frac{\cos \theta}{\Delta T / \Delta x} = \frac{1}{\tan \theta} \tag{14}$$

Equations 13 and 14 show, again using the fact that $T=0$ along the T-axis only when $X = X_0$:

$f(vo,x)=0$ for $x \neq xo$

$$\int_0^{\Delta x} f(vo,x)dx = \frac{1}{\tan \theta} = \frac{1}{dp(x)/dx} @ x = xo \qquad (15)$$

Equation 15 can now be used to evaluate equation (A4) for special case C. The result is:

$$g(v) = \int_{x\min}^{x\max} f(v,x)h(x)dx = \frac{h(x)}{p'(x)} @ x = p^{-1}(v) \qquad (16)$$

where $p'(x) = \dfrac{dp(x)}{dx} @ x = p^{-1}(v)$

where the term $p \neq (v)$ represents the inverse of $p(x)$ [i.e., $v = p(p(v))$].

Equation 16 was derived under the assumption that the value curve was monotonically increasing or decreasing. If the value curve is multi-valued, where the $v = v_o$ line is crossed for multiple values of x, say: xi, x2,,xN, then equation 16 must be evaluated for each crossing and the resulting g(v) is given by:

$$g(v) = \sum_{xi=1}^{N} \frac{h(xi)}{p'(xi)} \qquad (17)$$

There are also several special cases of interest. If the slope $p'(x)$ is zero over some range of *x*, say x_a to *xb*, *g(v)* in Equation 16 goes to infinity. However, the important term is the product *g(v)dv* representing the probability that an alternative has a value in the range from *v* to *v + dv*. In this case, *g(v)* looks like a Dirac delta function at the point *v* on the *v*-axis, with the integral across this point equaling the probability that the system performance falls in the range between x_a and *xb*. The other special case of interest is when the slope $p'(x)$ changes discontinuously at some point xo. In this case, Equation 16 can be evaluated on either side of x_o and *g(v)* has a finite value that changes discontinuously across the point $v_o = p^{-1}(x_0)$. However, such discontinuous changes in *g(v)* are not a problem and simply means the probability, *g(v)dv*, jumps in moving from one side of v_o to the other. Equations 16 and 17 can be evaluated properly to handle all the special cases.

As a parenthetical note, the fact that we have a vertically normalized pdf for *f(v,x)* does not generally guarantee that the same pdf is horizontally normalized and it generally is not, as Equation 15 clearly demonstrates. We could have elicited a horizontally normalized pdf by asking the SMEs what level of performance they would feel is appropriate for a given value level and derived the appropriate equations for that case, but then vertical normalization would not be generally guaranteed. Since value curves are most often generated by eliciting SME estimates for value for a given performance level and this is the only way values can be elicited for feature-based value functions (see Figure l), we will use only vertically normalized pdfs for *f(v,x)* in this chapter.

SUMMARY

This chapter has examined two sources of variability that are not generally treated in the books and papers on VFT: (1) mismatches between the developers of a VFM and the users/customers of the final system selected for acquisition in terms of their preference for how value increases as system performance increases over the range of interest and (2) variability on the value curves themselves. A mismatch between VFM developers and the users/customers can potentially lead to significant decision errors, as shown in Table 1, either selecting a system that is considered inadequate by the customers/users, rejecting a system that would be considered satisfactory by the customers/users, or selecting a more expensive system than considered necessary by the customers/users.

Variability in the value curves themselves can be a significant factor and value curve pdfs with standard deviations as large as 0.15 about a mean value of 0.5 have been observed in value functions developed by SMEs. Since assigning a value to a level of system performance is basically a subjective opinion of a SME, part of this variability may be the result of differing subjective views. Another source of such variability may be the group of SMEs developing value functions consists of a mix of SMEs with different preferences for value as a function of system performance.

The primary impact of such variability in system performance and value curve pdfs may be to reduce the statistical confidence in the decision maker that there is a significant difference in value between two alternative systems. Two recommendations for improving the decision process in terms of avoiding incorrect decisions or increasing confidence in the decision when using VFMs are to: (1) try to match the value preferences of the VFM developers with the user/customer value preferences and (2) focus first on reducing the dominant source of variability, either in the system performance distribution or the value curve pdf, then continue making reductions in tandem.

REFERENCES

Belton, V., & Stewart, T. J. (2002). Value function methods: Practical basics. In *Multiple Criteria Decision Analysis* (pp. 119–161). Springer. doi:10.1007/978-1-4615-1495-4_5

Dell'Ovo, M., & Oppio, A. (2018). Combining social and technical instances within design processes: a Value-Focused Thinking approach. In *the 87th Meeting of the European Working Group on Multicriteria Decision Aiding* (pp. 7-7).

Keeney, R. L., & McDaniels, T. L. (1992). Value-focused thinking about strategic decisions at BC Hydro. *Interfaces*, 22(6), 94–109. doi:10.1287/inte.22.6.94

Parnell, G. S., Terry Bresnick, M. B. A., Tani, S. N., & Johnson, E. R. (2013). *Handbook of decision analysis*. John Wiley & Sons. doi:10.1002/9781118515853

Chapter 5
Swing Weight Development for Software Platforms

ABSTRACT

The swing weight technique (SWT) is an approach for determining weighting factors indirectly through systematic comparison of attributes against the one deemed to be the most important. SWT consists of two general activities: (1) rank order attributes according to the relative importance of incremental changes in attribute values considering the full range of possibilities; and (2) select either the least or most important attribute as a reference point and assess how much more or less important the other attributes are with respect to the reference point. The purpose of this chapter is twofold. First, a new procedure to elicit, from a decision-maker, information regarding additive value weights (i.e., swing weights) is introduced. The procedure is a hybrid of the "balance-beam" method (BBM) and a dynamic "binary-like" interrogation (where the ith inquiry depends upon the answer to the $(j - 1)^{st}$ inquiry). Second, the maximum entropy methodology was used to demonstrate how to construct a set of additive value weights based solely on the elicited information.

INTRODUCTION

Maximum entropy methodology (MEM) is a well-established and valuable modeling tool which is applicable to a wide variety of problems, particularly those where uncertainty is involved (Squartini & Garlaschelli, 2017). Philosophically speaking, the MEM bridges the gap between what is known and unknown about a particular process or phenomenon. Specifically, it allows one to construct a model, which reflects precisely the information known about a process. Typically, this information consists primarily of observational data but may also include constraints on the process, which though unobserved for whatever reason, describe reasonable boundaries on the process. For example, consider a study of traffic flow at an Edge router. This may include the time-varying distribution of latency speeds obtained from packet captures, taken over a one-week period of each packet and the time interval (e.g., 10 milliseconds) during which a data packet passes through the router. Two servers connected with 100Gbps ethernet ran four virtual machines each and communications were conducted between each

DOI: 10.4018/978-1-6684-7766-3.ch005

virtual machine to test the performance of the Edge routers. The results showed that packet processing performance, which was 13.8Mpps using existing methods, was increased to 250Mpps, or about an 18-fold increase. A constraint might be to assume that the speed-arrival time pair, (s, t) is such that s < 250Mpps when server1 < t < server2; this includes the information that the pair (s, t) = (250, server1) never occurs. Though this information is not observed (we only monitor the packets for a week) it does reflect a reasonable limitation on the traffic flow process.

What is meant by the idea that a model precisely reflects the known information? To answer this, we must first discuss the concept of entropy. Entropy is a precise mathematical/probabilistic notion which provides a measure of information about a process; specifically, it measures the information contained in a probability distribution, obtained either theoretically or empirically (by sampled observations), describing the process (Greven et al. 2014). The product of applying the MEM is a conditional probability distribution, conditioned only on the data, which yields the maximum entropy. Colloquially speaking, we model precisely what is known and ignore all else. In other words, the MEM is a precise mathematical tactic, which avoids the unintentional incorporation of information from sources other than that provided by the data and/or plausible constraints.

The motivation for applying the MEM to issues in decision was aimed at how to deal with potential uncertainties and limitations inherent in the "industry-standard" methods used to construct utility curves and additive value functions (Keeney et al. 1993). In addition, based on these discussions, a limited literature search and the author's current awareness of the mainstream techniques for the construction of such objects, nowhere is the concept of maximum entropy introduced.

Common to many (if not all) of these discussions is the notion of constructing a "complete" function using incomplete information. The "raw" form of this information usually consists of responses, elicited from the decision-maker to well-designed sequences of questions posed by the analyst. The raw form (which may possess some numerical properties at the outset) is converted into appropriate sets of numerical values from which the function is constructed. Unfortunately, because of some subjectivity inherent in both the decision-maker responses to the questions and the conversion process used by the analyst, more information may be exhibited by the construct than that provided by the elicited responses. This is a natural phenomenon one should expect when transforming an incomplete and subjective data source (such as that representing the "feelings" of a decision-maker) into a deterministic data source, such as a well-defined mathematical function.

Such is precisely the case when constructing a multidimensional additive value function using single-dimensional value functions as the building blocks. Under certain preference conditions (specified in [Keeney et al. 1993]), the additive value function may be expressed as a convex combination of the single-dimensional value functions where each of these functions is multiplied by a constant referred to as an additive value weight. Henceforth, for reasons given in (Watson et al. 1987) and (Wall et al. 2022), we shall refer to an additive value weight as a swing weight. Assuming that each of the single dimensional value functions is accurate, the uncertainty of the additive value construct arises in the elicitation procedure used to obtain the swing weights. Among decision analysts, two of the most used elicitation procedures are the balance-beam method (outlined in [Watson et al., 1987)]) and the rank-order centroid (ROC) method (discussed in Olson & Dorai, 1992 and Solymosi & Dombi, 1986). In this chapter, we focus primarily on the balance-beam technique by first describing then modifying it. The proposed modifications involve changes to both (1) the elicitation process and (2) the post-elicitation conversion process whereby the decision-makers responses are transformed into specific numerical values for the weights. It is about this conversion process that the MEM offers a very natural approach to eliminating the potential introduction of extraneous information.

The layout of this chapter includes a brief primer on the fundamentals and jargon of a branch of decision theory known as multi-attribute value theory. Here, particular attention is given to the notions of actions, consequences, attributes, value functions and preference. For those unfamiliar with these concepts, we point the reader to (Keeney et al., 1993), which provides a well-written and in-depth introduction to decision theory. Next, we describe two currently practiced methods of swing weight elicitation/determination; these, as noted earlier, are the balance beam and ROC-methods. The purpose of considering the ROC-method is to show that, even though this technique elicits only ordinal information regarding the weights, it is not an MEM. With background on the balance beam and ROC methods in mind, we discuss our alternative elicitation technique which we refer to as binary descending bracketing (BDB) of the weights. Included in this discussion is the key notion of a structured elicitation algorithm. Finally, we apply the MEM to the swing weight information elicited via BDB; this result in a nonlinear constrained optimization problem whose solution yields the desired weights.

SOME FUNDAMENTAL NOTIONS OF MULTI-ATTRIBUTE VALUE THEORY

In decision theory, an attribute variable [1], X, is typically defined to be a resource available to a decision-maker (e.g., time, money, manpower, etc.). Correspondingly, we define x, the level of attribute X, to be a numerical measure of X. For practical purposes, $x[x^0, x^*]$ where x^0 and x^* are the minimum and maximum levels of X, respectively. This measure arises as a consequence of an action (decision) taken by a decision-maker. Associated with x is its value, $v(x)$, to the decision-maker where v is a value function $v: [x^0, x^*] \rightarrow [0, 1]$. Typically, v is a monotonically increasing function where, by convention, $v(x^0) = 0$ and $v(x^*) = 1$.

Should it be the case that multiple attributes, represented by a multidimensional vector of attribute variables $X = (X1, X2,....,X_m)$, must be considered, we are confronted with the problem of constructing a multi-attribute value function $v(x_1,....,x_m)$ using the information provided by the m one-dimensional (or single-attribute) value functions $v_1(x_1),....,v_m(x_m)$. Provided certain conditions hold (discussed in Keeney [1]), the multi-attribute value function may be written as a convex combination of single-attribute value functions. Such a function is referred to in the literature as an additive value function with defined as

$$v(x_1,...,x_m) = \sum_{i=1}^{m} w_i v_i(x_i) \tag{1}$$

where the m-long vector of constants, $w = (w_1, w_2,....,w_m)$, known as additive value weights, are chosen so that $w_i [0, 1]$ and

$$\sum_{i=1}^{m} w_i = 1 \tag{2}$$

For purposes here (as will be explained later), we shall interchangeably refer to the w_i as swing weights. Observe that if $\left(x_1^0,...,x_m^0\right)$ and $(x_1^*,...,x_m^*)$ are the m-dimensional attribute level coordinates representing the lowest and highest levels, respectively, of X then, by construct,

$$v : [x_1^0, x_1^*] \times [x_2^0, x_2^*] \times ... \times [x_m^0, x_m^*] \to [0,1]$$
$$v(x_1^0, ..., {}_m^0) = 0 \ and \ v(x_1^*, ..., x_m^*) = 1$$

(3)

In the context of an additive value function, it is clear that the swing weights represent the relative importance of the m attributes. Thus, a larger (smaller) weight indicates an attribute of greater (lesser) importance, relative to the other attributes, to the decision-maker.

Finally, we consider one more notion from decision theory, that of preference. Let Y be an attribute (single or multidimensional) and v be a value function defined as earlier with $v(y^0) = 0$ and $v(y*) = 1$. Consider two distinct levels, y_1 and y_2, of Y. We say that y_2 is preferred to y_1, denoted by $y_2 \gg y_1$, if and only if $v(y_2) > v(y_1)$. Further, we say that y_1 and y_2 are indifferent (denoted by $y_1 \sim y_2$) if and only if $v(y_1) = v(y_2)$. Observe that if Y is a single-dimensional attribute and v is monotonically increasing in the attribute level, $y_2 \gg y_1 \leftrightarrow y_2 > y_1$ and $y_1 \sim y_2 \leftrightarrow y_1 = y_2$.

DETERMINATION OF SWING WEIGHTS: ESTABLISHED METHODS

The decision-theoretic literature is rife with techniques for determining values for the swing weights. In addition, a number of papers have been written whereby these methods are compared (e.g., see Poyhonen & Ganakaubebm 2001, Wall et al., 2022). For most of these, part of their determination is based on an analyst's elicitation of preferences from the decision-maker. The elicited information is then processed using a mathematical or statistical procedure to produce the weights. Often, the distinguishing feature among swing weight assessment methodologies is the elicitation procedure. Based on his study in this area, this chapter tends to lean heavily toward the conclusion sited in (Watson et al., 1987, pp. 194-95) in their discussion of the bisection method of assessing value functions; a good elicitation philosophy is one which restricts the decision-maker to answering "yes"-or-"no" questions regarding preferences of one attribute over another. This tactic may be applied to the construction of swing weights as well. In the following sections, we briefly outline two procedures, established in the literature, to determine swing weights with the purpose of motivating the methodology proposed in the next chapter.

The Balance-Beam Method

The first of these is known as the balance-beam method. Here, the process permits the formation of boundaries, in the form of inequalities on each of the w_1, where the limits are simple linear combinations of other weights. Using these boundaries and additional elicitation, the decision-maker assigns specific values to the weights while simultaneously ensuring that the normality condition (Equation 2) is satisfied.

Essentially, this method is a three-stage procedure involving two types of elicitation questions which we shall dub binary and fuzzy. Binary elicitation, as implied by its name, involves the use of strictly yes/no-questions to obtain the preference information from the decision-maker. This information is in the form of the aforementioned inequalities. On the other hand, fuzzy elicitation requires the decision-maker to select a specific value of w_i from the continuous range defined by the inequality boundaries determined by binary elicitation on w_1. This being the case, more uncertainty is inherent in fuzzy elicitation than in binary elicitation.

Determination of w_i via the Balance-Beam Method

{1} Importance-Rank the Single-Dimensional Attributes $\{X_1, X_2, \ldots, X_m\}$

This is done using binary elicitation. Let $x^{(i)}$ be the m-long vector of attribute levels, for the multidimensional attribute $X = (X_1, \ldots, X_m)$, given by

$$x^{(i)} = (x_1^0, x_2^0, \ldots, x_{i-1}^0, x_i^*, x_{i+1}^0, \ldots, x_m^0) \tag{4}$$

Thus, $x^{(i)}$ is merely the multi-attribute level vector consisting of all of the lowest levels for the single-dimensional attributes except in the ith coordinate, where the corresponding single-dimensional attribute level is maximal. We refer to $x^{(i)}$ as a swing vector. Note that we may associate $x^{(i)}$ with the single-attribute variable X as these are in one-to-one correspondence. Next, in the context of attribute variables, let "$X_i > X_j$" denote the notion that "X_i is more important than X_j" and define importance by $X_i > X_j$ « $x^{(i)} \gg x^{(j)}$. Using at most $\dfrac{m(m-1)}{2}$ "binary" elicitation questions (i. e., "yes/no") of the form "is $x^{(i)} \gg x^{(j)}$ or $x^{(j)} \gg x^{(i)}$?" for $1 \le i < j \le m$, we may construct, from the original list $\{X_1, X_2, \ldots, X_m\}$ the permutation known as the importance-ranked attribute list $\{ \overline{X}_1, \overline{X}_2, \ldots, \overline{X}_m \}$ where $\overline{x}^{(i)} \approx \overline{x}^{(j)}$ whenever $i <$ j. Thus, $\overline{X}_1 > \overline{X}_2 > \ldots > \overline{X}_m$. In order to simplify the discussion, we tacitly disregarded, in the definition of importance, the possibility of indifference between the swing vectors $x^{(i)}$ and $x^{(j)}$ (i. e., $x^{(j)} \sim x^{(i)}$).

{2} Form Inequalities to "Bracket" the Weights (w_i)

This is accomplished using the importance-ranked attribute list and further binary elicitation. Let $\{X_1, X_2, \ldots, X_m\}$ be this list (dropping the "$\overline{X}$" notation). By definition (see Equation 3), this ordering induces the ordering $w_1 > w_2 > \ldots > w_m$ on the weights; the latter ordering provides the first bracketing inequalities on the weights. We henceforth refer to this ordering as the primary bracket on the weights.

Without loss of generality, let $i < j$ so that $X_i > X_j$. Define the multi-attribute level vector $x^{(i,j)}$ by

$$x^{(i,j)} = (x_1^0, \ldots, x_{i-1}^0, x_i^*, x_{i+1}^0, \ldots, x_{j-1}^0, x_j^*, x_{j+1}^0, \ldots, x_m^0) \tag{5}$$

Thus, in general, $x^{(i_1, i_2, \ldots, i_n)}$ is the multi-attribute level swing vector with component attributes $Xi_1, \ldots, Xi_n$ at their highest levels and all other component attributes X_j, for $j \notin \{i_1, \ldots, i_n\}$, at their lowest levels. Suppose we wish to form an additional inequality bracketing w_1 (other than $w_1 > w_2$). The analyst may use binary elicitation to obtain the following preference relations from the decision-maker:

$$x^{(2,3)} \gg x^{(1)} \text{ and } x^{(1)} \gg x^{(3,4)} \tag{6}$$

Together, these imply that $w_2 + w_3 > w_1 > w_3 + w_4$. This procedure may also be applied to each of $w_2, \ldots, w_m$ to obtain brackets on these weights as well. Note that, in general,

$$x^{(i_1,\ldots,i_Q)} \approx x^{(j_1,\ldots,j_R)} \Leftrightarrow \sum_{k=1}^{Q} w_{i_k} > \sum_{k=1}^{R} w_{j_k} \tag{7}$$

{3} Use the Inequalities (Brackets) and Fuzzy Elicitation to Assign Values to Weights

This is best illustrated with a hypothetical. Suppose we determine, through binary elicitation, that for the six weights $w_1,\ldots\ldots,w_6$,

$$w_2 + w_4 + w_6 > w_1 > w_2 + w_4, \; w_3 + w_4 = w_2, \; w_3 > w_4 > w_5 + w_6 \text{ and } w_5 > w_6 \tag{8}$$

where the last inequality (on w_6) is obtained because of the primary bracket which is always assumed to be in force. In addition, observe that indifferences sometimes arise; e. g., in the bracketing for w_2, the decision-maker is indifferent between the attribute levels $x^{(2)}$ and $x^{(3,4)}$ (i.e., $x^{(2)} \sim x^{(3,4)}$). To obtain values for the wi, a "bottom-up" approach is taken whereby we (a) set $w_6 = 1$, (b) use Inequalities (8) and fuzzy elicitation to obtain the remaining weights in the following order: w_5, w_4, w_3, w_2 and w_1 and (c) scale these by their sum so as to satisfy the normality condition. To this end, suppose the decision-maker feels that attribute X_5 is fifty percent more important than X_6. Then, since $w_6 = 1$, $w_5 = 1.5$. Next, it is decided that $x^{(4)}$ is preferentially midway between $x^{(3)}$ and $x^{(5,6)}$. Thus,

$$w_4 = \frac{1}{2}(w_3 + w_5 + w_6) = \frac{1}{2}(w_3 + 1.5 + 1) = \frac{1}{2}w_3 + 1.25 \tag{9}$$

Combining Equation (9) with the sole equality for w_2 in (8) yields

$$w_3 = \frac{2}{3}w_2 - 0.833 \; and \; w_4 = \frac{1}{3}w_2 + 0.833 \tag{10}$$

These constraints, along with the first the inequality for w_1 in (8) and the baseline assumption that $w_6 = 1.0$ gives

$$\frac{4}{3}w_2 + 1.833 > w_1 > \frac{4}{3}w_2 + 0.833 \tag{11}$$

At this point, we have gleaned as much information (about w_1 to w_4) as possible from Inequalities (8). In other words, a little fuzzier elicitation is required; specifically, this entails deciding first for w_2 then a second for w_1 based on the chosen value for w_2 and Inequality (11). Note that having decided upon w_2, the values of w_3 and w_4 are determined by (10). It is important to realize that though there is latitude in the selection of w_2, by no means can the choice be arbitrary. For example, try setting $w_2 = 2$. Doing so yields values of $w_3 = 0.5$ and $w_4 = 1.5$ thereby violating the primary bracket condition. With this in mind, it is decided that $x^{(2)}$ is preferred ten-to-one over $x^{(6)}$ or, equivalently, $w_2 = 10w_6$. This assignment yields $w_2 = 10$, $w_3 = 5.833$, $w_4 = 4.167$ and $15.167 > w_1 > 14.167$. For w_i, the decision-maker deems that w_1 is closer to 15.167 than 14.167 so the value $w_1 = 15$ is chosen. Finally, we normalize the raw weights to obtain $w_1 = 0.400$, $w_2 = 0.267$, $w_3 = 0.156$, $w_4 = 0.111$, $w_5 = 0.040$ and $w_6 = 0.026$. This completes our description of the balance-beam method.

The motivation for the terminology "swing" when referring to additive value weights and attribute vectors of the form $x^{(i)}$ (Equation (4)) arises from the notion of the change or swing in the additive value function (Equation (1)) when the level of X_i is increased from its minimum to its maximum value, while restricting all other attributes to their minimum levels. In fact, this change is precisely w_i. To see this, we merely evaluate Equation (1) at $x^{(i)}$; i. e.,

$$v(x^{(i)}) = v(x_1^0, x_2^0, ..., x_{i-1}^0, x_i^*, x_{i+1}^0, ..., x_m^0)$$
$$= \sum_{k=1}^{m} w_k v_k(x_k) = \sum_{k=1,k \neq i}^{m} w_k v_k(x_k^0) + w_i v_i(x_i^*) = 0 + w_i \cdot 1 = w_i \tag{12}$$

since $v_k(x_k^0) = 0$ and $v_i(x_i^*) = 1$ (by the definition of a single-attribute value function).

To simplify the remainder of the discussion, we shall use the terms "(multi)attribute levels" and "swing weights" interchangeably as illustrated by Equation (6). Eliciting preference inequalities and swing weight inequalities are one and the same. Keep in mind, however, that Equation (6) applies only to additive value weights and is not, in general, valid for any multi-attribute value function.

THE RANK-ORDER CENTROID (ROC) METHOD

The rank-order centroid method, developed by (Solymosi & Dombi, 1986) employs only ordinal information concerning the swing weights. Here, the only elicitation involved is that required to importance-rank the attributes; this is precisely Step {1} in the balance-beam method. In other words, the importance-ranked attributes lead directly to the primary bracket on the swing weights. The ordering information of the primary bracket, in turn, is used to produce the ROC-weights.

Suppose we are given the primary bracket $w_1 > w_2 > ... > w_m$ on the w_i. For the ROC method, strict preferential inequality (consequently, strict inequality of the weights) must be assumed. The weight w_k is computed by

$$w_k = \frac{1}{m} \sum_{i=k}^{m} \frac{1}{i} \text{ for } 1 \leq k \leq m \tag{13}$$

Olson & Dorai (1992), compare the ROC method to the analytic hierarchy process (AHP) method where the latter requires additional elicitation steps, just as with the balance-beam technique. Their conclusion is that the AHP method is only marginally more accurate than the ROC method but only at the expense of eliciting, from the decision-maker, a potentially large number (proportional to m^2) of pairwise comparisons among the attributes.

Olson & Dorai (1992) describes the method by which (Solymosi & Dombi, 1986) derive their result:

"...preference information between criteria yields knowledge about the bounds of specific weight values. Individual weights could take on a range of values. S/D used the centroid of the bounded area as a likely estimate of the true weights implied by the preference statements. The basis for this approach is to minimize the maximum error by finding the weights in the center of the region bounded by the decision-makers ordinal ranking of factors."

Here, a "region" refers to the bounds on the weight w_i implied by the bracketing inequality $w_{i-1} > w_i > w_{i+1}$, i.e., the open interval (w_{i+1}, w_{i-1}).

It is the opinion of the author that the above explanation for (3.10) is nebulous. There is, in fact, a sound and certainly more intuitive statistical argument justifying this formula. Let $W = (W_1, W_2, ..., W_m)$ be an m-long random vector with the properties that (1) W_k assumes values in [0, 1] for $1 \leq k \leq m$ and (2) $\sum_{k=1}^{m} W_k = 1$. A specific m-long value of W is commonly referred to as a random simplex while W is an m-long simplex random vector. Suppose we select a value of W $[0,1]^m$ in the most <u>uniform</u> manner possible given the constraints W_k [0, 1] and $\sum_{k=1}^{m} W_k = 1$. This is done using the joint density

$$f_W(w_1, w_2, ..., w_m) = (m - 1)! \tag{14}$$

Let $W_{(1)}$ be the random variable for the largest of $\{W_1, ..., W_m\}$, $W_{(2)}$ be the second largest, $W_{(k)}$ be the kth largest and so on. Thus $\hat{W} = (W_{(1)}, W_{(2)}, ..., W_{(m)})$ is the m-long ordered simplex random variable corresponding to W, whose <u>joint density is given by Equation (14)</u>. In the statistical parlance, $W_{(k)}$ is referred to the kth order statistic for the random variables $\{W_1, ..., W_m\}$ and $1 \leq k \leq m$.

The significance of $\hat{W}$ is that it is directly related to selecting a set of m weights given <u>only</u> the primary bracket (i. e., $w_1 > w_2 > ... > w_m$). That is, with nothing other than ordinal information regarding the weights, it seems reasonable to assign to w_k its expected value, $E[W_{(k)}]$. It can be shown, albeit nontrivially, that if the m-long random vector of weights is selected according to (14), then

$$E[W_{(k)}] = \frac{1}{m} \sum_{i=k}^{m} \frac{1}{i} \tag{15}$$

which is precisely the assignment proposed by S/D. Loosely speaking, if we simulate $\hat{W}$ by generating a large sample of independent ordered m-long simplexes, the average value of the kth largest weight approaches, via the strong law of large numbers, $m^{-1} \sum_{i=k}^{m} i^{-1}$. Additional study might consider the degree to which $W_{(k)}$ wanders from its mean. This degree may be quantified by the standard deviation. For example, considering the largest weight, w_1, we set $w_1 = E[W_{(1)}]$ and can show that its standard deviation is given by

$$\sigma_{W_{(1)}} = \sqrt{\frac{1}{m(m+1)} \sum_{i=1}^{m} \frac{1}{i^2} - \frac{1}{m^2(m+1)} \left(\sum_{i=1}^{m} \frac{1}{i} \right)^2} \tag{16}$$

which is $0(\frac{\pi}{m\sqrt{6}}) as\ m \rightarrow \infty$

THE BINARY DESCENDING BRACKETING / MAXIMUM ENTROPY (BDB/ME) METHOD

As an alternative to the established techniques discuss thus far, we propose a method that employs (1) binary elicitation to form bracketing inequalities on the additive value (swing) weights and (2) a maximum entropy calculation, based on these inequalities, to specify these weights. This method, the binary descending bracketing / maximum entropy (BDB/ME)-method, may be regarded as a hybrid of the balance-beam and centroid methods. Like both, the first step in BDB/ME is to importance-rank the attributes thus establishing a primary bracket on the swing weights. As with the balance-beam, additional binary elicitation is used to obtain more informative or refined bracketing inequalities on the weights. Using these refined brackets, the BDB/ME technique outputs maximum entropy estimates for the weights. This ensures that only the preference information about which the decision-maker is certain (i.e., the information supplied by the bracketing) contributes to the weight estimates. The notion of maximum entropy is somewhat like the approach taken by the centroid method. Recall that the centroid method uses the expected value of the kth-order statistic (for $1 \leq k \leq m$), of the non-informative prior distribution

$$f_W(w_1, w_2, \ldots, w_m) = (m - 1)! \tag{17}$$

on the coordinates of an m-long simplex, as an estimate for w_k. The term "non informative prior" is merely the Bayesian parlance for selecting w_1 to w_m, "as uniformly as possible" on $[0, 1]$, subject to the normality constraint $\sum_{i=1}^{m} w_i = 1$.

How does the BDB/ME method distinguish itself from the balance-beam and centroid approaches? Consider first the balance-beam method. Recall that the balance-beam includes both binary and fuzzy elicitation. The binary elicitation results in brackets for the weights but is not sufficient to produce actual values. A weight value is generally specified by requiring the decision-maker to make an educated guess (the fuzzy elicitation) on the interval established by the bracketing inequalities. The BDB/ME-method does not embrace the concept behind the additional fuzzy elicitation but rather treats the bracketing information as the limit of the decision-makers certainty regarding preferences. Thus, it regards conclusions drawn from fuzzy elicitation as not necessarily valid. In response to this, the BDB/ME method produces weights based solely on the information provided by the bracketing inequalities generated by binary elicitation. This is accomplished by treating the m-long weight vector $w = (w_1, w_2, \ldots, w_m)$ as a discrete probability distribution whose entropy is to be maximized, subject to the constraints imposed by the bracketing; the weights are then specified as the solutions to the appropriate Lagrange multiplier equations. On the other hand, the centroid method may be considered to lie at the other end of the spectrum; the only information used is that contained in the primary bracket. Thus, it ignores any additional information, regardless of how certain the decision-maker feels, which may substantially sharpen the upper/lower boundaries on a given preference.

In the next two sections, we discuss the BDB/ME in detail. The next section is devoted to the description of the binary descending bracketing (BDB) algorithm with emphasis on structured elicitation; this notion allows one to logically automate the elicitation process. The basic strategy of the algorithm is introduced using a "pan scale-and-weights" concept. Using the resulting qualitative description of BDB and the precise notion of refinement brackets (to be defined), a user-friendly graphical representation of the algorithm is constructed whereby all of the possible elicitation paths for bracketing each weight may be visualized. Having the bracketing information (inequalities) for each of the weights obtained from the BDB algorithm details the maximum entropy calculations necessary to produce specific values for the weights.

BINARY DESCENDING BRACKETING: A STRUCTURE ELICITATION ALGORITHM

{1} Structured Elicitation: Automating the Elicitation Process

An elicitation algorithm which produces a definite outcome (such as an inequality on each of $w_1,...,w_m$) on the basis of a finite <u>recursive</u> sequence of choices, where each choice is selected from a finite set of choices, we call a structured elicitation algorithm. By recursive, we mean that each choice depends on the choice immediately preceding it. Structured elicitation is the essential feature of the BDB algorithm. The philosophy behind this type of procedure is to simplify or, to some extent, automate the elicitation process. Doing so prevents the analyst from eliciting a potentially meandering sequence of preferences whose outcome likely produces a set of inequalities no more informative than those produced by BDB. By design, BDB provides an orderly fashion for refining a primary preference (swing weight) bracket using a "reasonably small" number of binary (yes/no) elicitation inquiries. Refining a bracket on a weight refers to the process of sharpening the upper a/or lower bound on the weight under consideration. More detail on refining shall be discussed in a forthcoming section of this chapter.

Technically speaking, the algorithm is not truly binary; rather, at each step in the bracketing process, the decision-maker is asked to select one of four disjoint possibilities represented symbolically by the set $\{>, <, =, ?\}$. However, as only one choice is allowed per inquiry, a question involving four choices may be viewed as a set of at most three ordered binary questions: ">"? (yes/no), "<"? (yes/no) and "=" (yes/no). The first "yes" response yields a selection from $\{>, <, =\}$ and terminates the questioning. If the responses are all "no", the selection "?" (an indecision point) is chosen by default. The point here is that responses to this type of inquiry are easy to elicit from the decision maker.

When we consider a graphical representation of the algorithm, namely a bracketing tree, the reader may visualize the elicitation process as a descending "flow" through the tree from top to bottom. Moving from a node (which represents an inquiry regarding bracketing) at one level in the tree to a node one level "below" involves making a choice of one of two possible nodes at the lower level. This action accounts for the use of the term "binary descending".

{2} The BDB Algorithm I: A "Pan Scale-and-Weights" Concept

Consider an ordinary two-pan balancing scale and a set of m distinct ordered weights, w_1, with $w_1 > w_2 > ... > w_m$. The game is to express, as closely as possible, a given weight in terms of the next smallest weight and some combination of the remaining smaller weights, as needed. Specifically, the procedure might be physically envisioned as follows:

[1]   Place the largest weight, w_1, in the left pan. Place w_2 in the right pan. Clearly, the left pan is lower than the right (i. e., the left pan outweighs the right).

[2]   Starting with w_3, place this weight into the right pan. Consider the following four possible (disjoint) decisions:

(a)   Inequality (>): the left pan remains lower than the right ($w_1 > w_2 + w_3$),

(b)   Inequality (<): the right pan is clearly lower than the left ($w_1 < w_2 + w_3$),

(c)   Indifference (=): the right pan and left pans achieve an equilibrium and remain level with one another ($w_1 = w_2 + w_3$) and

(d)   Indecision (?): the left and right pans seem to oscillate about an equilibrium level thereby indicating an indecision point for w_1; that is, $w_1 \; ? \; w_2 + w_3$ where ? lies in the set {>, <, =, ?}.

[3]   Consider the decision made in Step [2] (precisely one of the four possible listed). This determines the next step in the elicitation procedure.

If [2] (a) occurs: add w_4 to the right pan and repeat Step [2] to determine which of the four decisions results from comparing the sum $w_2 + w_3 + w_4$ to w_1.

If [2] (b) occurs: w_1 is bracketed (bounded) above by $w_2 + w_3$. Remove w_3 from the right pan and replace it with w_4. Repeat Step [2] to determine which of the four decisions results from comparing the sum $w_2 + w_4$ to w_1.

If [2] (c) occurs: elicitation is complete on w_1 since we have obtained an equality in terms of smaller weights. Return to Step [1] and begin elicitation on w_2 by placing this weight in the left pan and placing w_3 (by itself) in the right pan.

If [2] (d) occurs: elicitation should terminate and only the bracketing information established <u>just prior</u> to the point of indecision should take precedence. In this case, the bracketing information is $w_1 > w_2$. Return to Step [1] an begin elicitation on w_2 by placing this weight in the left pan and placing w_3 (by itself) in the right pan.

[4]   Repeat Steps [1] - [3] until either:

(1)   a lower bound, involving the lowest weight, w_m, is obtained for w_1,

(2)   an upper bound on w_1 is obtained which involves w_m,

(3)   an equality (indifference) is obtained for w_1, or

(4)   an indecision point is reached whereby only the bracketing information on w_1, just prior to the point of indecision, should be considered.

Based on the procedure of Steps [1] - [3], precisely one of the above four alternatives must occur.

[5]   Repeat [1]-[4] for w_2, w_3 and so on.

Clearly, this scale-and-weights algorithm relates directly to the corresponding elicitation procedure (for bracketing swing weights) between the analyst and the decision-maker. The scale, used to compare w_i to combinations of smaller physical weights, is merely replaced by the decision-maker who must make the comparisons between the swing weight w_i to additive combinations chosen from $\{w_{i+1}, \ldots, w_m\}$.

{3} Refinement Brackets

Recall the term, "refining a primary bracket" introduced in the first section of the chapter. When $i <$ m, we may consider the lower bound portion, $\{w_i > w_{i+1}\}$, of the primary bracket $\{w_{i-1} > w_i > w_{i+1}\}$ on the weight w_i. This portion shall be referred to as the partial primary bracket on w_i. Starting with the partial primary on w_i (for $1 \le i \le m - 1$) the outcome of the BDB algorithm is (a) a lower bound, (b) an upper bound, or (c) a lower and an upper bound on w_i, or (d) an equality. Next, we formally define a refinement of the partial primary bracket as a mapping, R, of $\{w_i > w_{i+1}\}$, to yet another bracket which assumes precisely one of the following forms listed below.

For a_k, b_k $\{0,1\}$, R: $\{w_i > w_{i+1}\} \to \Omega$ where Ω is one of the following:

(i) $\quad \Omega : \left\{ w_i > w_{i+1} + \sum_{k=1+2}^{m} a_k w_k \right\}$ \hfill (18)

$$\Omega : \left\{ w_i > w_{i+1} + \sum_{k=1+2}^{m} a_k w_k \right\} \tag{18}$$

(ii) $\quad \Omega : \left\{ w_i < w_{i+1} + \sum_{k=1+2}^{m} a_k w_k \right\}$ \hfill (19)

(iii) $\quad \Omega : \left\{ w_{i+1} + \sum_{k=1+2}^{m} b_k w_k > w_i > w_{i+1} + \sum_{k=1+2}^{m} a_k w_k \right\}$ \hfill (20)

where a_m and b_m are not simultaneously zero and

(iv) $\quad \Omega : \left\{ w_i = w_{i+1} + \sum_{k=1+2}^{m} a_k w_k \right\}$ \hfill (21)

As noted earlier, the term "refinement" is chosen to represent the fact that the resulting bracket is sharper than the primary bracket. For example, suppose, starting with primary partial $w_2 > w_3$, we find, after a couple of iterations of Steps [1]-[3] of the BDB, that $w_2 > w_3 + w_5 + w_6$. Clearly, the second inequality is sharper in the sense that the lower bound, $w_3 + w_5 + w_6$, is closer to w_2 than w_3 itself. Here, we would describe the sum $w_3 + w_5 + w_6$ as a lower bound refinement. The same principle applies to upper bound refinements. The bracket, Ω, resulting from a refinement mapping R is referred to as a refinement bracket.

If the iterations of Steps [1]-[3] of the BDB result in a refinement bracket on w_i ($i < m$) involving w_m (the lowest weight), then

(1)   The inequality (5.1a), with $a_m = 1$, is a sharpest lower-bound refinement given the weights $w = (w_1, w_2, ..., w_m)$,

(2)   The inequality (5.1b), with $a_m = 1$, is a sharpest upper-bound refinement given the weights $w = (w_1, w_2, ..., w_m)$,

Consider Inequality (5.1 a), with $a_m = 1$. The lower bound on w_i possesses the form $w_i > w_{i+1} + \sum_{k=1+2}^{m-1} a_k w_k + w_m$. Since w_m is the lowest weight available, there are no additional smaller weights upon which to make inquiries. This implies that, without changing any of the a_k (for $i + 2 \leq k \leq$ m-1) the right side of the inequality can no longer be increased with the potential of sharpening the lower bound. Further, by design of the BDB algorithm, if indeed any of these a_k are changed from zero to one, the right side will increase so as to reverse the inequality. A similar argument may be made regarding the sharpest upper bound refinement, Inequality (5.1b) with $a_m = 1$.

{4} The BDB Algorithm II: A Graphical Representation

At this point we urge the reader to review Steps [1]-[3] of the BDB procedure above as the following discussion is based on these steps. In lieu of expressing the generalized form of the BDB algorithm using complicated (cumbersome) lines of pseudocode, a graphical approach is adopted which enables one to easily visualize the flow of the elicitation and the iterative development of refinement bracketing. Simply put, the BDB algorithm may be graphically expressed as a binary decision tree where (1) the top level node of the tree is defined by the weight to be bracketed and the next smallest weight, (2) each of the nodes in the proceeding levels represents an elicitation question (comparison) as outlined in Step [2] of the BDB (to refine the bracketing) and (3) the edges linking the levels represent the actions taken, as outlined in Step [3] of the BDB. In fact, the term "Binary Descending Bracketing" is based on this tree structure, i.e., the tree is binary and the flow of the elicitation is descending from tree top to bottom. In the current context, as alluded to earlier, the term "Binary" is not altogether accurate. This is due to the fact that there are actually four Step [2] choices possible and that two of these, namely [2] (c) (indifference) and [2] (d) (indecision), are omitted from the graphical representation. The reason for this is that these choices do not affect the downward flow of elicitation as represented by the Y and N-edges. When one of [2] (c) or [2] (d) is chosen, a final decision is made in Step [3] ("If [2] (c) occurs" or "If [2] (d) occurs") and no further elicitation is required. A node at which the answer to the inquiry is either (a) an "Indifference (=)", (b) an "Indecision (?)", or (c) an inequality involving the lowest weight, is deemed a terminal node. A terminal node which involves the lowest weight, w_m, is appropriately referred to as a bottom node. At a bottom node, one additional inquiry must be considered.

To illustrate the graphical approach, we shall examine the case for m = 7 and consider all the possibilities for bounding w_1 (in terms of the remaining six weights). This is accomplished by the "top-down" directed graph (or BDB-tree for short) shown in Figure 1. The BDB tree consists of nodes which represent inquiries (or comparisons) and edges which represent actions resulting from the answers to the inquires. It should be noted that, due to space considerations, not all the terminal nodes involving the lowest weight (in this case, w_7) show the edges representing the final possible actions to be taken based on the last inquiry.

Specifically, a node represents an inquiry about the <u>truth of Inequality (18)</u> and is labeled by the subscripts for the weights in this inequality. Thus, a node with label "(2, a, b, c)" denotes the inquiry

$$\text{Node: } (2,a,b,c)° \text{ "Is } w_1 > w_2 + w_a + w_b + w_c? \text{"} \tag{22}$$

Note each of the node labels starts with a "2" as w_1 is to be bounded by an expression involving the 2nd largest weight as per the intention of the BDB algorithm. Also observe that $2 < a < b < c$.

Figure 1. Binary Descending Bracketing Tree

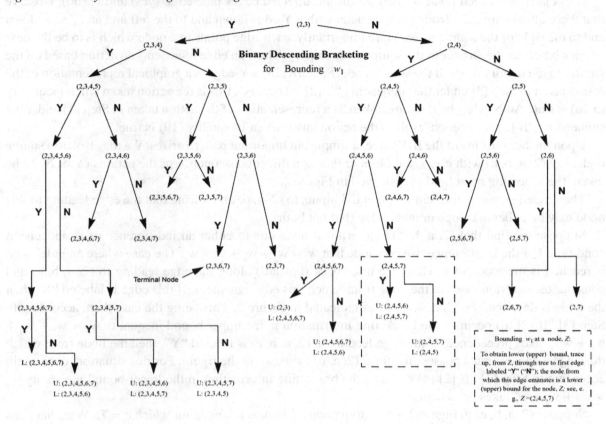

Figure 2. Possible actions (N or Y) for inquiry at node (2, a, b, c)

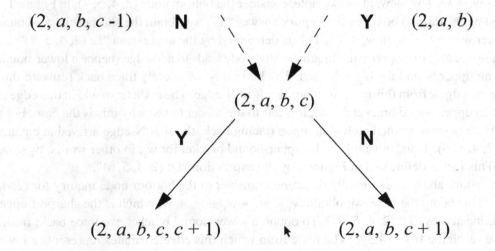

Associated with each node are two downward directed edges labeled Y (yes) and N (no). Observe that these always emanate from a source node with a Y-edge down and to the left and an N-edge down and to the right of the source node. More importantly, each edge points to a node which is to be the next inquiry based on the answer to the source node inquiry. Thus, an edge represents an action based on the answer to the inquiry made at the source node. Specifically, a Y-edge is a graphical representation of the action taken in Step [3] under the subheading "If [2] (a) occurs"; this is the action taken when Inequality (5.1a) is true. An N-edge, by the same token, is a representation of the action taken in Step [3] under the subheading "If [2] (b) occurs:"; this is the action taken when Inequality (19) is true.

Upon further scrutiny of the BDB-tree, a simple but important pattern arises. We may isolate a source node, say (2, a, b, c) with c < 7 and observe that as a direct consequence of the actions (Y or N) to be taken, the following must hold as displayed in Figure 2.

The dashed arrows, representing potential inputs to (2, a, b, c), indicate that the edge leading to this node may be either a Y-edge or an N-edge (but not both).

Suppose we find that (2, a, b, c) is a terminal node due to either an indifference or an indecision condition. For the indifference, we conclude that $w_i = w_2 + w_a + w_b + w_c$. The case where an indecision is reached is more complex. Here, we trace back (upward) along the edge leading to (2, a, b, c) and consider the decision made at the node from which this edge emanates. If this edge is labeled "N" then the node is described by (2, a, b, c - 1) as indicated in Figure 2. This being the case then, according to Step [3] "If [2] (d) occurs", the bracketing information in the upper-bound inequality $w_1 < w_2 + w_a + w_b + w_{c-1}$ takes precedence. If the edge leading to (2, a, b, c) is labeled "Y", then the node from which this edge emanates must possess the form (2, a, b) as shown in the figure. For this situation, once again according to Step [3] "If [2] (d) occurs", the bracketing information in the lower-bound inequality $w_1 > w_2 + w_a + w_b$ takes precedence.

Suppose (2, a, b, c) in Figure 2 is a bottom node (in Figure 1, a node for which c = 7). What happens when we reach a bottom node? As noted earlier, we consider one more inquiry. If the edge emanating from (2, a, b, c) in an N-edge, we produce a sharpest upper bound bracket for w_1; this is $w_1 < w_2 + w_a + w_b + w_e$. If the emanating edge is a Y-edge, a sharpest lower bound refinement for w_1 is established; this is $w_1 > w_2 + w_a + w_b + w_,$. For example, consider the bottom node (2, 4, 5, 7), in Figure 1, which is highlighted by the dashed box. For the inquiry answer "Y", we obtain the sharpest lower-bound refinement bracket $w_1 > w_2 + w_4 + w_5 + w_7$. This is delineated by the expression "L: (2, 4, 5, 7)".

Returning (2, a, b, c), suppose the inquiry at this node leads to a Y-edge (hence a lower-bound refinement) but an upper bound for w_1 is desired. To obtain this, we merely trace back (upward through the tree) along the edges, from this node, until we reach an N-edge. The node from which this edge emanates represents an upper bound bracket for w_1; it is left to the reader to see why this is the case. For the node (2, 4, 5, 7), we observe immediately that, upon tracing back, the first N-edge arrived at emanates from the node (2, 4, 5, 6). Thus, this node is the upper-bound bracket for w_1; in other words, $w_i < w_2 + w_4 + w_5 + w_6$. This fact is delineated in Figure 1 by the expression "U: (2, 4, 5, 6)".

The procedure above is essentially the same if answer to the bottom-node inquiry for (2, 4, 5, 7) is an N-edge. This being the case, we obtain $w_1 < w_2 + w_4 + w_5 + w_7$ which is the sharpest upper-bound bracket, delineated by "U: (2, 4, 5, 7)". To obtain a lower-bound bracket, we trace back, from (2, 4, 5, 7), until we reach the first Y-edge. The node from which this edge emanates represents a lower-bound bracket (again, we leave this as an exercise for the reader). In this case, we obtain $w_1 > w_2 + w_4 + w_5$. This fact is delineated by "L: (2, 4, 5)" in Figure 1. In general, this trace-back rule can be used not only at a bottom node, but <u>any terminal node </u>to obtain a lower (upper)-bound bracket on w_1. To obtain a lower-bound (upper-bound) bracket, we trace back (or up the tree, if you prefer), from the terminal node, along the edges until we reach the first edge labeled "Y" ("N"). The node from which this edge emanates represents the combination of weights which provide the lower-bound (upper-bound) bracket for w_1. It should be noted it is not always possible to produce both an upper and lower bound for a terminal node. Consider, for example, the terminal node given by (2, 3, 4, 5, 6, 7) in Figure 1. If the inquiry answer from this node is "Y" then, using the trace-back rule, there is no "N"-edge from which an upper bound can be established. Common sense reveals why this is so; all of the weights less than w1 have been used to construct the lower bound.

Yet another advantage of the graphical representation is the fact that the BDB trees for bracketing w_2, w_3 and so on are embedded in the tree for w_1! Figure 3, which is essentially a reprint of Figure 1, illustrates the subtree for bracketing w_2 using a larger font for the node "coordinates" involved in the bracketing. In this case, for example, the top of the BDB tree for w_2 would be (3, 4). The next level below is {(3, 4, 5), (3, 5)} where (3, 4, 5) prevails if the edge from (3, 4) is a Y and (3, 5) prevails if the edge from (3, 4) is an N. In short, Step [5] of BDB procedure on p. 14 is represented by the act of "eliciting" a terminal node in the subtree for each of the w_i. The subtree for w_7 is trivial; here, there is no lower bound in the sense of (5.1a) and the sharpest upper bound is merely w_6. It remains an exercise for the reader to locate the embedded subtrees for w_3, w_4 and so on.

Figure 3. BDB Tree showing embedded subtree for w2

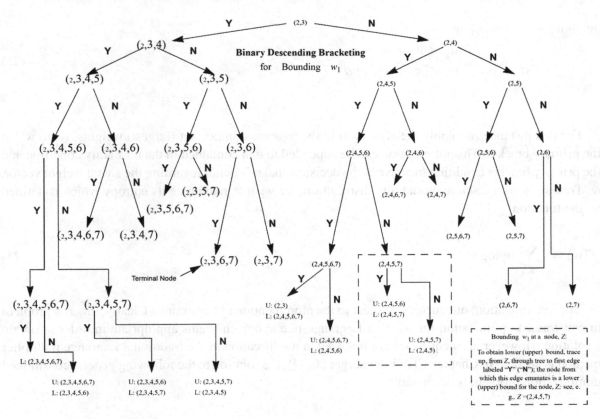

It should be emphasized that while the BDB tree is useful for enumerating and visualizing all possible elicitation sequences, the BDB procedure as presented Section {2} should suffice for implementation purposes. For m weights, the BDB tree has $2^{m-2} - 1$ nodes so that other than for small values of m, it is clearly impractical as an illustration tool.

In practice, when more than a few weights are considered, it is possible to arrive at contradictory brackets involving inconsistent inequalities. This, in part, is likely because it is often difficult for a decision-maker to distinguish preference between two "consecutive" low priority attributes (e. g., X_{15} and X_{16}) among a large number (say m > 10). To avoid this shortcoming when faced with a "large" value of m, one might only seek refinements on the k largest of the m weights while retaining the primary bracket $w_{k+1} > w_{k+2} > \ldots > w_m$ on the remaining m – k weights.

The choice of k is a matter of joint judgement on the part of the decision-maker and analyst. One possible criterion for its selection should be the repeatability of preference bracketing. That is, barring any substantial changes in preferences, the value of k chosen should permit the decision-maker to repeat the elicitation procedure and, in the short term, however one defines this, arrive at the same refinement brackets on the w_i.

MAXIMUN ENTROPY CALCULATIONS

Suppose we consider the following bracketing information, on $w = (w_1, w_2, \ldots, w_7)$, obtained as a result of implementing the BDB algorithm:

$$w_2 + w_4 + w_6 + w_7 > w_1 > w_2 + w_4 + w_6,$$
$$w_2 = w_3 + w_5 + w_7,$$
$$w_3 < w_4 + w_5, \text{ and} \tag{23}$$
$$w_4 > w_5 + w_7$$

For this instance, we apply the algorithm to the four most important (largest) weights, w_1 to w_4, in the primary bracket. This information can be appended to that contained in the normality condition and the primary bracket condition to arrive at the decision-maker's belief regarding the swing weight vector, w. Treating w as a discrete probability distribution, we wish to maximize its entropy which is defined by the function

$$f(\mathbf{w}) = -\sum_{i=1}^{7} w_i \log w_i \tag{24}$$

The maximization, of course, is subject to the aforementioned constraints. Clearly, this is a problem in constrained optimization for which a Lagrange-like approach seems appropriate in order to obtain a solution. However, as inequalities are involved, a modification to the traditional Lagrange multiplier method is needed. In Chapter 10 of Luenberger (1984), the solution to the following general constrained minimization problem is discussed:

minimize : $f(\mathbf{x})$ *with* $x \in \Omega \subset E^m$

subject to : $h_1(\mathbf{x}) = 0, ..., h_l(\mathbf{x}) = 0$ $(l \leq m)$ (25)

$\qquad\qquad g_1(\mathbf{x}) \leq 0, ..., g_p(\mathbf{x}) \leq 0$

where the functions f, h_i and g_j are C^2 (i. e., possess continuous second partial derivatives). The swing weight problem with constraints given by Equation (23) may be recast as an instantiation of this general form with m = 7, l = 2 and p = 10:

subject to: $\qquad h_1(\mathbf{w}) = \sum_{i=1} w_i - 1 = 0$ (normality condition on w_i),

$$h_2(\mathbf{w}) = w_2 - (w_3 + w_5 + w_7) = 0 \text{ (other equality constraints)},$$

$$g_j(\mathbf{w}) = w_{j+1} - w_j \leq 0 \quad \text{for } 1 \leq j \leq 6 \text{ (primary bracket constraints)},$$

$$g_7(\mathbf{w}) = w_1 - (w_2 + w_4 + w_6 + w_7) \leq 0$$

$$g_8(\mathbf{w}) = w_3 - (w_4 + w_5) \leq 0 \qquad \text{(upper-bound constraints)},$$

and

$$g_9(\mathbf{w}) = w_2 + w_4 + w_6 - w_1 \leq 0$$

$$\qquad\qquad\qquad\qquad\qquad \text{(lower-bound constraints)}.$$

$$g_{10}(\mathbf{w}) = w_5 + w_7 - w_4 \leq 0 \; .$$

$\qquad$ (26)

Here, we observe that, for the function described by Equation (24), maximizing is equivalent to minimizing on the domain .

Consider the general-case Equations (25). To determine a solution to these, we require some definitions and supplementary concepts. Suppose $x^* \in \Omega$ satisfies and for $h_i(x) = 0$ $(1 \leq i \leq l)$ and $g_j \leq 0$ for $1 \leq j \leq p$. An inequality constraint, $g_j(x)$, is active at x^* whenever; otherwise, when $gj(x^*) < 0$, g_j is inactive at x^*. Let J be the subset of indices in the set $\{1, 2, ..., p\}$ such that $g_j(x^*) = 0$ for $j \in J$. x^* is said to be a regular point of the constraints if gradient vectors $\nabla h_i(x^*)$ and $\nabla g_i(x^*)$ are linearly independent for $(1 \leq i \leq l)$ and $j \in J$. We state the first-order necessary conditions for x^* being a relative minimum (i. e., a solution) for the problem (25):

KUHN-TUCKER CONDITIONS (FIRST-ORDER NECESSARY)

Let x^* be a relative minimum point for the problem described by Equations (25). Let h(x) denote the l-long vector-valued function $h(x) = (h_1(x), ..., h_l(x))$ and similarly for the p-long vector-valued function

$g(x)$. Suppose x^* is a regular point for the constraints. Then there is a column vector $\mu \geq 0$ with $\mu \in E^p$ and a column vector $\lambda \in E^l$ such that

$$\nabla f(x^*) + \lambda T^\nabla h(x^*) + \mu T \nabla^g(x^*) = 0; \ \mu Tg^{(x^*)} = 0 \tag{27}$$

where $\nabla h(x)$ is the $l \times m$ matrix of partials $[aij_= \dfrac{h_i(x)}{x_i}]$, $\nabla g(x)$ is the $p \times m$ matrix $[bi_{j=} \dfrac{g_i(x)}{x_i}]$ and 0, on the right side of Equation 27, is the zero-vector in E^m. Note that "T" is the transpose operator while the $\nabla h(x)$ and $\nabla g(x)$ – matrices are each evaluated at the critical point x^*.

We remind the reader that the gradient operator, ∇f, on a vector-valued function, $f(x)$, with $x \in E^m$, is the vector function ($\dfrac{f}{x_1}, \ldots, \dfrac{f}{x_m}$). In essence, to find a potential relative minimum, x^*, we must find a solution to the $m + p + l$ system of equations given by Equations (26) (m equations), (27) (p equations) and the l equality constraints compactly expressed by $h(x^*) = 0$; these are solved for the unknowns $x_1^*, \ldots, x_m^*, \mu_1, \ldots, \mu_p$ and $\lambda_1, \ldots, \lambda_l$. In addition, using x^*, we must determine the $\widehat{p} + l$ gradient vectors $\nabla h_i(x^*)$ and $\nabla g_j(x^*)$ for $1 \leq i \leq l, j \in J$ and $\widehat{p} = |J|$. These vectors must be linearly independent so as to ensure that x^* is a regular point.

Unfortunately, though the Kuhn-Tucker conditions are necessary, they are not sufficient to guarantee that x^* is a strict relative minimum. For sufficiency, we must consider an additional second-order condition requiring that (1) f, g and h be C^2-functions (vector functions) and (2) the Hessian matrix $L(x^*) = F(x^*) + \lambda^T H(x^*) + \mu^T G(x^*)$ be positive definite on the tangent plane containing the gradients $\nabla h_i(x^*)$ and $\nabla g_j(x^*)$ for $j \in J$; this plane is characterized, at the regular point x^*, by the set $M = \{y \in E^m; \nabla h(x^*) y = 0, \nabla g_j(x^*) y = 0, j \in J\}$ where y is an m-long column vector. Recall that the Hessian of $y(x)$, $Y(x)$, is the $m \times m$ matrix of second partials $\left[\dfrac{\partial^2 y}{\partial x_i \partial x_k} \right]$; L above is actually a linear combination of the three Hessians F, H and G. When x is specified (e.g., $x = x^*$), the Hessian is evaluated at the specified point. Usually, verifying that a candidate solution satisfies these conditions is computationally intensive. However, it may be possible to circumvent the second-order sufficiency conditions using Convex Programming (Rao, 79).

CONVEX PROGRAMMING

Consider the constrained minimization problem in Equations (25). Suppose the functions $f(x)$, $h(x) = (h_1(x), \ldots, h_l(x))$ and $g(x) = (g_1)(x), \ldots, g_p(x))$ are convex and C^1. A regular point, x^*, for the constraints and satisfies Equations (27) if and only if x^* is a global minimum for (25). To paraphrase, this powerful result states that, for an optimization involving a convex objective function with convex constraints, the Kuhn-Tucker first-order conditions are necessary and sufficient for a regular point to be a global minimum.

Under most circumstances, establishing the convexity requirement is more difficult than applying the second-order criterion. However, the case described by Equations (26) is an exception. In fact, we may generalize this instantiation of BDB/ME with the purpose of showing that any such problem is one in convex programming.

To this end, let w = (w$_1$, w$_2$,..., w$_m$) be the m-long row vector of swing weights. Next, let l and p be the number of equality constraints (l ≤ m) and inequality constraints, respectively. Then our generalization of Equations 26 is

$$minimize: \quad f(w) = \sum_{i=1}^{m} w_i \log w_i \ with \ w \in \Omega = [0,1]^m \subset E^m$$

$$subject \ to: \quad Aw^T - N = h(w)^T = 0 \ and \ Bw^T = g(w)^T \leq 0$$

(28)

Here, A = [a$_{i,j}$] is the l x m matrix, with a$_{i,j}$ ∈ {-1, 0, 1}, representing the equality constraints. The first row of A represents the normality condition; that is, a$_{i,j}$ = 1 for 1 ≤ j ≤ m. N is the l-long column vector (1,0,...,0)^T. B = [b$_{i,j}$] is the p x m matrix with b$_{i,j}$ ∈ {-1, 0, 1} and

$$
B = \begin{bmatrix}
-1 & 1 & 0 & \cdots & \cdots & \cdots & \cdots & \cdots & \cdots & \cdots & 0 \\
0 & -1 & 1 & 0 & \cdots & \cdots & \cdots & \cdots & \cdots & & 0 \\
0 & 0 & -1 & 1 & 0 & \cdots & \cdots & \cdots & \cdots & & 0 \\
\circ & \circ & \circ & \circ & \circ & & & \circ & \circ & & \circ \\
\circ & \circ & & & & & & \circ & \circ & & \circ \\
0 & \cdots & & \cdots & \cdots & \cdots & \cdots & 0 & -1 & & 1 \\
b_{m,1} & b_{m,2} & \cdots & \cdots & \cdots & \cdots & \cdots & \cdots & b_{m,m} & & \\
b_{m+1,1} & b_{m+1,2} & \cdots & \cdots & \cdots & \cdots & \cdots & \cdots & b_{m+1,m} & & \\
\circ & \circ & & & & & & & \circ & & \\
\circ & \circ & & & & & & & \circ & & \\
b_{p,1} & b_{p,2} & \cdots & \cdots & \cdots & \cdots & \cdots & \cdots & b_{p,m} & &
\end{bmatrix}
\begin{matrix}
\leftarrow primary \ bracket \\
\leftarrow primary \ bracket \\
\leftarrow primary \ bracket \\
\\
\\
\leftarrow primary \ bracket \\
\leftarrow up/low \ bound \ bracket \\
\leftarrow up/low \ bound \ bracket \\
\\
\\
\leftarrow up/low \ bound \ bracket
\end{matrix}
$$

(29)

The B-matrix represents the inequality constraints. Specifically, the first m-1 rows give the primary bracket constraints while the remaining p − m + 1 rows reveal the upper and lower-bound constraints obtained by BDB elicitation. Finally, h(w)^T = (h1(w), h2(w),...,h$_l$(w))^T and g(w)^T = (g$_1$(w), g$_2$(w),... ,g$_p$(w))^T are the l and p-long column vectors representing the vector-valued functions, h and g respectively, on the right sides of Equations (28). Equations 28 clearly reveal that the constraints in any BDB/ME problem are, by construct, linear; this greatly simplifies the proof that Equations 29 represent a convex programming problem.

Having established that the BDB/ME is a convex programming problem, there is still the matter of ensuring that a candidate solutions, w*, which satisfies h(w*)^T = 0 and g(w*)^T ≤ 0, is indeed a regular point. Recall that J is the subset of the indices {1, 2,..., p} such that if i∈ J the ith entry of the p-long column vector g(w*)^T is zero (i.e. i∈ J Þ g$_i$(w*) = 0). Next, using the fact that Bw^T = g(w)^T, we observe that, for 1 ≤i≤p and 1≤j≤m,

$$\nabla g(w) = \left[\frac{\partial g_i(w)}{\partial x_j}\right] = B \tag{30}$$

which is independent of w. Similarly, for $1 \leq i \leq p$ and $1 \leq j \leq m$,

$$\nabla h(w) = \left[\frac{\partial h_i(w)}{\partial w_j}\right] = A \tag{31}$$

Denote row i of B by the m-long vector B(i). Let $\bar{B}$ be the |J| x m matrix submatrix of B whose rows, $\bar{B}$ (k) ($1 \leq k \leq |J|$), $g_k(w^*) = \bar{B}$ (k) $\bullet$ w* = 0. That is, $\bar{B}$ is the submatrix of B whose rows represent the inequality constraints which are active at w*. For $\hat{p}$ = |J|, let C be the $(1 + \hat{p})$ x m matrix

$$C = \left[\frac{A}{B}\right] \tag{32}$$

For w* to be a regular point for the constraints h(w) and g(w), the rank of C must be $1 + \hat{p}$; in other words, the rows of C must be linearly independent.

Possessing the theory necessary for solving the convex programming problem (28), we resume with the case study given by Equations (26). In the language of Equations (28), the case study becomes

$$\text{minimize:} \quad f(w) = \sum_{i=1}^{7} w_i \log w_i \quad \text{with} \quad w \in \Omega = [0,1]^7 \subset E^7$$

$$\text{subject to:} \quad \begin{bmatrix} 1 & 1 & 1 & 1 & 1 & 1 & 1 \\ 0 & 1 & -1 & 0 & -1 & 0 & -1 \end{bmatrix} \begin{bmatrix} w_1 \\ w_2 \\ w_3 \\ w_4 \\ w_5 \\ w_6 \\ w_7 \end{bmatrix} - \begin{bmatrix} 1 \\ 0 \end{bmatrix} = h(w)^T = \begin{bmatrix} 0 \\ 0 \end{bmatrix} \text{and}$$

$$
\begin{bmatrix}
-1 & 1 & 0 & 0 & 0 & 0 & 0 \\
0 & -1 & 1 & 0 & 0 & 0 & 0 \\
0 & 0 & -1 & 1 & 0 & 0 & 0 \\
0 & 0 & 0 & -1 & 1 & 0 & 0 \\
0 & 0 & 0 & 0 & -1 & 1 & 0 \\
0 & 0 & 0 & 0 & 0 & -1 & 1 \\
1 & -1 & 0 & -1 & 0 & -1 & -1 \\
0 & 0 & 1 & -1 & -1 & 0 & 0 \\
-1 & 1 & 0 & 1 & 0 & 1 & 0 \\
0 & 0 & 0 & -1 & 1 & 0 & 1
\end{bmatrix}
\begin{bmatrix}
w_1 \\
w_2 \\
w_3 \\
w_4 \\
w_5 \\
w_6 \\
w_7
\end{bmatrix}
= \mathbf{g(w)}^T \leq
\begin{bmatrix}
0 \\
0 \\
0 \\
0 \\
0 \\
0 \\
0 \\
0 \\
0 \\
0
\end{bmatrix}
$$

$$(33)$$

To solve, (33), we begin by writing out the Kuhn-Tucker conditions (Equation 27) with m = 7, 1 =2 and p =10. Starting with Equation (27) and using the results in Equations (30) and (31), we get

$$
\nabla f(w^*) + \lambda^T \nabla h(w^*) + \mu^T \nabla g(w^*) = 0 \text{ } and \text{ } \mu^T \nabla g(w^*) = 0 \text{ } with \text{ } 0 \in E^7
$$
$$
\log w^* + \overline{1} + \lambda^T A + \mu^T B = 0 \text{ } and \text{ } \mu^T(Bw^*) = 0
$$

$$(34)$$

In above, log w = (log w1,...,log w7), $\overline{1}$ = (1,1,...,1) ∈ E7 and μ 3⁰. These equations are to be solved for w* = (w1*,...,w7*), T = (1,2) and μT = (μ1,... μ10). writing out Equations (35), along with those for equality constraints, in all their glory, we obtain

Table 1. Solution to the Constrained Optimization Equations (26)

i→	1	2	3	4	5	6	7	8	9	10..
w_i^*	0.3943	0.2113	0.1057	0.1057	0.0773	0.0773	0.0284			
μ_i	0	0	0.5016	0	0.0016	0	0	0	0.8140	0.8128
λ_i	0.7446	-1.004								

$$\log w_1^* + 1 + \lambda_1 - \mu_1 + \mu_7 - \mu_9 = 0$$

$$\log w_2^* + 1 + \lambda_1 + \lambda_2 + \mu_1 - \mu_2 - \mu_7 + \mu_9 = 0$$

$$\log w_3^* + 1 + \lambda_1 - \lambda_2 + \mu_2 - \mu_3 + \mu_8 = 0$$

$$\log w_4^* + 1 + \lambda_1 + \mu_3 - \mu_4 - \mu_7 - \mu_8 + \mu_9 - \mu_{10} = 0 \qquad \text{Kuhn-Tucker Conditons (6.5a)}$$

$$\log w_5^* + 1 + \lambda_1 - \lambda_2 + \mu_4 - \mu_5 - \mu_8 + \mu_{10} = 0$$

$$\log w_6^* + 1 + \lambda_1 + \mu_5 - \mu_6 - \mu_7 + \mu_9 = 0$$

$$\log w_7^* + 1 + \lambda_1 - \lambda_2 + \mu_6 - \mu_7 + \mu_{10} = 0$$

$$\mu_j(w_{j+1}^* - w_j^*) = 0; \quad 1 \le j \le 6 \qquad \text{Kuhn-Tucker Conditions (6.5b)}$$

$$\mu_7(w_1^* - w_2^* - w_4^* - w_6^* - w_7^*) = 0$$

$$\mu_8(w_3^* - w_4^* - w_5^*) = 0 \qquad \text{Kuhn-Tucker Conditions (6.5b)}$$

$$\mu_9(w_2^* + w_4^* + w_6^* - w_1^*) = 0$$

$$\mu_{10}(w_5^* + w_7^* - w_4^*) = 0$$

$$\Sigma_{i=1}^{7} w_i^* - 1 = 0 \qquad \text{Equality Constraints}$$

$$w_2^* - w_3^* - w_5^* - w_7^* = 0. \qquad (6.13)$$

Solving these equations for the nineteen unknown's yields:

Note that the vector μ satisfies $\mu \ge 0$. Next, we observe that set of active g_j-constraints, according to the Kuhn-Tucker conditions (6.5b), are those for which $g_j(w^*) = 0$. The set of indices for which this is the case is J= {3, 5, 9, 10}. Forming the matrix C, as per Equation (32) we get

$$C = \begin{bmatrix} A \\ \overline{B} \end{bmatrix} = \begin{bmatrix} 1 & 1 & 1 & 1 & 1 & 1 & 1 \\ 0 & 1 & -1 & 0 & -1 & 0 & -1 \\ 0 & 0 & -1 & 1 & 0 & 0 & 0 \\ 0 & 0 & 0 & 0 & -1 & 1 & 0 \\ -1 & 1 & 0 & 1 & 0 & 1 & 0 \\ 0 & 0 & 0 & -1 & 1 & 0 & 1 \end{bmatrix} \tag{36}$$

with Rank(C) = 6. Thus, the gradient vectors for the equality constraints, $\Delta h(w^*)$ and the relevant gradient vectors (i.e., those corresponding to the active constraints) chosen from $\Delta g(w^*)$ are linearly independent. Hence, w^* is a regular point and the solution to Equations (26) (see table above) is indeed globally valid, according to Proposition 23. The reader might have noticed that in transforming the "original" problem in Equations (23) into the problem of Equations (26), the problem involving strict inequalities was transformed into one where the inequalities are not strict. This implies that the solution (w^*) for the ME swing weight vector may satisfy neither the strict primary nor secondary upper/lower bound inequalities.

In fact, because the BDB/ME problem is convex with linear constraints, several of the components of w^* are likely to be boundary points. This is indeed the case observed in Table 1, particularly where $w_3^* = w_4^*$ and $w_5^* = w_6^*$. To circumvent this issue, one may modify the problem described by Equa-

Table 2. Updated Solution to Equations (26) - strict inequality bracketing

i→	1	2	3	4	5	6	7	8	9	10
w_i^*	0.3974	0.2153	0.1176	0.1076	0.0745	0.0645	0.0231			
μ_i	0	0	0.6422	0	0.1698	0	0	0	0.8242	0.9844
λ_i	0.7471	-1.035								

tions (26) by choosing > 0 and insisting that, for the primary and secondary upper/lower bound brackets:

$w_j - w_{j+1} \geq \varepsilon$ for $1 \leq j \leq 6$ (primary brackets)

and

$w_2 + w_4 + w_6 + w_7 - w_1 \geq \varepsilon$, $w1 - (w2_+ w4_+ w6_) \geq \varepsilon$,

$w4_+ w5 - w3 \geq \varepsilon$, and $w4 _- (w5 +_w 7)_\geq \varepsilon$ (secondary brackets) $\tag{37}$

To avoid selecting an inappropriately large &, we suggest that ≤ m-2 ʷhere m is the dimension of the swing weight vector. Imposing this additional requirement on the bracketing, the Kuhn-Tucker conditions in Equation (35) become

$$\mu_j(w_{j+1}{}^* + \varepsilon - w_j{}^*) = 0; \quad 1 \le j \le 6$$

$$\mu_7(w_1{}^* + \varepsilon - w_2{}^* - w_4{}^* - w_6{}^* - w_7{}^*) = 0$$

$$\mu_8(w_3{}^* + \varepsilon - w_4{}^* - w_5{}^*) = 0 \qquad \text{Kuhn-Tucker Conditions (6.5b)}$$

$$\mu_9(w_2{}^* + w_4{}^* + w_6{}^* + \varepsilon - w_1{}^*) = 0$$

$$\mu_{10}(w_5{}^* + w_7{}^* + \varepsilon - w_4{}^*) = 0$$

$$(38)$$

Using $= 0.01$, we substitute these conditions for the original ones in Equation (35) and solve, once again, for the nineteen unknowns. Table 2 below displays the updated solution for w*. The C-matrix (Equation (36)) remains unchanged so that the updated w* is guaranteed to be a regular point and, consequently, a valid solution to the constrained optimization.

MAXIMUM ENTROPY VS. THE RANK ORDER CENTROID

A final note regarding maximum entropy swing weight vectors is in order. In the first section, we mentioned that the purpose of considering the ROC-method is to show that, even though this technique elicits only ordinal information regarding the weights, it does not produce the maximum entropy swing weight vector. To see this, we may construct a swing weight vector (or a class of vectors) in E^7 which possess more entropy than the vector

$$\widehat{w} = (\widehat{w}_1, \ldots, \widehat{w}_7) \ where \ \widehat{w}_k = E[W_{(k)}] = \frac{1}{7}\sum_{i=k}^{7}\frac{1}{i} \tag{39}$$

and $E[W_{(k)}]$ is defined in Equation (15). Consider the problem

$$minimize: \quad f(\mathbf{w}) = \sum_{i=1}^{7} w_i \log w_i \quad \text{with} \quad \mathbf{w} \in \Omega = [0, 1]^7 \subset E^7$$

$$subject \ to: \quad h_1(\mathbf{w}) = \sum_{i=1}^{7} w_i - 1 = 0$$

$$g_j(\mathbf{w}) = w_{j+1} + \varepsilon - w_j \le 0 \quad \text{for } 1 \le j \le 6 \quad \text{(primary bracket)}$$

$$(40)$$

where s > 0. This problem, for suitably selected, has solution $w_j^* = w_7^* + (7 - j)$ for $1 \leq j \leq 6$. Using the normality condition, we determine that $w_7^* = 1/7 — 3$ so that

$$w^* = \left(\frac{1}{7} + 3\varepsilon, \frac{1}{7} + 2\varepsilon, ..., \frac{1}{7} - 3\varepsilon\right) \tag{41}$$

The entropy of $\widehat{w}$ $is - f\left(\widehat{w}\right)$ or

$$\sum_{j=1}^{7}\left(\frac{1}{7}\sum_{i=j}^{7}\frac{1}{i}\right)\log\left(\frac{1}{7}\sum_{i=j}^{7}\frac{1}{i}\right) = 1.644 \tag{42}$$

Suppose = 0.01. The entropy of w* is

$$-f(w^*) = \sum_{j=1}^{7}\left(\frac{1}{7} - (j-4)\varepsilon\right)\log\left(\frac{1}{7} - (j-4)\varepsilon\right) = 1.936 \tag{43}$$

which is greater than that for $\widehat{w}$.

CONVEXITY OF THE BINARY DESCENDING BRACKETING / MAXIMUM ENTROPY (BDB/ME) PROBLEM

Recall the generalization of the BDB/ME problem in Equation 20. For the m-long swing weight vector $W = (w_1, ..., w_m)$ with l equality constraints $(1 \leq m)$ and p inequality constraints, we have

$$\text{minimize}: \quad f(W) = \sum_{i=1}^{m} w_i \log w_i \ \text{with} \ W \in \Omega = [0,1]^m \subset E^m$$
$$\text{subject to}: \quad AW^T - N = h(W)^T = 0 \ \text{and} \ BW^T = g(W)^T \leq 0 \tag{44}$$

Here, A = $[a_{i,j}]$ is the 1 x m matrix, with $a_{i,j}$ {-1, 0, 1} representing the equality constraints. The first row of A represents the normality condition; that is, $a_{1,j} = 1$ for $1 \leq j \leq m$. N is the m-long column vector $(1, 0, ..., 0)^T$. B = $[b_{i,j}]$ is the p x m matrix with $b_{i,j}$ {-1, 0, 1} and

$$B = \begin{bmatrix} -1 & 1 & 0 & \dots & \dots & \dots & \dots & \dots & \dots & \dots & 0 \\ 0 & -1 & 1 & 0 & \dots & \dots & \dots & \dots & \dots & \dots & 0 \\ 0 & 0 & -1 & 1 & 0 & \dots & \dots & \dots & \dots & \dots & 0 \\ \circ & \circ & \circ & \circ & \circ & & & \circ & \circ & & \circ \\ \circ & \circ & & & & & & \circ & \circ & & \circ \\ 0 & \dots & & \dots & \dots & \dots & \dots & 0 & -1 & & 1 \\ b_{m,1} & b_{m,2} & \dots & \dots & \dots & \dots & \dots & \dots & & b_{m,m} \\ b_{m+1,1} & b_{m+1,2} & \dots & \dots & \dots & \dots & \dots & \dots & & b_{m+1,m} \\ \circ & \circ & & & & & & & & \circ \\ \circ & \circ & & & & & & & & \circ \\ b_{p,1} & b_{p,2} & \dots & \dots & \dots & \dots & \dots & \dots & & b_{p,m} \end{bmatrix}$$

← *primary bracket*
← *primary bracket*
← *primary bracket*

← *primary bracket*
← *up/low bound bracket*
← *up/low bound bracket*

← *up/low bound bracket*

(45)

To establish that Equations (44) represent a convex programming problem we need to show that Ω is a convex set and that the functions f, g and h, defined on Ω are convex. First, we remind the reader of the definitions of convex sets and convex functions.

Definition (*Convex Set*). A set $\Omega \subset E^m$ is said to be convex if for every x_1 and $x_2 \in \Omega$ and every real number $\alpha \in (0,1)$, the point $\alpha x1 + (1-\alpha)x2 \in \Omega$.

Definition (*Convex Function*). A funciton f defined on a convex set Ω is said to be convex if, for every $x1, x2 \in_\Omega$ and every $\alpha \in [0,1]$ the following holds:

$$f(\alpha x1 + (1-\alpha)x2) \leq \alpha f(x1) + (1-\alpha)f(x2)$$

(i) Convexity of $\Omega = [0, 1]m$. Suppose x, y Ω. . Then, for any α (0, 1) we have $\alpha x + (1-\alpha)y = \alpha(x1,...,xm) + (1-\alpha)(y1,...ym)$ where $xi, yi [_0, 1]$. Then $0 \leq \alpha xi + (1-\alpha)yi \leq 1$. So, if $wi = \alpha_x i + (1-\alpha)yi$ then either $xi < w_i < y_i$ or $i < w_i < x_i$. Thus, for $1 \leq i \leq m$, wi $[_0, 1]$. Then w = $\alpha x + (1-\alpha)$ y 0 which establishes that Ω is convex.

(ii) Convexity of g and h-Functions. A linear function on Ω, $g(x) = \Sigma_{i=1}^m cixi$ with x Em and real-valued constants ci i_s, by its very nature, convex though degenerately so (strict equality). That is, for x, y $\Omega = [0, 1]m$ and α [0,1] we have

$$g(\alpha x + (1-\alpha)y) = \sum_{i=1}^{m} c_i(\alpha x_i + (1-\alpha)y_i)$$

$$= \alpha \sum_{i=1}^{mi} c_i x_i + (1-\alpha)\sum_{i=1}^{m} c_i y_i \qquad (46)$$

$$= \alpha g(x) + (1-\alpha)g(y)$$

(iii) <u>Convexity of f(w).</u> We employ the following characterization of convexity:

Let f C^2 (i. e., f is a twice continuously differentiable function). Then f is convex over a convex set Q containing an interior point if and only if the Hessian matrix F off is positive semi definite throughout Ω.

In other words, we must show that for w = $(w_1,...,w_m)$ Ω, wFw^{T} ^{3} 0 where F is the m x m Hessian F = $[\partial^2 f/\partial w_i \partial w_j]$ $(1 \leq i, j \leq m)$ and $\Omega = [0, 1]^m$ is the convex space of interest. To this end, we note that for f(W) = $\sum_{i=1}^{m} w_i \log w_i$,

$$\frac{\partial^2}{\partial w_i \partial w_j} f(w) = \begin{cases} 0 & i \neq j \\ w_i^{-1} & i = j \end{cases} \qquad (47)$$

From Equation (A2), it is easy to see that F = Diag$[w_1^{-1}, w_2^{-1}, ..., w_m^{-1}]$ where all of the entries either zero (off-diagonal) or positive (on-diagonal). Finally,

$$\mathbf{wFw}^{T} = (w_1,...,w_m) \begin{bmatrix} w_1^{-1} & 0 & ... & ... & 0 \\ 0 & w_2^{-1} & 0 & ... & 0 \\ 0 & 0 & \circ & ... & 0 \\ \circ & \circ & \circ & \circ & 0 \\ 0 & ... & ... & 0 & w_m^{-1} \end{bmatrix} \begin{bmatrix} w_1 \\ \circ \\ \circ \\ \circ \\ w_m \end{bmatrix} = I_m \cdot \begin{bmatrix} w_1 \\ \circ \\ \circ \\ \circ \\ w_m \end{bmatrix} = \sum_{i=1}^{m} w_i = 1 > 0 \qquad (48)$$

In closing, the purpose of this chapter was twofold. First, a new procedure to elicit, from a decision-maker, information regarding additive value weights (a.k.a. swing weights) is introduced. The procedure is a hybrid of the "balance-beam" method and a dynamic "binary-like" interrogation (where the jth inquiry depends upon the answer to the (j - 1)st inquiry). Second, using the maximum entropy methodology, we demonstrate how to construct a set of additive value weights based solely on the elicited information.

REFERENCES

Greven, A., Keller, G., & Warnecke, G. (Eds.). (2014). *Entropy* (Vol. 47). Princeton University Press.

Keeney, R. L., Raiffa, H., & Meyer, R. F. (1993). *Decisions with multiple objectives: preferences and value trade-offs*. Cambridge university press. doi:10.1017/CBO9781139174084

Luenberger, D. G. (1984). *Linear and Nonlinear Programming* (2nd ed.). Addison-Wesley Publishing Company Inc.

Olson, D. L., & Dorai, V. K. (1992). Implementation of the centroid method of Solymosi and Dombi. *European Journal of Operational Research, 60*(1), 117–129. doi:10.1016/0377-2217(92)90339-B

Pöyhönen, M., & Hämäläinen, R. P. (2001). On the convergence of multiattribute weighting methods. *European Journal of Operational Research, 129*(3), 569–585. doi:10.1016/S0377-2217(99)00467-1

Rao, S. S. (1979). *Optimization (Theory and Applications)*. Wiley Eastern Limited.

Solymosi, T., & Dombi, J. (1986). A method for determining the weights of criteria: The centralized weights. *European Journal of Operational Research, 26*(1), 35–41. doi:10.1016/0377-2217(86)90157-8

Squartini, T., & Garlaschelli, D. (2017). *Maximum-Entropy Networks: Pattern Detection, Network Reconstruction and Graph Combinatorics*. Springer. doi:10.1007/978-3-319-69438-2

Wall, E. S., Rinaudo, C. H., & Salter, R. C. (2022). Comparing Weighting Strategies for SME-Based Manufacturability Assessment Scoring. In *Recent Trends and Advances in Model Based Systems Engineering* (pp. 485–492). Springer. doi:10.1007/978-3-030-82083-1_41

Watson, S. R., Buede, D. M., & Buede, D. M. (1987). *Decision synthesis: The principles and practice of decision analysis*. Cambridge University Press.

Chapter 6
Utility Curves for
Decision Making

ABSTRACT

A utility curve, from the risk assessment standpoint, provides a scaled/relative relationship between the value of achieving a goal or reward versus the expenditure of resources required to attain this goal. This chapter focuses on selecting, in an "unbiased" fashion, such a curve using only a minimum of knowledge. The notion of unbiased is expressed in the form of a well-defined "no-preference" rule. In design analyses, which involve trading off one property of a system with one unit of measure for a property of a system with a different unit of measure, it is often helpful to explicitly state the trade-off relationship between the measurement parameters by developing utility functions for each. These functions can be elicited from individuals via a series of preference questions. This chapter addresses how to develop "no-preference" utility curve equations using three points. Of all possible functions, which include these points, a no-preference utility curve, according to some well-defined measure of preference, is the most measure-neutral.

INTRODUCTION

The purpose of constructing a utility function via a no-preference rule is precisely analogous to that of constructing a probability model using maximum-entropy methods. In practice, an analyst is faced with forming a probability model of a real-world process, using a limited amount of data obtained by observing the process (Du et al., 2020). The strategy of constructing a "best" probability model, based only upon the information revealed by the observations, is the cornerstone of the maximum entropy method (Wu, 2012). In essence, the information contained in the probability model (as measured by entropy) should be no greater than the information contained in the observations (Yang & Sen, 1996). The approach applied in this chapter is conceptually the same. However, because we are considering utility functions instead of probability models, we substitute, for maximum entropy, a well-defined measure of "no-preference".

This chapter will develop two types of utility curves, each based on a one of two no-preference rules. For purposes of this discussion, the general form assumed for the utility curve will be that which is di-

DOI: 10.4018/978-1-6684-7766-3.ch006

minishing, as x increases and is concave-down. However, without loss of generality, the results obtained for this curve are equally applicable to three other types of utility functions encountered in trade-off design. These are: (1) a concave-up decreasing function, (2) a concave-down increasing function and (3) a concave-up increasing function. Finally, we shall show that each of the latter three problems is equivalent, up to a simple transformation, to the decreasing/concave-down function.

A utility curve, for purposes of this discussion, provides a scaled/relative relationship between the value of achieving a goal or reward versus the expenditure of resources required to attain this goal (Abbas, 2003). For example, this might be a successful attack on a cryptosystem while the resources expended are typically computer time, manpower, etc. Specifically, let x denote the relative value of one's resources, that is $0 \le x \le 1$, while letting $f(x)$, with $0 \le f(x) \le 1$, denote the relative value of the expected reward received as a result of expending resources valued at x. We call the function, $f(x)$, a utility curve for the resources, x. The general form of $f(x)$ to be considered here possesses the following characteristics:

1. $f(x)$ is a strictly decreasing function on $x \in [0, 1]$; i.e.
    $x_2 > x_1 \rightarrow f(x_2) < f(x_1)$ for all $x_1, x_2 \in [0,1]$,
2. f is piecewise continuous on $[0, 1]$ and
3. $f(0) = 1$ and $f(1) = 0$

When f(x) possesses the strictly decreasing property, we say that it is a diminishing utility curve (DUC); that is, the greater the relative expenditure of resources, the lesser the relative value of achieving the intended goal. Thus, in the extreme, f attains a maximum value of one (100% utility) when the goal is achieved without expending any resources (i.e., x = 0) and attains a minimum of zero when one must apply all the available resources (x = 1) to the problem at hand.

Of particular interest is a class DUCs, one of which is represented in Equation 1. Specifically, consider the region in the x-y plane, R, given by

$$R = \{(x,y) \ni 0 \le x, y \le 1 \text{ and } 1 - x < y\} \quad (1)$$

That is, R is the semi-open region bounded by the lines y = 1, x = 1 and y = 1- x. By the "semi-open" region we mean that the points, (x, y), on the boundary line y = 1 - x are not included in R. Next, suppose $p = (\hat{x},\hat{y}) \in R$ is given. Having chosen p, we seek a C^2-smooth function on [0,1], f(x) = h(x), with the following well-defined requirements (see p. 3):

(r1) $h'(x) \le 0$ at $x=0$ and $h'(x)<0$ for $0<x \le 1$,
(r2) $h''(x)<0$ for $0 \le x \le 1$,
(r3) $h(0)=1$,
(r4) $h(1)=0$, and
(r5) $h(\hat{x}) = \hat{y}; \quad (\hat{x}, \hat{y}) \in R$

By C^2-smooth, we mean that h, h' and h'' are continuous in R. Note, by necessity, that we must have $h(x) \ge g(x)$ on [0, 1] where $g(x)$ is given by

Figure 1. General properties of h(x)

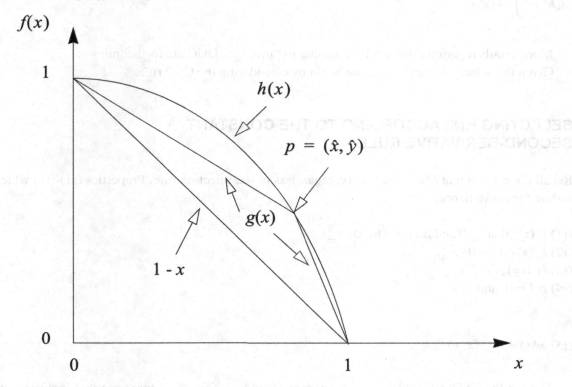

$$g(x) = \begin{cases} \left(\dfrac{\hat{y}-1}{\hat{x}}\right)x + 1; & 0 \leq x \leq \hat{x} \\ \left(\dfrac{\hat{y}}{\hat{x}-1}\right)(x-|1); & \hat{x} < x \leq 1 \end{cases} \qquad (2)$$

The significance of *g(x)* shall be made apparent during the discussion of one of the no-preference rules for selecting *h(x)*.

A selection via a no-preference rule is one whereby a choice is made which, by some well-defined measure, is "neutral" or "average", according to some desired property. The two no-preference rules we consider are:

(I) Constant Second-Derivative (CSD) - choose *h(x)* so that $h''(x) = k < 0$ where *k* is a constant. That is, there is no reason to assume (or prefer, if you will) that the rate of decrease of h is greater or lesser for one value of *x* over another.

(II) Median Average Utility (MAU) - find a DUC, *M(x)*, which, in some sense, is an "average" utility curve out of "all possible DUCs ("*h(x)'s*")" satisfying Properties (r1)-(r5). In this instance, the measure used to compare DUCs is an integral functional, *A(h)*, which maps *h(x)* to a positive real number which, in turn, represents the average utility, on [0, 1], of the DUC, *h(x)*. That is,

$$A(h) = \int_0^1 h(x)dx \tag{3}$$

More details regarding the precise meaning of "average" DUC are forthcoming. Given the selection rules above, we begin by considering the CSD rule.

SELECTING H(X) ACCORDING TO THE CONSTANT SECOND-DERIVATIVE RULE

Recall the criteria that $h(x)$ must satisfy, regardless of the selection rule, Properties (r1)-(r5) which we restate for convenience:

(r1) $h'(x) \leq 0$ at $x=0$ and $h'(x) < 0$ for $0 < x \leq 1$,
(r2) $h''(x) < 0$ for $0 \leq x \leq 1$,
(r3) $h(0)=1$,
(r4) $h(1)=0$, and

$$\text{(r5)} \quad h(\hat{x}) = \hat{y}; \quad (\hat{x}, \hat{y}) \in R \tag{4}$$

Though the CSD-rule adds only one more constraint, $h''(x) = k$, it turns out that inclusion of this condition completely determines the form of $h(x)$. In fact, such an h exists only if the given point, p ($\hat{x}, \hat{y}$), satisfies certain requirements as well. Starting with $h''(x) = k$, we have, after two indefinite integrations

$$h''(x) = \frac{d^2}{dx^2} h(x) \Rightarrow h(x) = \frac{1}{2} kx^2 + C_1 x + C_2 \tag{5}$$

where C_1 and C_2 are constants of integration. Next, using (r3) and (r4), we obtain

$$h(x) = \frac{1}{2} kx^2 - \left(\frac{k}{2} + 1 \right) x + 1 \tag{6}$$

According to (r5), we see that $\hat{y} = \frac{1}{2} k\hat{x}^2 - \left(\frac{k}{2} + 1 \right) \hat{x} + 1$ from which we obtain k as a function of the known point, p, in R (see Eq. (1)); i.e.,

$$k = \frac{2(\hat{y} + \hat{x} - 1)}{\hat{x}^2 - \hat{x}} \tag{7}$$

We note that for k to even be at all defined, we must initially restrict $\hat{x}$ to the open interval, (0, 1), where, incidentally, $\hat{x}^2 - \hat{x} < 0$. Next, as $p \in R$, we have $\hat{y} + \hat{x} - 1 > 0$ so that $k < 0$ in R (except when $\hat{x}T\{0,1\}$). Since $k < 0$ in R, Property (r2) is satisfied.

Now, we need to determine the constraints on p to ensure that (i) $h(x) > 1 - x$ on (0, 1), (ii) $h'(x) < 0$ on (0,1) and (iii) $h'(0) \leq 0$. For (i), we observe that

$$h(x) - (1 - x) = \frac{1}{2}kx^2 - \left(\frac{k}{2} + 1\right)x + 1 - (1 - x)$$

$$= \frac{1}{2}kx^2 - \frac{k}{2}x = \frac{k}{2}x(x - 1) > 0 \tag{8}$$

since $x > 0$ on (0, 1) while k and $x - 1$ are both negative on (0, 1); thus, (i) is true regardless of the choice of p. For $h'(x)$, we observe that $h'(x) = kx - (k/2 + 1)$. Now, at $x = 0$, the following must be satisfied:

$$h'(0) = -\frac{k}{2} - 1 = \frac{1 - \hat{y} - \hat{x}}{\hat{x}^2 - \hat{x}} - 1 = \frac{1 - \hat{y} - \hat{x}^2}{\hat{x}^2 - \hat{x}} \tag{9}$$

since $\hat{x}T(0,1)$, we observe that $\hat{x}^2 - \hat{x} < 0$ which, in turn, forces the condition $1 - \hat{y} - \hat{x}^2 \geq 0$ Turning to $h'(1)$, we have

$$h'(1) = \frac{k}{2} - 1 = \frac{\hat{y} + \hat{x} - 1}{\hat{x}^2 - \hat{x}} - 1 = \frac{-(1 - \hat{x})^2 + \hat{y}}{\hat{x}^2 - \hat{x}} \tag{10}$$

since $k/2 - 1 < 0$. The points, $p = (\hat{x}, \hat{y})$, which satisfy Inequality (10) must satisfy the constraint - ($1 - \hat{x})^2 + \hat{y} > 0$ Combining constraints, we observe that for both $h'(0) \leq 0$ and $h'(1) < 0$ to be simultaneously satisfied, we must have

$$1 - \hat{x}^2 \geq \hat{y} > (1 - \hat{x})^2 \tag{11}$$

since $h'(x)$ is a linear function of x on [0, 1] and if p satisfies Inequality (11) then both $h'(0) < 0$ and $h'(1) < 0$ from which we may conclude that, for choices of p which satisfy Inequality (11), $h'(x) < 0$ for all x on (0,1). Hence, assuming the validity of Inequality (11), Property (r 1) is satisfied. Further, since we assumed at the outset that $p = (\hat{x}, \hat{y}) \in R$, the condition comprising the right half of Inequality (11) is superfluous because, in R, $\hat{y} > 1 - \hat{x}$.

To summarize, selecting $h(x)$ according to the CSD-rule is possible provided that the given point, $p = (\hat{x}, \hat{y}) \in R$, satisfies $1 - x^2 \geq \hat{y}$. For such a p, we have

$$h(x) = \frac{1}{2}kx^2 - \left(\frac{k}{2} + 1\right)x + 1 \quad \text{and} \quad k = \frac{2(\hat{y} + \hat{x} - 1)}{\hat{x}^2 - \hat{x}} \tag{12}$$

UPPER AND LOWER-BOUND DIMINISHING UTILITY CURVES IN R

The second no-preference rule we consider is based on average utility. As mentioned above, if $h(x)$ is a DUC (defined on [0, 1]), then the functional which measures the average utility of h is the integral form

$$A(h) = \int_0^1 h(x)dx \tag{13}$$

The focus of the next two chapters is to construct a technique for computing the median average utility curve. To understand the term "median", we must first discuss the concept of upper and lower-bound DUCs on the region R (defined by Equation (1)).

Once again, we consider the region R, a given point $p = (\hat{x}, \hat{y})$ and H, the set of all functions, $h(x)$, satisfying Properties (r1)-(r5). Looking at Figure 1, it is apparent that $g(x)$ (Equation [2]) is a lower bound curve for any such $h(x)$. That is, for any $h(x)$, $h(x) \geq g(x)$ for all x ∈ [0, 1]. However, note that g(x) ≠ H because g is not C²-smooth on [0, 1] (it is not differentiable at p). We may view g as a "limiting" or the "greatest lower bound"-curve obtained by forming any sequence of functions in H, say {$h_1(x)$, $h_2(x),\ldots h_N(x),\ldots$}, with the property that $j > i \rightarrow 0 > h''_j(x) > h''_i(x)$ for all x ∈ [0, 1] and with the limiting properties

$$\lim_{N \to \infty} h''_N(x) = 0 \,\forall x \in [0,1] \quad \text{and} \quad \lim_{N \to \infty} h'_N(x) = \begin{cases} \dfrac{\hat{y} - 1}{\hat{x}} & 0 \leq x \leq \hat{x} \\[2mm] \dfrac{\hat{y}}{\hat{x} - 1} & \hat{x} < x \leq 1 \end{cases} \tag{14}$$

Observe that these limiting properties, taken together, completely determine $g(x)$. Clearly, because of these limiting properties, g should be taken as our lower-bound DUC even though it is not in *H*. Finally, because of this construct, it is also clear that the average utility of g is the greatest lower bound on the average utility of each h in *H*; that is

$$A(g) = \int_0^1 g(x)dx \leq A(h) \quad (\forall h \in H) \tag{15}$$

With the lower-bound DUC established, we turn to the much more difficult problem of determining the upper-bound DUC in *H*, which we denote henceforth by $G(x)$. That is,

$$G(x) = Arg \max_{h(x) \in H} \{A(h)\} \tag{16}$$

where $G(x)$ is the function in H which maximizes $A(h)$; in other words, $G(x)$ maximizes the average utility functional. At first glance, as difficult as this problem is, the solution to this problem (unique or otherwise) might be determined by the methods of variation calculus (Leitmann, 2013). However, upon a cursory inspection of Leitmann (2013) the techniques for finding the extrema of $A(h)$ seem to be based only on the assumption that h is C^2-smooth and that the initial constraints, $h(0) = h_0$ and $h(1) = h_1$, are given. The latter two constraints correspond to Properties (r3) and (r4). However, if it exists, which considers additional constraints along the lines of (r1), (r2) and (r5). Therefore, determining a general function or class of functions in H which maximize A is, currently, elusive.

Considering this complication, we shall limit our discussion to that of extremizing A under the assumption that $h(x)$ is a polynomial of a specified degree. Why do we choose polynomials? There are four reasons:

1. All polynomials (with real coefficients) are C^2-smooth on $[0, 1]$ (or any interval, for that matter),
2. polynomials are easy to integrate,

3. a function, h(x), possessing a polynomial form, $h(x) = \sum_{i=1}^{n} a_i x^i$ will afford a translation of the constraints (r1)-(r5) into a system of <u>linear</u> (simple) equations and inequalities involving the unknown coefficients, a_i and

4. we may "fine-tune" or extend, if you will, the function h(x) by adding as many parameters (in the form of polynomial coefficients) as we wish.

Therefore, unless additional knowledge regarding the possible form of $G(x)$ is given, polynomials seem to be an appropriate way to proceed.

Before beginning our quest for $G(x)$, it is prudent at this point to simplify one of the constraints, namely (r1). Intuitively, it seems reasonable that any candidate for a concave-down C^2-smooth curve which maximizes the area underneath it should possess zero slope at $x = 0$, as allowed by (r1). In effect, this allows the candidate function to attain larger values, in "δ-neighborhoods" of zero, than candidate functions whose first derivative is strictly less than zero at $x = 0$. Naturally, one would expect that functions with larger values on $[0, 1]$ produce larger integrals over $[0, 1]$. In addition, knowing that $h''(x) < 0$ for all x in $[0, 1]$ and $h'(0) = 0$ <u>implies</u> that $h'(x) < 0$ for $0 < x \leq 1$; thus, (r1) is, at least in part, redundant. Consequently, we prefer to rewrite (r1) as

$$(r1') \ h'(0) = 0 \tag{17}$$

We are now ready to consider some examples.

Example 1: The General Cubic

Given $p = (\hat{x}, \hat{y}) \in$ R, determine a, b, c and d so that $h(x) = G(x)$, given by the cubic $G(x) = ax^3 + bx^2 + cx + d$, maximizes $A(h)$ under our constraints (r1')-(r5).

Solution:

First, we see that

$$\int_0^1 G(x)dx = \int_0^1 (ax^3 + bx^2 + cx + d)dx = \frac{a}{4} + \frac{b}{3} + \frac{c}{2} + d \tag{18}$$

so that our problem is to determine

$$\underset{a,b,c,d}{Max}\left\{\frac{a}{4} + \frac{b}{3} + \frac{c}{2} + d\right\} \tag{19}$$

subject to:

(i) $G'(0)=0$,
(ii) $G''(x)<0$ for $0\leq x\leq 1$,
(iii) $G(0)=1$,
(iv)   (iv) $G(1)=0$, and

(v) $G(\hat{x}) = \hat{y}; \quad (\hat{x}, \hat{y}) \in T$ \hfill (20)

From (iii) and (iv), we see that $d= 1$ and $a + b + c = -1$, respectively. From (*i*), we observe that

$$G''(0) = 0 \Rightarrow (3ax^2 + 2bx + c)\big|_{x=0} = 0 \Rightarrow c = 0 \tag{21}$$

so that $a + b = -1$ or $b = -(1+ a)$. Next, considering (*v*) above, we have

$$G(\hat{x}) = a\hat{x}^3 + b\hat{x}^2 + c\hat{x} + d = \hat{y} = a\hat{x}^3 - (1+a)\hat{x}^2 + 1 \tag{22}$$

from which we obtain

$$a = \frac{\hat{y} + \hat{x}^2 - 1}{\hat{x}^3 - \hat{x}^2} \tag{23}$$

At this point, we run into a problem. Using constraints (i), (iii), (iv) and (v), we have completely determined our cubic. That is, a is computed from the given point, $(\hat{x}, \hat{y})$, using (23), b is computed from a by $b = -(1 + a)$ and we already determined that c and d are 0 and 1, respectively. All that remains is to check to see if (ii) holds; that is, if

$$G''(x) = 6ax + 2b = 6\left[\frac{\hat{y} + \hat{x}^2 - 1}{\hat{x}^3 - \hat{x}^2}\right]x - \frac{\hat{y} + \hat{x}^3 + 1}{\hat{x}^3 - \hat{x}^2} < 0 \ \textit{for all} \ x \in [0,1] \tag{24}$$

Strict Inequality (24), in turn, can only be assessed upon specifying $(\hat{x}, \hat{y})$. In short, if a point, p = $(\hat{x}, \hat{y})$ is specified so that (24) holds, then the cubic is completely determined as well as the value of its integral on [0,1]; that is, due to the strength of the restrictions (i) - (v), we are, essentially, <u>trivially</u> maximizing Equation (19) over a <u>single</u> value of a, namely that given by (23). In addition, we must ensure our result is a "legal" one by checking Inequality (24).

For example, take the point, $p = (\frac{3}{4}, \frac{1}{2})$. It is left to the reader to ensure that this point lies in R (see Equation (1). This p yields $a = -\frac{4}{9}$ and $b = -\frac{5}{9}$. Next, we check Inequality (24) by observing that, for $x \in [0, 1]$,

$$-\frac{34}{9} \leq 6ax + 2b = -\frac{24}{9}x - \frac{10}{9} \leq -\frac{10}{9} < 0 \tag{25}$$

Thus, the cubic, $h(x) = G(x) = -\frac{4}{9}x^3 - \frac{5}{9}x^2 + 1$, satisfies (i)-(v). Its integral on [0,1] is $\frac{19}{27}$ which, in turn, is found by substituting $a = -\frac{4}{9}$, $b = -\frac{5}{9}$, $c = 0$ and $d = 1$ into the formula in Equation (2).

To summarize Example 1, the five requirements, (r1')-(r5), are very restrictive on the general cubic; that is, a four-parameter (a, b, c and d) polynomial leads to at most one solution in R satisfying (r1')-(r5) which, in turn, makes the maximization step (2) trivial. Clearly, if we wish to be less restrictive (and avoid "trivial" maximums), functions with more than four parameters should be considered. Perhaps we should increment the complexity of the cubic by surveying the general quartic.

<u>Example 2:</u> The General Quartic

Given $p = (\hat{x}, \hat{y}) \in$ R, determine a, b, c and d so that $h(x) = G(x)$, given by the cubic $G(x) = ax^4 + bx^3 + cx^2 + dx + e$, maximizes $A(h) = \int_0^1 h(x)\,dx$ under our constraints of Properties (r1')-(r5).

Solution:

First, we see that

$$\int_0^1 G(x)dx = \int_0^1 (ax^4 + bx^3 + cx^2 + dx + e)dx = \frac{a}{5} + \frac{b}{4} + \frac{c}{3} + \frac{d}{2} + e \tag{26}$$

so that our problem is to determine

$$\underset{a,b,c,d,e}{Max} \left\{ \frac{a}{5} + \frac{b}{4} + \frac{c}{3} + \frac{d}{2} + e \right\} \tag{27}$$

subject to: constraints (i)-(v) listed in Equation (20).

From (iii) and (iv), we see that e = 1 and a + b + c + d = -1, respectively. From (i), we observe that

$$G'(0) = 0 \Rightarrow (3ax^2 + 2bx + c)\big|_{x=0} = 0 \Rightarrow c = 0 \tag{28}$$

so that a + b + c = -1 or

$$c = -(1 + a + b) \tag{29}$$

Next, considering (v), we have

$$\hat{y} = a\hat{x}^4 + b\hat{x}^3 + c\hat{x}^2 + 1 \tag{30}$$

which, when the point $p = (\hat{x}, \hat{y},) \in R$ is specified, may be used to generate yet another linear relationship between a, b and c. Consider the point $p = (\frac{3}{4}, \frac{1}{2})$ (as we did in Example 1). Using Equation (30) for this p yields:

$$81a + 108b + 144c = -128 \tag{31}$$

When this equation is used in conjunction with Equation (E2.4), we obtain

$$63a + 36b = -16 \text{ or } b = -\frac{4}{9} - \frac{7}{4}a \tag{32}$$

as well as

$$c = -\frac{5}{9} + \frac{3}{4}a \tag{33}$$

Using these expressions for b and c (in terms of a) along with the restriction on the second derivative, $h''(x) < 0$, for $x \in [0, 1]$ and the fact that we already have determined $d = 0$ and $e = 1$, we restate our optimization problem, for $(\hat{x}, \hat{y}) = \left(\frac{3}{4}, \frac{1}{2} \right)$, as

Find: $\displaystyle Max_a \left\{ \frac{1}{80} a + \frac{19}{27} \right\}$

Subject to: $\displaystyle a\left(12x^2 - \frac{21}{2}x + \frac{3}{2} \right) < \frac{8}{3}x + \frac{10}{9}$ for all $x \in [0,1]$

(34)

Clearly, the largest value of a for which (34) holds is the one which maximizes the guar-tic integral, $\displaystyle \frac{a}{80} + \frac{19}{27}$, on [0,1]. The key to finding this value of a lies in the behavior of the polynomials $12x^2 - \dfrac{21}{2} + \dfrac{3}{2}$ and $\dfrac{8}{3}x + \dfrac{10}{9}$ on [0,1]. The plot of these functions, on [0,1], is given in 2.

Note that (*i*) the roots of $12x^2 - \dfrac{21}{2}x + \dfrac{3}{2}$, namely $x = \dfrac{1}{16}(7 \pm \sqrt{17})$ both lie in [0,1], (ii) the graph of this quadratic is concave-up and, consequently, (iii) the abscissa of the minimum, $x = \dfrac{7}{16}$, also lies in [0,1]. More importantly, however, is that fact that the locations of these roots and the minimum are invariant under multiplication of the quadratic polynomial by a constant (namely, a). This implies that multiplying the polynomial $12x^2 - \dfrac{21}{2}x + \dfrac{3}{2}$ by a, "shifts" its graph up or down while preserving the location of the roots, minimum and concavity. Keeping this in mind, upon further inspection of Figure 2, it becomes clear that the value of a we seek is the largest one for which the plot, on [0, 1], of a($12x^2 - \dfrac{21}{2} + \dfrac{3}{2}$) lies entirely below the graph of the line $\dfrac{8}{3}x + \dfrac{10}{9}$ (this is a graphical description of Inequality (34)). Based on the concavity property of the quadratic, it is clear that (34) will hold on [0, 1] if it holds at x = 0 and x = 1. This, in turn, implies that following conditions hold simultaneously:

(1) $\dfrac{3}{2}a < \dfrac{10}{9} \Rightarrow a < \dfrac{20}{27}$ (*at x = 0*) and

(2) $3a < \dfrac{34}{9} \Rightarrow a < \dfrac{34}{27}$ (*at x = 1*)

(35)

Hence, (34) holds whenever $a < 20/27$. Let $\epsilon > 0$ be an arbitrarily small constant. All the above suggests that we set

$a = \dfrac{20}{27} = \varepsilon, \; b = -\dfrac{4}{9} - \dfrac{7}{4}a = -\dfrac{47}{27} + \dfrac{7}{4}\varepsilon, \; c = -\dfrac{3}{4}\varepsilon, \; d = 0, \text{ and } e = 1 \text{ making}$

(36)

$h(x) = G(x) = \left(\dfrac{20}{27} - \varepsilon \right)x^4 - \left(\dfrac{47}{27} - \dfrac{7}{4}\varepsilon \right)x^3 - \dfrac{3}{4}\varepsilon x^2 + 1$

which possesses a maximum integral of $\dfrac{1}{80}a + \dfrac{19}{27} \approx \dfrac{77}{108}$. G(x) is plotted in Figure 3.

Figure 2. Plots of $12x^2 - \dfrac{21}{2}x + \dfrac{3}{2}$ and $\dfrac{8}{3}x + \dfrac{10}{9}$

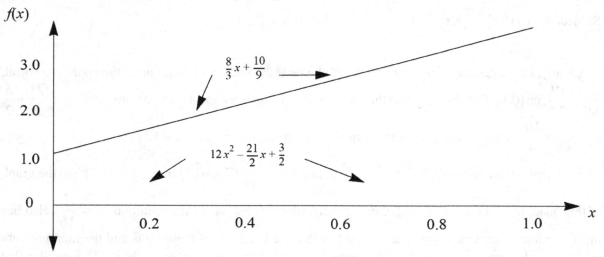

We consider one more polynomial example to illustrate the increasing complexity of the optimization resulting from increasing the degree of $h(x)$. In addition, this affords an opportunity to observe yet another maximum value of $A(h) = \int_0^1 h\big(x\big)\,dx$ to see how it varies with the degree of $h(x)$ while keeping $(\hat{x}, \hat{y})$ fixed.

Example 3: The Quintic Passing Through $(\hat{x}, \hat{y}) = (\dfrac{3}{4}, \dfrac{1}{2})$

Using the procedure in Example 4, determine the degree 5 polynomial, $G(x) = ax^5 + bx^4 + cx^3 + dx^2 + ex + f$ passing through $p = (\dfrac{3}{4}, \dfrac{1}{2}) \in R$, which maximizes the values of $\int_0^1 h\big(x\big)\,dx$ under the constraints listed in (20).

Solution:

We seek a, b,…,f which maximizes

$$\int_0^1 G(x)\,dx = \frac{a}{6} + \frac{b}{5} + \frac{c}{4} + \frac{d}{3} + \frac{e}{2} + f$$

Subject to:

(i) $G'(x) = 5ax^4 + 4bx^3 + 3cx^2 + 2dx + e = 0$ (at $x=0$),

Figure 3. G(x), passing through desired point, $(\hat{x}, \hat{y}) = (\frac{3}{4}, \frac{1}{4})$

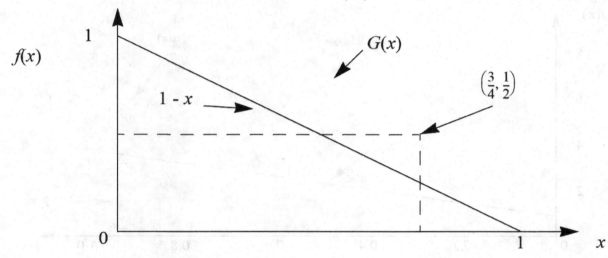

(ii) $G''(x) = 20ax^3 + 12bx^2 + 6cx + 2d < 0$ $(x \hat{I}[0,1]$,

(iii) $G(0) = f = 1$

(iv)   (iv) $G(1) = a + b + c + d + e + f = 0$, and

(v) $G\left(\frac{3}{4}\right) = a\left(\frac{3}{4}\right)^5 + b\left(\frac{3}{4}\right)^4 + c\left(\frac{3}{4}\right)^3 + d\left(\frac{3}{4}\right)^2 + e\left(\frac{3}{4}\right) + f = \frac{1}{2}$ (37)

After a bit of simplifying, the problem above reduces to finding

$$\underset{a,b}{Max}\left\{\frac{5}{192}a + \frac{1}{80}b + \frac{19}{27}\right\}$$

Subject to:

$$a\left(20x^3 - \frac{111}{8}x + \frac{21}{8}\right) + b\left(12x^2 - \frac{21}{2}x + \frac{3}{2}\right) < \frac{8}{3}x + \frac{10}{9}$$ (38)

Notice the strong similarity between the problem in (38) and that of (34). One might say that (29) is "embedded" in (38) since the set of polynomial terms (in x) in the former lie entirely in the set of the latter. The difference, of course, is that we must consider two parameters versus the one parameter in (32). The approach to solving this problem, however, is much like that used in Example 2; that is, the solution hinges on a sound understanding of the properties of the polynomials

Figure 4. Plots of μ(x), β(x), and $\frac{8}{3}x+\frac{10}{9}$

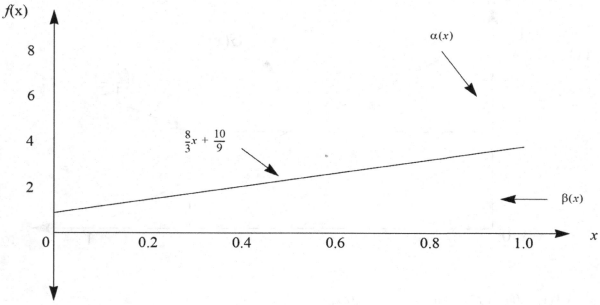

$$\alpha(x) = 20x^3 - \frac{111}{8}x + \frac{21}{8} \quad \text{and} \quad \beta(x) = 12x^2 - \frac{21}{2}x + \frac{3}{2} \tag{39}$$

on the interval [0, 1]. To achieve this, we once again appeal to graphical methods as displayed in Figure 4.

As indicated in Figure 4, both μ(x) and β(x), are concave-up on [0, 1]. Therefore, so is any linear combination μ(x) + β(x), provided a and b are nonnegative and not simultaneously zero. Thus, to ensure that aμ(x) + b$\beta(x) < \frac{8}{3}x+\frac{10}{9}$ on [0, 1], we need only to check the endpoints (as we did in Example 2). Specifically, the restriction (38) may be rewritten as the following set of linear constraints with a and b not simultaneously zero:

$$\begin{cases} a\alpha(0) + b\beta(0) < \dfrac{10}{9} \\ a\alpha(1) + b\beta(1) < \dfrac{34}{9} \end{cases} \text{or} \begin{cases} \dfrac{21}{8}a + \dfrac{3}{2}b < \dfrac{10}{9} \\ \dfrac{35}{4}a + 3b < \dfrac{34}{9} \end{cases} \text{and } a,b \geq 0 \tag{40}$$

Thus, our problem now reduces to finding $\max_{a,b}\left\{\frac{5}{192}a+\frac{1}{80}b+\frac{19}{27}\right\}$ subject to the above strict inequalities in a and b.

One may recognize this as a simple linear programming problem where the expression to be extremized, $\frac{5}{192}a + \frac{1}{80}b + \frac{19}{27}$, called the objective function (Luenberger & Ye, 1984). Assume, for the

Figure 5. Plot of the constraints (4)

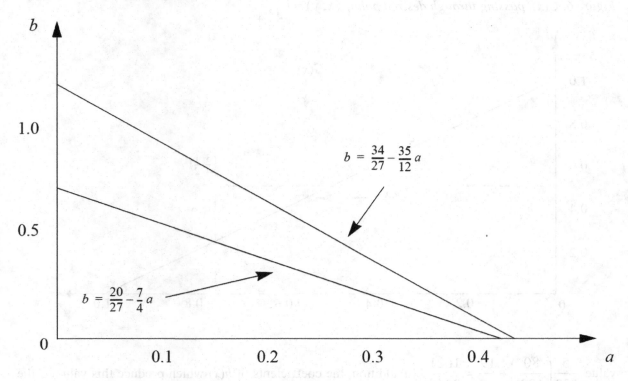

moment, that the inequalities (40) are not strict. The procedure for solving this linear programming problem rests on graphing the constraint inequalities. The result of this graph is a convex polygonal region (known as the feasible region) in the a/b-plane where every point, (a, b), in this region satisfies the constraints (40). A fundamental result of linear programming theory states that a linear objective function will achieve its maximum (minimum) value at one of the vertices of the feasible region (Rao, 2019). In view of this, we present Figure 5; observe that the feasible region satisfying (40) is that bounded by the lines $a = 0$, $b = 0$ and $b = \dfrac{20}{27} - \dfrac{7}{4}a$.

For the case where the inequalities are not strict, the vertices of this region are $(0, 0)$ and $(0, \dfrac{20}{27})$ and $(\dfrac{80}{189}, 0)$ where the maximum of the objective function occurs at the latter point. However, since Inequalities (40) are strict, the feasible region is actually the one shown in Figure 5 but with the boundary deleted. Thus, our estimate for the location, in the a/b-plane, of the maximum of the objective function is $a = \dfrac{80}{189} - \epsilon(\epsilon > 0$, arbitrarily small) and $b = 0$, a form like that of Example 2. Thus, the maximum value of the objective function (hence the maximum value of $A(h) = \int\limits_0^1 h(x)\, dx$ is estimated by the

Figure 6. G(x), passing through desired point, $(\hat{x}, \hat{y}) = (\frac{3}{4}, \frac{1}{4})$

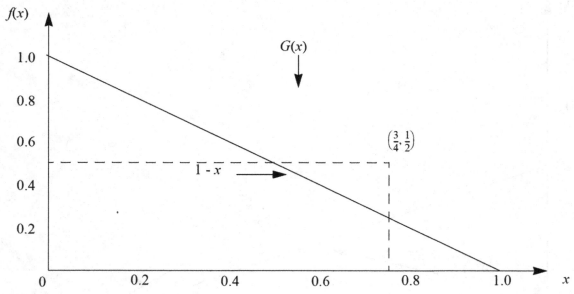

value $\frac{5}{192}\left(\frac{80}{189}\right) + \frac{19}{27} = \frac{1621}{2268}$. In addition, the coefficients of $h(x)$ which produce this value of the

integral are given by $a = \frac{80}{189} - \epsilon$, $b=0$, $c = -\frac{269}{189} + \frac{37}{16}T$, $d = -\frac{21}{16}T$, $e=0$ and $f = 1$ so that

$$G(x) = \left(\frac{80}{189} - \varepsilon\right)x^5 - \left(\frac{269}{189} - \frac{37}{16}\varepsilon\right)x^3 - \frac{21}{16}\varepsilon x^2 + 1 \qquad (41)$$

This $G(x)$ is plotted in Figure 6.

SUMMARY

Results of Examples 1-3

At this point, we summarize the results obtained for our polynomial-type upper-bound curves, $G(x)$. As defined earlier, let $\& > 0$ be an arbitrarily small positive constant. We have:

Degree	$G(x)$	$\int_0^1 G(x)\,dx$
3	$-\dfrac{4}{9}x^3 - \dfrac{5}{9}x^2 + 1$	$\dfrac{19}{27} = 0.70370$
4	$\left(\dfrac{20}{27} - \varepsilon\right)x^4 - \left(\dfrac{47}{27} - \dfrac{7}{4}\varepsilon\right)x^3 - \dfrac{3}{4}\varepsilon x^2 + 1$	$\dfrac{77}{108} - \dfrac{\varepsilon}{80} \approx 0.71296$
5	$\left(\dfrac{80}{189} - \varepsilon\right)x^5 - \left(\dfrac{269}{189} - \dfrac{37}{16}\varepsilon\right)x^3 - \dfrac{21}{16}\varepsilon x^2 + 1$	$\dfrac{1621}{2268} - \dfrac{5\varepsilon}{192} \approx 0.71473$

Each of the $G(x)$ satisfies all of the criteria set forth in the list (20) on page 8.

THE MEDIAN AVERAGE UTILITY DIMINISHING UTILITY CURVES

Given some point, $p = (\hat{x}, \hat{y}) \in R$, let $g(x)$ be the limiting lower-bound DUC defined by Equation (2). Next, suppose we have determined some upper-bound polynomial-form DUC, $G(x)$, using the constraints of Equation (20). Then a natural definition of a median DUC might be

$$M(x) = \frac{1}{2}[g(x) + G(x)] \tag{42}$$

Clearly, Equation (42) is inspired by the notion of the median of a probability distribution. That is, if $f_x(x)$ is a probability density function whereby the probability that $X \le k$ is given by

$$\Pr[X \le k] = \int_{-\infty}^{k} f_X(x)dx \tag{43}$$

then the median of f_x, m, is that value of k for which

$$\Pr[X \le m] = \int_{-\infty}^{m} f_X(x)dx = \int_{m}^{\infty} f_X(x)dx \tag{44}$$

That is, m is the value which divides the area under the density function in half. In a similar fashion, $M(x)$ may be viewed as a curve which, in the sense of average utility, divides the space of DUCs, satisfying (2), in "half"; that is, M(x) is the DUC possessing the arithmetic mean average utility of the maximum and minimum possible average utilities of all possible DUCs passing through the point, p. To see this, observe that the space of all possible DUCs through p is essentially represented by the "area" between $G(x)$ and $g(x)$, on [0,1]. Next, we show that half of this area lies above $M(x)$ and half lies below. To this end, we have, for the area between $M(x)$ and $g(x)$,

Figure 7. Median DUC (M(x)) for the Degree Five Polynomial

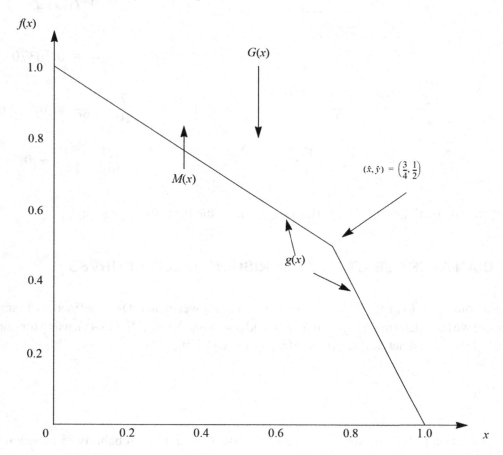

$$\int_0^1 [M(x) - g(x)]dx = \int_0^1 \left[\frac{1}{2}[G(x) + g(x)] - g(x)\right] dx = \int_0^1 \frac{1}{2}[G(x) - g(x)]dx \qquad (45)$$

where the rightmost side of Equation (4.3) is precisely half of the area between $G(x)$ and $g(x)$.

Consider the quintic (degree five polynomial) of Example 3 in the preceding chapter. Applying Equation (41) to this G(x), for the point $(\hat{x}, \hat{y}) = (\frac{3}{4}, \frac{1}{2})$, we obtain

$$M(x) = \begin{cases} \frac{1}{2}\left[\left(\frac{80}{189} - \varepsilon\right)x^5 - \left(\frac{269}{189} - \frac{37}{16}\varepsilon\right)x^3 - \frac{21}{16}\varepsilon x^2 - \frac{2}{3}x + 2\right]; & 0 \le x \le \frac{3}{4} \\ \frac{1}{2}\left[\left(\frac{80}{189} - \varepsilon\right)x^5 - \left(\frac{269}{189} - \frac{37}{16}\varepsilon\right)x^3 - \frac{21}{16}\varepsilon x^2 - 2x + 3\right]; & \frac{3}{4} < x \le 1 \end{cases} \qquad (46)$$

This function is plotted, along with $G(x)$ (Equation (41)) and $g(x)$ (Equation [2]), in Figure 7.

To summarize, one may think of $M(x)$ as a no-preference rule in the sense of it possessing the median average utility; that is, it is "average utility-neutral" with respect to the median.

THE EQUIVALENCE OF UTILITY CURVE PROBLEMS

(With Respect to the Average Utility Measure)

The purpose of the forthcoming is to justify the claims that the problems of finding a concave-up/decreasing, concave-down/increasing and concave-up/increasing no-preference curve, with respect to the average utility measure (Equation [15]), are equivalent. We accomplish this by showing that the problem of determining the upper and lower-bound DUC which are concave-up is equivalent, up to a simple transformation, to the concave-down DUC problem previously discussed. Once establishing this, the median average concave-up DUC maps, under this transformation, into the median average concave-down DUC. Similar arguments may be constructed to prove the equivalence of the concave-down and concave-up IUCs to the concave-down DUC.

Specifically, for the concave-up DUC problem, let J be the set of all C^2-smooth functions, $j(x)$, on $(0, 1)$, satisfying

(s1) $j'(x) = -\infty$ at $x=0$ and $-\infty < j'(x) < 0$ for $0 < x \leq 1$,

(s2) $j''(x) > 0$ for $0 < x \leq 1$

(s3) $j(0) = 1$

(s4) $j(1) = 0$, and

(s5) $j(\hat{x}) = \hat{y}$; $(\hat{x}, \hat{y}) \in Q$

where $Q = \{(x, y)\} \in 0 \leq x, y \leq 1 \text{ and } y < 1 - x\}$, the point $(\hat{x}, \hat{y}) \in Q$ is given and $j(x)$ is continuous at zero but not differentiable there. Observe that Q is the semi-open region bounded the lines $x = 0$, $y = 0$ and $y = x - 1$. Clearly, all such functions, j, lie in the region bounded by the lines $x = 0$, $y = 0$ and the function $g(x)$ given by

$$g(x) = \begin{cases} \left(\dfrac{\hat{y}-1}{\hat{x}}\right)x + 1; & 0 \leq x \leq \hat{x} \\ \left(\dfrac{\hat{y}}{\hat{x}-1}\right)(x-1); & \hat{x} < x \leq 1 \end{cases} \tag{47}$$

which is Equation (2). Note, since each $j(x) \in J$ is concave-up, that we may view $g(x)$ as a limiting or "least upper bound"-curve for the functions in J in much the same way it was viewed as the "greatest lower bound"-curve for the functions in H (see Equation (37)).

Recall the functional, which defines the average utility of the function, $j(x) \in J$, given by

$$A(j) = \int_0^1 j(x)dx \tag{48}$$

and observe, by construct, that $A(j) \leq A(g)$ for all $j(x)$ in J. The optimization problem here analogous is to determine which function in J minimizes the average utility, i.e., we seek $F(x) \in J$ with

$$F(x) = \underset{j(x) \in J}{Arg \min} \{A(j)\} \tag{49}$$

Further it is critical to observe that if $F(x)$ minimizes $A(j)$ then it simultaneously maximizes the value of $\int_0^1 (1 - j(x)) dx$.

Recall that H is the set of C2-smooth functions, on $[0, 1]$, which satisfy properties (r1)-(r5). Having established the problem for the concave-up DUC, we introduce a transformation

(i) which maps the region bounded by $g(x)$, $x = 0$ and $y = 0$ (where the point $(\hat{x}, \hat{y},) \in Q$) into the region bounded by lines $g(x)$, $x = 1$ and $y = 1$ (where the point $(\hat{x}, \hat{y})$ lies in R (see Equation (1))) and

(ii) where the image, under this transformation, of each function in J is a function in H. In particular, the image of $F(x) \in J$ is precisely the function $G \in H$ where G is defined in Equation (39). That is, $G(u)$ is the upper bound concave-down DUC in the $(u\text{-}v)$-plane.

Let T be a transformation which maps the $(x\text{-}y)$-plane to the $(u\text{-}v)$-plane according to

$T: (x,y) \rightarrow (u,v)$ with $u = 1-y$ and $v = 1-x$

To begin, consider (i) above. Note that the lines $x = 0$ and $y = 0$ map to the lines $v = 1$ and $u = 1$, respectively. Note too that the line $y = 1 - x$ maps to $v = 1 - u$ in the $(u\text{-}v)$-plane. Also, as stated in the definition of Q, the inequality $y < 1 - x$ maps to the inequality $1 - u < v$ in the $(u\text{-}v)$-plane. Thus, in total,

$$Q_{xy} = \{(x,y) \ni 0 \leq x,y \leq 1 \text{ and } y < 1-x\} \rightarrow R_{uv} = \{(u,v) \ni 0 \leq u,v \leq 1 \text{ and } 1-u < v\} \tag{51}$$

so that the set Q maps onto the set R. Next, note that if $(\hat{x}, \hat{y}) \in Q$ (Q_{xy}) then $(\hat{u}, \hat{v}) \in R$ (R_{uv}). Finally, for the function $g(x)$, we first consider the interval $0 \leq x \leq \hat{x}$. Here, when $x = 0$, $y = g(x) = g(0) = 1$ and when $x = \hat{x}$ we see that $y = \hat{y}$; . So, according to Equation (50), we note that $0 \leq x \leq \hat{x} \rightarrow 1 \geq y \geq \hat{y} \rightarrow 0 \leq u \leq \hat{u}$. Also, since $y = g(x) = [(\hat{y} - 1)/\hat{x}]x + 1$, we have

$$x = \frac{\hat{x}}{\hat{y} - 1}(y - 1) \Rightarrow v = \frac{\hat{v} - 1}{\hat{u}}u + 1 \tag{52}$$

so that v is precisely $g(u)$ (i.e., substitute v for y and u for x in Equation (47) while the domain is precisely $0 \leq u \leq \hat{u}$. An analogous result is used to obtain the mapping of $g(x)$ to g on the interval $\hat{u} < u \leq 1$. The preceding argument allows us to conclude that

$$\{(x,y) \ni 0 \leq x,y \leq 1 \text{ and } y \leq g(x)\} \rightarrow \{(u,v) \ni 0 \leq u,v \leq 1 \text{ and } g(u) \leq v\} \tag{53}$$

which is the claim in (i). Intuitively speaking, the region on the right-hand side of Equation (53) may be obtained from that on the left-hand side by reflecting the latter about the line $y = 1 - x$. To see this, the reader is encouraged to sketch both regions for a valid choice of $(\hat{x}, \hat{y}) \in Q_{xy}$.

Now we establish (ii) above. This demonstration requires that we prove the following:

(D1) T transforms the constraints (s1) - (s5), in the $(x$-$y)$-plane, into the constraints and (r1)-(r5), in the $(u$-$v)$-plane, with the exception of the definition of $h''(u)$ at $u = 0$.

(D2) T transforms the integral $\int_0^1 (1 - j(x))dx$ in the $(x$–$y)$-plane into the integral $\int_0^1 h(u)\,du$ in the $(u$–$v)$-plane.

Of course, our proof is dependent upon the assumption that the functions in J are invertible (i.e., j^{-1} exists where $j^{-1}(j(x)) = x$) but not necessarily invertible in closed-form.

For (1), we begin by defining the point sets ∂x_y and $¡u_v$ by

$\partial x_{y=} \{(x,y) \ni 0 \leq x, y \leq 1 \text{ and } y \leq g(x)\}$ and

$\Upsilon_{uv} = \{(u,v) \ni 0 \leq u, v \leq 1 \text{ and } g(u) \leq v\}$ (54)

and observe that $T: \partial x_y \to Yu_v$. Hence, as $j(x) \in J$, the point $(x, j(x)) \in \partial xy_m$ aps to the point $(u, v) \in ¡uv$ where $u = 1 - j(x)$ and $v = 1 - x$. Writing v as a function of u yields

$v = h(u) = 1 - j^{-1}(1 - u) = 1 - c(1 - u)$ (55)

where $c(y)$ is the inverse function of $j(x)$ (i.e., $c(j(x)) = x$). Next, we look at the criteria that j satisfies, namely (s1)-(s5). Through the action of T, we may transform these constraints on j into constraints on h defined on Y_{uv}. Starting with (56), we have

$j(0) = 1 \Rightarrow c(1) = 0 \Rightarrow h(0) = 1 - c(1) = 1$ (56)

Next, using (57),

$j(1) = 0 \Rightarrow c(0) = 1 \Rightarrow h(1) = 1 - c(0) = 0$ (57)

From (58), Equation (55) and the definition of T,

$j(\hat{x}) = \hat{y} \Rightarrow c(\hat{y}) = \hat{x} \Rightarrow h(\hat{u}) = 1 - c(1 - \hat{u}) = 1 - c(\hat{y}) = 1 - \hat{x} = \hat{v}$ (58)

The constraints (sl) and (s2), in the $(x$-$y)$-plane, require a bit more effort to transform into constraints in the $(u$-$v)$-plane. In fact, we need two results regarding the relationship between the derivatives of a function and its inverse. To this end, let p and q be twice differentiable functions with $q = p^{-1}$ so that $q(p(x)) = x$. Denote $p(x)$ by y. Then, using the classic chain rule for computing derivatives of composite functions we obtain, by differentiating both sides of $q(p(x)) = x$ with respect to x,

$$\frac{dq}{dx} = \frac{dq}{dy} \cdot \frac{dy}{dx} = q'(y) \cdot p'(x) = \frac{dx}{dx} = 1 \Rightarrow q'(y) = \frac{1}{p'(x)} \tag{59}$$

for all x where $p'(x) \neq 0$. Next, we require an expression for $q''(y)$. We use Equation (59), the product rule for differentiation and a second application of the chain rule. First,

$$q(y) = q(p(x)) = x \Rightarrow \frac{d^2q}{dx^2} = 0 \tag{60}$$

by observing that $d^2(x)/dx^2 = 0$. In addition,

$$
\begin{aligned}
\frac{d^2q}{dx^2} &= \frac{d}{dx}\left[\frac{dq}{dx}\right] = \frac{d}{dx}\left[q'(y) \cdot p'(x)\right] \\
&= \frac{d}{dx}\left[q'(y)\right] \cdot p'(x) + q'(y) \cdot \frac{d}{dx}p'(x) \\
&= \left(\frac{d}{dy}\left[q'(y)\right] \cdot \frac{dy}{dx}\right) \cdot p'(x) + q'(y) \cdot p''(x) \\
&= q''(y) \cdot \left(p'(x)\right)^2 + \frac{1}{p'(x)} \cdot p''(x) = 0
\end{aligned} \tag{61}
$$

from which we conclude that

$$q''(y) = -\left[\frac{1}{p'(x)}\right]^3 \cdot p''(x) \tag{62}$$

provided $p'(x)$ is nonzero at the points of interest.

For (s1), we have $j'(0) = -\infty$ and $j'(x) < 0$ for $0 < x \leq 1$. Noting that $T: j(x) \to h$ we have, via Equation (55),

$$\frac{dv}{du} = h'(u) = \frac{d}{du}\left[1 - c(1 - u)\right] \tag{63}$$

Recalling that $y = 1 - u$ (via T) and that c is the inverse function of j we get, using Equation (59),

$$h'(u) = -c'(1 - u) = -\frac{dc(1 - u)}{d(1 - u)} \cdot \frac{d(1 - u)}{du} = \frac{dc(y)}{dy} = \frac{1}{j'(x)} \tag{64}$$

Observe that for $0 < x \leq 1$, $1/j'(x) < 0$ so that $h' < 0$ for $0 < u \leq 1$. As $j'(x)$ is negatively infinite at $x = 0$ then $h' = 0$ (in the limit) when $u = 1 - j(0) = 0$. This confirms (s1) $\to$ (r1).

Turning to (s2), we use Equation (62), to obtain

$$h''(u) = -c''(1-u) = -\frac{d}{du}\left[\frac{dc(1-u)}{du}\right]$$

$$= -\frac{d}{du}\left[\frac{dc(1-u)}{d(1-u)}\cdot\frac{d(1-u)}{du}\right] = \frac{d}{du}\left[\frac{dc(1-u)}{d(1-u)}\right] \qquad (65)$$

$$= \frac{d\left[\frac{dc(1-u)}{d(1-u)}\right]}{d(1-u)}\cdot\frac{d(1-u)}{du} = -c''(y) = \left[\frac{1}{j'(x)}\right]^3\cdot j''(x)$$

From Equation (65) and the conditions $0 < x \le 1$, $j''(x) > 0$ and $j'(x) < 0$, we conclude that $h'' < 0$ for $0 < u \le 1$ which confirms (s2) → (r2) up to the definition of $h''(0)$. This competes the demonstration of (D1 above).

Finally, for D2 above, consider the integral $\int_0^1 (1 - j(x))\, dx$ for a function $j(x)\, \epsilon\, J$. By the preceding, we are guaranteed that $y = j(x)$ maps to some function, $v = h\, \epsilon\, H$, under the transformation $u = 1 - y$ and $v = 1 - x$. Thus, the integral in the $(x$-$y)$-plane transforms into the $(u$-$v)$-plane by first observing that

$$\int_0^1 (1 - j(x))\, dx = \int_0^1 (1 - y)dx = \int_0^1 u\, dx \qquad (66)$$

Next, we see that, as $v = 1 - x$, $dx = -dv = -d(h)(u)) = -h'(u)du$. Also, since the variable of integration changes from x to u, we must transform the interval of integration as well. To this end, we see that $x = 0 \Rightarrow v = 1 = h \Rightarrow u = 0$ and, similarly, $x = 1 \Rightarrow u = 1$. Therefore, continuing with Equation (66),

$$\int_0^1 (1 - j(x))\, dx = \int_0^1 u\, dx$$

$$= \int_0^1 u\cdot(-h'(u)du) = -\int_0^1 u\cdot h'(u)du \qquad (67)$$

$$= -\left[u\cdot h(u)\,|_0^1 - \int_0^1 h(u)du\right] = \int_0^1 h(u)du$$

In short, the integral $\int_0^1 (1 - j(x))\,\mathrm{dx}$ in the (x-y)-plane transforms to the integral $\int_0^1 h(u)\, du$ in the $(u$-$v)$-plane. This completes the proof of (D2).

Recall, at the outset, that we noticed if $F(x)$ is defined by Equation (49), then

$$F(x) = \underset{j(x)\in J}{Arg\max}\left\{\int_0^1 (1 - j(x))\, dx\right\} \qquad (68)$$

Clearly, Equations (67) and (68) together imply that if $F(x)$ is the $j(x)$ which maximizes the integral $\int_0^1 (1 - j(x))\, dx$ in the (x-y) plane then $T\!: F(x) \to G(u)$ where $G(u)$ is the $h(u)$ which maximizes $\int_0^1 h(u)\, du$

in the $(u\text{-}v)$-plane. That is, G is the solution to Equation (16). This completes the proof of the assertion (ii) under the equivalence of utility curve problems (with respect to the average utility measure) section above.

To review, we list the "converted" criterion in the (u-v)-plane:

(s1*) $h'(0)=0$ and $h'(u)<0$ for $0<u\leq1$,
(s2*) $h''(u)<0$ for $0<u\leq1$,
(s3*) $h(0)=1$,
(s4*) $h(1)=0$, and

$$(\text{s5*})\ \ h(\hat{u}) = \hat{v};\ \ (\hat{u},\hat{v}) \in R \tag{69}$$

Observe that, up to the definition of $h''(0)$, $(s1*)$-$(s5*)$ is precisely the criteria (r1)-(r5). This implies that T maps a function $j(x)$ in J to a function h in H. In addition, T maps the $(x\text{-}y)$ minimization problem of Equation (49) into the $(u\text{–}v)$-maximization of $\int_0^1 h(u)\,du$ (Equation (16)). Therefore, the problem of determining a lower-bound concave-up DUC satisfying (s1)-(s5) is equivalent to determining an upper-bound DUC satisfying (r1)-(r5) (up to the definition of $h''(0)$).

In the next section, we discuss the application of theory above to the construction of an appropriate transformation, one for each of the three other desired UCs, of the concave-down DUC.

EQUIVALENCE TRANSFORMATIONS AND THEIR APPLICATION TO UTILITY CURVES CONSTRUCTION

The preceding is essentially a formal argument which states that any concave-down DUC satisfying constraints (r1)-(r5) may be transformed into a concave-up DUC satisfying constraints (s1)-(s5) and vice versa.; in addition, the transformation maps the upper (lower)-bound/concave-down DUC into the lower (upper)-bound/concave-up DUC. Keep in mind that references to upper-bound concave-down and lower-bound concave-up are those where the bounding is with respect to the average utility functional $\int_0^1 h(u)\,du$. To elucidate on the theory presented thus far, we outline a specific procedure for constructing a lower-bound concave-up DUC by first constructing the appropriate upper-bound concave-down DUC and applying the inverse transformation, T^{-1}, of Equation (50) where

$$T^{-1}: (u,v) \rightarrow (c,y) \text{ with } y=1-u \text{ and } x=1-v \tag{70}$$

By doing this, we need only to consider the methods for computing the curve itself; the simple transformation completes the construction.

To Obtain the Concave-Up Lower-Bound DUC, $F(x)$, satisfying (s1)-(s5):

1. Let $q = (\hat{x}, \hat{y}) \epsilon Q = \{(x,y) \ni 0 \leq x, y \leq 1$ and $y < 1 - x\}$ be the given "third" point that $F(x)$ must pass through (the other two points being $(0, 1)$ and $(1, 0)$). Transform q in the $(x\text{-}y)$-plane into $p = (\hat{u}, \hat{v})$ in the $(u\text{-}v)$-plane by applying T accordingly, i.e., $\hat{u} = 1 - \hat{y}$ and $\hat{v} = 1 - \hat{x}$.

2. Using $p = (\hat{u}, \hat{v})$, determine the upper-bound concave-down DUC, $v = G$, in the $(u\text{-}v)$-plane. G (6) satisfies (r1)-(r5) and Equation (16).

3. Using T^{-1}: $x = 1 - v = 1 - G$ and $y = 1 - u = F(x)$, numerically generate $F(x)$ by computing/ plotting a sufficient number of points, i.e., compute $(x,y) = (x, F(x)) = (1 - G, 1 - u)$ by selecting $u \epsilon [0, 1]$ and computing G. Note, from the discussion above, that $F(x)$ satisfies (s1)-(s5) and Equation (49).

4. Using the points $(0, 1)$, $(1, 0)$, $q = (\hat{x}, \hat{y})$ and those $(x, F(x))$ plotted in (3), interpolate to complete the sketch of $F(x)$.

In Step (3) above, it is emphasized that $F(x)$ be numerically generated. The reason for this is the fact that it may not be possible to express $F(x)$ as a closed-form function of x. For example, suppose we determine that the degree-five upper-bound concave-down DUC for $q = (\hat{x}, \hat{y})$ is of the form $v = G = au^5 + bu^3 + c$ where a, b and c are determined by the methods above. Now, from T^{-1}, we see that $F(x) = 1 - u = 1 - G^{-1}(1 - x)$ where G^{-1} where G^{-1} is the inverse of the quintic polynomial, G. However, computing u as a function of x, namely $G^{-1}(1 - x)$, implies that we must solve for u in $1 - x = au^5 + bu^3 + c$ as an explicit function of x. As this is a degree five polynomial, such a solution does not, in general, exist. Pragmatically speaking, $G^{-1}(1 - x)$ is seldom expressible as a closed form function of x. Consequently, this is the case for $F(x)$ as well.

Recall Equation (54) which defines the regions ∂x_y and Yu_v, that contain the points $(x, j(x))$ (concave-up DUC) and (u, h) (concave-down DUC), respectively. As noted earlier, the transformation T: $\partial xy \rightarrow$ ¡uv¡s merely a reflection of the region ∂xy, about the line $y = 1 - x$. Consequently, when the graphs of $j(x)$ and $u(h)$ are plotted in the same physical space (i.e. the x-and u-axis coincide and the y- and v-axis coincide), they too are reflections of each other over $y = 1 - x$ ($v = 1 - u$). This suggests that to construct an upper-bound concave-down increasing utility curve (IUC), h, in the $(u\text{-}v)$-plane from an upper-bound concave-down DUC curve, $j(x)$, in the $(x\text{-}y)$- plane, we employ the transformation

T: $u = 1 - x$ and $v = y$ (71)

which represents a reflection of the graph of $j(x)$ about the line $x = \dfrac{1}{2}$. Thus, T transforms $j(x)$ which satisfies (r1)-(r5) into h satisfying

(t1) $h'(1) = 0$ and $h'(u) > 0$ for $0 \leq u < 1$,
(t2) $h''(u) < 0$ for $0 \leq u \leq 1$,
(t3) $h(0) = 0$,
(t4) $h(1) = 1$, and

(t5) $h(\hat{u}) = \hat{v}$; $(\hat{u}, \hat{v}) \in R_{uv}$ (72)

Table 1. Summary of Transformations T: (x, j(x)) → (u,h) for Utility Curves

T	Curve Type	Concavity	"Extreme" Curve	$A(h) = \int_0^1 h(u)\,du$
u = 1 - y, v = 1 - x	DUC	Up	Lower Bound	Minimized
u = 1 - x, v = y	IUC	Down	Upper Bound	Maximized
u = x, v = 1 - y	IUC	Up	Lower Bound	Minimized

where $R_{uv} = (u, v) \in 0 \leq u, v \leq 1$ and $u < v\}$. In addition, T: F(x) → G where j(x) = F(x) maximizes $A(j) = \int_0^1 j(x)\,dx$ and h = G maximizes $A(h) = \int_0^1 h(u)\,du$. That is, T maps the upper-bound concave down DUC into the upper-bound concave-down IUC.

Starting again with a concave-down DUC, j(x), one may obtain a concave-up IUC a reflection of j(x) about the line $y = \dfrac{1}{2}$. Thus, *T* assumes the form

T: u=x and *v=1–y* $\qquad\qquad\qquad\qquad\qquad\qquad\qquad\qquad\qquad$ (73)

which transforms j(x) into h with

(w1) $h'(0)=0$ and $h'(u)>0$ for $0 \leq u < 1$,
(w2) $h''(u)>0$ for $0 \leq u \leq 1$,
(w3) $h(0)=0$,
(w4) $h(1)=1$, and

(w5) $h(\hat{u}) = \hat{v};\quad (\hat{u}, \hat{v}) \in R_{uv}$ $\qquad\qquad\qquad\qquad\qquad\qquad\qquad$ (74)

where $R_{uv} = \{(u,v) \ni 0 \leq u, v \leq 1$ and $v < u\}$. Further, *T: F(x) → G(u)* where *j(x) = F(x)* maximizes $A(j) = \int_0^1 (x)\,dx$ and h = G minimizes $A(h) = \int_0^1 h(u)\,du$. In other words, *T* maps the upper-bound concave-down DUC into the lower-bound concave-up IUC.

Table 1 above summarizes the results obtained when *T* is applied to the concave-down DUC curve, *j(x)*. The rightmost two columns specify the type of extreme curve, with respect to the measure of average utility (i.e., *A(h)*), obtained by transforming the upper-bound concave-down DUC in the (*x-y*)-plane into the (*u-v*)-plane.

CONCLUSION

Based on the preceding examples, it is quite evident that, even for functions as simple as polynomials, finding an *h(x)* which maximizes *A(h)*, under the constraints (r1)-(r5), is hardly trivial. Despite this, polynomials are, computationally speaking, a far better alternative to candidates using exponential, logarithmic, or trigonometric terms, particularly when extending $h(x)$ by adding additional shaping parameters. For example, using a term like ax^5 might be preferable to using something like e^{ax} since the former is linear in the shape parameter, a, while the latter is not. This characteristic difference comes into play when trying to express the integral objective function and the constraints in terms of simple functions of the shape parameters, which must then be manipulated to determine the optimal form of $h(x)$, namely $G(x)$.

Under the assumption that $A(h)$ be maximized over the space of degree-n polynomials, consider the results for our degree three, four and five $G(x)$-polynomials listed in the SUMMARY section (p. 15). Clearly, as the degree increases, so does $\int_0^1 G(x)\,dx$, but only marginally; this makes sense as we would expect that if n is the degree of $G(x)$ then

$$\lim_{n\to\infty} \int_0^1 G(x)\,dx = \Omega < 1 \tag{75}$$

where the upper bound, Ω follows from the fact that $G(x)$, by definition, must lie entirely in the region bounded by $x = 0$, $y = 0$, $x = 1$ and $y = 1$. The limit, Ω, appears to be ~ 0.72. Based on these results, a degree five polynomial appears to be a suitable solution for $(\hat{x}, \hat{y}) = \left(\dfrac{3}{4}, \dfrac{1}{2}\right)$. However, the preceding observations account for the behavior $A(G)$ for merely a single value of $(\hat{x}, \hat{y})$ in R. Further testing should be performed by varying $(\hat{x}, \hat{y})$ to obtain a more comprehensive assessment of the viability of this methodology.

To illustrate the notion of "further testing", consider the integral maximizing polynomials, for a fixed value of $(\hat{x}, \hat{y})$, in the "SUMMARY" table on p. 16. Denote the degree-n maximizing polynomial by $G_n(x)$ with $\int_0^1 G_n(x)\,dx > \int_0^1 G_{n-1}(x)\,dx$ for $n = 3, 4$ and 5. Some questions to answer are:

(1)   Is $\int_0^1 G_n(x)\,dx > \int_0^1 G_{n-1}(x)\,dx$ true for all $(\hat{x}, \hat{y}) \in R$?

(2)   Is there some "closed-form" analytic expression, in terms of $\hat{x}$, $\hat{y}$, and n, for $\left|\int_0^1 \{G_n(x) - G_{n-1}(x)\}\,dx\right|$? Or, at the least, is there a simple asymptotic expression (in n)?

(3)   Does $\int_0^1 G_n(x)\,dx > \int_0^1 G_{n-1}(x)\,dx \Rightarrow G_n(x) > G_{n-1}(x)$ for all $x \in [0, 1]$?

The answer to (3) is "no", as revealed by the counterexample illustrated in Figure 8.

Figure 8. Plot of $G_5(x) - G_4(x)$

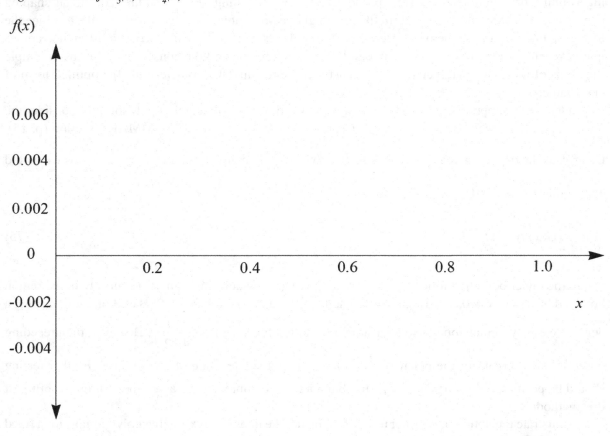

REFERENCES

Abbas, A. E. (2003, March). An entropy approach for utility assignment in decision analysis. In. AIP Conference Proceedings (Vol. 659, pp. 328–338). American Institute of Physics. doi:10.1063/1.1570550

Du, Y. M., Ma, Y. H., Wei, Y. F., Guan, X., & Sun, C. P. (2020). Maximum entropy approach to reliability. *Physical Review. E, 101*(1), 012106. doi:10.1103/PhysRevE.101.012106 PMID:32069657

Leitmann, G. (2013). *The calculus of variations and optimal control: an introduction* (Vol. 24). Springer Science & Business Media.

Luenberger, D. G., & Ye, Y. (1984). *Linear and nonlinear programming* (Vol. 2). Addison-wesley.

Rao, S. S. (2019). *Engineering optimization: theory and practice.* John Wiley & Sons. doi:10.1002/9781119454816

Wu, N. (2012). *The maximum entropy method* (Vol. 32). Springer Science & Business Media.

Yang, J. B., & Sen, P. (1996). Preference modelling by estimating local utility functions for multiobjective optimization. *European Journal of Operational Research, 95*(1), 115–138. doi:10.1016/0377-2217(96)00300-1

Chapter 7
Attack Adaptation Patterns for Defensive Operations

ABSTRACT

The mission of cyber defenders is as monumental as it is unprecedented: protect information systems from ongoing cyber-attacks while simultaneously fortifying those systems against tomorrow's unrealized threats. The pressing imperative to react quickly to these constant attacks makes it difficult to find the time and resources needed to build capabilities focused on anticipating tomorrow's threats before they result in costly systems damage or information leakage. This chapter focuses on the role defensive measures play in spurring cyber-attack adaptation, especially with respect to malware. While the need to react to today's attacks will likely persist indefinitely, this chapter aims to begin helping defenders and researchers channel its wealth of tacit knowledge, deep expertise, and sophisticated capabilities into establishing more anticipative defensive postures.

INTRODUCTION

Cyber-Assurance is defined as a means of Internet of Things (IoT) smart devices and networks providing the opportunity of automatically securing themselves against security threats (Brooks, 2020). The concept of cyber-assurance must provide embedded security within these IoT devices to allow these new networks to operate correctly even when subjected to a cyber-attack. Cyber-attacks and the individuals who perpetrate them cannot be divorced from their surrounding social, political, economic and technological contexts — the cyber-attack "ecosystem" (see Figure 1).

This ecosystem influences the intentions and motivations of these individuals and thus impacts the way in which they adapt to defenses. This chapter begins with the creation of a framework for better understanding the exogenous forces that shape the opportunity space for attackers and affect how attacks evolve over time.

Outlined in Table 1 below, these ecosystem components affect how attacker strategies and tactics evolve.

While this model for the cyber-attack ecosystem is not comprehensive, it provides analysts and researchers with a structure for diagnosing and assessing the enablers, constraints and actors shaping

DOI: 10.4018/978-1-6684-7766-3.ch007

Figure 1. Cyber Attack Ecosystem Analytic Approach

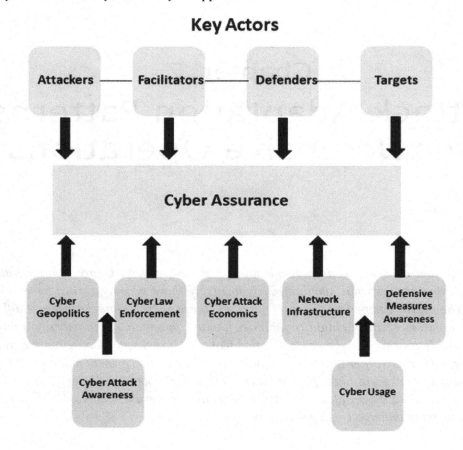

the attack opportunity space. This structure also allows for more robust Cyber awareness on the part of defenders, an important asset in anticipating how defensive measures might influence how attackers adapt. Armed with a more complete picture of an attacker's opportunity space, defenders can better assess how the introduction of a new defensive measure interacts with and affects that space. The ability of defenders to identify the range of opportunities available to adaptive attackers can be the difference between a defensive campaign that impedes attacker success and one that only serves to inspire attacker adaptation. In the latter case, defensive measures can generate attacks that are more dangerous or difficult to mitigate. The ecosystem framework above informs the attack adaptation taxonomy outlined in this chapter by illustrating the enablers and constraints that factor into an attacker's decision to pursue a particular adaptation strategy when confronted with disruptive defensive measures.

Attacker Motives

Behind every cyber-attack are individuals with missions and motives ranging from financial gain and prestige to intelligence gathering and information warfare (Huskaj et al., 2020). These motives influence both the adaptive strategies that attackers develop as well as their level of persistence in pursuing their goals and objectives. As a result, attacker motivations have a significant impact on how rapidly and in

Table 1. Cyber Attack Enablers & Constraints

Ecosystem Component	Description	Examples
Cyber Geopolitics	The role of states and international structures in cyber arenas	State strategy, state budget, clandestine operations, international agreements, interstate cyber tensions
Cyber Law Enforcement	Laws and enforcement measures designed to address malicious cyber activity	Legislation, law enforcement, jurisprudence
Cyber Attack Economics	Economic opportunities and constraints surrounding malware production and use, as well as attack capability development and services	Malware marketplaces, attack functions for sale, botnet operations and services, extortion, product sales and advertising, stolen goods and information, contract hacking
Network Infrastructure	Local and regional technological facilitators of cyber-attack delivery and impact	Internet capacity, mobile telephony, operating systems
Defensive Measures Awareness	Attacker knowledge of public or target-specific defenses	Updates and patches, anti-virus and detection software, professional and academic defensive measures research, attack countermeasures
Cyber Attack Awareness	Public knowledge of cyber-attack-related threats	Knowledge of publicized threats and vulnerabilities, reactive damage mitigation tools, anticipative attack prevention tools
Cyber usage	Geographically differentiated trends in cyber usage and user preferences	Preferences for operating systems, hardware platforms, legitimate software, illegitimate software, web-based applications
Key Actors		
Attackers	Actors involved in malicious vulnerability discovery, code creation or dissemination, attack executions, or other malicious activities	Criminals, terrorists, intelligence services, armed forces, non-criminal hackers
Facilitators	Actors in academia, industry, or other areas contributing to malware, exploits, or vulnerability-related knowledge or providing attack –supporting services	Computer researchers and academics, white/grey hat hackers, malware vendors, financiers, communication enablers
Defenders	Actors engaged in cyber defense, whether for their own systems or those of an affiliate/associate	Software providers, anti-virus companies, state institutions, corporate security, security researchers
Targets	Actor targeted by a cyber-attack, or the victims of an indiscriminate attack	Individuals, corporations, organizations, state institutions

what ways attackers adapt in response to defensive measures. For these actors, carrying out cyber-attacks is their business and defenders need to understand the operational priorities that make up the "business models" those different attackers pursue.

This chapter focuses on better understanding these models by representing the attacker value chain — the operational tactics that attackers use in carrying out their missions — for example, actors primarily motivated by financial or political gain. Focusing on financially and political motivated actors offers several analytic advantages for understanding attacker adaptation more broadly:

1. The illicit malware economy is a major driver of innovation in global attacker' tactics and strategy,
2. Financially motivated actors follow structured business models, making it more feasible —through open-source research — to surface patterns in how they respond to defensive measures,

Figure 2. Financially Motivated Cyber Attack Value Chain

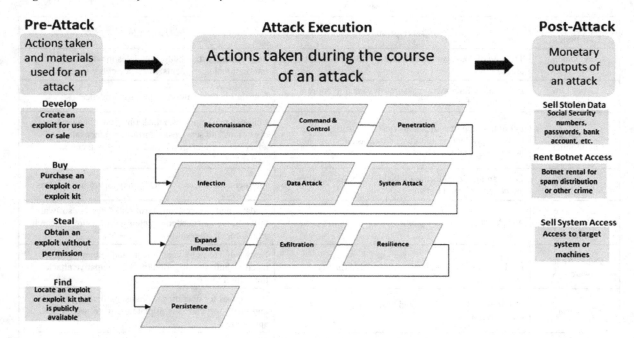

3. Innovations and strategies from the malware economy are appropriated by ideologically motivated or state-backed actors as well as other entities seeking to steal intelligence information or undermine US interests and

4. There is a growing body of evidence suggesting that the activities of financially motivated actors, such as botnet operators, can easily be leveraged by states in times of conflict.

As shown in Figure 2, the range of operational priorities for financially and political motivated attacker's model "value chain" before, during and after an attack is carried out. Such a structured lens serves as a basis for better understanding exactly how attackers operate and where their operations are likely to be most sensitive to defensive measures.

As identified above, Figure 2 demonstrates how such a value chain can be applied to a particular class of actors. Different areas of the attacker value chain are "activated" or "deactivated" depending on their relevance and importance to the attacker. In this chapter, the author applied value chain analysis to different models to understand how certain defensive measures influences parts of an attacker's overall operations.

Analytic Payoff

Identifying an attacker's operational priorities based on their motives supports analysis of how particular defensive measures will spur attacker adaptation. An attacker's choice to pursue one of the adaptation strategies outlined in this chapter is influenced by the extent to which those defenses influence the most vital parts of an attacker's value chain — these represent key vulnerabilities because undermining them would disrupt the attack. Defenders must remember, however, that these areas are also trigger points:

attackers interested in maintaining their attack capabilities are more likely to innovate and adapt when defensive pressure is exerted on vital operational priorities.

This type of analysis can help defenders identify the areas for which attackers are likely to invest in developing new capabilities more broadly, as these are important for maintaining an attack operation. For instance, defenders might use knowledge of vital attack capabilities to understand how and why attackers update attack capabilities included in exploit kits. Because of these applications, the attack value chain served as a useful analytic lens for surfacing the adaptation patterns outlined in this chapter.

Cyber-Assurance Patterns

Using the analytic frameworks outlined above, this chapter identifies the attack adaptation patterns presented in the sequential sections. Across all these attacker adaptations, defensive measures play a central role in inspiring how attackers adapt and change. While not comprehensive, these adaptation patterns collectively make up a taxonomy of attack adaptation that can be used to advance research and understanding of how cyber-attacks evolve in response to defensive measures.

RECOGNITION

What is the Assurance Strategy?

Recognition includes the identification of a cyber-attack being performed leading to the fortification of smart ICDs before gaining access to IoT networks and systems (Brooks, 2020). Attackers routinely rely on superior agility to overcome defensive obstacles: the ease with which they can "pack up and move" their operations is a critical asymmetry that often gives attackers the upper hand. Once a cyber-attack has been launched, the key is to recognize this action before malicious activity hits. While many of the adaptation strategies outlined in this chapter highlight how attackers adapt to defensive measures by improving their attack capabilities, attackers also circumvent defenses through migration — relocating their operations to new technology platforms, online services, attack campaigns, or geographic locations.

How do Attackers Implement the Strategy?

Recognition adaptation occurs when defensive measures disrupt attackers familiar or established operating environments, most commonly involving the institution of new technical barriers, heightened law enforcement scrutiny, or the implementation of constrictive regulatory or legal conditions. Open-source research suggests that attackers implement migratory adaptation in the following ways:

When defensive measures obstruct system intrusions that use conventional attack avenues such as email or remote protocols, attackers migrate to new or uncommon infection vectors where targets are more trusting of a particular technology platform or less aware of the latest threats. Rather than attempting to defeat defensive measures, actors who pursue this approach aim for more vulnerable avenues for attack — and the range of potential infection vectors is constantly expanding. This has been exemplified by some attackers shifting from using malicious email attachments to using increasingly popular social media platforms such as Facebook (e.g., Meta) and Twitter. Illicit marketplaces for malware and attack capabilities have matured rapidly as cyber-attacks have become an increasingly lucrative business.

Hackers use web forums and other communications channels to advertise and sell products to potential customers. When these forums or exchange services are compromised by defenders, hackers migrate to alternative online services. With an abundance of online vendors and service providers offering channels for exchanging funds and data, dismantling an online service used by attackers seldom deters them from continuing to develop and sell attack capabilities.

In many instances, defenders attempt to undermine attacks through engaging in a war of attrition, persistently raising the cost of doing business for attackers until those costs outweigh the attack's rewards and the attacker abandons the attack. These apparent defensive successes, however, may lead attackers to choose displacement — abandoning their current attack operations only to start a new attack of equal or greater strength. Not only are these new attacks unencumbered by the defensive scrutiny directed at the original attack, but they often also incorporate improved versions of the same technologies used in the original attack. Defenders then face new attacks that may be stronger and smarter because attackers can apply technical and operational lessons learned from the previous attack. Further, defenders must identify and scrutinize these new attacks all over again, resulting in additional expenditure of defender resources.

Attacker migration also demonstrates that hackers are acutely aware of the fact that cyber regulations and law enforcement differ from country to country, making some countries more attractive than others as staging areas for attacks. When attackers encounter regular or heightened disruptions from defenders or regulators, many engage in geographic migration, shifting their operations to new regions or countries with more permissive regulatory or law enforcement conditions. This migration can be either virtual (such as routing through foreign servers) or physical (attackers moving to other countries where they can operate more freely). The lack of international coordination on cyber-laws and law enforcement makes migration a simple and attractive option for many attackers. As broadband penetration rates continue to climb internationally, the opportunity space for geographic migration grows with it.

What are the Implications for Protecting Systems?

Tighter cyber security, heightened law enforcement and new regulations drive attackers to migrate to more favorable environments where defenders have a lighter presence or less influence. As a result, attacker migration generally (though not always) flows toward Eastern Europe and Asia, often to adversary countries. These countries often offer attackers the benefit of corrupt law enforcement, less restrictive legal environments and sufficient internet infrastructure to execute attacks. Over time, this has accelerated the maturation of malware and hacker markets in these areas, giving adversary states and intelligence services greater access to new attack technologies developed in these markets.

To better anticipate when and where this type of adaptation is likely to take place, analysts and researchers would benefit from a framework for mapping cyber-security and regulatory conditions across a wide range of relevant countries. Such a framework would be used to track sudden or significant changes in the cyber security, regulatory and law enforcement contexts across regions and countries where cyber-attackers and developers are active. In addition, it would provide analysts and researchers with a standardized platform for analyzing attackers' evolving and shifting opportunity space, allowing organizations to better anticipate attacker migration in response to recent defensive measures or long-term trends.

Defensive Action
- ○ Block communications ports on a machine, preventing infection by remote access
- ○ Increase law enforcement activity, e.g., dismantling botnet command and control servers

Adaptive Response
- ○ Infection Vector Migration: Attackers circumvent blockages by exploiting different infection vectors such as social media or removable devices.

FORTIFICATION

What is the Assurance Strategy?

Fortification means to apply automatic embedded network protection techniques in ICD devices for protecting IoT devices and networks during a cyber-attack (Brooks, 2020). Identifying and blocking malicious activity is the cornerstone of most strategies for defending against cyber-attacks and a critical reason why disguise is so valuable to attackers. As anti-virus and defender tactics have evolved, attackers have developed sophisticated camouflage strategies mimicking, co-opting, or hiding in legitimate communications channels and platforms in order to blend in with normal system activity.

How do Attackers Implement the Strategy?

Attackers have developed innovative tactics to avoid being identified and thwarted. If successful, these camouflage tactics allow attackers to "go about their business" without fear of defender intervention. Open-source research suggests attackers will employ camouflage in the following ways:

Many defensive fortification strategies rely on recognizing abnormal network behavior as an indicator of malicious intrusion, often leading defenders to block channels and programs that are used to bring malware into a system. When confronted with this defense, attackers may respond by co-opting normal system processes for malicious purposes. For instance, when defenders block entry ports, attackers may shift to penetrating systems via normal communications ports — such as port 80 (most often used for HTTP) — in order to avoid further defender scrutiny. Defenders may search for spikes in network traffic to detect attackers whose mission is to exfiltrate data, only to find that attackers mimic normal network behavior by exfiltrating data in smaller packets that blend into routine traffic. Moreover, when faced with firewalls or antivirus programs that block certain file types, attackers may bypass these added defenses using legitimate packers or by binding malware to approved file extensions — co-opting legitimate software to bypass defenses. Each of these tactics represents a carefully crafted innovation designed to circumvent specific defenses.

Fortification strategies, however, are not only used within compromised networks. Publicly available web services offer a growing repertoire of legitimate tools that can used for executing attacks and attackers are developing innovative camouflage tactics for hiding their activities in the cloud. Attackers often hide in the noise generated by legitimate, high-traffic communications channels, such as freely available email or popular blog hosting services. For example, botnet operators have used Twitter to send commands to botnets, relying on the constant stream of communications across Twitter's networks to hide ongoing operational instructions. The business models of these online services work to attackers' advantage since service providers optimizing for customer experience would likely oppose imposing greater restrictions and surveillance on these high-traffic channels.

What are the Implications for Protecting Systems?

Because cyber security strategies have long relied on establishing a clear distinction between what is malicious versus what is "normal," attackers have had good reason to improve their ability to fortify their activities over time. To complicate matters further, any efforts to add security barriers or heighten scrutiny of system abnormalities run counter to prevailing commercial trends that value user experience and seamless web access — which bodes well for attackers looking for more ways to disguise their operations.

Many of the tools used by attackers to implement camouflage strategies are linked to publicly available technologies, offering defenders a window into what might come next in camouflage tactics. In order to better anticipate future attacker camouflage tactics, defenders could develop a framework for assessing the potential malicious use of emerging technologies and online services. Such a framework would provide analysts and researchers with guidelines for identifying new technologies that could be used by attackers, as well as a structured approach for thinking about the variety of ways in which those technologies might enable new camouflage tactics.

Defensive Actions
- ○ Block malicious threats with firewalls and intrusion prevention systems
- ○ Disable command and control servers so that attackers cannot communicate with compromised computers

Adaptive Responses
- ○ Co-opting Legitimate Software: Attackers use legitimate packers or bind malware to seemingly normal files to make malware undetectable. In emerging technologies framework would facilitate more anticipative analysis of emerging threats to systems. An emerging technologies framework could help analysts identify and anticipate similar patterns on platforms and technologies that become widely used in the coming years.
- ○ Hide in the Noise: Communicate through high-volume, trusted protocols that provide cover for malicious activity Botnet operators need to communicate with compromised computers to provide them with updates and instructions. Without this command-and-control capability, the botnet is essentially worthless, as it cannot be used to carry out any of its profitable activities such as DDoS attacks or spam campaigns. Given the importance of command and control, defenders have focused efforts on disrupting command and control capabilities, including server takedowns and blocking websites that compromised computers check for updates

REESTABLISH

What is the Assurance Strategy?

Reestablishment is a means to return the ICDs to its operational condition after the cyber-attack through remapping to a different route since the ICD was under attack (Brooks, 2020). Because today's attackers are often able to easily navigate computer networks once they have gained access, any network is only as secure as its weakest point. Often this weak point is best captured by the idiom: "The greatest threat to a network sits between the keyboard and the back of the chair," implying that human error is the easiest and therefore most attractive vulnerability for attackers to exploit. As technical defenses become more sophisticated, reestablishment strategies are increasingly attractive for attackers —exploiting human ignorance or naïveté to penetrate an otherwise protected system.

How do Attackers Implement the Strategy?

Reestablishment often occurs when technical defensive measures sufficiently disrupt an attacker's approach by blocking access to a system or network and continuing to process the data. By increasing the difficulty of penetrating a system through technical means, defenders can unwittingly make human users — so-called "soft" targets — a more attractive option.

While it is impossible to catalog all of the ways in which a human might be deceived, open-source research suggests that attackers frequently use social engineering to deceive targets in the following two ways: (1) the global expansion of online services and social connectedness has created numerous opportunities for attackers to benefit from the reputations and reliability of everything from international banks and government agencies to social networks and private contact lists. As these opportunities continue to expand, attackers frequently exploit user trust in order to fool targets into believing that they are communicating with reliable contacts. Once this false trust is established, targets willingly grant system privileges. Exploiting these trust relationships is attractive to attackers because trust relationships that are established offline without the attacker's involvement or investment — such as trust in a reputable company or a close associate — can lull users into drawing a false linkage between offline and online trust. These attacks often include targeted, convincingly legitimate messages, commonly referred to as "spear phishing." These messages may appear to come from trusted contacts and may urge the target to open an attachment or click on a link laced with malware. Attackers have even been known to intercept ongoing dialogues between contacts and then pose as one of the parties involved, a trust exploitation tactic known as "man in the mailbox." Trust exploitation has the added benefit of allowing attackers to repurpose or reuse old exploits that have already been identified by automated defenses such as anti-virus software: in these cases, the human infection vector offers a way around heightened technical barrier.

Secondly, because social engineering is such a widespread cyber-attack strategy, efforts have been made to educate the public about what to look for and how to stop these attacks. In response to heightened user education, however, attackers can exploit user ignorance by making simple adjustments in their attack approach that make the attack less predictable or recognizable. For example, when the LoveLetter worm spread across the globe in 2000, significant media attention trained the public to avoid opening emails with the subject line "ILOVEYOU." Copycat hackers, however, quickly began disseminating the same exploit in emails with modified subject lines in order to obviate increased levels of user awareness. Exploiting user ignorance allows attackers to find a path of least resistance for infecting a target system: with this approach, attackers can rely on what their targets do not know as a means of penetrating or attacking systems and networks.

What are the Implications for Protecting Systems?

Despite its simplicity relative to technical attack strategies, deception through social engineering remains one of the most successful cyber-intrusion strategies. Deception can render major R&D investments in technical defenses immediately obsolete and can do so at the low cost of sending a well-crafted email or leaving a malware-laced USB drive in an area with regular foot traffic in the hope that someone might pick it up. These types of attacks routinely target important systems.

There can never be a "perfect patch" for deception: humans will always remain an imperfect element in the security of any system or network. Knowing this, however, defenders can become more anticipative of attacks that utilize deception by tracking employee threat awareness in real time. Rather than focusing solely on training programs that seek to make those in contact with computer systems better informed, defenders could conduct threat awareness diagnostic surveys to identify gaps in overall user awareness.

Such diagnostics could help analysts and researchers had better identify human vulnerabilities in networks, augmenting their ability to anticipate likely targets for future attacks on systems. This strategy would not necessarily rely upon the success of subsequent training in order to protect systems but would rather alert network defenders as to the vulnerabilities that might be exploited by attackers.

Defensive Action
- ○ Increase public awareness and education about malware threats
- ○ Network firewalls, intrusion prevention systems or software patches block known malicious threats from entering a system or network

Adaptive Response
- ○ Exploit User Ignorance: Attackers diversify their approach to spreading malware so that education is rendered ineffective
- ○ Exploit User Trust: Attackers shift to email or other infection vectors to get users to voluntarily grant access to malicious code

SURVIVABILITY

What is the Adaptation Strategy?

Survivability as the capability of an entity to continue its mission even in the presence of cyber-attacks, internal failures, or accidents; these services should be survivable in order to support the important missions (Brooks, 2020). Hacker networks rely on the fluid transmission of ideas and technology to stay abreast of the latest and most advanced attack capabilities. Relying on online communications channels, however, is a double-edged sword: online hacker networks are vulnerable to intrusion from unwelcome visitors such law enforcement, intelligence agencies, or competitors. Similarly, ongoing attack operations are also susceptible to intrusion by defenders or competing attackers. Attackers adapt to these intrusions through network hardening, imposing stiffer barriers to entry and tighter trust layers on their networks and communications channels.

How do Attackers Implement the Strategy?

When defenders or other actors intrude on attacker networks, attackers can pursue either a technical or a social strategy for survivability through network hardening. Hackers can add technical capabilities to their attacks to secure networks of infected machines or take operations further "underground" by establishing stricter control over social activities and communications channels. Open-source research suggests that attackers can implement network hardening through one of the following ways: first, hardening can be technical in nature when defenders monitor attacker activities or seek out vulnerabilities in attacker networks. This defensive strategy can yield vital information for thwarting cyber-attacks but can also lead attackers to harden an attack's technical defenses, making attack technology more situationally aware and aggressive. For instance, the largest and most successful botnets are also the most likely to attract attention from intrusive defenders aiming to identify vulnerabilities or pinpoint the offline location of botnet operators. Botnet operators often respond to defender intrusions and anti-virus updates with entrenchment — adding technical capabilities such as updating malware on infected machines with the ability to attack anti-virus software. Hardening the botnet in this way can come at the cost of slower infections and botnet growth as interactions with other computers become more restricted, but the adaptation provides the benefit of making the botnet a harder target for defenders or rivals.

Secondly, network hardening can also be social in nature when attackers implement hardening tactics that more tightly monitor and control attack-related communications. When defenders compromise attacker communications channels, attackers frequently increase their focus on operations security (OPSEC) to protect themselves from further exposure. There are several ways that attackers increase OPSEC, including communicating only with individuals possessing trusted reputations or affiliations, or increasing the barriers to entry for participation in a hacker forum or marketplace. Such heightened barriers could include instituting trial periods to vet a new member's intentions, new member initiation rites, subscription fees, or a required personal recommendation from a trusted forum member. This socially oriented hardening makes it harder for defenders to track important actors and their activities.

What are the Implications for Protecting Systems?

Network hardening demonstrates how attackers might react to intrusive defensive measures like malware market infiltrations. By prompting sophisticated actors to go "underground," defenders lose to ability to stay on top of the latest exploits and trends in the cyber-attack arena. Driven largely by private sector actors such as anti-virus companies and software vendors, the technical arms race between attackers and defenders is likely to make entrenchment a cyber-security reality for years to come.

Defensive Action
  - Block communications ports, preventing emails or remote directions from being delivered to or sent from the infected system
  - Disrupt exploit sales by infiltrating hacker networks to identify and arrest hackers

Adaptive Response
  - Operations Security (OPSEC): Market participants fortify the marketplace by creating barriers to entry or the market. In the hacker forum vBulletin, new members are not permitted to contact other forum members directly until they post comments at least five times and the forum moderator vets their posts. This simple vetting mechanism allows the moderator to

      assess an actor's character and intentions before allowing him or her to become a full-fledged member of the network with unfettered access.

   ◦ Entrenchment: Attackers focus on strengthening the existing network of infected machines, such as updating malware to attack anti-virus or building defenses so that other attackers cannot infiltrate their botnet. For example, iIn response to Conficker's rapid growth, defenders developed a patch to protect systems from the worm and anti-virus software to remove it from infected machines. Thus, Conficker's later variants shifted the focus to hardening the botnet against defensive measures and rival attackers and no longer attempted to propagate to new systems. These versions of the worm had added capabilities allowing it to attack antivirus software. In addition, the worm patched the vulnerability through which it had originally infected each target machine, securing the botnet against being taken over by other attackers.

However, defenders could make considerable headway in slowing the advancement of attacker OPSEC if they better understood how attackers structure their communications, modes of data and monetary exchange and trust relationships. Analysts and researchers already possess a wealth of tacit knowledge and expertise about these attacker dynamics, but they need a system for institutionalizing this knowledge and making it actionable.

Developing a shared framework for mapping hacker professional and social networks would facilitate formalizing and institutionalizing tacit knowledge about attacker communications channels, social and professional hierarchies, barriers to entry into attacker communications channels and attacker responses to intrusions (whether from defenders or other attackers). Armed with a structured approach for understanding attacker professional and social network dynamics, defenders could better navigate hacker networks while reducing the likelihood of unwittingly instigating network hardening. Further, this system would allow defenders to identify vulnerabilities or security gaps that could be used against attackers themselves, i.e., for intelligence gathering.

CYBER ASSURANCE AWARNESS

What is the Assurance Strategy?

Cyber-attack capabilities such as mutating malware and polymorphic code have greatly diminished the efficacy of malware signature recognition — arguably the foundation of the anti-virus industry — as a viable defensive tool. Some defenders have responded with behavior-based detection that runs suspect programs in virtualized environments in order to observe and identify malicious activity. This approach has proven to be a promising alternative to traditional signature-based detection. Attackers have responded to these more sophisticated defenses through heightened Cyber Assurance, using attack tactics or technologies capable of diagnosing the malware's operating environment and adjusting attack behavior accordingly.

How do Attackers Implement the Strategy?

When attackers suspect that defenders are watching ongoing malicious activity, attackers may attempt to outsmart defenders by altering an attack's behavior based on its hardware and software environment.

Cyber awareness also allows attackers to obtain better information about what defenders are trying to do to thwart the cyber-attack. Open-source research suggests that attackers pursue Cyber awareness using one or both of the following tactics:

Defensive strategies that seek to isolate and observe malicious activity may prompt attackers to invest in deeper Cyber awareness. Conducting network diagnostics allows botnet operators and other attackers to determine if their attack has been compromised by a honeypot or virtual machine, either of which could compromise the secrecy of their attack tools or offline identity. In the case of botnet operators, these diagnostics often use defenders' legal and ethical constraints against the defenders themselves: if malicious activity launched through a suspected honeypot is blocked or obstructed, it may indicate that a honeypot operator is trying to avoid engaging in illicit activity, such as sending spam or launching a DDoS attack. Upon recognizing the defender's presence, the attacker may then isolate the honeypot, potentially rendering it useless to the defender.

Attackers also use Cyber awareness to make their attacks more difficult to detect and this capability can be coded into malware itself in response to behavior-based defenses. In these cases, attackers deploy "smart" malware capable of recognizing when defensive scanning is taking place and consequently remaining dormant or benign until after this scanning is complete. Once cleared by behavior-based defenses, attacks are allowed into the target system where they can commence malicious activity. A similar tactic is used for websites laced with malicious programs — when interacting with an automated web crawler, the websites will not return malware and are therefore not catalogued as dangerous for web users. Bolstered by search engine optimization (SEO) poisoning tactics, these malicious websites can attract a high volume of visitors, so their ability to hide from automated defender systems creates a serious threat to global user and system security.

What are the Implications for Protecting Systems?

Attacker adaptation involving Cyber awareness has led to attacks that are increasingly difficult to observe and track. Further, this adaptation allows attackers to learn about defender tactics and capabilities, which can strengthen their ability to make future attacks more potent and insidious. All of these attacker adaptations, however, rely on defenders behaving predictably, whether due to the legal constraints they face or the network diagnosis tools they use to detect attacks. In order to undermine Cyber awareness adaptation, leaders could investigate strategies for randomizing defenses that would make it more difficult for attackers to diagnose defender presence on a network or deploy smart malware capable of recognizing when it has bypassed defensive barriers. In doing so, leaders would benefit from both researching technical tools for randomizing defenses and reaching out to experts within and outside of an organization who could shed light on defensive randomization best practices in fields such as personnel security, border protection, or private sector industries invested in defending against intrusions or manipulation, such as the banking and casino gaming industries.

Defensive Action
  ◦   Defenders infiltrate and observe a botnet using honeypots or virtual machines
  ◦   Seek to identify and flag malicious websites using an automated web crawler
Adaptive Response
  ◦   Network Diagnostics: Run tests to determine the number of honeypots in the network. When defenders can infiltrate botnets with honeypots or virtual machines, they can observe attacker

communications and tactics. In some cases, defenders may even be able to reverse engineer the attack and create effective defenses that will increase the costs of doing business for attackers. Botnet operators can detect these machines by instructing all machines in the botnet to send malicious traffic to another machine within the botnet itself. Security researchers and other defenders are bound by ethical and legal obligations not to perform malicious activity and therefore the botnet operators can observe which machines fail to carry out the malicious commands. These machines can then be isolated from the botnet or not given further instructions, preventing the outside observer from monitoring botnet activity.

- Deploy "Smart" Malware: Malicious website recognizes when it is interacting with a web crawler and does not deliver malware. "Drive-by downloads" have been used by attackers to deliver malware to web users. To drive users to these malicious sites, attackers use SEC) poisoning to position these sites at the top of popular search engine results. Google, Yahoo and other search engines use automated web crawlers to search for and flag these websites hosting malicious content. In response, attackers have added the ability for websites to recognize these crawlers and imitate good behavior until unsuspecting internet users are directed to the site.

COMPLEXITY

What is the Assurance Strategy?

When a successful defensive measure is executed in cyberspace, it can come at the cost of defenders revealing their strategies or capabilities, potentially resulting in an information asymmetry that attackers can exploit in subsequent attacks. These circumstances also help attackers better understand structural vulnerabilities in their own operations, since successful defenses can highlight shortcomings in attacker structures and strategies, especially when those defenses involve actively undermining attacker systems. When attackers recognize these shortcomings, they can respond by introducing complexity into their attacks — changing the structure and operations of their attack for the purpose of confusing or misleading defenders.

How do Attackers Implement the Strategy?

There are myriad ways in which attackers may introduce complexity, including creating an attack that mutates or has a redundant and decentralized structure. These characteristics help the attack seem erratic and unpredictable to defenders who might try to disrupt the attack operation. Open-source research indicates that complexity can be introduced in one or more of the following ways:

If defenders can recognize discrete attack code signatures, attackers will use mutation in order to trick defenses. Polymorphism (the ability of malware to frequently change its code signature) has become a common feature in cyber-attacks, causing the volume of malware samples in the wild to expand rapidly every day. The sheer number of distinct attack technologies in the wild makes the global cyber-attack environment an increasingly complicated and messy place for defenders to navigate efficiently. As a result, anti-virus companies have struggled with the fact that they can no longer account for every variant of malicious code in their malware definition libraries.

Attackers who are threatened by defenders may choose to restructure an existing attack in one of several ways to make it more complex and difficult to undermine. If defenders disable fundamental capabilities of an attack, such as the command-and-control structure of a botnet, attackers will innovate quickly to avoid losing control over the attack. Attackers may build redundancy into the command-and-control structure so that if defenders disable one server host, communications can be channeled along a different pathway in the structure. Alternatively, attackers may decentralize the operating structure by shifting to a peer-to-peer structure, which makes it difficult for defenders to find and take advantage of a single point of failure in the attack structure. This adaptive response to defensive measures leads to attacks that are not only more robust and elusive, but also more likely to utilize available cloud services, often unknowingly implicating licit services such as free webmail clients.

Finally, when defenders disrupt attacks by identifying malicious signals or processes, attackers may introduce complexity by programming infected systems to create noise — false indicators of operational activity — that obfuscates vital attack operations and misdirects defender investigations. This occurs most often with botnets that instruct compromised machines to check a high volume of random websites as if they are receiving instructions from the botnet operator, making it difficult for defenders to differentiate signal from noise. This adaptive tactic prevents defenders from successfully interfering with vital command and control activities.

What are the Implications for Protecting Systems?

Adaptation strategies that introduce complexity into attacks are particularly problematic because they are inexpensive for attackers but costly for defenders. A small investment that makes an attack more complex can demand expensive and time-consuming countermeasures from defenders. In this situation, the attack-defend arms race is skewed heavily in favor of the attackers. Furthermore, engaging in this arms race by deploying new defensive measures against increasingly complex attacks can make the problem worse — as defenders up the ante, attackers will be further motivated to introduce greater complexity into their attack strategies.

In the face of attackers who adapt by introducing complexity into their attack structures and operations, there is a growing imperative for defenders to be able to navigate changing attack environments as efficiently as possible. To facilitate more fluid coordination between defenders across departments and areas of expertise, organizations could start by developing a standardized lexicon for analyzing and diagnosing attack strategies and tactics. Formalizing the language that analysts and researchers use in their assessments of attacks would make inter-departmental and automated information sharing easier. At the same time, updating this lexicon on a regular basis would help ensure that tacit knowledge acquired by senior analysts and managers is efficiently disseminated to new analysts and researchers. By establishing shared terminology and defining concepts in the cyber-attack space, defenders would be better equipped to quickly make sense of new attacker behaviors that make the space more complex.

Defensive Action
- ○ Disrupt command and control servers so that attackers cannot communicate with compromised machines
- ○ Disrupt command and control servers so that attackers cannot communicate with compromised machines

Adaptive Response
- ○ Decentralization: Attackers shift to peer-to-peer or other decentralized command structure
- ○ Redundancy: Set up a nested and redundant hosting model so traffic can be rerouted in the event of a server takedown

CONCLUSION

If defenders anticipate possible attacker reactions before implementing defenses, they will be better prepared to manage and defeat the attacker strategies and tactics that evolve in response to defensive measures. The attack adaptation taxonomy developed in this chapter is designed to help defenders achieve this goal. This taxonomy is grounded in frameworks for understanding the broader context in which attackers exist enablers and constraints that attackers face, their motivations and sensitivities and the ways in which they interact with and respond to defensive measures.

This chapter is a first step in a larger effort to help leaders become more anticipative of this evolutionary process by developing more robust and future-oriented cyber defense strategies. This could eventually include the formation of automated predictive threat models capable of anticipating attacker adaptation. The taxonomy of attack adaptations outlined in this chapter also underscores two important lessons for defenders:

- First, defenders play a significant role in driving attack adaptation: Sometimes defenders shape attack adaptation intentionally, while in other instances defenders unwittingly create the impetus for attackers to develop stronger, more dangerous attack strategies and technologies. The evolution of cyber-attacks over the past three decades demonstrates that attackers routinely develop new capabilities or target new systems in response to the defensive measures that disrupt them. To avoid making cyber defense problems worse in the long term, defenders should critically assess how new defensive strategies and tactics may inspire attacker adaptation.
- Second, continuing to engage in the "they attack, we react" dynamics of today's cyber arms race puts defenders at a disadvantage. As defenders put new defensive measures in place to combat known threats, agile attackers are constantly adapting to launch new classes of attacks that push current defenses toward obsolescence. This status quo, however, is not necessarily permanent. Anticipative capabilities such as those outlined in this chapter could help break this cycle. Unlike many of its adversaries who focus on narrow missions and often operate with limited resources, organizations have the resources and expertise to take a "big picture" perspective of the cyber-attack space, giving defenders insights into important systemic forces and dynamics of which US adversaries may be unaware. Doing so means building analytic capabilities that address the full spectrum of enablers, constraints and motivations that influence attack adaptation.

The number of daily cyber-attacks targeting systems will undoubtedly expand in the years to come, stretching the ability of defenders to efficiently deploy precious human and technical resources. The critical strategic question is whether defenders will continue to engage in a cyber-arms race that, up to this point, appears to overwhelmingly favor the interests, capabilities and missions of adversaries. The alternative to this cycle of attacker action followed by defender reaction lies in defenses that are designed to be anticipative rather than reactive — defenses that give the organizations greater leeway to shape the attack opportunity space from the outset. Developing research and analytic capabilities that use patterns in attack adaptation against attackers themselves is an important first step in creating cyber defense strategies better suited to the challenging and complex mission of today's cyber-defenders.

REFERENCES

Brooks, T. (2020). An internet control device embedded sensor agent. *International Journal of Internet of Things and Cyber-Assurance*, *1*(3-4), 267–290. doi:10.1504/IJITCA.2020.112534

Huskaj, G., Iftimie, I. A., & Wilson, R. L. (2020, June). Designing attack infrastructure for offensive cyberspace operations. In *European Conference on Information Warfare and Security*, ECCWS (pp. 473-482).

Chapter 8
Intelligence Modeling Cyber–Physical Systems for the Internet of Things

ABSTRACT

Cyber-physical systems and internet of things (IoT) networks will form a universal computing environment which will motivate much of modern technological growth. Cyber-physical systems arise from the tight integration of physical processes, computational resources, and communication capabilities: processing units monitor and control physical processes by means of sensor and actuator networks. With regards to the level of operations, the cyber-physical systems platform should achieve the integration of various security controls (e.g., access, authentication, etc.), essential internet of things elements and processes (e.g., integration of systemic power from the smart grid, sensors, tags, etc.) even from the integration of new processes and information implementations. Intelligence depends on storage and sharing of large amounts of data. This chapter introduces a new model for cyber-attack defense modeling required to address cyber-physical attacks.

INTRODUCTION

Recently, great advances have been made towards realizing artificial intelligence based on the access to very large and efficient data and services in cyber space. The precision and real-time nature of artificial intelligence is the foundation for decision-making. Cyber physical systems that are based on the integration of human and artificial intelligence functions may greatly raise the decision-making quality. With respect to artificial intelligence information flow, a cyber-physical systems platform should cover the sensor and information networks so that the networks can work together as a whole. This also includes malicious detection, information transmission and processing networks into the cyber-physical systems platform and ensuring full network coverage and linkage in all the areas where information must reach. Only by first properly handling the relationship between human and machines can the advantages of the cyber physical systems for decision-making be brought into play and can the expected efficacies be achieved.

DOI: 10.4018/978-1-6684-7766-3.ch008

The word "intelligence" is used to denote two different but related concepts: (1) problem solving capacity (like in "artificial intelligence") and information gathering and analysis (like in "signal intelligence"). These two concepts are studied in two separate research areas, by two separate research communities, although the problem-solving capacity plays an important role in information gathering and analysis, while information gathering and analysis is a necessary for problem solving. Cyber physical systems introduce new dimensions and fundamental new problems in both realms of intelligence.

Traditional system analysis and control methods can not explicitly consider the impacts towards the internet of things architecture. It is usually assumed that all IoT system 'things/objects' (e.g., smart devices, etc.) data will be received and processed timely, accurately, and reliably. In current grid systems, the main control objectives include large-scale power plants, protective relays, and reactive power consumption devices (Lin et al., 2011). Since the number devices to be controlled are relatively small and most control actions are completed based on local information; therefore, the traffic of the communication network is not very congested. In addition, existing power communication networks are not open access networks which are relatively independent and do not have many interfaces with external networks (Tomsovic et al., 2005). Because of these characteristics of the current grid systems, the impacts of the cyber system on grid system analysis and control can be largely neglected.

The above assumption, however, no longer holds for satellite networks, mobile networks, embedded systems, wireless networks, radio frequency identification (RFID) and even the Internet. For example, since the number of smart devices in the future smart grid environment can be massive (e.g., a single distribution network may cover thousands of distributed generators, electric vehicles, and controllable loads) and each smart device needs to exchange status information, market-related information and control signals with the control center in the future; thus, the data traffic can be extremely heavy (Lee & Seshina, 2011). On the other hand, since a communication channel does not exist between distributed smart devices and a control center, the most economical way to implement the communication is by utilizing an existing general-purpose communication network (e.g., the Internet or mobile phone network). Since a general communication network is a public characteristic and usually covers a large geographical space, the communication delay and data loss will be non-neglectable and can significantly degrade the control system performance. Moreover, since computing and sensing devices determine the amount of data injected into the network, the performance of control system will also be significantly affected. In summary, the performance of the cyber-infrastructure has great impacts on these types of operations and must be taken into consideration properly.

All these approaches fall into the concept of a cyber-physical system (CPS) as displayed in Figure 1, which are systems deployed in large geographical areas and generally consist of a massive number of distributed computing devices tightly coupled with their physical environment (Lee & Seshia, 2011). The frontier between CPS and IoT has not been clearly identified since both concepts have been driven in parallel from two independent communities (i.e., sensor networks and RFID, respectively), although they have always been closely related.

Intelligence depends on storage and sharing of large amounts of data. Recently, great advances have been made towards realizing artificial intelligence based on the access to very large and efficient data and services in cyber space[1]. The precision and real-time nature of artificial intelligence is the foundation for decision-making. Cyber physical systems that are based on the integration of human and artificial intelligence functions may greatly raise the decision-making quality. With respect to artificial intelligence information flow, a cyber-physical systems platform should cover the sensor and information networks so that the networks can work together as a whole. This also includes malicious detection, information

Figure 1. Cyber-Physical Systems

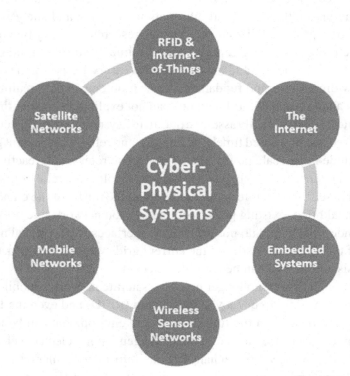

transmission and processing networks into the cyber-physical systems platform and ensuring full network coverage and linkage in all the areas where information must reach. Only by first properly handling the relationship between human and machines can the advantages of the cyber physical systems for deci-sion- making be brought into play and can the expected efficacies be achieved.

Cyber physical system components consist of computational computer systems platforms, physical/environmental devices and the network which captures the source of information and is the source of all information used in the processing of data throughout the system (see Figure 1) (Lee & Seshia, 2011). From an intelligence defense perspective, the basic task of a cyber-physical system is to support the defense for the network through detecting technical loopholes and topographic structures from the various networks and the data/information stored inside the system. By searching, discovering and determining tactical and technical parameters of wireless equipment and systems, discovering irregularities of electronic tags and their threat levels and analyzing tags/readers strong and weak access points provides the interoperability for organizing and carrying out defense. The defense in the cyber physical systems is to guarantee that the network, devices and system performs its normal functions. The concrete tasks are mainly, through multiple means and methods, to guarantee the normal operations of a user's own computing device or network system, guarantee the processing of secure data transmissions and defend against malicious intrusions.

These components in Figure 2 are responsible for the processing, transferring and collecting of infor-mation respectively and jointly determine the overall performance of the system. These types of cyber-physical systems can be used for the detection, identification, surveillance, tracking and location of all

Figure 2. Cyber Physical System Components

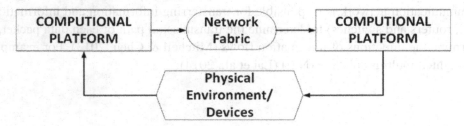

acoustic, electrical, magnetic and mechanical signals in networks. The cyber physical system is mainly responsible for the security of the data through screening, identification, computation and encryption of original information (Cardenas et al. 2008; Lee & Seshia, 2011). For example, as data is obtained by digital sensors/tags/actuators, information will be fed directly into the network for computation (or storage) and non-digital information must be encoded to become digital information before it can be processed. The cyber physical system supporting the system and the wide application of modern information technology (IT) can turn the network into an unobstructed, grid-style entity with revolutionary changes in data transmission methods, modes and processing alike. In terms of physical structure, the cyber physical system will include power generation (e.g., water, oil, etc.), mass transportation (e.g., smart vehicles, etc.), distribution (e.g., electricity, gas, etc.), sensors, process control and industrial automated networks; these network types will include wireless grids, satellites, microwave relay, mobile, clouds, wired, etc. The cyber physical system resistibility to the various security threats, such as hacking of the network, electromagnetic attacks, data theft and disruption by denial-of-service (DoS), consists of integrating this defense into entities the functions of the system monitoring and control (e.g., issue of warnings, launching of counterattacks, etc.).

INTELLIGENCE AS PROBLEM SOLVING

Intelligence as problem solving is an evolutionary process. In contrast with evolution of life, which is based on natural selection, intelligence is based on artificial selection: the candidate solutions are created, tested and the successful ones are stored and used to steer further search for improved solutions. Natural selection is enabled by heredity, i.e., the organisms' capability for self-reproduction and for encoding and retaining the selected features and properties. Artificial selection of intelligent behaviors requires a similar capability. John von Neumann observed and spent his last days pondering the fact that a computer with sensors and actuators is capable of self-reproduction and that every artificial system capable of self-reproduction has to satisfy the definition of a computer with sensors and actuators (Ellery, 2016). A cyber physical system is a network of computers with sensors and actuators.

As such, intelligence is thus also a computational process, as coding, variation, testing and storage of new solutions subsumes under a general form of programming, just like heredity as the foundation of natural selection and life, is a form of programming. Since the cyber physical architecture is a network of systems, its basic state can therefore be formulated as a network flow model. Any system architecture, sensing devices and some computing devices are the sources of information flow; their functions are to generate information and then eject into the communication network. Other computing devices are at the end of information flow, since they are used to receive the information and conduct necessarily analysis. The communication network is responsible for transferring information and information exchange devices (e.g., routers and switches) to determine the transmission path of each data packet, or in other words, determine the directions of information flows (Mitchell & Chen, 2013). For example, consider a directed weighted multi/graph G = (N,E) (Lai et al., 2014):

where:

$N=$ is the set of communication nodes in the graph. Each node can represent a computing access point, communication or sensing device, or their combination.

$E=$ represents the set of edges (e.g., communication links) in the graph.

For any information exchange device $n \in N$, denote $_nC$ asset information exchange capability with the unit as bit\second (bps) or megabits\second (Mbps); and denote $_nD$ as the delay in device n.

For any communication link l: $(i,j) \in E$, denote its bandwidth as $_lB$ or $_{ij}B$, with the unit as bps or Mbps. Note that since G is a directed graph, $_{ij}B$, does not necessarily equal $_{ij}B$.

The communication delay in the link is represented by $_lD$ or $_{ij}D$.

Assume that S information sources exist in the cyber physical system and denote (), Sk_{ij} as the data rate with the unit as bps or Mbps of the information flow injected into the cyber physical system by source k. i and j are respectively the source node and end node of the information flow.

Note that it is not required that i and j are connected directly. d represents the distance in the total communication path and L_{tot} is the total path loss during communications. Therefore, the cyber physical system model can then be described by the following equations (Lai et al., 2014):

Regarding the communication node information balance equation, for any communication node $n \in N$, its information inflow and outflow should be equal (Lai et al., 2014):

$$\sum_{(i,n) \in E} S_{i,n} + \sum_{k=1}^{Sv} S_n(k) = \sum_{(n,j) \in E} S_{n,j} + \sum_{k=1}^{Mv} O_n(k) \tag{1}$$

where: $(i,n) \in E$ and $(n,j) \in E$ indicate that nodes i and j are connected with node n directly. $_{iv}S$ and $_{vj}S$, represent respectively the data rate of the information flow from node i to node n and from node n to node j. $_vS$ denotes the number of information sources located at node v. $S(k)_v$ is the data rate of the information flow injected by source k at node v. $_vM$ represents the information flow ended at node v. $O(k)_v$ is the data rate of the information flow k which is ended at node v (Lai et al., 2014).

Regarding the communication node flow limit constraint, any node $n \in N$, its information inflow should not exceed its information exchange ability as described by (Khazaei et al., 2011):

$$0 \leq \sum_{(i,n) \in E} S_{i,n} + \sum_{k=1}^{Sv} S_n(k) \leq C_n \rightleftharpoons \tag{2}$$

As it pertains to the link information flow limit constraint, for any link $(i,j) \in E$, its information flow should not exceed its bandwidth (Lai et al., 2014):

$$0 \leq S_{i,j} \leq B_{i,j} \rightleftharpoons \tag{3}$$

Finally, as it relates to the total path loss for each communication node in the cyber physical system, it's described by (Giannattasio et al., 2009):

$$L_{tot}(d) = \left(\frac{\lambda}{4\pi d_0}\right)^2 \times \left(\frac{d}{d_0}\right)^n \tag{4}$$

Using the equations above, intelligence can be derived out of the cyber physical system. When the information volume injected into the node and link does not exceed their exchange and transmission limits, the cyber-physical system is in its operational. Since the data is passed directly to and from the actual physical transmission medium and bypass layers three through seven of the open system interconnection (OSI) communications protocol[1], the synchronous signals are sent as rapidly as possible between the actual devices (Giannattasio et al., 2009). Based on the traffic of the network, a data packet will have seven different pass to select and therefore, the cyber physical system may have several differing working states. The purpose of the analysis is to obtain a feasible working environment based on solving Eqns. (1) – (4). The optimal working environment can be attained by solving the optimal routing problem in Eqns. [1-2], which is an optimization problem subject to constraints in Eqns. (1) – (4). By performing the analysis, the information flows of all the links in the network can be obtained and whether a network can support the operation of a specific control system for a cyber-physical system can then be determined.

The above analysis can determine the information paths flows in the network. Ideally, the volume of information flows of all nodes and links should be smaller than their exchange and transmission limits; if this holds, the cyber physical system would be considered in its operational (Lai et al., 2014). In practice, however, some information sources may inject into the network a large amount of data, beyond the capability of the network (Lai et al., 2014). This will consequently cause a significant communication delay and data loss known as communication network congestion (Lai et al., 2014, Singh & Gupte, 2005). When congestion occurs, the cyber physical system will enter a dynamic process and return to the steady state through the application of a communication network control mechanism. In the actual operation of communication networks, congestion can be frequently observed. Therefore, it is essential to develop an appropriate dynamic model of the cyber physical system to assess the performance and abnormal operating states.

The dynamic model of the communications network can be formulated based on the OSI model developed by the international organization for standardization (ISO). Regarding intelligence, the main interest will be in the communication delay and data loss, hence only the network layer and transport layer will be considered. In the network and transport layer, routers, access points, communication links and congestion control protocol(s) act as a key control mechanism for handling communication network congestion (Lai et al., 2014). Routers and communication links usually have memory buffers; once a data packet reaches the router or communication link, it will be stored in the buffer before the process; the memory buffer can usually be model as a queue and the size of the memory buffer is called the maximum queue size (Lai et al., 2014). For example, take the TCP/IP network; the congestion control protocol can mitigate congestion in two ways: First, the information volume injected into the network can be decreased and this can be implemented by reducing the congestion window size of some nodes. Second, some data packets with a lower priority can be deleted proactively from the memory buffer to avoid the memory buffer overflow and further data loss. Because of the congestion control protocol, the congestion window size and queue size will vary dramatically when network congestion occurs; thus, they can be selected as the state variables of the dynamic model. The outputs of the cyber physical system can usually be set as the communication delays and data loss rates of information flows. Like conventional control systems, the note $X(t)$ as the state variable vector, $Y(t)$ as system output vector and $u(t)$ as the control signal vector, then the dynamic model of the communication network can be expressed as (Lai et al., 2014):

$$X(t) = f(X,u) \tag{5}$$

$$Y(t) = g(X,u) \tag{6}$$

For different working states of the communication network, the cyber physical system model will be different taken into consideration that the TCP/IP network as an example; a queue can transit between three different states: empty, non-empty and full (Bohacek et al., 2003, Hespanha, 2004, Lai et al., 2014). Also, corresponding to different congestion conditions, the TCP protocol has three different working states: slow start, congestion avoidance, fast recovery (Bohacek et al., 2003, Hespanha, 2004, Lai et al., 2014). For all these working states, the differential equations should be different. Therefore, to handle the state transition of the communication network, it can be combined with differential equations to form the mathematical model of the communication network (Hespanha, 2004, Lai et al., 2014). The automation can describe the discrete state transition of the communication network; for each state of the automation, the dynamic behaviors of the cyber physical system can be modeled with corresponding differential equations which is called the hybrid system modeling approach of the communication network (Hespanha, 2004, Lai et al., 2014).

The computing devices can be modeled based on queuing theory and stochastic processes (Singh & Gupte, 2005; Khazaei, et al., 2011; Newell, 2013). A computing device usually consists of a processor and a memory buffer. Once arrived, a computing task will be stored in the buffer and then be processed based on the principle of "first-in-first-out" (Khazaei et al., 2011). Therefore, the computing device can be modeled with the D/G/c/∞ or M/G/c/ ∞ queues in the queuing theory (Khazaei et al., 2011). In the queue name, the first character represents the probability distribution of the arriving frequency of computing tasks: "D" indicates that computing tasks will reach the computing device with a deterministic frequency, "M" indicates that the arriving frequency will follow a Markov process (e.g. Poisson process or Binomial process), "G" means that the processing time of a computing task follows a Gaussian procedure, "c" indicates that the computing device can parallel process at most c tasks and Symbol "∞" means that memory buffer can store infinite computing tasks since (currently) the cost a storage device is very low and a computing device usually has a very large storage space (Rybko & Stolyar, 1992; Kelly, 2011; Newell, 2013). Therefore, the assumption is that the size of the computing device's buffer is nearly infinite (Rybko & Stolyar, 1992; Kelly, 2011; Newell, 2013). In other words, no computing tasks should be lost due to the memory buffer overflows and within an environment, the computing task must include power system analysis (e.g., power flow calculation and dynamic security assessment) and control strategy calculations.

The distributions of the arriving frequency and processing time of each computing task should be carefully selected based on its characteristics. With these distributions, the performance indices of computing devices (e.g., the average processing time of each task) can be estimated (Kelly, 2011). It then further calculates the data rate of the information flow injected by a computing device (e.g., the data rate of the control signal) (Kelly, 2011). For a sensing device, its mainly consider the probability distribution of its data rate. The possible models include continuous stochastic process (e.g., Wiener process), Markov process (e.g., Poisson process and fat-tailed process (e.g., the Pareto process) (Kelly, 2011). By integrating the models of computing devices, communication networks and sensing devices, the dynamic model of the cyber physical system can be obtained. Based on the developed dynamic model, dynamic analysis can be carried out to calculate the key performance indices of the cyber physical system when it is disturbed by congestions or faults. The output of the dynamic analysis is usually the time varying paths of communication delay and data loss rate and can eventually be conducted through cyber physical system simulations.

Two widely used methods for simulating cyber-physical systems are the so-called discrete even simulation and fluid simulation (Lee & Seshia, 2011; Lin, 2011; Guseva et al., 2018). The discrete event simulation obtains the system-wide dynamics by simulating the behaviors of each data packet and can achieve superior accuracy; its major a disadvantage is very low computational efficiency (Guseva et al., 2018). The packet level simulation can be performed offline to estimate the working status of the cyber system and the parameters of the dynamic model can be estimated based on results of the packet level simulation (Lin, 2011, Lai, 2014). Different from the discrete event simulation, the fluid simulation calculates the system performance indices (e.g., the queue size, congestion window size, link information flow) by calculating the time-domain solution of the proposed dynamic model directly. The computational speed of the fluid simulation is much faster than that of the packet level simulation and can be used for the online performance assessment of the cyber system. Some classical methods for solving ordinary differential equations, such as the Runge-Kutta method, can be applied directly in the fluid simulation (Lin et al., 2011; Lai et al., 2014; Guseva et al. 2018).

AGGREGATING CYBER INTELLIGENCE

Intelligence is physical. Search for new solutions is performed in a process of hypothesis formation and testing. Testing usually requires interactions with physical world. In science, these interactions are steered using experimental methods. Although it does not involve physical experiments, even purely mathematical problem solving usually goes through an empiric trial-and-error phase, where general hypotheses are tested on special cases. Geometric puzzles are often solved through physical interaction. In a sense, geometry is problem solving through interaction with the physical space of diagrams, using our visual sensors and drawing actuators. In a broader sense, all of mathematics can be viewed as problem solving using mathematical notations and text as the external states. To multiply large numbers, we use physical interaction with pencil and paper to support and extend our internal short-term memory. The algorithms that we use in mathematical calculations are usually physical interactions: with paper, abacus, calculator. — Intelligence is usually a physical behavior, in animals, in humans and presumably in cyber physical systems. Artificial intelligence also evolves its solution through an inductive process of hypothesis testing. Self-Reproduction physical intelligence is realized with no internal states.

Traditional system analysis and control methods can not explicitly consider the impacts towards intelligence derived from system architectures. It is usually assumed that all system's data will be received and processed timely, accurately and reliably for adequate decision-making. For example, in current grid systems, the main control objectives include large-scale power plants, protective relays and reactive power consumption devices (Tomsovic et al., 2005). Since the number devices to be controlled are relatively small and most control actions are completed based on local information; therefore, the traffic of the communication network is not very congested. In addition, existing power communication networks are not open access networks which are relatively independent and do not have many interfaces with external networks (Arnold, 2010). Because of these characteristics of the current grid systems, the impacts of the intelligence aspects towards cyber on grid system analysis and control can be largely neglected.

The above assumption, however, no longer holds for cyber intelligence gathering relating to satellite networks, mobile networks, embedded systems, wireless networks, radio frequency identification (RFID) and even the Internet. For example, since the number of smart devices in the future smart grid environment can be massive (e.g., a single distribution network may cover thousands of distributed generators, electric vehicles and controllable loads) and each smart device needs to exchange status information, market-related information and control signals with the control center in the future; thus, the data traffic can be extremely heavy (Yan et al., 2012). On the other hand, since a communication channel does not exist between distributed smart devices and a control center, the most economical way to implement the communication is by utilizing an existing general-purpose communication network (e.g., the Internet or mobile phone network). Since a general communication network is a public characteristic and usually covers a large geographical space, the communication delay and data loss will be non-neglectable and can significantly degrade the control system performance. Moreover, since computing and sensing devices determine the amount of data injected into the network, the performance of control system will also be significantly affected. In summary, the performance of the cyber-infrastructure has great impacts on these types of operations and must be taken into consideration properly.

The physical structure of the cyber physical system will include automatic monitoring of performance indicators. There may potentially be thousands of sensors, tags, actuators, network data center facilities and wireless access points, which will be widely distributed on the network. As it is nearly impossible to effectively monitor and manage them manually, the cyber physical system must be employed to carry out automatic monitoring and management performed at various locations (Brooks et al., 2014). Only in this way can failures in the system be detected and diagnosed immediately to ensure the stability of the system. The automatic adjustment of the structure of the network will be subjected to substitutions within different vendor facilities and space in different time frames. There will also be constant realignments and changes of technology and consequential changes of the flow of data/information in the network. Therefore, the structure of the cyber physical system must be modified accordingly. For instance, in a typical grid network system, there are sufficient routes for point-to-point transmission, but because of the instantaneous property of information transmission, there is a need for high-speed selection of routes (which is impossible to be accomplished manually in the environment) (Brooks et al., 2014). This will only be achieved through an automatic selection based on real-time monitoring of the quality of the various data routes and the allocation of bandwidth for processing. There will be a vast amount of information to process in an infinite number of bandwidths, but this will require the use of technology and the system to have the capability of allocating bandwidths automatically per the state of flow of data.

As it pertains to intelligence, it is necessary to develop a cyber physical system covering the physical and wireless space. In wireless operations, there will be no boundary to the cyber-space realm which will extend to anywhere on the Internet. Therefore, the cyber physical system is not only confined to the actual network with devices, hardware and software, but should also involve the whole dimensions of a cyber physical system strategy. In this cyber physical system -dimensional environment, the main mode of transmissions of information is wireless (e.g., ultra-short wave, satellite, etc.). The cyber physical system platform must combine defense and security into a single, unified entity. Each of the cyber physical system components not only can act separately and independently in a time segment and area during operations but must also be integrated to form a single operation system. Hence, the cyber physical system platform not only has to cover and connect the various systems in the network but should also be able to separate or realign the various components based on the changes in the environment.

With respect to information flow, the cyber physical system platform should cover the sensor and information networks so that the networks can work together as a whole. This also includes malicious detection, information transmission and processing networks into the cyber physical system platform and ensuring full network coverage and linkage in all the areas where information should reach. With regards to the level of operations, the cyber physical system platform should achieve the integration of various security controls (e.g., access, authentication, etc.), essential network elements and processes (e.g., integration of systemic power from the smart grid, sensors, tags, etc.) even from the integration of new processes and information implementations. For example, the smart grid relies heavily on the underlying communication network to collect system information and transfer control signals (Lin et al;, 2011). Therefore, the failures of switches, communication links and servers will downgrade the communication network performance and threaten the security of the smart grid. In practice, attackers can disable a switch, a communication server, or a communication link by launching a denial-of-services/ distributed denial-of-service (DoS/DDos) attack; or they can simply destroy these devices physically if not well protected. Even without an attacker, these devices may also experience random hardware/ software faults. It is therefore important to quantitatively measure the impacts of device failures on the overall performance of the network.

Networks use high-capacity and high-speed transmission of data processing and full compatibility in various formats. To meet this requirement, the network provides many different methods of data transmissions; these various transmission modes and methods are used in combination and through the development of optical cables and satellite systems for long-distance transmissions. The bandwidth of data transmissions is extensive; various frequencies such as high frequency (HF), extremely low frequency (ELF), ultra-high frequency (UHF), etc. are utilized and with the bandwidths being allocated automatically per the properties of the information transmitted. Furthermore, the system has a high compatibility which can handle various formats of information such as voice, data, images and multi-media documents at the same time. The capability of uninterrupted wireless data processing at any time and under any circumstances, through standardization of transmission of information in various systems, is required even under hostile conditions to satisfy the requests of devices accessing the network. As such, physical layer monitoring through a cyber physical system will be essential in the network.

Several physical layer parameters can be monitored and incorporated into the network. These may include the observed transmission signal strength, the observed round-trip time (RTT) measurement between pairs of communication devices (station and access point) and the identification of unique artifacts resulting from the transmit characteristics of transceiver prints from radios. Physical layer attribute monitoring is typically incorporated into an anomaly-based detection scheme (Berthier et al., 2010). In the simplest case, alarms will be raised when a predetermined threshold value has been breached. More sophisticated approaches will incorporate statistical and learning based approaches. The vagaries of the cyber physical system and the high rate of false positives associated with anomaly-based detection systems suggest that such approaches will be noisy. The monitoring of physical layer parameters can be performed entirely passively and does not require that the cyber physical system reveal its presence to participants of the network and the parameters being monitored are difficult to fabricate and therefore not easily spoofable. Having the infrastructure in place to monitor physical layer parameter can be used to aid the localization of rogue devices and are most effective with the radio propagation characteristics of the environment are known in advance- either through empirical analysis or through the construction of computer-based models.

Data quality from the processing of information in cyber-physical systems is essential. Regular monitoring and correction of divergence in cyber physical system data processing quality includes performing quality control over the data transmitted and the monitoring of any loss, miscoding and leaking of data during transmission and it carries out quality control over the transmission channels and detects such failures as channel congestion, interference, short-circuit and disconnection in a timely manner (Tang et al., 2010). Correction of divergence also consists of the recovery of and supplements to miscoded information the repair of the defect of leakage of information. The timely adjustment of information with falling quality and automatic switching to the best routing by making use of the multi-directional routing feature of the cyber physical system for information physical device security is important (Trapp, 1994). Data automation for the processing of information should include the automatic filtering of malicious data. For data processed within the cyber physical system, the cyber physical system automatically identifies and classifies the various parameters like the data source, nature, properties, status and distribution and must discard the malevolent data but retain the valid and necessary information automatically. Data being processed in this manner will thus become useful information and after categorizing the collected data, the cyber physical system proceeds with its allocation.

CYBER PHYSICAL VIRUSES: A PROBABILISTIC MEASUREMENT FOR ATTACKS

The fundamental theorem of computation enables the construction of computer viruses: they perform a function and reproduce several copies of themselves, or mutated copies (towards selection of the fittest), or modified copies (towards increased malice). Cyber physical systems implement a physical function and may reproduce copies of themselves, or mutations, or weaponized versions, which will reproduce further copies of these malicious entities, also known as a computer virus. As a component of malware, a virus is essentially a piece of software that is capable of infecting other programs by self-replicating and modifying the operating system (OS) or the application's portable executable (PE) files (Wu & Irwin, 2016). This modification includes a copy of the virus program, which propagates to infect other programs in other hosts or devices (Wu & Irwin, 2016). Like biological viruses, a computer virus carries within its instruction code, the recipe for replicating itself.

Executed software viruses in physical environments, e.g., Flame, etc., and physical zombies, e.g. software that takes over physical behavior, can perform any function, e.g., download files and execute programs and may progress from dormancy; where it lies in wait of a triggering event, to either propagation where it uses exploits for replication to other hosts, or to an event that causes it to execute a payload that may include information stealing. For example, two most common compartments that exist in essentially every epidemic model are susceptible (S) and infected (I) (Anderson & May, 1992, Nowzari et al., 2016). In models that contain only these two compartments, a given population is initially divided into them, with S represents individuals who are healthy but susceptible to becoming infected and I represent individuals who are infected but can recover (Nowzari et al., 2016).

Heckerman (1990) three-state compartmental susceptible-protected-infected-susceptible model identifies an individual i in the infected state I transitions to the healthy or susceptible state S with a natural recovery rate δ; an individual in the susceptible state transitions to the protected state P at a rate fi (p^s, p^l, p^p) that depends on the entire network state and to the infected state at a rate βY_i proportional to the number of infected neighbors Y_i possessed by node i; an individual in the protected state transitions to the infected state at a rate $\beta_0 Y_i$, where $\beta_0 < \beta$ captures the fact that this individual is in a less susceptible state than normal, for instance, due to behavioral changes or vaccination.

The action of malicious objects (e.g., viruses) throughout a computer network can be studied by using mathematical models (Aron et al., 2002; Balthrop, et al., 2004; Billings et al., 2002, Mishra & Saini, 2007a; Mishra & Saini, 2007b). Mishra & Saini, (2007a) researched a susceptible (S) – exposed (E) – infectious (I) – quarantined (Q) – recovered (R) (SEIQRS) model for the transmission of malicious objects in computer networks. The authors identified a population size $N(t)$ is partitioned into subclasses of nodes which are susceptible, exposed (infected but not yet infectious), infectious, quarantined and recovered, with sizes denoted by $S(t)$, $E(t)$, $I(t)$, $Q(t)$, $R(t)$ respectively and identified their SEIQRS model with cyber mass action incidence as:

$$S'(t) = A - \beta SI - dS + \eta R,$$

$$E'(t) = \beta SI - (d + \mu)E,$$

$$I'(t) = \mu E - (d + \alpha + y + \delta)I,$$

$$Q'(t) = \delta I - (d + \alpha + \in)Q,$$

$$R'(t) = \gamma I + \in Q - (d + \eta)R, \tag{7}$$

Where parameters A, d, β are positive constants and μ, γ, δ, ϵ, η and α are nonnegative constants. The constant A is the recruitment rate of susceptible nodes to the computer network, d is the per capita natural mortality rate (that is the crashing of nodes due to the reason other than the attack of malicious objects), μ is the rate constant for nodes leaving the exposed class E for infective compartment, δ is the rate constant for nodes leaving the infective compartment I for quarantine compartment, α is the disease related death rate (crashing of nodes due to the attack of malicious objects) constant in the compartments I and Q; γ, ϵ are the rates at which nodes recover temporarily after the run of anti-malicious software and return to recovered class R from compartments I and Q respectively; η is the loss of immunity rate constant (Mishra & Saini, 2007a). The way to control the spread of worms for the nodes which are highly infected is to be kept in isolation for some time, which may help to reduce the transmission of infection to susceptible nodes and the infected files are quarantined to reduce the further transmission of malicious objects in computer networks.

Malicious objects (e.g., viruses) are injected into computer networks through cyber-attacks from insiders (malicious or non-malicious) or hostile outsiders (external entities), also known as adversaries, through various means (e.g., email, thumb drives, etc.). A cyber-attack contains 3 main elements: (1) the OBJECT being attacked, (2) the BEHAVIOR of the attack and the EFFECT of the attack (see Figure 3).

Figure 3. General Attack Taxonomy

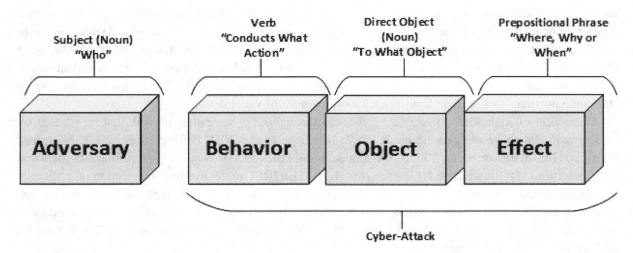

Cyber physical systems depend on proper operation and are susceptible to cyber-physical attacks consisting of cyber and physical components. Since cyber-attacks generally take the form of viruses, malware, or denial-of-service (DoS) attacks with the goal of disabling computers or networks, there numerous techniques exist for modeling and defending against cyber-attacks. When evaluating which cyber-attack to attempt regarding the infection of viruses in cyber-physical systems, adversaries consider three high-level aspects of the outcome of executing the attack: (1) the resources required to execute the attack (resources expended [RE]), the likelihood of success of the attack (probability of success - p(s)) and the likelihood of being detected given attempt of the attack (probability of detection – p(d)).

The likelihood of a cyber-attack refers to the change or probability of a security incident or event occurring that would result in a cyber-attack. The likelihood can be estimated as an absolute probability, as the chance that something will occur over a defined period (e.g., over the next year) or as a percentage chance of occurrence. Cyber-attacks that succeed or those that are not likely to succeed, require resources that exceed an adversaries' available resources, are easy to detect and/or do not accomplish the adversary's goals. Therefore, monetary resources expended (RE) measures the marginal resources required to execute the cyber-attack and includes funds, time, manpower, equipment, etc., and excludes general development costs – the one-time expenses required to develop the attack. The probability of success (p(s)) measures the likelihood that the attack will succeed and includes the notions of the challenge the attack presents to the attacker's capabilities and the random nature of circumstances surrounding the attack. The probability of detection measures the likelihood that a defender will detect an attack. Therefore, the aggregation of the RE *parameter* is simply the sum of the RE *of* the individual attack steps that constitute an attack:

$$RE = \sum_{i=1}^{n} RE_i \tag{8}$$

where:

RE = aggregate monetary resources expended of the attack

RE_i = the RE required for each attack step that constitute the attack
n = total number of attack steps in the attack

The aggregation of probability of success is the product of $p(s)$ of the individual attack steps:

$$P(s) = \sum_{i=1}^{n} P_i \tag{9}$$

where:

$P(s)$ = probability that the attack will succeed
p_i = probability of success of attack step i
n = total number of attack steps in the attack

The aggregation of probability of detection is 1 minus the product of $(1 - p(d))$ of the individual attack step:

$$P(d) = 1 - \sum_{i=1}^{n} (1 - p_i) \tag{10}$$

where:

$P(d)$ = probability that the attack will be detected
p_i = probability of detection of attack step i
n = total number of attack steps in the attack

Utility functions/curves based on classic utility theory exhibit an upward concavity, a downward concavity, or the absence of concavity (linearity) (Starmer, 2000; Von Neumann & Morgenstern, 2007). In addition, utility curves can be positively or negatively sloped, based on whether more of a parameter is better or worse than lass of that parameter. Each utility function has values ranging from zero (worst case) to one (best case) for that parameter. Each adversary has an associated utility function (i.e., a preference for a specific virus attack with respect to a security parameter [e.g., intrusion detection system, anti-virus software, etc.]) for each of the security parameters: RE, $p(s)$ and $p(d)$. After aggregating the scores with respect to RE, $p(s)$ and $p(d)$ for all attacks, an adversary utility curve should be defined to determine the utility value of the attack to each applicable adversary, with respect to each security parameter (e.g., RE, $p(s)$, $p(d)$). Using the utility curves for each of the security parameters, determine the utility of each attack for each applicable type of adversary. That is, for each system attack, determine $U(RE_a)$, $U[P(s)_a]$ and $U[P(d)_a]$ for each applicable adversary:

where:

RE_a = cost of attack a
$P(s)_a$ = probability of success of attack a
$P(d)_a$ = probability of detection of attack a
$U(RE_a)$ = the adversary utility for attack a derived from the cost parameter
$U[P(s)_a]$ = the adversary utility for attack a derived from the probability of success parameter
$U[P(d)_a]$ = the adversary utility for attack a derived from the probability of detection parameter

Then, calculate the attack utility (AU) of each attack to each adversary using the following formula:

$$AUa = W_{RE}*U\left(RE_{a}\right)+W_{p(s)}*U\left[p(s)_{a}\right]+W_{p(d)}*U\left[p(d)_{a}\right] \tag{11}$$

where:

a = attack index

AU_{a} = overall utility of attack a

RE_{a} = RE required for attack a

$P(s)_{a}$ = probability of success of attack a

$P(d)_{a}$ = probability of detection of attack a

W_{RE} = the adversary weight of RE parameter

$W_{p(s)}$ = the adversary weight of probability of success parameter

$W_{p(d)}$ = the adversary weight of probability of detection parameter

$U(RE_{a})$ = the adversary value of attack a with respect to the RE required for the attack

$U[P(s)_{a}]$ = the adversary value of attack a with respect to the $p(s)$ required for the attack

$U[P(d)_{a}]$ = the adversary value of attack a with respect to the $p(d)$ required for the attack

The overall attack utility is a function of the attack characteristics, adversary preferences and impact. The attack utilities provide system architects/designers a metric to identify the most serious concerns to the baseline system with the higher attack utilities representing more preferred attacks. These types of mathematical models will help in finding the probability of a system being infected by any computer virus or a group of computer viruses at any time specifically dealing with the speed of breeding of the viruses and the adversary injecting the virus into the network (Mishra & Saini, 2007a; Mishra & Saini, 2007b).

However, this assumption may not be accurate depending on the time scale of a virus diffusion process. For instance, in the context of computer viruses, the network of devices in nodes is constantly changing through technological improvements (e.g., wireless, Internet of Things, etc.). Hence, a device-varying network model might be more appropriate, although more challenging, to analyze and devise. There is still a little bit of work analyzing these types of device-varying models, which seems to be a promising new branch of research. Extensions to the cyber-attack defense modeling and defense methodologies are required to address cyber-physical attacks. These models can be useful in designing defenses against malicious computer virus attacks and will help in carrying out analysis and verification by simulation.

CONCLUSION

CPS and IoT systems will possess a function of automatic identity recognition. First, the IoT system should automatically recognize and verify the identities of 'things/objects' that have gained random access to the IoT system; it should be able to distinguish whether the information that has entered the IoT system is valid from legitimate sources or a potential adversary. The environment surrounding the IoT is extremely harsh and there are many factors posing tremendous threats to the validity of its architecture which can seriously affect the functions of the IoT system and even its existence. Therefore, future research on CPS and how they should be able to monitor the IoT environmental parameters automatically and issue warnings in time to respective individuals or organizations is warranted. When an attack, which is threatening the security of the IoT system has escalated to a certain level to reach safety coefficient values, the IoT system should be able to carry out an evaluation of the level of safety automatically. While issuing warnings and providing detection and protection automatically, the CPS system should also be able to connect to corresponding counter-attack systems or defense systems in accordance with IoT standards to give protection to the IoT system and to launch effective counterattacks.

The CPS model proposed needs further development, testing and implementation into an actual IoT environment for validity. The IoT architecture will be one of the most powerful platforms for computer networking. A wide range of communication networks, from a single local area network (LAN) to global satellite networks will support in this new IoT environment. With the incorporation of a broad suite of protocols and technologies, new development environments to enable modeling of all IoT network types and technologies to perform both fluid simulation and discrete event simulation will be used to analyze network performance and obtain key performance indices.

REFERENCES

Anderson, R. M., May, R. M., & Anderson, B. (1992). *Infectious diseases of humans: dynamics and control* (Vol. 28). Oxford university press.

Arnold, O., Richter, F., Fettweis, G., & Blume, O. (2010, June). *Power consumption modeling of different base station types in heterogeneous cellular networks. In 2010 Future Network & Mobile Summit*. IEEE.

Aron, J. L., O'leary, M., Gove, R. A., Azadegan, S., & Schneider, M. C. (2002). The benefits of a notification process in addressing the worsening computer virus problem: Results of a survey and a simulation model. *Computers & Security, 21*(2), 142–163. doi:10.1016/S0167-4048(02)00210-9

Balthrop, J., Forrest, S., Newman, M. E., & Williamson, M. M. (2004). Technological networks and the spread of computer viruses. *Science, 304*(5670), 527–529. doi:10.1126cience.1095845 PMID:15105484

Berthier, R., Sanders, W. H., & Khurana, H. (2010, October). Intrusion detection for advanced metering infrastructures: Requirements and architectural directions. In *2010 First IEEE International Conference on Smart Grid Communications* (pp. 350-355). IEEE. 10.1109/SMARTGRID.2010.5622068

Billings, L., Spears, W. M., & Schwartz, I. B. (2002). A unified prediction of computer virus spread in connected networks. *Physics Letters. [Part A], 297*(3-4), 261–266. doi:10.1016/S0375-9601(02)00152-4

Bohacek, S., Hespanha, J. P., Lee, J., & Obraczka, K. (2003, June). A hybrid systems modeling framework for fast and accurate simulation of data communication networks. In *Proceedings of the 2003 ACM SIGMETRICS international conference on Measurement and modeling of computer systems* (pp. 58-69). 10.1145/781027.781036

Brooks, T., Kaarst-Brown, M., Caicedo, C., Park, J., & McKnight, L. W. (2014). Secure the edge? Understanding the risk towards wireless grids Edgeware technology. *International Journal of Internet Technology and Secured Transactions 8, 5*(3), 191-222.

Cardenas, A. A., Amin, S., & Sastry, S. (2008, June). Secure control: Towards survivable cyber-physical systems. In *2008 the 28th International Conference on Distributed Computing Systems Workshops* (pp. 495-500). IEEE.

Ellery, A. (2016, October). John von Neumann's self-replicating machine—Critical components required. In *2016 IEEE International Conference on Systems, Man, and Cybernetics* (SMC) (pp. 000314-000319). IEEE. 10.1109/SMC.2016.7844259

Giannattasio, G., Erfanian, J., Wills, P., Nguyen, H. Q., Croda, T., Rauscher, K., & Wong, K. D. (2009). A guide to the wireless engineering body of knowledge (WEBOK). John Wiley & Sons.

Guseva, E., Varfolomeyeva, T., Efimova, I., & Movchan, I. (2018, May). Discrete event simulation modelling of patient service management with Arena. []. IOP Publishing.]. *Journal of Physics: Conference Series*, *1015*(3), 032095. doi:10.1088/1742-6596/1015/3/032095

Heckerman, D. (1990). Probabilistic similarity networks. *Networks*, *20*(5), 607–636. doi:10.1002/net.3230200508

Hespanha, J. P. (2004, March). Stochastic hybrid systems: Application to communication networks. In *International Workshop on Hybrid Systems: Computation and Control* (pp. 387-401). Springer. 10.1007/978-3-540-24743-2_26

Khazaei, H., Misic, J., & Misic, V. B. (2011). Performance analysis of cloud computing centers using m/g/m/m+ r queuing systems. *IEEE Transactions on Parallel and Distributed Systems*, *23*(5), 936–943. doi:10.1109/TPDS.2011.199

Lai, M., Yang, H., Yang, S., Zhao, J., & Xu, Y. (2014). Modeling and Analysis of the Cyber Infrastructure for Vehicle Route Optimization. In *Optimization and Control Techniques and Applications* (pp. 255–269). Springer. doi:10.1007/978-3-662-43404-8_14

Lee, E. A., & Seshia, S. A. (2011). Introduction to embedded systems. *A cyber-physical systems approach*, 499.

Lin, H., Sambamoorthy, S., Shukla, S., Thorp, J., & Mili, L. (2011, January). Power system and communication network co-simulation for smart grid applications. In *ISGT 2011* (pp. 1–6). IEEE. doi:10.1109/ISGT.2011.5759166

Mishra, B. K., & Saini, D. (2007a). Mathematical models on computer viruses. *Applied Mathematics and Computation*, *187*(2), 929–936. doi:10.1016/j.amc.2006.09.062

Mishra, B. K., & Saini, D. K. (2007b). SEIRS epidemic model with delay for transmission of malicious objects in computer network. *Applied Mathematics and Computation*, *188*(2), 1476–1482. doi:10.1016/j.amc.2006.11.012

Newell, C. (2013). *Applications of queueing theory* (Vol. 4). Springer Science & Business Media.

Rybko, A. N., & Stolyar, A. L. (1992). Ergodicity of stochastic processes describing the operation of open queueing networks. *Problemy Peredachi Informatsii*, *28*(3), 3–26.

Singh, B. K., & Gupte, N. (2005). Congestion and decongestion in a communication network. *Physical Review. E*, *71*(5), 055103. doi:10.1103/PhysRevE.71.055103 PMID:16089586

Starmer, C. (2000). Developments in non-expected utility theory: The hunt for a descriptive theory of choice under risk. *Journal of Economic Literature*, *38*(2), 332–382. doi:10.1257/jel.38.2.332

Tang, L. A., Yu, X., Kim, S., Han, J., Hung, C. C., & Peng, W. C. (2010, December). Tru-alarm: Trustworthiness analysis of sensor networks in cyber-physical systems. In *2010 IEEE International Conference on Data Mining* (pp. 1079-1084). IEEE. 10.1109/ICDM.2010.63

Tomsovic, K., Bakken, D. E., Venkatasubramanian, V., & Bose, A. (2005). Designing the next generation of real-time control, communication, and computations for large power systems. *Proceedings of the IEEE*, *93*(5), 965–979. doi:10.1109/JPROC.2005.847249

Trapp, T. J. (1994). *Network synchronous data distribution system*. U.S. Patent No. 5,280,477. Washington, DC: U.S. Patent and Trademark Office.

Von Neumann, J., & Morgenstern, O. (2007). Theory of games and economic behavior. In *Theory of games and economic behavior*. Princeton university press.

Wu, C. H. J., & Irwin, J. D. (2016). *Introduction to computer networks and cybersecurity*. CRC Press. doi:10.1201/9781466572140

Yan, Y., Qian, Y., Sharif, H., & Tipper, D. (2012). A survey on smart grid communication infrastructures: Motivations, requirements and challenges. *IEEE Communications Surveys and Tutorials*, *15*(1), 5–20. doi:10.1109/SURV.2012.021312.00034

ENDNOTE

[1] In the Open System Interconnection (OSI) model, a communication network can be divided into seven layers (i.e. physical, data link, network, transport, session, presentation, application layers) based on their functions (http://www.iso.org).

Chapter 9
Review of Probability Elicitation and Examination of Approaches for Large Bayesian Networks

ABSTRACT

Probability elicitation is the process of formulating a person's knowledge and beliefs about one or more uncertain quantities into a joint probability distribution for those quantities. The important point is that the goal of elicitation is to capture a person's knowledge and beliefs based upon their current state of information. Consequently, the results of elicitation need be only good enough to make reasoned decisions or reasonable inferences. This chapter identifies how to elicit probabilities for large conditional probability tables in Bayesian networks. This chapter looks at Bayesian networks which are statistical models to describe and visualize in a compact graphical form the probabilistic relationships between variables of interest; the nodes of a graphical structure correspond to the variables, while directed edges between the nodes encode conditional independence relationships between them.

INTRODUCTION

A Bayesian network (BN) is an acyclic directed graph in which the vertices or nodes represent random variables and the directed arcs indicate probabilistic dependence (Kuipers et al., 2022). Each random variable is defined by a set of mutually exclusive and exhaustive states. The arcs in the network define probabilistic dependence between pairs of variables; the direction of the arc indicates which conditional probability distribution has been captured. Probability theory prohibits cycles in such a network; a cycle is a sequence of arcs that starts at one node and leads back to the same node. Each variable then contains a probability distribution conditioned on the nodes having arcs into the node in question (called the parents of the node). For variables with discrete states the probabilistic dependence of a random variable on its parents is captured in a conditional probability table (CPT). For each unique combination of the states of the parent variables, a distribution over the states of the dependent variable is specified.

DOI: 10.4018/978-1-6684-7766-3.ch009

As displayed in Figure 1 four variables (or nodes) are shown for a model of the weather in order to predict the chance of light, moderate or heavy rain during a farmer's planting season. The boxes show the probability distributions that are contained within each node. Note how the probability table expands as there are larger numbers of parents (entering arcs).

Figure 1. Sample Bayesian Network Showing Conditional Probability Tables

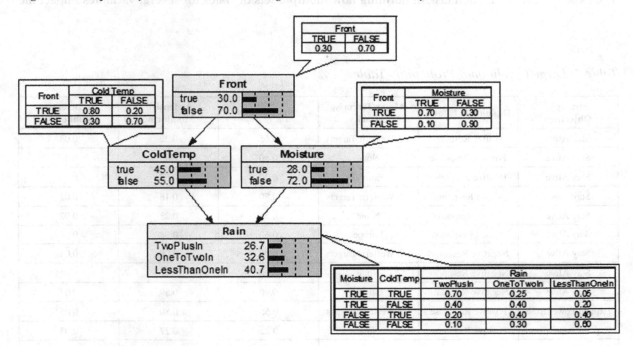

BNs are rooted in statistics, computer science and artificial intelligence; and are structured using conditional probability and Bayes' theorem, which capture dependency among system components (Hosseini & Ivanov, 2020). BNs are structured using conditional probability and Bayes' theorem, which capture dependency among system components (Hosseini & Ivanov, 2020). Traditionally, Bayesian network structure learning is often carried out at a central site, in which all data is gathered. However, in practice, data may be distributed across different parties (e.g., companies, devices) who intend to collectively learn a Bayesian network but are not willing to disclose information related to their data owing to privacy or security concerns (Ng & Zhang, 2022). BN's benefits are: (1) its high flexibility to model any causal relationships; (2) its capability to integrate information from any kind of sources, including experimental data, historical data and prior expert opinion and (3) its capability to answer probabilistic queries about them and to find out updated knowledge of the state of a subset of variables when other variables (the evidence variables) are observed (Rohmer, 2020).

For a BN, we may consider a network large if it contains variables with a large number of states, CPTs with a large number of distributions and/or a large number of variables. Acquiring numbers is only a part of the overall network engineering process. Experts are required to identify relevant variables, define their states and dependencies among the networks. These are commonly referred to as the structure of the network while the probability distributions are called the parameters of the network. We define the probability elicitation size of a network to be the number of probabilities that need to be elicited from experts.

Large CPTs present elicitors not only with the challenge of eliciting a large number of distributions that need to be consistent with one another, but also with simply navigating through large CPTs to compare closely related distributions with one another. Large CPTs also present problems for experts. The experts have the mental task of defining how multiple sets of states for several variables impact the

Table 1. Large Conditional Probability Table

Strategic Objectives	Diplomatic Efforts	Major Terrorist Attacks	Status Quo	Defensive Monitoring	No Defensive Monitoring
Stay Alive	Positive Response	US Western Targets	0.65	0.32	0.03
Stay Alive	Positive Response	None	0.50	0.45	0.05
Stay Alive	Positive Response	Europe	0.30	0.63	0.07
Stay Alive	Mixed Response	US Western Targets	0.80	0.18	0.02
Stay Alive	Mixed Response	None	0.70	0.28	0.02
Stay Alive	Mixed Response	Europe	0.60	0.38	0.01
Stay Alive	Negative Response	US Western Targets	0.90	0.09	0.01
Stay Alive	Negative Response	None	0.90	0.42	0.01
Stay Alive	Negative Response	Europe	0.90	0.59	0.03
Expand Power Base	Positive Response	US Western Targets	0.55	0.80	0.05
Expand Power Base	Positive Response	None	0.35	0.27	0.03
Expand Power Base	Positive Response	Europe	0.10	0.39	0.06
Expand Power Base	Mixed Response	US Western Targets	0.70	0.50	0.10
Expand Power Base	Mixed Response	None	0.55	0.13	0.04
Expand Power Base	Mixed Response	Europe	0.35	0.17	0.10
Expand Power Base	Negative Response	US Western Targets	0.10	0.25	0.03
Expand Power Base	Negative Response	None	0.70	0.42	0.06
Expand Power Base	Negative Response	Europe	0.55	0.59	0.02
Expand Power Base	Negative Response	US Western Targets	0.35	0.80	0.10
Power in Region	Positive Response	US Western Targets	0.10	0.27	0.02
Power in Region	Positive Response	None	0.70	0.39	0.03
Power in Region	Positive Response	Europe	0.55	0.50	0.06
Power in Region	Mixed Response	US Western Targets	0.35	0.13	0.03
Power in Region	Mixed Response	US Western Targets	0.10	0.17	0.10
Power in Region	Mixed Response	None	0.70	0.25	0.05
Power in Region	Negative Response	Europe	0.55	0.42	0.06
Power in Region	Negative Response	US Western Targets	0.40	0.59	0.01
Power in Region	Negative Response	US Western Targets	0.85	0.85	0.03
Power in Region	Negative Response	None	0.75	.037	0.07

conditional probabilities of the states for the target variable being assessed. See Table 1, which is taken from a notional model about whether Iran is creating a nuclear weapon.

While these techniques are useful in reducing the elicitation size of a network, this chapter is concerned primarily with non-deterministic, discrete CPTs, whose parents have dependent causal influences. These are tables for which distributions for every combination of states of the parents must be elicited.

When data is available, knowledge engineers take advantage of BN learning algorithms to fill in parameters. Sometimes, data is used to fill some cells of a CPT and experts fill in the remaining cells. Data may be derived from real world cases or other models such as simulations. In other cases, very large BNs may be built from a knowledge base of network fragments. Some top historical examples of large networks for which probability elicitation from experts has been documented are:

- The QMR-DT BN2O network was a medical diagnostic network having 600 disease nodes, 4000 possible findings and 40,000 links between diseases and findings. It used a noisy-or interaction model as an approximation so that approximately as many probabilities as links were required (D'Ambrosio, 1994).
- The BN for Computer-based Patient Case Simulation (CPCS) included 448 variables, 908 arcs and required 560 probabilities. It used a generalization of the noisy-or for its CPTs. (Pradhan et al., 1994).
- The esophageal cancer network contained almost 3000 probabilities (van der Gagg et al., 1999).
- The risk influence network contained 94 nodes, 104 links and 4719 probabilities (Hudson et al., 2001).
- A network for detecting swine flu [37] contains over 2400 probabilities for 42 variables (Geneen & van der Gaag, 2005).
- The University of Kentucky Bayesian Advisor Project model's probabilistic dependencies among university courses. A large university can easily have 3000 courses (Dekhytar, 2002).

This chapter contains six more major sections: accepted elicitation processes, expertise and probability elicitation, methods for eliciting probabilities, Bayesian network elicitation for large tables, conducting tests during probability elicitation and sensitivity and conclusions. Probability elicitation is almost always part of a model construction process. Elicitation of probabilities within the context of an iterative systems engineering methodology is examined in the next section titled Accepted Elicitation Processes. Here we summarize processes in the literature and propose our vision of the process.

Elicitation itself has numerous uncertainties. Experts arrive with different amounts and types of expertise. Humans tend to have biases that may skew the elicitation process. The elicitation method may be unfamiliar to the experts. The section, Expertise and Probability Elicitations, discusses human biases; dealing with multiple experts; and the reliability of different types of experts. Methods for Eliciting Probabilities (the fourth section) have been a subject of research for more than forty years. In much early work, the emphasis was on eliciting probabilities for single events. Eliciting distributions was also of interest. With the introduction of BNs twenty years ago, populating CPTs became a concern. Generally, one associates a facilitator with probability elicitation. However, the requirement to fill numerous CPTs in large BNs and the capability to develop graphical user interfaces has led to the use of computer-supported graphical tools to elicit probabilities. The section titled; Methods for Eliciting Probabilities covers methods that range from those for eliciting probabilities for single events to those for specifying continuous distributions.

The following section describes elicitation approaches for large CPTs in BNs. The section covers methods for specifying conditional probabilities as well as methods for navigating through large CPTs. The emphasis in this section is on automated tools for BNs. The section titled, Conducting Tests during Probability Elicitation, covers methods for 'testing' just elicited probabilities during an elicitation session. Although this topic has not been covered in the literature, the author has found it to be of great value in their personal experience. Three types of tests are covered in this section: consistency, coherence and what-if/sensitivity.

The final section, Summary and Conclusions, summarizes our findings and lays out our recommendations for future research. As a part of the recommendations, we also specify an approach for measuring elicitation quality. Measuring the quality of an elicitation process requires measuring how accurate the elicited values are, how efficient the process is and the quality of the process as perceived by the experts themselves. How to measure the accuracy of the elicited results depends upon the nature of the objective of the model being constructed. Efficiency includes not only the time required to capture probabilities, but also the time to train the experts. Experts not only need to find the process easy to perform but must also feel comfortable about the numbers that they are giving.

ACCEPTED ELICITATION PROCESSES

In this section we first summarize previous historical research regarding the role of probability elicitation within the context of BN construction and use. We then present our view of the overall BN construction process and the role of probability elicitation within that process.

Those who construct BNs for practical applications need to treat it as a system engineering process. Nicholson (2003) proposes that the life cycle of a BN follows an iterative approach that includes the following steps:

1. Building the BN
   a. Obtain variables, structure, parameters and preferences
   b. When data is available, combine expert elicitation with knowledge discovery
2. Validation/Evaluation
   a. Exercise network with selected cases,
   b. Perform sensitivity analysis,
   c. Test for accuracy
3. Field Testing
   a. Carry out alpha/beta testing,
   b. Perform acceptance testing
4. Industrial Use
   a. Collect statistics
5. Refinement
   a. Update procedures,
   b. Perform regression testing

In this process, the role of eliciting probabilities is confined to the first step. Feedback is provided by steps two through four.

Laskey & Mahoney (2000) broke the network construction task into the following steps:

1. Developing the network structure.
   a. Identify the variables of interest,
   b. Define their possible states and
   c. Indicate relationships among the variables.
2. Eliciting the probabilities and
3. Evaluating the resulting network
   d. Examine its behavior using a set of cases and
   e. Perform sensitivity analyses.

These steps are often overlapping as well as iterative. For example, because thinking about the probabilities raises questions about definitions and dependencies, elements of the network structure are frequently modified during probability elicitation. Often, it is best to develop a small segment of the network structure; then elicit and evaluate; and if satisfied, continue developing another small segment of the network; etc. Evaluation techniques, restricted to limited subsets of the network, are often used to provide immediate feedback during the probability elicitation.

Wang (2000) describes the probability elicitation itself as an iterative process with the following steps:

1. Setup
   a. Select expert(s)
   b. Train expert(s)
   c. Identify aspects of problem to elicit
2. Elicit discrete probability distributions or summaries of continuous distributions
3. Fit probability distribution to the summaries (if using continuous distributions)
4. Assess adequacy of the elicitation.

Notably, the setup stage listed here is missing in the previous process descriptions. Yet this stage is vitally important. In selecting the experts, the BN constructor needs to be aware of the scope of their expertise. One option is to elicit different parts of a network using different experts. Another option is to combine the opinions of experts whose knowledge overlaps.

Training is another important aspect of setup. It is important that the experts understand what is being asked of them. The obvious purpose of training is to familiarize the experts with the elicitation techniques that will be used during the elicitation sessions. A second purpose is to educate the experts so as to minimize the biases that characterize probability elicitation.

The traditional probability elicitation process for a CPT of a single variable conditioned on several others, first proposed by (Spetzler & Stael von Holstein, 1975) and updated by (Merkhofer, 1987), has five steps:

1. Motivating the experts about the importance of their task,
2. Structuring the definition of the variable for which the probabilities are being elicited,
3. Conditioning the probability distribution upon both the explicit variables in the model as well as the average values of important variables that have been left out of the model (here is where the elicitor must combat the many cognitive biases to which humans are susceptible),

4. Asking the questions that the expert(s) will answer to provide the probability distributions (see the next section) and

5. Verifying that the expert(s) are really comfortable with and believe the results (this is where we check consistency with other distributions in the conditional table and coherence of the marginal distribution after the table is completed).

PROPOSED PROCESS

The proposed integration of these processes is shown in Figure 2. The core process appears at the top: build, validate, use and refine the BN. There are feedback loops between the first two and last two functions. The block of boxes down the left-hand side, which points to the top left box, decomposes the "Build the Bayesian Network" function. The blocks of boxes pointing to the block on the left-hand side provide a decomposition of the probability elicitation sub-functions within the decomposition of "Build the Bayesian Network". There are three more decompositions: the first is for "Prepare the Experts"; the second is to "Elicit the Needed Probabilities"; the last is for "Test the Added Nodes and Refine".

The first function, "Build the Bayesian Network", is the one of interest for this chapter and is broken into four sub-functions shown vertically on the left-hand side of Figure 2. To the extent feasible, we provide some training for the experts. Often, we will simply work with them to set the probabilities for a few nodes in a small BN. Then we show them how the network behaves in response to the probabilities embedded in the BN. This provides the experts with immediate feedback on the impact of the probabilities that they provide. It also helps them feel more comfortable with the BN.

Figure 2. Building a Bayesian Network

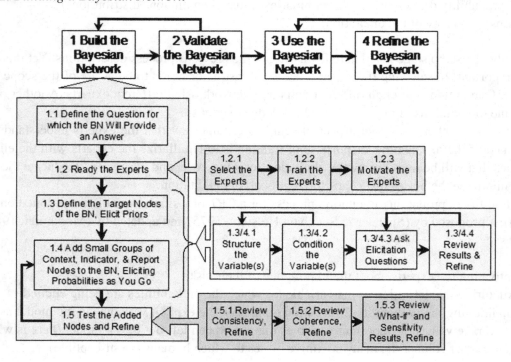

We use a canonical representation of BNs (Mahoney et al., 2005). In this representation, we separate the variables into different classes, depending upon their function within the network: context, causal, hypothesis, indicator and report (see Figure 3). Hypothesis nodes, sometimes called target nodes, are those variables that are of interest to the network's user. Context nodes set the stage for other nodes in the network. Often their values are known to the network's user. Context nodes influence some or all of the other classes of variables and so have arcs into the other nodes. The causes or conditioning variables of the hypothesis nodes have arcs into the hypothesis nodes. Indicators are features of the hypotheses or context that are observable. The indicator nodes have arcs entering them from the nodes for which they are indicators; the most important are the hypothesis indicators, but there are often important indicators of the context nodes as well. Finally, there are often reports from sensors, humans, tests, etc. that provide information about the indicators and perhaps some context nodes. There is an important distinction between our uncertainty about the domain and our uncertainty in the reports. Domain uncertainty is uncertainty about the 'world' that our BN represents. Uncertainty about a report's accuracy needs to be modeled based on the reporting entities' characteristics that affect their capability to report truthfully.

Figure 3. Building a Bayesian Network

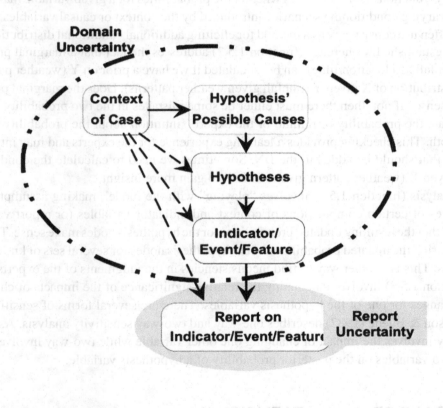

To build a BN, we always need to start with the purpose (question(s) to be answered) of any model; this is function 1.1 in Figure 2. The questions that need to be answered allow us to structure the target or hypothesis nodes of the BN (function 1.3). We have found that the experts get significant insight into their model if we initially elicit the prior probabilities of these target nodes without any conditioning variables. Then as we elicit the conditional distributions, we create an active learning process that puts their training into immediate practice. The experts realize how uncertain they are about what the probabilities are and are anxious to start adding conditioning variables.

Once we have established the hypothesis nodes, we ask the relevant experts about some important conditioning (context or causal) nodes to add or some important indicator nodes to add (function 1.4). We structure these variables in terms of the relevant states or possibilities and then begin eliciting the probability distributions. As small groups of probability nodes are added to the BN along with the appropriate conditional probability distributions, we test these results (function 1.5). The tests include consistency, coherence and what-if/sensitivity analysis. They provide immediate feedback to the experts so that problems with the elicited network may be discovered during the elicitation process. These tests do not replace the core process step "Validate the Bayesian Network", but they do make this step much easier to complete.

Consistency (function 1.5.1) addresses whether the probabilities for a given variable make sense with respect to the varying conditioning scenarios introduced by the context or causal variables for the given variable. We often use consistency as a method for eliciting additional conditional distributions once one distribution is established. Coherence (function 1.5.2) addresses the fact that a marginal probability for variable X (rainfall at a location/time) can be calculated if we have a prior on Y (weather patterns) and a conditional distribution of X given Y (rainfall given weather patterns). Does the marginal probability on rainfall make sense? If not, then there must either be some mistakes in the two probability distributions used to calculate the probability of rainfall or the experts' intuition about the probability of rainfall is incorrect or both. This checking provides a learning experience for the experts and may introduce some new variables that should be added to the BN. Sometimes we need to calculate the conditional probability of Y given X (weather pattern given rainfall) to gain more insight.

What-if analysis (function 1.5.3) involves "playing" with the model, making assumptions that we know the values of certain combinations of context and indicator variables (or report variables) and evaluating whether the resulting updated probabilities for the hypothesis nodes make sense. Typically, this involves comparing the updated probabilities of the hypothesis nodes for several sets of known values for the other nodes. This is another way to find inconsistencies in the judgments of the experts. Sensitivity analysis (function 1.5.3) involves calculating the relative significance of the impacts of changes in one variable on changes for one of the hypothesis variables. There are several forms of sensitivity analysis available. Watson & Buede (1987) describes one-way and two-way sensitivity analysis. As their names imply, one-way involves the impact of changing one other variable while two-way involves the impact of changing two variables on the posterior probability of a hypothesis variable.

EXPERTISE AND PROBABILITY ELICITATION

This section is concerned with characteristics of experts from whom probabilities may be elicited and address's function 1.2 of Figure 2. The first subsection addresses the calibration of experts and the heuristics/biases exhibited by all humans in making probability statements. The second subsection describes ways in which the judgments of multiple experts may be combined. The final subsection presents research on the reliability and consistency of different types of experts.

CALIBRATION AND BIASES IN PROBABILITY ELICITATION

This subsection first describes how to establish how well calibrated experts are when they provide probability judgments. The second subsection describes some of the many heuristics and biases that humans have in providing expert judgments.

Before discussing the overconfidence that most people exhibit when making probability statements, we need to define calibration. Calibration means that when an expert states that a specific event has a probability of 0.9 of happening, this event fits into an ensemble (or group) of events, all of which have a probability of 0.9. So, we should see that 90% of the events in this ensemble do occur for the expert to be calibrated. So, if an expert says 100 events of various sorts have a probability of 0.9 of occurring over the course of a year, roughly 90 of those events should occur. Similarly, 70% should occur for events assigned a probability of 0.7 and so on. We can plot the probabilities that an expert assign and the percentages of events occurring as shown in Figure 4. Here, the stated probabilities are on the horizontal axis and the frequencies of occurrence are on the vertical axis. Many people are well-calibrated at the 50-50 point; this is a point of symmetry for events that have two states (happen or do not happen). However, many people do not exhibit this symmetry at 50-50; for these people we see underprediction or overprediction.

Overconfidence includes the overprediction and overextremity cases shown in this figure. Overconfidence means estimating probabilities that are closer to 1.0 than should be the case if overconfidence is present. For overextremity experts provide probabilities that re too high for likely events (probability greater than 0.5) and too low for unlikely events (probability less than 0.5).

Short-term weather forecasters are the only group that has demonstrated good calibration (Murphy & Winkler, 1984). The standard reasons given for this calibration are that short-term weather forecasters get nearly immediate feedback about whether they were right or wrong on a continuous basis. Also, (at least in the past) the weather forecasters were paid a salary based on what is called a "proper scoring rule". A proper scoring rule is a transformation of the probability estimated into a reward such that the estimator is motivated to provide their true belief rather than an over or underestimate. An example of a proper scoring rule *is* $k \bullet ln(p)$ (p is the probability given by the expert and k is a constant).

Figure 4. Representation of Calibration of Probability Judgments

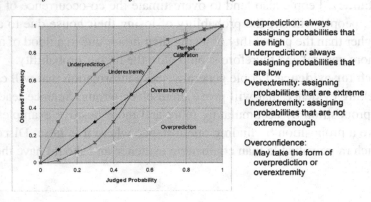

It is well known that humans are overconfident in making most probability judgments; that is, humans think they know more than they do (Lichtenstein & Newman, 1967; Yates et al., 1998; Klayman et al., 1999). There is some evidence that people are almost always likely to be overconfident on hard questions but underconfident on easy questions (Lichtenstein et al., 1982). The overconfidence bias manifests itself in at least two ways. First, people will express greater confidence that they are right than is justified by the data (including their own real-life experiences). Second, when asked for a probability distribution on a variable, the variance for that variable will almost always be too small; the distribution will be too narrow.

In their foundational work on judgment under uncertainty, Tversky & Kahneman (1974) discuss common biases of humans when asked for probability judgments:

- **Representativeness**: In making predictions, humans will make their judgments based upon current descriptions and not consider how relevant the description is to the prediction or the reliability of the evidence.

- **Base rate neglect**: Humans tend to judge descriptions of others by how representative the description is of a category. In doing this they usually ignore the prior probability for the category. Interestingly, persons don't ignore the prior if they are given no other information.

- **Small sample fallacy**: Humans tend to ignore sample sizes when making probability judgments. They expect small samples to mirror the statistics of the population. Consequently, they will overconfidently predict tails if heads appears in four out of the first five flips of a fair coin.

- **Regression fallacy**: Humans tend to assume that relative performance is consistent from test to test. So, they expect those who perform best on one test will continue to do so. However, individuals vary in their performance from one test to the next.

- **Availability**: Humans tend to attach higher probability to events that they recall readily. Recent events, or those that are more salient to the individual, impact their perception of the frequency of such events. How readily an event may be imagined may also be a factor. For example, accidents that make the news are judged more likely as accidents than are just as likely accidents that do not tend to make the news. Specifically, a death by a firearm assault is about as likely as death by accidental falling; yet most people would think the former is much more likely than the latter due to firearm assaults appearing the news more often.

- **Anchoring and Adjustment**: Humans will often start with an initial value and adjust away from it to obtain related values. In general, such adjustments are insufficient, being biased towards the starting value.

- **Conjunction fallacy**: People also tend to overestimate the co-occurrence of conjunctive events. As an example, people will say the probability of losing their house due to a flood caused by a hurricane is higher than the probability of losing their house due to a flood of any sort. Clearly the latter case is more general and therefore should have the higher probability.

- **Selective search for evidence**: People generally seeks information that will confirm their beliefs rather than seeking evidence that will prove themselves wrong. Science teaches us that we can never prove a proposition by accumulating more and more positive examples that it is true, but we can disprove a proposition by finding one instance where it is false. Disconfirming evidence is therefore much more valuable than confirming evidence and should have the effect of reducing our overconfidence.

DEBIASING STRATEGIES FOR PROBABILITY ELICITATION

One of the challenges in training experts for a probability elicitation is to reduce their biases. A number of approaches for debiasing experts have been proposed.

Historically, significant psychological research was done in this area through 1980. Lichtenstein et al. (1982) summarizes the state of the art as of 1980. Fischhoff (1982) suggests the following elicitation support techniques that might be promising in helping experts avoid many of the biases.

- Faulty Tasks
  - Unfair task
- Raise stakes
- Clarify instructions/stimuli
- Discourage second-guessing
- Use better response modes
- Ask few questions
  - Misunderstood task
- Demonstrate alternative goal
- Demonstrate semantic disagreement
- Demonstrate impossibility of task
- Demonstrate overlooked distinction
- Faulty Judges
  - Perfectible individuals
- Warn of problem
- Describe problem
- Provide personalized feedback
- Train extensively
  - Incorrigible individuals
- Replace them
- Recalibrate their responses
- Plan on error
- Mismatch between Judges and Tasks
  - Restructuring
- Make knowledge explicit
- Search for discrepant information
- Decompose problem
- Consider alternative situations
  - Education
- Rely on substantive experts
- Educate from childhood

Klayman et al. (1999) demonstrates an example of task restructuring that works; namely, changing the way the question is asked. Much of the research on overconfidence has been to elicit the fractals for a specific random variable such as "How many calories are there in 1/2-cup of bread pudding?" [Klayman et al. (1999), p. 218]. However, if the question is changed to a two-choice question such as

"Which of these nations has higher life expectancy, averaged across men and women: (A) Argentina, or (B) Canada?" followed by an expression of confidence, Klayman et al. (1999) show there is much less overconfidence with the two-choice response but still some overconfidence in the statement of confidence (see the discussion of indirect versus direct elicitation techniques in the section on Methods for Eliciting a Single Probability). The direct techniques would be expected to have much higher overconfidence issues than the indirect techniques.

Larrick (2004) suggests the following structure for debiasing:

- Motivational strategies
  - Incentives (e.g., proper scoring rule for salary for weather forecasters)
  - Accountability (responsible for explaining judgment)
- Cognitive strategies
  - "Consider the opposite" (ask "What are some reasons why my judgment might be wrong") – there is evidence this reduces overconfidence, hindsight bias and anchoring effects (Arkes, 1991; Mussweiler et al., 2000).
  - Training in rules such as sunk costs and law of large numbers (works for these simple issues)
  - Training in representations (examples include reasoning about frequencies reduces the chances of reduced effects of the conjunction fallacy compared to reasoning about probabilities) – this is an example of restructuring the task
  - Training in biases (little research on the effectiveness of this)
- Technological strategies
  - Group decision making (there are possibilities for both improvement and worsening)
  - Linear models, multiattribute utility analysis and decision analysis
    § Proper and improper linear models (there is substantial evidence that linear models when they are appropriate (proper) and inappropriate (improper) are better than intuitive judgment)
    § Multiattribute utility analysis (little research on the effectiveness of this)
    § Decision analysis (little research on the effectiveness of this)
  - Decision support systems (little research on the effectiveness of this)

WAYS TO INCORPORATE JUDGMENTS FROM MULTIPLE EXPERTS

Typically, we want to obtain probability assessments from multiple experts so that we are not dependent upon one person's judgment. Naturally, there are several approaches for gathering judgments from multiple experts:

- Elicit individual probability distributions, then combine these distributions mathematically
  - Take a weighted average of the individual distributions
- Weight probabilities for fixed values of X
- Weight values of X for fixed fractiles across distributions
- Compute the geometric mean (with weights) for fixed values of X
  - Embed these distributions into a multivariate named distribution (e.g., the normal) or a hierarchical probability distribution

- ○   Use the axiomatic Bayesian approach defined by (Morris, 1977; Morris, 1983). This method uses Bayes rule by using the probability distributions of the experts as likelihood information to update the decision maker's prior probability distribution to get a posterior probability distribution given the inputs of the experts
- Elicit individual probability distributions, then use a group process (e.g., Delphi or nominal group technique) to create a consensus distribution
- Elicit a consensus distribution directly from the group of experts without establishing a unique distribution for each expert. This can be done via a decision conference (Phillips, 1999).

These last two approaches are termed "behavioral" methods. An intuitive approach would be to "eyeball" some combination of individual expert judgments. Each of these approaches has advantages and disadvantages. Clemen & Winkler (1999) conclude:

"We have reviewed a variety of methods for combining probability distributions in risk analysis. The empirical results reviewed above suggest that mathematical aggregation outperforms intuitive aggregation and that mathematical and behavioral approaches tend to be similar in performance, with mathematical rules having a slight edge. A comparison of behavioral approaches yields no clear-cut conclusions. As for mathematical combination methods, simple combination rules (e.g., a simple average) tend to perform quite well. More complex rules sometimes outperform the simple rules, but they can be somewhat sensitive, leading to poor performance in some instances. All of these conclusions should be qualified by noting that they represent tendencies over a series of different empirical studies, generally conducted in an experimental setting as opposed to occurring in the context of a real-world risk analysis. These studies do not, unfortunately, directly assess the precise issue that needs to be addressed. For the purpose of the typical risk analysis in which probability distributions are to be combined, but limited past data are available, the real question is, "What is the best way to combine the judgments?" Thus, while we should pay careful attention to available empirical results and learn from them, we should think hard about their generalizability to realistic risk-analysis applications."

We would add that the behavioral approaches are the most difficult to replicate in research settings and therefore are most likely to have performance characteristics that lie outside the envelope of the empirical research results. Phillips (1999) work was not available when the Clemen & Winkler (1999) paper was written; this work by Phillips provides a very convincing argument for the use of a behavioral approach.

CAN EXPERTS PROVIDE RELIABLE, CONSISTENT PROBABILITY JUDGEMENTS?

With the advent of artificial intelligence and the resulting search for experts by knowledge engineers, psychologists began asking how to define and identify experts. Historically people have defined experts as follows (Weiss & Shanteau, 2004):

- "A man who has made all the mistakes which can be made in a very narrow field" (Niels Bohr)
- "One who predicts the job will take the longest and cost the most" (Arthur Bloch)
- "A damn fool a long way away from home" (Carl Sandberg)

- "A man who has stopped thinking" (Frank Lloyd Wright)
- "One who can take something you already know and make it sound confusing" (Anonymous)

Weiss & Shanteau (2004) explore this question of experts in some detail and identify the following three statistical characteristics that ought to be present among the experts in any field:

- Consensus: between-expert reliability
  - Medical Pathologists: 0.55
  - Short term weather forecasters: 0.95
- Internal consistency: within-expert reliability across judgments
  - Medical Pathologists: 0.50
  - Short term weather forecasters: 0.98
- Increasing within-expert reliability with experience
  - Student auditors: 0.66
  - Mid-level auditors: 0.76
  - Full partner auditors: 0.83

The second tier of bullets shows some statistical results from several different fields of study that claim to have experts.

Weiss & Shanteau (2004) then proceed to summarize eight different domains of study (e.g., short-term weather forecasters, polygraphers) in four levels of expertise on the basis of the first two measures discussed above. (Data on increasing within-expert reliability was not readily available for many domains.) The lowest level of expertise reviewed was random; these were domains in which the consensus and internal consistency did not justify relying on the experts compared to flipping a coin. The next level up was called restricted; here the experts were better than flipping a coin, but their judgments should be highly suspect and used with caution. The third level of expertise was called competent; here the experts could be relied upon to be substantially better than flipping a coin but still were not what some people might consider experts. The fourth and highest level was called "Aided Decisions" because the experts in this domain could truly be relied upon to improve the ability of other people in their domain to make decisions as shown in Table 2.

Table 3 shows the grouping of a much larger set of domains, based upon the expert judgment of a set of psychologists. The domains shown in italics are those repeated from the table above, which were based on data as well as expert judgment. Assuming this table is correct, we can see some trends across domains that cause them to be placed more to the right or more to the left in such a table. The domains on the left are relatively stable in terms of their "facts" compared to those on the right. Also, the domains on the left deal more with science and logic while those on the right are more heavily skewed towards people.

Tetlock (1999) addressed the limited ability of political science analysts to make correct judgments about future events. Table 4 shows some of Tetlock's key results. Again, we find political science experts to be little better than chance and subject to significant overconfidence. The following quotation from Tetlock (2002) summarizes the meaning of this table.

"Tetlock (1999) drew on a longitudinal data base of predictions of a wide array of outcomes from 1985 to 2010. This chapter considers the predictions that experts offered for the 5-year futures of the Soviet Union in 1988, of South Africa in 1989, of Kazakhstan in 1992, of the European Monetary Union in 1991 and of Canada in 1992. … All participants received some graduate training in social science or

Table 2. Levels of Expertise for Domains of Study [Weiss & Shanteau, 2004]

Aided Decisions	Competent	Restricted	Random
Short-Term Weather Forecasters Consensus: 0.95 Int'l Cons: 0.98	Livestock Judges Consensus: 0.50 Int'l Cons: 0.96	Clinical Psychologists Consensus: 0.40 Int'l Cons: 0.44	Stockbrokers Consensus: 0.32 Int'l Cons: 0.40
Auditors Consensus: 0.76 Int'l Cons: 0.90	Grain Inspectors Consensus: 0.60 Int'l Cons: 0.62	Parole Officers Consensus: 0.55 Int'l Cons: 0.50	Polygraphers Consensus: 0.33 Int'l Cons: 0.91

Table 3. Broader Assessment of Domains by Four Levels of Expertise [Weiss & Shanteau, 2004]

Aided Decisions	Competent	Restricted	Random
Short-Term Weather Forecasters	Chess Masters	Clinical Psychologists	Polygraphers
Astronomers	Livestock Judges	Pathologists	Managers
Test Pilots	Grain Inspectors	Psychiatrists	Stockbrokers
Auditors	Photo Interpreters	Student Admissions	Parole Officers
Physicists	Soil Judges	Intelligence Analysts	Court Judges

history, specialized in one or more of the regions under examination and earned their livelihoods either as advanced graduate students in comparative politics and international relations (n = 58), university professors (n = 51), policy analysts (n = 17), intelligence analysts in government service (n = 39), or journalists in the employ of the mass media (n = 9).

… "Among other things, experts responded to a working-style questionnaire (designed, in part, to assess individual differences in preferences for parsimony and explanatory closure) and also rated a number of probabilities necessary for comparing their belief updating with the normative Bayesian model. Respondents were given detailed guidance on how to use the subjective-probability scales that ranged from 0 to 1.0. Experts rated their probabilities that: (1) their interpretations of the underlying forces operating in the scenario was correct (e.g., that their theory or model of the Soviet Union was correct) (prior probability of H); (2) the most influential alternative interpretation of the underlying forces was correct (e.g., that a different theory or model of the Soviet Union was correct) (prior probability of H~); (3) various possible futures for [x] would occur, assuming that: (a) their own understanding of the underlying forces shaping events was correct (conditional probability of outcome given H); and (b) the most influential alternative interpretation of the underlying forces was correct (conditional probability of outcome given H~). The 'possible futures' were designed to be logically exclusive and exhaustive. For example, in the Soviet case, the scenarios included a strengthening, a reduction, or no change in communist party control.

"After the specified forecasting interval had elapsed, 78% of the original forecasters were successfully contacted and questioned again. After exploring experts' ability to recall their original answers, experts were reminded of the original forecasts and confidence estimates. Experts rated their agreement with 9 propositions that could theoretically either cushion the disappointment of "disconfirmation" or deflate the euphoria of 'confirmation.' Experts also answered 'retrospective-probability' questions that assessed the degree to which they updated their prior probabilities in an approximately Bayesian fash-

Table 4. Tetlock's Key Results [Tetlock, 2004]

Predicting the Future of	Status of Forecast	Judged Prior Probability (Before Outcome Known)	Judged Posterior Probability (After Outcome Known)	Bayesian Predicted Posterior Probability
Soviet Union	Inaccurate	0.74	0.70	0.49
	Accurate	0.69	0.83	0.80
South Africa	Inaccurate	0.72	0.69	0.42
	Accurate	0.70	0.77	0.82
EMU	Inaccurate	0.66	.068	
	Accurate	0.71	0.78	0.85
Canada	Inaccurate	0.65	0.67	0.39
	Accurate	0.68	0.81	0.79

ion (although this was done in only 4 of the 7 forecasting domains examined here). The retrospective probabilities were compared with the posterior probabilities derived by combining the relevant prior probabilities and conditional probabilities collected at the pre-test (described in the paragraph above). ... Across all seven domains, experts were only slightly more accurate than one would expect from chance (the proverbial dart-throwing, blindfolded chimpanzee who poses such tough competition for financial forecasters). Almost as many experts as not thought that the Soviet Communist Party would remain firmly in the saddle of power in 1993, that Canada was doomed by 1997, that neo-fascism would prevail in Pretoria by 1994, that the EMU would collapse by 1997, that Bush would be reelected in 1992 and that the Persian Gulf crisis would be resolved peacefully. Moreover, although experts only sporadically exceeded chance predictive accuracy, they regularly assigned subjective probabilities that exceeded the scaling anchors for 'just guessing'. Most experts, especially those who valued parsimony and explanatory closure, thought they know more than they did. Moreover, these margins of error were larger than those customarily observed in laboratory research on the calibration of confidence. Across all predictions elicited across domains, experts who assigned confidence probabilities of 80% or higher were correct only 45% of the time, a hit rate not appreciably higher than that for experts who endorsed the "just guessing" subjective probabilities of 0.50 and 0.33 (for 2 and 3 outcome scenarios, respectively). Expertise thus may not translate into predictive accuracy, but it does translate into the ability to generate explanations for predictions that experts themselves find so compelling that the result is massive over-confidence." (Tetlock, 2002).

METHODS FOR ELICITING PROBABILITIES

This section addresses the "Ask Elicitation Questions" which is function 1.3/4.3 of Figure 2. The topics included here are a discussion of methods for eliciting a single probability (probability of a Heads resulting from a coin toss), extremely low probabilities (probability of being struck by lightning in a single year), a probability distribution for a continuous random variable (number of inches of rainfall during a year) and a probability distribution for a discrete random variable (number of Category 4 or greater hurricanes in a single hurricane season).

METHODS FOR ELICITING A SINGLE PROBABILITY

Many methods have been developed for eliciting a single probability about an event from an expert. Some are direct, in that they ask the expert to reply with a number and some are indirect, the expert replies with a relationship (e.g., greater than another probability) and the numbers are inferred/calculated from the relationships. Special attention is given to using words for expressing probabilities since experts seem to prefer this and much has been devoted to this topic.

DIRECT METHODS

Consider an example in which we are seeking a probability distribution on the amount of rainfall in a particular farming region during the planting season, which is 3 weeks long.

Table 5. Direct Methods for Eliciting a Single Probability

Method	Query
Direct (asking for numbers)	What is the probability that an event (there will be more than $\underline{2}$ inches of rainfall) will take place?
Fractiles (percentiles)	What is the probability that the rainfall will be less than or equal to $\underline{2}$ inches?
Quantile (inverse of fractile)	What amount of rainfall is associated with a probability of $\underline{0.5}$, such that it is equally likely that the rainfall will be above or below that value. (Note, other fractiles will have some ratio other than equally likely; .8 would be 4 times more likely to be below versus above.)
Odds (Log odds, Log-log odds – not shown)	What are the odds (1 chance in ?) that there will be $\underline{2}$ inches or less of rain? Note, ? can range from a number near zero to a number near infinity.
Analytical Hierarchy Process (numerical mode)	How many times more likely is it that there will be less than $\underline{2}$ inches of rain compared to more than equal to $\underline{2}$ inches of rain? The answer can be larger or smaller than 1.0.
Confidence intervals	How many times out of 1000 samples would less than $\underline{2}$ inches of rain?

Underlined quantity is a reference point supplied by the elicitor.
This reference point can be varied as needed, say to one or a half inch.

INDIRECT METHODS

Indirect methods ask for relationships that can be converted to numbers. These relationships either use words to represent numbers or are asking for ordinal judgments that can be combined to produce an estimate of the ratio scale for probabilities. Examples of indirect methods are:

- Words with numbers attached (see the Appendix)
- Hypothetical data (in light of sample evidence)
- Standard gambles
- Probability wheel (or other device) as metric
- Bar graphs (pie chart slices)

- Analytical Hierarchy Process (verbal or graphical mode)
- Ranking most likely; conversion to numbers (e.g., rank order centroid)
- Conjoint analysis
- Balance beam comparisons

Note, the last three will be discussed later. They typically require more possibilities than an event and its complement.

Table 6. Indirect Methods for Eliciting a Single Probability

Method	Query
Words with numbers attached	Which of the following words best describes your uncertainty that there will be less than 2 inches of rain?
Standard gambles	Is the probability of getting less than 2 inches of rain larger or smaller than drawing a club from a deck of 52 playing cards?
Probability wheel (or other device) as metric	Is the probability of getting 2 inches or less of rain bigger or smaller than the pointer landing on orange after spinning the wheel?
Bar graphs (pie chart slices)	Is the probability of getting 2 inches or less of rain more or less likely than the percent of space taken by the bar graph?
Analytical Hierarchy Process (verbal or graphical mode)	The same as in Table 5 above for direct methods, except the expert selects a word from a list or slides a bar graph to provide the judgment.
Ranking a set of events from most to least likely; then conversing these ranks to numbers (e.g., rank order centroid)	Rank order the events from most to least likely (make sure they are mutually exclusive and collectively exhaustive). Then use a formula such as rank order centroid to calculate the probabilities; $$w_i = \left(\frac{1}{K}\right)\sum_{j=i}^{K}\left(\frac{1}{r_j}\right)$$
Conjoint Analysis	Establish rank order relations (e.g., more likely, equal or less likely) between combinations of the events. Use these relations to infer a set of numbers that best meets the constraints of the relations.

Methods for Eliciting Extremely low Probabilities

The elicitation of low probability events is often very important in decision analysis and forecasting. Yet, this is a very difficult task for experts. The most common approach for helping experts think through this elicitation is to develop a set of reference events for which frequency information is available, giving anchors to the experts for using their expertise and selecting some events that seem to be similar. For example,

- Is this event more likely than getting a straight flush, pat hand in five cards draw poker?
- Is this event more likely than getting a straight flush, pat hand in five cards draw poker twice in a row?

Methods for Eliciting Probability Distributions for Continuous Random Variables

There are four primary methods for eliciting the probability distribution of a continuous random variable, such as the amount of rainfall during a year at a given location.

- Assume a named distribution, elicit the two or three key parameters necessary. For a normal distribution it would be the mean and standard deviation (Gokhale & Press, 1982). This is a quick and dirty method that is appropriate if analytic methods using calculus are being used but adds error when we need to create discrete distributions for decision trees or BNs.
- Break X (amount of rainfall) into segments, elicit probabilities or fractiles for each segment. This is an extension of the fractile method for events.
- Define key fractiles (e.g., 0.5 (median), 0.75, 0.25), elicit the values of X (amount of rainfall) that are associated with these fractiles and use as is.
- Define key fractiles (e.g., 0.5 (median), 0.75, 0.25), elicit the values of X (amount of rainfall) that are associated with these fractiles and fit a named distribution to this data.

For example, you can examine the following six methods of eliciting the correlation coefficient between weight and height in a population of male MBA students.

1. Verbal (non-numeric) description on a 7-point scale ranging from `very strong negative relationship' to `very strong relationship'.
2. Direct statement by specifying a value between -1 and 1.
3. Given a randomly selected person's percentile for weight, direct statement about that person's percentile for the height.
4. Given the random selection of two people and conditional on person A having greater weight than person B, direct assessment of the probability that person A also has greater height than person B.
5. Given a randomly selected person, direct assessment off the probability the person is below a specified percentile for both variables.
6. Given a randomly selected person and conditional on the person being below a specified percentile for weight, direct assessment of the probability that the person is also below that percentile for height.

Methods for Eliciting Probability Distributions for Discrete Random Variables

A discrete random variable is one that has more than two possible states but less than an infinite number, typically discrete random variables have three to seven states. A probability is needed for each state; these probabilities need to sum to 1.0.

The key methods for eliciting probability distributions for discrete random variables are the same as those discussed in the section above titled "Methods for Eliciting a Single Probability". The most commonly used (in our experience) are:

- Direct assignment of a probability to each segment of the random variable
- Analytical hierarchy process (numerical, verbal or graphical mode)
- Verbal categories for each segment of the random variable, then normalize to sum to 1.0
- Ranking the segments and then computing probabilities based on some formula using the ranks as inputs
- Probability wheel with as many different colored sections as there are segments for the variable
- Bar graph adjustments for each segment of the random variable, then normalize to sum to 1.0 (note this is the same as the graphical mode for the Analytical Hierarchy Process)
- Balance beam (or some other conjoint analysis technique) on the segments of the random variable, then normalize to sum to 1.0

This last approach is the most accurate in our opinion. Other approaches that we have good success with are the bar graph adjustments, verbal word assignments and direct assignments (with a lot of discussion and coaching of the experts). However, there are many concerns for eliciting probabilities from experts such as the following:

- Be very vigilant for overconfidence. This can be seen in probability distributions with little variance and numbers too close to zero and one (an example of a small variance). This can be combated by
  ○ First asking for the probabilities of the tails of the distribution for a continuous variable or the probabilities for the least and most likely states of a discrete distribution. For continuous distributions, give the experts many examples of how the extremes could occur, then ask them for their probabilities, then ask them to explain the reasons that might be in a newspaper article saying one of the extremes did occur, then ask them to update their judgments.
  ○ For a discrete random variable, ask them to think of many reasons why the least likely segment could occur, or the most likely segment could not occur. In some cases, we have set ground rules that the experts could not use numbers higher than 0.9 or 0.95 and lower than 0.1 or 0.05.
- Fight the use of zero or one for probabilities. Suggest these numbers mean the expert would be willing to accept the death penalty if the event with a zero probability did occur or the event with a probability of one did not occur.
- Review specific cognitive biases with the experts from time to time.

BAYESIAN NETWORK ELICITATION FOR LARGE TABLES

The graphical structure of a BN reveals dependencies and independencies among a set of variables of interest. The underlying parameters of a BN are distributions. Variables with parents within the network require the specification of conditional probability distributions. BNs provide benefits in knowledge representation and efficient inference computation; methods to improve these two benefits have developed in tandem with the proliferation of personal computers and their associated graphical user interfaces. Consequently, approaches for eliciting probabilities for BNs take advantage of computer-based graphical and computational tools.

In this section, we first present a general approach for eliciting probabilities within the context of a BN. Then, we present methods for eliciting conditional probability distributions for one or more conditioning variables (probability of rainfall during a year given the presence or absence of El Nino) and for a large table of conditional probability distributions when several conditioning variables are needed (probability of rainfall during a year given various country locations, weather patterns and environmental conditions).

ELICIATATION APPROACH ELEMENTS

A Bayesian network probability elicitation approach is a set of techniques used to elicit the numbers in the CPTs of a BN. An elicitation approach must address three types of elicitation issues: eliciting probabilities within a single distribution; eliciting several related distributions within the context of a single CPT; and comparing the impacts of closely related variables on one another.

Many of the techniques for eliciting single probabilities and distributions are described above in the Methods for Eliciting Probabilities section. Much of the elicitation literature was written before BNs with reasonably friendly user interfaces were available. Relatively little research has been done for eliciting probabilities using the software interfaces of available BN software. Also, because BN inference algorithms for continuous variables are not widely available, elicitation research has been almost exclusively for networks with discrete variables.

Within distribution: These techniques are designed to elicit numbers for a single distribution. The expert is asked for probabilities of specified states of a variable under a stated set of conditions. As with any distribution, the expert may be asked to compare the probability of one state with that of another and ensure that all of the probabilities sum to one. For example, a transportation expert is asked to classify trucks by their length. In this case a truck is defined as the combination of the actual truck and any trailers it may be hauling as shown in Figure 5. SUVs are specifically not counted as trucks, even though they may be built on a truck frame. The expert is given three well-defined categories. The 'long' category is defined as trucks over 35 feet in length. These include large moving vans, oil tank trucks, etc. The 'short' category includes trucks that are less than 15 feet in length. Many light trucks fit in this category. The general knowledge incorporated in this distribution is that most (5/8) trucks are long, only a few (1/8) are short and the rest (1/4) are in the middle.

Figure 5. Truck Length

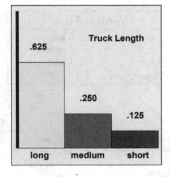

Within CPT: These techniques require the expert to make judgments about distributions within a single CPT. The expert may be asked to compare distributions in making her judgments. Extending our previous example, suppose we have a length distribution for different types of vehicles. Two of those types may be trucks and cars. While we can elicit the distributions independently, we often want to compare them to make sure that they have the right relationship with one another. Our general knowledge is that cars are shorter than trucks. The two distributions shown in Figure 6 represent that knowledge visually. If we were to do a similar distribution for buses, we would expect it to look more like the truck distribution than the car distribution.

Figure 6. Truck & Car Length

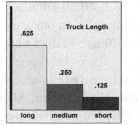
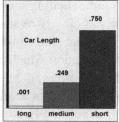

Figure 7. CPT for Truck & Car Lengths

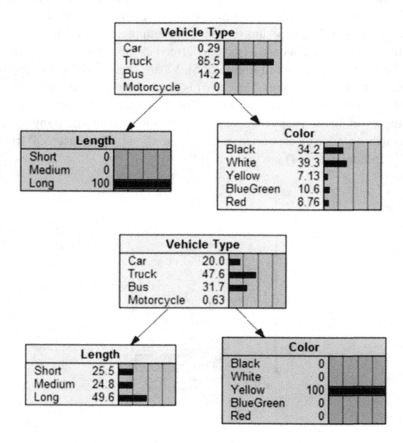

Between CPTs: Using BN tools the impact of just elicited distributions on closely related variables can be presented to the experts. This feedback may lead to revised distributions. For example, we may be setting up a sensor along the highway to count vehicles of different types. The sensor can detect two things, the length of the vehicle and its color (assume for this example that there are only five possible colors: black, white, yellow, blue/green and red). We have elicited the CPTs for these variables in the network as shown in Figure 7.

The top network displays the impact of knowing that the length of a vehicle is 'Long'. As expected, it provides strong evidence for 'Truck' and 'Bus' over 'Car' and 'Motorcycle'. Color is not quite so discriminatory. But knowing that a vehicle is 'Yellow' pushes up the posterior belief in 'Bus', reflecting our knowledge that school busses are yellow.

STRATEGIES FOR COMPLETING LARGE CPTs

One of the critical issues in large CPTs is how to make the elicitation process as painless as possible for the experts. This issue has received very little attention in the literature. This section is based entirely on the work done by the authors. Our previous discussion has addressed some ways to reduce the size of the large CPT. We have found three useful ways to proceed when all of these methods have been utilized and a large CPT is still present. By large we mean at least three conditioning variables and 15 or more conditioning sets of states in the table.

1   Build and complete a table one variable at a time. Pick the variable that you or the experts feel has the biggest impact and complete a table with just this variable. Then add the second variable to the table. In most BN packages, the numbers for the first variable will be present in this table for all rows (or columns in some packages) that the states from the first variable apply. Often there is one state for the second variable that is a neutral or most common state that can be associated with the probabilities assigned previously for the first variable (if not, then this method is not useful. Stop and try one of the other methods). Then assess probabilities for the other states of the second variable for each state of the first variable, paying attention to how these numbers change from those previously assessed. Add the third variable and repeat, etc.

2   Begin with the big CPT and find those combinations of conditioning states that produce the largest and smallest probabilities for each state of the variable of interest in the CPT. For example, in the above table for grades in courses, what combination of grades produces the highest probability of an A in the course being addressed and a D in the course being addressed. Then check to see if these combinations also produce the lowest probability of an A and a D (probably in reverse order); if not, find out which combinations do and assess those. Remember, caution the experts on being overconfident in these cases and ask the experts for reasons why people might do poorly in the past but then start doing better or vice versa. Next find some most likely conditioning combinations and assess those. By the time ten to fifteen combinations have been completed in a table like that shown above, the experts can begin seeing trends in the columns and start using logic to interpolate the extreme values and then complete the intermediate values. This is where the ability to change the order of the conditioning variables in the table has great value.

3   Spend time with experts searching for sets of conditioning events that will have the same probability assignments. Reasons for this happening in the table above might include:

a. When a grade of D is obtained in a course that is the key prerequisite for the course of interest, the grades in the other prerequisites do not matter very much.

b. When a grade of A is obtained in two of the three courses that are prerequisites, it does not matter so much what the grade in the third course is.

When there is sufficient commonality for conditioning events, the number of real distributions for a big table is dramatically reduced (note, this approach can be combined with either of the two above).

I suggest the first and third methods above are the ones to try first. The second method is available if either of the first two will not help.

CONDUCTING TESTS DURING PROBABILITY ELICITATION

As stated in the section titled above, Accepted Elicitation Processes, facilitators frequently conduct tests of an elicited BN. The tests include consistency, coherence and what-if/sensitivity analysis. It is the authors' experience that carrying out limited testing during a probability elicitation session improves both the elicited distributions and the confidence of the experts in those distributions. This cyclic iteration between structuring variables, eliciting the numbers and testing also generates frequent changes in the activities of the experts, making it possible to have longer, more productive sessions with the experts. This limited testing does not replace more thorough sensitivity analyses and more extensive case-based testing. The availability of graphical tools for BNs makes testing during an elicitation session feasible.

We generally restrict elicitation-session testing to a few closely related variables in the network; for example, we may consider a variable and its immediate parents and/or children. These are the variables whose probabilities have been just elicited, so the thought processes of the experts are fresh in everyone's minds. By keeping the network fragment small, the experts can more readily evaluate the effects of any computations: for example, we may ask the expert to judge the effects of evidence upon another closely related variable.

In this section we show how some of the available BN tools may be used for testing in the context of an elicitation session. The primary requirements for using these tools are that they impose a minimal burden on the expert(s) and that they produce comprehensible and relevant results quickly.

Consistency Testing

Consistency testing involves the comparison of distributions within a single CPT. To ease the mental burden on experts, distributions being compared should be placed side-by-side. Tools that support rearranging the order of parent variables and hiding distributions that are not of current interest facilitate side-by-side comparisons.

Consider the following example. An on-call expert is asked about commuting time from the central office to a remote location under a set of conditions that include: time of day, day of the week and weather. Figure 8 shows a graphical view of the network. Suppose that the expert has already specified the 48 distributions for the 'Commuting Time' variable of the network. To verify that those distributions are consistent with her knowledge, she is reviewing the elicited distributions of the table. Figure 9 shows two different views of the table.

Figure 8. Commuting Time Network Showing Marginal for Commuting Time

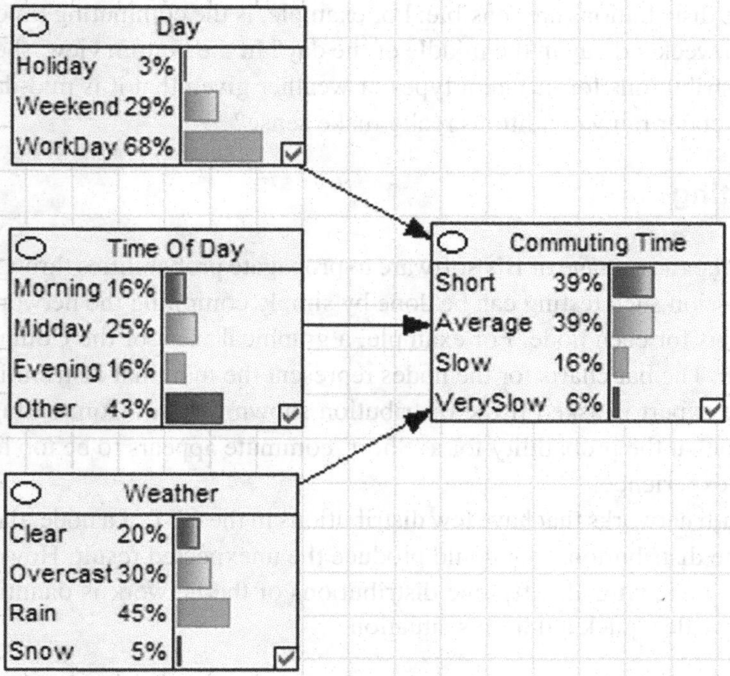

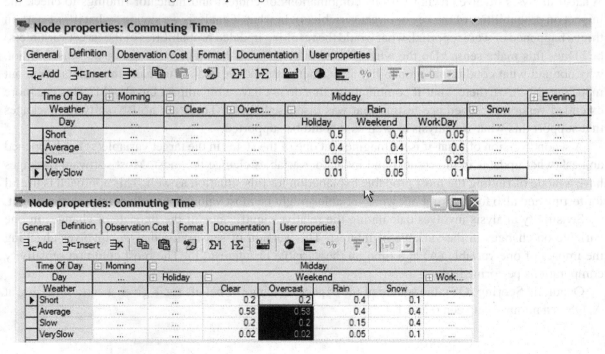

Figure 9. Consistency Testing by Comparing Distributions.

In the top view, the expert is asked to compare the commuting time distributions for rainy conditions during the mid-day hours across different days of the week. While making these comparisons she is asked to judge whether the distributions are sensible: For example, is the commuting time for a workday really longer than that of a weekend day in the middle of the day? In the bottom view, she is asked to compare commuting time distributions for different types of weather given that it is mid-day on a weekend. Do shorter travel times under rainy conditions really make sense?

Coherence Testing

Coherence testing takes advantage of BN software to propagate probabilities throughout a network. During an elicitation session such testing can be done by simply compiling the network to get the posterior marginal distributions for each node. For example, a graphical view of the Commuting Time network is shown in Figure 8. The bar charts for the nodes represent the marginal distributions for each variable in the network. The expert is asked if the distribution shown for the 'Commuting Time' node makes sense. She may note that the probability for a 'Short' commute appears to be too high, because it is not consistent with her experience.

When dealing with networks that have few distributions in the CPT of a node, the facilitator may have the expert review the distributions that could produce the unexpected result. However, in cases such as this one, the task of reviewing all fifty-one distributions of the network is daunting. The next section shows a tool that provides quick aid in this situation.

WHAT-IF/SENSITIVITY ANALYSIS

What-if analysis involves trying various combinations of context and indicator findings to check the impact on probabilities of the key or target variable(s). In what-if analysis we saying "what if" we certain things happened or were reported, what would the resulting updated probabilities of the target variable(s) be? Does this make sense? Do the what-if combinations with the biggest change make sense? If not, why not and what conditional probability assessments should we change to make the results come out more sensibly? Are there what-if combinations that do not have a big impact but should? This is a more extended version of coherence testing that was discussed above. There are no BN software packages that support this what-if analysis as well as it could be supported.

A second version of what-if is to imagine that one of the states in the target variable(s) has happened and ask what updates in the context and indicator variables change the most. Most software packages have a mode of finding the most probable explanation for this situation as well. This approach is useful for testing and also for figuring out what variables might be most valuable to collect information about.

Sensitivity analysis involves calculating the relative significance of the impacts of changes in one variable on changes in the variable of interest. This version of sensitivity analysis involves checking the impact of one variable (A) at a time on the variable of interest (T). The most common sensitivity computations performed are:

Quadratic Scoring (QS): the square of the expected change of beliefs for T given a certain finding at A. QS is a number between 0 and 1.

$$QS = \sum_a \sum_t p(a,t)[p(t \mid a) - p(t)]^2 \tag{1}$$

Variance Reduction (VR): the expected reduction in variance of T given a certain finding at A. VR is a number between 0 and the marginal variance of T. Note $\bar{t}$ is the marginal mean of t. Also note, the VR does not work for variables that are not defined quantitatively.

$$VR = \sum_t \left[p(t)[t - \bar{t}]^2 \right] - \sum_t \left[p(t \mid a) \left[t - \left(\sum_a tp(t \mid a) \right) \right]^2 \right] \tag{2}$$

Entropy Reduction or Mutual Information (MI): the expected reduction in entropy of T given a certain finding at A. MI is a number between 0 and the marginal entropy of T.

$$MI = \sum_t \sum_a p(a,t) \ln \left[\frac{p(a,t)}{p(a) p(t)} \right] \tag{3}$$

To discover which distributions are causing the 'Short' commute to have such a high value, the facilitator may make use of a quick sensitivity analysis that suggests relevant modifications to the network. In this case, the facilitator elicits the probability below which the expert believes the probability for 'Short' should be and the tool makes the suggestions as displayed in Figure 10. In this case, the expert believes that the marginal probability of 'Short' should be less than 0.3. The tool provides two suggestions: the proportion of the "Time of Day" for 'Other' should be less than 0.28 or the probability of 'Weather' being 'Snow' should be greater than 0.90. The expert realizes that she had not considered that 'Other' is defined to be a percentage of the hours of the day. This explains her belief that the probability for 'Short' is too high. She may subsequently change the definition of 'Time of Day' to be the probability of commuting at the specified time of day.

Figure 10. Sensitivity Analysis Example

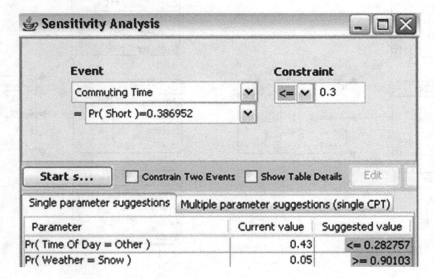

These single parameter suggestions require that a single probability distribution is changed. The expert may believe that these suggestions are not acceptable. To achieve her desired marginal belief for 'Short', she may wish instead to make several changes to the CPT for the variable 'Commuting Time'. The sensitivity tool will make such a recommendation by shifting probability from 'Short' to other states of the variable 'Commuting Time' as displayed in Figure 11.

Whether this type of blanket modification is acceptable is up to the expert. If it is not, the facilitator may walk the expert through some relevant cases to discover why the posterior for short may be so high. In this case, the expert looks at the cases for the workday morning commute and the workday mid-day commute as displayed in Figure 12. The expert decides that some of the problem lies in the distributions

Figure 11. Recommended CPT Changes.

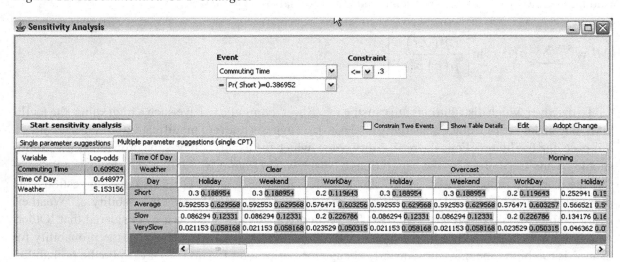

Figure 12. Comparing Cases

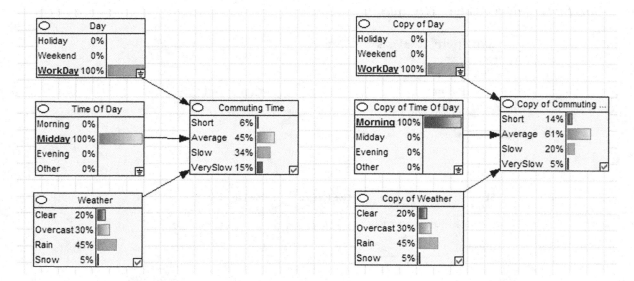

for workday morning commutes. She may choose to make the modifications herself or use the sensitivity tool to make a recommendation.

Recommended Accuracy Measures

In a BN, we are interested in the behavior of a group of related variables, not just the accuracy of a single elicited probability. Judging the behavior depends upon the purpose of the network. For diagnostic networks, one is interested in the posterior probabilities of hypothesized explanations. For predictive networks, one may be interested in the distributions of predicted effects.

There are several shortcomings associated with the measures described for the diagnostic networks of the previous section. Measures that consider only the hypothesis with the highest posterior do not discriminate among different posterior probabilities: a 0.51 posterior will be treated equally with a 1.0 posterior. The second is that some measures are meaningful only for binary variables. For example, receiver operator characteristic (ROC) curves only compare correct hypotheses with false alarms. Another issue is that priors are ignored. For example, if a prior for the correct classification moves from 0.9 to 0.6, the classification is still considered correct even though the model is behaving erroneously.

Consider a diagnostic network. When used in practice, one would expect that after some evidence has been applied to the network, the posterior probability of the correct diagnosis would be relatively high. If the evidence applied to the network is strong, one might expect the posterior of the correct diagnosis to be above 0.9. However, if the evidence is incomplete or weak, one might be satisfied that the posterior of the correct diagnosis is significantly higher than it's prior. In a medical situation, the doctor in the first case may proceed to treatment. In the second situation, the doctor may order additional tests to gather more information. In both cases, the network's performance is good enough to make a decision.

To respond to these issues and to produce an information theoretic measure, Hope & Korb. (2004) developed a Bayesian information reward. It has the following characteristics: 1) it applies to multinomial distributions; 2) it provides a positive reward when the posterior of the correct state is greater than its prior or when the posterior of an incorrect state is less than its prior; 3) no reward is provided for the posterior of a state when it is equal to its prior; 4) it provides a negative reward otherwise, one that is -¥ for giving an incorrect state a posterior of 1.0 or the correct state a posterior of 0.0. The Bayesian information reward applies to a set of k classes with estimated probabilities p_i' and priors p_i, where i is an element of the set (1, ..., k) The Bayesian information reward is calculated as shown below.

$$IR_B = \frac{\sum_i I_i}{k} \tag{1}$$

where $I_i = I_i^+$ for the true class and $I_i = I_i^-$, otherwise and where

$$I_i^+ = \log \frac{p_i'}{p_i} \text{ and } I_i^- = \log \frac{1 - p_i'}{1 - p_i}. \tag{2}$$

Now, consider a predictive situation. We are trying to understand the risk of some event. For example, the expert may have no trouble predicting the height of the average storm surge. However, the issue is the probability that the height of a storm surge will exceed a certain value. In this case, we are concerned not with the highest probability, but the probability of a relatively rare event. It is important that the expert get the tails of the distribution over storm surge correct. It makes a difference in the possible responses of civil authorities.

Chan & Darwiche (2002) developed a measure for probability distributions that bounds belief change. Unlike the commonly used Kullback Leibler divergence, it has the desirable property of being a true distance measure as displayed in the following formula. Pr represents the prior probability for the states, w, of a variable. Pr' represents the posterior probability distribution. The formula involves the ratio of posterior to prior values for two states; the state with the maximum natural log of the ratio and the state with the minimum natural log. The resulting value is always positive.

$$D(\text{Pr}, PU \underset{=}{def} \ln \max_w \frac{PU(w)}{\text{Pr}(w)} - \ln \min_w \frac{PU(w)}{\text{Pr}(w)'} \ln - \ln \tag{3}$$

Recommended Efficiency Measures

While the above measures give us a way of measuring accuracy, in some situations, one may not have a standard against which to compare the accuracy of elicited numbers. In those cases, there is a requirement to generate a surrogate for 'accurate' numbers. There are several approaches for doing so.

1. Assuming that the network goes through several spirals of a spiral development process, the distributions of the initial elicitation may be compared with those of the final form of the network. In this case, the final numbers in the network act as the ground truth against which the initial numbers may be compared.
2. For a diagnostic network, one may use evidence for a set of cases, either real or hypothetical, to instantiate the network. Then the posteriors of the variable of interest may be used to generate the Bayesian information reward.
3. For a predictive network, the case evidence produces one or more distributions of interest. Experts could conceivably give expectations about the distributions of interest and then we could compare the network's results with those produced by the experts using a Chan-Darwiche measure.

Efficiency is measured as work product per unit time. The work product in this case is a set of probabilities. However, because we are working in the context of a BN, we want to consider the probabilities in the context of distributions of CPTs within a network fragment.

While we are primarily interested in facilitating the elicitation of probabilities, the setup prior to that includes training the experts in the procedures to be used and making sure that the variables and their states are well-defined and the network structure is clearly explained. This also increases the overall time it takes to do an elicitation.

We can measure time to elicit probabilities for different granularities of the network. Possible measures are:

1. Time to elicit single probabilities.

2.　Time to elicit a distribution.
3.　Time to elicit a CPT.
4.　Total time to elicit the network fragment.

Recommended Expert Comfort Measures

We can compare the comfort levels of the experts across the different parts of the elicitation by surveying the experts. Such a survey would include the questions such as the following.

1.　At the beginning of the elicitation, the facilitator explained the procedures to be used.
　　a.　Were the directions clear?
　　b.　Were the examples provided relevant to the task?
　　c.　Were the procedures easy to understand?
2.　The network's variables, their states and dependencies are defined before the probability elicitation begins.
　　a.　Were the definitions of the variables and their states precise and complete?
　　b.　Were the dependencies between the variables clearly explained?
　　c.　Were you comfortable giving probabilities for the variables of interest?
3.　During the elicitation, you were asked to provide three types of judgments:
　　a.　Probabilities for the first distribution of a variable given a set of conditions,
　　　　i.　Did you feel comfortable giving your judgments?
　　　　ii.　Were the procedures easy to use?
　　b.　Subsequent distributions for a variable given varying sets of conditions.
　　　　i.　Did you feel comfortable giving your judgments?
　　　　ii.　Were the procedures easy to use?
　　　　iii.　Did previously elicited distributions influence your judgments about subsequent distributions?
　　　　iv.　When providing a judgment about a distribution, did you revise your judgments about previously elicited distributions?
　　c.　Feedback on the local behavior of the BN.
　　　　i.　Did you feel comfortable giving your judgments?
　　　　ii.　Were the procedures easy to use?
　　　　iii.　Did the feedback make you feel more comfortable with the final version of the network?
4.　Do you feel comfortable with the final version of the BN?
5.　Value of the model/process
　　a.　Is the model produced by this process of value to you?
　　b.　Was the process itself of value to you in clarifying your thinking about the problem at hand?
　　c.　Would you participate in future sessions to produce additional models?

WEIGHING THE ELICITATION RESULTS

Which of the above measures is of most importance depends upon the situation. Experts are notoriously difficult to obtain for elicitation sessions, simply because they tend to be very busy. So, one wants to encourage their current and future participation in several different ways:

1. Having the elicitation be efficient, thus reducing the time spent by an expert during elicitation
2. Having the elicitation use a method that the experts are comfortable with, thus increasing their confidence in the final model.
3. Having the resulting model and/or process be of practical use to the experts.

So, at least in initial work with experts, the comfort of the experts should come first, followed closely by efficiency and then the accuracy of the network.

SUMMARY

The research and application associated with elicitation of probability distributions suggests too many people that probabilities can be elicited from experts but must be done carefully and should be subjected to significant testing and skepticism when finished. Our discussion of experts and expertise in varying domains suggests that there are some domains where eliciting probabilities should be considered more of an educational exercise for the experts than an approach for producing numbers that will be useful to decision makers. Nonetheless, this can still be a valuable service. Other domains contain experts that can produce probability judgments that will be useful to decision makers.

Humans are subject to many biases and employ many heuristics when providing probabilities. There are some approaches to combating the effects of these biases and heuristics, but more are needed. Training can help and should be undertaken both before and during the elicitation process. Restructuring the variables in question so that the expert is more at ease and has more understanding is also a very valuable step in debiasing. Finally, the tendency towards of overconfidence for difficult tasks (which encompasses almost all real-world applications) needs to be understood and constantly addressed by both the expert and the person doing the elicitation. This is probably the single most important aspect since experts discard many probability analyses because the overconfidence of the experts is so obvious.

There are many questioning techniques for use in probability elicitation. In general, there has been insufficient research on which techniques are best. A general conclusion is that the indirect techniques are better than the direct techniques because the experts are more comfortable and overconfidence is less of a problem. However, there are many indirect techniques available and little guidance on which to select. Combining techniques is a recent trend that will most likely continue. Recent research on using words during elicitation shows that his approach works about as well as others. The evidence is that words should not be used to communicate the results.

REFERENCES

Arkes, H. R. (1991). Costs and benefits of judgment errors: Implications for debiasing. *Psychological Bulletin*, *110*(3), 486–498. doi:10.1037/0033-2909.110.3.486

Chan, H., & Darwiche, A. (2002). When do numbers really matter? *Journal of Artificial Intelligence Research*, *17*, 265–287. doi:10.1613/jair.967

Clemen, R. T., & Winkler, R. L. (1999). Combining probability distributions from experts in risk analysis. *Risk Analysis*, *19*(2), 187–203. doi:10.1111/j.1539-6924.1999.tb00399.x

D'Ambrosio, B. (1994). Symbolic probabilistic inference in large BN20 networks. In *Uncertainty Proceedings 1994* (pp. 128–135). Morgan Kaufmann.

Dekhytar, A. J. Goldsmith, (2002). *The Bayesian Advisor Project*. ENGR. http://www.cs.engr.uky.edu/~goldsmit/papers/papers.html

Fischhoff, B. (1982). Debiasing. In D. Kahneman, P. Slovic, & A. Tversky (Eds.), *Judgment under uncertainty: Heuristics and biases* (pp. 422–444). Cambridge Univ. Press. doi:10.1017/CBO9780511809477.032

Garthwaite, P. H., Kadane, J. B., & O'Hagan, A. (2005). Statistical methods for eliciting probability distributions. *Journal of the American Statistical Association*, *100*(470), 680–701. doi:10.1198/016214505000000105

Geenen, P. L., & Van Der Gaag, L. C. (2005). Developing a Bayesian network for clinical diagnosis in veterinary medicine: from the individual to the herd. In *Proceedings of the Third Bayesian Modelling Applications Workshop*, Edinburgh.

Hope, L. R., & Korb, K. B. (2004, December). A Bayesian metric for evaluating machine learning algorithms. In *Australasian Joint Conference on Artificial Intelligence* (pp. 991-997). Springer, Berlin, Heidelberg. 10.1007/978-3-540-30549-1_91

Hosseini, S., & Ivanov, D. (2020). Bayesian networks for supply chain risk, resilience and ripple effect analysis: A literature review. *Expert Systems with Applications*, *161*, 113649. doi:10.1016/j.eswa.2020.113649 PMID:32834558

Hudson, L. D., Ware, B. S., Laskey, K. B., & Mahoney, S. M. (2001) *An Application of Bayesian Networks to Antiterrorism Risk Management for Military Planners*. George Mason University C4I Center Technical Report C4I-05-01.

Klayman, J., Soll, J. B., Gonzalez-Vallejo, C., & Barlas, S. (1999). Overconfidence: It depends on how, what, and whom you ask. *Organizational Behavior and Human Decision Processes*, *79*(3), 216–247. doi:10.1006/obhd.1999.2847 PMID:10471362

Kuipers, J., Suter, P., & Moffa, G. (2022). Efficient sampling and structure learning of Bayesian networks. *Journal of Computational and Graphical Statistics*, *31*(3), 1–12. doi:10.1080/10618600.2021.2020127

Laskey, K. B., & Mahoney, S. M. (2000). Network engineering for agile belief network models. *IEEE Transactions on Knowledge and Data Engineering*, *12*(4), 487–498. doi:10.1109/69.868902

Lichtenstein, S., & Newman, J. R. (1967). Empirical scaling of common verbal phrases associated with numerical probabilities. *Psychonomic Science*, *9*(10), 563–564. doi:10.3758/BF03327890

Mahoney, S. M., Buede, D. M., & Tatman, J. A. (2005). *Patterns of Report Relevance*. In Proceedings of the 3rd Bayesian Modelling Applications Workshop of the 21st Conference on Uncertainty in Artificial Intelligence (UAI-2005), Edinburgh, UK.

Merkhofer, M. W. (1987). Quantifying judgmental uncertainty: Methodology, experiences, and insights. *IEEE Transactions on Systems, Man, and Cybernetics*, *17*(5), 741–752. doi:10.1109/TSMC.1987.6499281

Morris, P. A. (1977). Combining expert judgments: A Bayesian approach. *Management Science*, *23*(7), 679–693. doi:10.1287/mnsc.23.7.679

Morris, P. A. (1983). An axiomatic approach to expert resolution. *Management Science*, *29*(1), 24–32. doi:10.1287/mnsc.29.1.24

Murphy, A. H., & Winkler, R. (1984). Probability forecasting in meteorology. *Journal of the American Statistical Association*, *79*, 489–500.

Mussweiler, T., Strack, F., & Pfeiffer, T. (2000). Overcoming the inevitable anchoring effect: Considering the opposite compensates for selective accessibility. *Personality and Social Psychology Bulletin*, *26*(9), 1142–1150. doi:10.1177/01461672002611010

Ng, I., & Zhang, K. (2022, May). Towards federated bayesian network structure learning with continuous optimization. In *International Conference on Artificial Intelligence and Statistics* (pp. 8095-8111). PMLR.

Nicholson, A., Boneh, T., Wilkin, T., Stacey, K., Sonenberg, L., & Steinle, V. (2013). *A case study in knowledge discovery and elicitation in an intelligent tutoring application*. arXiv preprint arXiv:1301.2297.

Phillips, L. D. (1999). Group elicitation of probability distributions: are many heads better than one? In *Decision Science and Technology* (pp. 313–330). Springer. doi:10.1007/978-1-4615-5089-1_17

Pradhan, M., Provan, G., Middleton, B., & Henrion, M. (1994). Knowledge engineering for large belief networks. In *Uncertainty Proceedings 1994* (pp. 484–490). Morgan Kaufmann. doi:10.1016/B978-1-55860-332-5.50066-3

Rohmer, J. (2020). Uncertainties in conditional probability tables of discrete Bayesian Belief Networks: A comprehensive review. *Engineering Applications of Artificial Intelligence*, *88*, 103384. doi:10.1016/j.engappai.2019.103384

Spetzler, C. S., & Stael von Holstein, C. A. S. (1975). Exceptional paper—Probability encoding in decision analysis. *Management Science*, *22*(3), 340–358. doi:10.1287/mnsc.22.3.340

Tetlock, P. E. (1999). Theory-driven reasoning about plausible pasts and probable futures in world politics: Are we prisoners of our preconceptions? *American Journal of Political Science*, *43*(2), 335–366. doi:10.2307/2991798

Tetlock, P. E. (2002). Cognitive biases in path-dependent systems: Theory driven reasoning about plausible pasts and probable futures in world politics. Inferences, Heuristics and Biases: New Directions in Judgment under Uncertainty, New York.

Tversky, A., & Kahneman, D. (1974). Judgment under Uncertainty: Heuristics and Biases: Biases in judgments reveal some heuristics of thinking under uncertainty. *Science, 185*(4157), 1124–1131. doi:10.1126cience.185.4157.1124 PMID:17835457

van der Gaag, L., & Reenooij, S. (2001). Analysing Sensitivity Data from Probabilistic Networks. In *Uncertainty in Artificial Intelligence: Proceedings of the Seventeenth Conference*. Morgan Kaufmann.

van der Gaag, L., Reenooij, S., Sitteman, C. L. M., Aleman, B. M. P., & Taal, B. G. (1999). How to Elicit Many Probabilities. In *Uncertainty in Artificial Intelligence: Proceedings of the Fifteenth Conference*. Morgan Kaufmann.

Wang, H., & Druzdzel, M. (2000). User Interface Tools for Navigation in Conditional Probability Tables and Elicitation of Probabilities in Bayesian Networks, in *Proceedings of the Sixteenth Conference on Uncertainty in Artificial Intelligence*. Morgan Kaufmann, San Francisco.

Weiss, D. J., & Shanteau, J. (2004). The vice of consensus and the virtue of consistency. *Psychological investigations of competent decision making*, 226-240.

Yates, J. F., Lee, J. W., Shinotsuka, H., Patalano, A. L., & Sieck, W. R. (1998). Cross-Cultural Variations in *Probability Judgment Accuracy: Beyond General Knowledge Overconfidence. Organizational Behavior and Human Decision Processes, 74*(2), 89–117. doi:10.1006/obhd.1998.2771 PMID:9705815

APPENDIX: WORDS TO PROBABILITY INTERVAL

The interval constitutes a 100% upper and lower bound for the probability that is not known with certainty. The actual endpoints of the intervals are not as sensitive to error in interval probability modeling as one might expect. Therefore, the numbers need not be perfectly justified or agreed upon.

Wording	Translation to Probability Interval
Absolutely certain	[0.999, 1.00]
Almost certain	[0.99, 1.00]
Extremely probable	[0.95, 1.00]
With very high probability	[0.90, 1.00]
Highly probable	[0.85, 1.00]
Very probable	[0.75, 1.00]
Very likely	[0.70, 1.00]
Very good chance	[0.65, 1.00]
Strong chance	[0.65, 1.00]
Quite probable	[0.60, 1.00]
Probable	[0.50, 0.90]
Likely	[0.50, 0.85]
Good chance	[0.50, 0.85]
Even chance	[0.45, 0.55]
Estimated, judged, predicted	[0.10, 0.45]
Believed, deemed, potential	[0.10, 0.45]
Possible, plausible	[0.05, 0.45]
Some chance	[0.00, 0.45]
Somewhat unlikely	[0.00, 0.40]
Unlikely	[0.00, 0.35]
Improbable	[0.00, 0.30]
Very unlikely	[0.00, 0.20]
Little chance	[0.00, 0.20]
Highly improbable	[0.00, 0.10]
With very low probability	[0.00, 0.10]
Slight chance	[0.00, 0.10]
Unknown	[0.00, 1.00]
Extremely unlikely	[0.00, 0.02]
Remote	[0.001, 0.01]
Almost impossible	[0.001, 0.01]
Impossible	[0.00 0.001]
Probability is about P	[P-0.10, P+0.10]

Chapter 10
Modeling Parameters and Techniques for Risk Modeling

ABSTRACT

To make more informed cyber-assurance decisions, the information security community needs better models to evaluate and predict future adversarial behavior and greatest return-on-investment in defensive measures. In addition, adversary characterization information on their success rate, resources expended, risk perception, and attack decision trade-off preferences are almost always derived from observable characteristics and rarely directly acquired. Rather than abdicate use of analytical techniques or resort to using less rigorous modeling techniques because of a lack of available data, this chapter proposes a set of techniques to be used to capture the best available information at the time for use in more rigorous models, and provides insight into the level of confidence the authors have in this data. From this information, one can also then derive modeling estimation parameters to meet the need for specific confidence levels. It can also provide us guidance on how to invest to improve our data estimates.

INTRODUCTION

Information security researchers also have not been collecting information on how well various defensive actions mitigate adversary behavior, their degradation on mission critical performance, or their costs and schedule impacts. Whether we choose to model this attack/defense scenario or not, this is precisely the information that is needed to make sound risk management decisions.

We are forced to make decisions at the time a decision must be made under uncertainty using the quantity and quality of the data that we have at hand and the insights that we can derive from our existing decision support processes, both intuitive and analytical. As a result of this uncertainty surrounding the availability and reliability of data to support these risk management decisions, detailed models have not been developed and where models have been using simplistic rudimentary heuristic models using descriptive data with vague units of measure have been employed to fill the vacuum.

DOI: 10.4018/978-1-6684-7766-3.ch010

In general, risk modeling is about defining the likelihood of specific events that lead to harmful consequences and the extent of harm caused if that event were to occur. Therefore, the four primary concepts that we need to model are:

A.   Define the Harmful Event
B.   Estimate the Likelihood of a Harmful Event
C.   Estimate the Extent of Harm caused if the Harmful Event occurs
D.   Determine the relationship between the output Value of Risk and the input parameters "Likelihood of a Harmful Event" and "Extent of Harm" caused by the Harmful Event.

For modeling purposes, ideally, we would like precisely defined events and natural units of measure. In the case of "Likelihood", a natural measure would be the probability that the event would happen within some time window or conditioned on some event within a time window. For "Extent of Harm" a natural measure would be some unit of value such as $, time, or utility. The relationship between the input and the output can be assumed to be any Risk = f(Likelihood, Extent of Harm). Common functions are the Expected Harm function where Risk = Likelihood * Extent of Harm [if likelihood is expressed in probability and Extent of Harm is expressed in a value measure]. Expected Harm is not always a good function to represent the risk tolerance of a risk manager especially with very low likelihood and very high extents of harm or very high likelihood and very low extents of harm.

But "Harmful Events" are difficult to precisely define, probabilities and values are difficult parameters to estimate with empirical data and especially without empirical data and risk tolerance functions that are difficult to elicit. So, our risk estimates contain uncertainty, which is natural for the type of data being collected. Complicating the definition, collection and computation issue is the fact that when it comes to the risks associated with malicious attacks, we are dealing with conscious deliberately chosen behaviors. So, the "Estimate of the Likelihood of a Harmful Event" needs to be split up into a pair of conditioned and unconditioned probabilities:

p(malicious event) = p(malicious event attempted) * p(malicious event succeeds given attempted)
p(e) = p(attempt) * p(success|attempt)

We still have the same problems associated with the p(success|attempt) parameter, but the p(attempt) parameter requires us to make estimates about the probability an adversary will decide to attempt any attack p(attack) and the probability they will select a specific attack p(select).

CYBERASSURANCE METRICS

Information security professionals are in need of some sound and meaningful metrics to allow us to transform CyberAssurance from its current art or alchemy state into a science and associated engineering discipline. While I don't have "the answer", I'll offer some of my thoughts and experience that may provide ideas to build upon when considering specific metrics an analytical framework that can use those metrics to provide insights to support design and risk management decisions.

One area that hampers us in defining good metrics is a lack of common definitions (Hopkin, 2018). We have plenty of glossaries and approved definitions, but these authorities often contradict one another, are not applicable to an sound analytical framework and/or they don't correspond to or resonate with the language used by subject matter experts (SMEs) that are practitioners of CyberAssurance. In the Cybersecurity field I find it hard to have everyone in the same meeting use the same definition for words such as security, risk, vulnerabilities, threats, attacks, adversaries, countermeasures, security controls, or impact. If we can't even have a common definition, we certainly can't make much progress on how to "measure" these. Yet these are the basic concepts that we deal with in Information Assurance. Unfortunately, even if we were to find a common definition, these still fall into the category of the "things I need that can't be directly measured".

After working with and evaluating many "security" and "risk" methodologies, I've come to some opinions.

1. We need to start someplace and establish some basic definitions, principles and beliefs. Where I am right now in my thinking is that I start with some premises:

    a. The goal of any system is to provide functional support to a mission and an information system is to provide functional support through the information that it provides. Therefore, the benefit derived from a system is directly derived from the benefit the system provides to a mission.

    b. Information systems operate in hostile and malicious environments where environmental factors and malicious attacks can degrade the ability of systems to provide optimal functionality to support the mission through system or component failure or data denial of service, system modification or degradation of data integrity and/or loss of data confidentiality.

    c. These environmental factors can lead to stochastic failure or degradation events that can be studied through failure analysis and malicious attacks lead to stochastic events conditioned on the probability of attempt of the malicious activity.

    d. Risk is a concept that is useful in understanding the potential for future harm derived from malicious and non-malicious events and the concept of risk is composed of two elements: the likelihood that the event will occur and the amount of harm that result given the event occurs. Risk is not a parameter that is directly measurable and is a function of directly measurable and indirectly measurable parameters as well as the value system of those perceiving the risk.

2. To define "risk" we need to define the specific consequences in question, understand the events (environmental or malicious) that can bring about those consequences and measure or estimate the likelihood those events will occur and assign a value to the extent of harm to the mission if those consequences are realized.

    a. For failure events we often have empirical data that we can draw upon to make estimates for the likelihood of those types of events.

    b. For malicious events we are at a loss for measuring p(attempt of an attack out of a menu of possible attacks) because p(attempt) is adversary and situation dependent. Yet because the likelihood of malicious events are conditioned on p(attempt) we must come up with estimates on p(attempt) to be able to continue the parallel analysis of malicious and non-malicious events. This is where failure analysis and malicious event analysis seem to diverge and we begin to see many different approaches to estimating things that we can measure and somehow translate them into estimates on the measures that we need.

    c. The difficulty of estimating p(attempt) is exacerbated by the fact that we "see" only a portion of the "successes" and only a portion of the "attempts" so our empirical data may not be representative of what is really going on in a specific situation and by the fact that an adversary may employ an entirely different strategy in a different situation.

    d.   While the likelihood of a malicious event is difficult to develop good metrics for, we as a community seem to also have a problem defining good metrics for the harm or impact caused by a successful event. I believe there are sound techniques that can be used to help us gain estimates on both the likelihood and impact parameters that we need for this risk perspective.

3.   One of the technique areas that we've explored is utility theory to help us develop estimates on the harm or impact AND on the likelihood of malicious events.

    a.   For harm or impact valuation, it is a direct use of utility theory in measuring characteristics of the system that are meaningful to the system user and developing utility curves as a function of those measures.

    b.   We have also used utility theory to help build estimates on the likelihood of events by trying to imagine an adversary's decision-making process on how to select an attack to attempt from a menu of attacks. Our assumption is that they, like others faced with decisions across multiple criteria will select attacks that are more "attractive" to them than attacks that are less "attractive" to them and that the attractiveness of attacks to an adversary are a function of an attack:

Probabilistic Payoff Utility, which is a function of:

Payoff

p(success|attempt)

Probabilistic Risk from Response Utility, which is a function of:

p(detection)

p(attribution|detection)

p(response|attribution)

harm of response

Probabilistic Risk from Unintended Consequences Utility, which is a function of:

p(unintended consequences)

harm of unintended consequences

Resource Utility, which is a function of:

Resources to acquire unrealized Access, Knowledge and Capability

Resources to further reduce Attack Risk

Resources to Execute Attack

[These are general concepts that can be refined and tailored for specific analyses]

Likewise, if we can make estimates on these characteristics of attacks and can develop the utility curves and trade-off swing weights from an adversary situational perspective, we can draw upon decision analysis to help rank order and compare these attacks by their "attractiveness" to specific adversaries in specific situations. We believe there is a correlation between attack "attractiveness" (or utility) and an adversary's p(attempt) but defining a defendable correlation function is still an ongoing effort.

From a Defensive perspective, our defensive measures can be viewed as features in our system (technical and procedural) that we control that change the fundamental characteristics of the attack (e.g., payoff, p(success|attempt), p(detection), etc.) and there-by the attack's attractiveness and corresponding p(attempt). If we had some estimate on a threshold of "attractiveness" beyond which an adversary would not attempt, we could begin to define cost-effective defenses to try to bring the attack values below that threshold. But that is an adversary situational dependent threshold that we would have to estimate and direct data on that threshold is not readily available. We have to look at other ways to estimate p(attempt) and possible thresholds.

The only benefit of a security measure is to allow for greater functionality of the system to support the mission within a hostile and malicious environment (Boranbayev et al., 2022). We can also use utility theory to trade-off the "attack attractiveness reduction" that we obtain from a set of defensive measures with whatever performance degradation is caused by those defensive measures, its acquisition and operational costs and its schedule costs. We can again use decision analysis as a framework for trading off these defensive measures to gain insight into optimal defensive strategy.

A State Space Modeling for CyberAssurance model is theoretical. I believe there is a lot of potential mileage in analysis that we can get if we can define:

A. The states to reflect:
1. The access and privilege acquired by an adversary relative to a defensive boundary established by our various defensive mechanisms,
2. The system attack knowledge possessed by possessed by an adversary,
3. The system attack capability possessed by an adversary.
4. The resources available that can be translated into access, privilege, knowledge and capability.
5. The level of risk of harm an adversary is exposed to.
B. The transitions to represent sets of attacks against those defensive boundaries to transition to a new state; and
C. The "treasures" that are acquired by adversaries with successful attacks. Such as:
1. Degradation of the Confidentiality of a Set of Mission Data
2. Degradation of the Integrity of a Set of Mission Data
3. Degradation of the Availability of a Set of Mission Data

To use this type of model though requires "metrics" that support developing state values and transition probabilities.

Another thought in considering the modeling of an adversary exploiting the Information Assurance aspects of a system seems that in many ways, modeling the CyberAssurance of a system may be similar to modeling adventure type video games such as "Halo[1]" where:

- The Adversary is the game character
- The System is the immersive environment
- The Defensive Measures are the barriers and opponents impeding progress
- Knowledge, Capability and Resources are weapons, information and abilities, acquired by the character in traversing the environment
- Access is the room, location, or level the character currently occupies
- Mission or Data Impact is the successful completion of the game mission or a level of the game.

CYBERASSURANCE FOR RISK-BASED DECISION-MAKING

Making sound risk management decisions regarding information security that is vital to the effective accomplishment of an organization's mission activities is becoming more and more important as our operations become more and more dependent upon the availability, integrity and confidentiality of critical sets of information (Hubbard, 2020). To make better and more informed risk management decisions, a discipline of "CyberAssurance for risk-based decision-making" is slowly evolving to capture data that is relevant to the risk management decision and to interpret the meaning of that data for the decision-makers with respect to the risk management decisions they must make. There are many issues and challenges associated with developing a sound risk management decision analysis process that is faithful to the "observations" as described by the input data, sound in its transformation of input data to analytical results and an honest interpretation of those results in a form and format that helps decision-makers gain meaningful insights with respect to the risk management decisions they are faced with.

Often risk management decision analyses are treated, reviewed, critiqued and interpreted using a "natural science" perspective. In the natural sciences, we take measurements of well-defined phenomenon or events using instruments with known levels of precision relative to a well-defined scale with a well-defined unit of measure and we have well defined rules for analyzing and aggregating these measurements. We also have well defined rules for defining characteristics about the number of significant digits, confidence level, or distribution of the results. But when these results are applied to the decisions at hand, it takes a knowledgeable individual to "interpret" these results relative the decisions at hand. These interpretations can either be done by the decision-maker themselves or by the analyst and presented in a form and format that helps the decision-maker.

Unfortunately, often risk management decisions are dealing with potential future phenomenon or events for which we may not have any past empirical measurements or estimates that are representative of these future events. In lieu of hard statistical evidence, we are forced to use whatever past, somewhat related empirical evidence we have and project that insight in past situations to entirely different future situations using the knowledge, insight and experience of "Subject Matter Experts" (SMEs). Where and when we have empirical data directly related to the phenomenon, we want data on, we should use that. But when we are projecting our known information into different or future events, we need to rely on the subjective estimates of our SMEs. This introduces such issues as:

1. Limitations on the ability or precision of SMEs making estimates on the phenomenon in question.
2. Biases influencing a SMEs in making these estimates.
3. Errors introduced by misunderstanding of the SME on the phenomenon or event on which they are asked to provide estimates.
4. Differences of opinion on estimates by different SMEs.
5. Inability to measure the accuracy of a SMEs estimate.

Faced with the need to make a risk-management decision at a specific time with the information available, a decision maker has several options:

A. They can determine that they do not have the empirical evidence they need, choose not to collect SME estimates and make the risk management decision based on their own current knowledge and their own interpretation of the existing data relative to the decision. In this case, the decision is that both the empirical and SME generated data and insights do not have sufficient credibility relative to the insights of the decision-maker in order to justify using them in an analysis.

B.   They can choose to use only the empirical evidence and apply the results of the data from a specific past situation to a potentially future different situation. In this case, the decision is that the empirical evidence is sufficiently representative of the future different situation to be able to credibly use it and that the SME generated data and insights do not have sufficient credibility to use.

C.   They can simply ask a set of available SME's their opinion and do a personal interpretation of how to best use that information. In this case, the decision is that the general opinions and insights of SMEs have value to help inform decision-makers but not sufficient definition or credibility to warrant use in an analysis, or

D.   They can choose to do a formal analysis using the empirical and subjective SME data and insights using available techniques to minimize some of the issues associated with SME generated data and document and highlight to decision-makers the source and usefulness of the insights gleaned from this data. In this case there is a decision that a formalized definition and analysis of SME estimates may yield additional credible insights not provided by the decision-maker's personal interpretations and experience, analysis of the empirical evidence, or informal opinions of a set of SMEs.

Because SME generated data estimates are a statement of "belief" about a specific phenomenon or event, the analysis should be looked at from a "social science" analysis perspective rather than a "natural science" analysis.

Another way in which many risk management decision analyses should social science analyses lies in the fact that for analysis of malicious attacks, they involve a conscious decision by an individual to behave in a way that will cause harm. This is what makes it so difficult to generate estimates on the probability that an adversary will attempt a specific attack out of a menu of possible actions against a specific target within a specific time window [e.g., p(attack attempt)] to be used in a likelihood of event calculation in the form of:

p(attack success) = p(attack attempt) * p(attack success given attack attempt)

Yet in order to do a likelihood analysis of conscious malicious events we need values on the p(attack attempt) derived from either empirical data or derived from SME estimates. This piece of data is very difficult to derive from empirical evidence alone because of the sparse data sets we have and the applicability of existing data sets to the situations being studied. Our alternatives are to try to define a "likelihood" score independent of p(attempt), use imperfect empirical data for p(attempt), or use subjective SME "belief" data to derive a p(attempt).

Even in developing estimates on the impact or harm of an event to an entity, organization and/or mission requires a subjective or "belief" estimate on the "value" or "degree of harm" caused by the event. We can measure various properties, but "value" is an individual or organization belief that we can derive from either observing value-based behavior over time, or by asking for subjective SME opinions that are susceptible to the issues listed above. Both of these options have their foundations in social science analysis techniques instead of the empirical or natural science analysis techniques.

SCENARIO

As decision and risk analysts, it is important that the ideal technique for aggregating attacks would use probabilities and cost data. Unfortunately, this data is very difficult to obtain due to the large number of potential adversaries, scenarios and attack objectives. Subject matter experts have been unwilling or unable to estimate this data. This scenario examines several other attack value aggregation techniques and compares their worth based on:

- Closeness to the preferred, but currently intractable approach,
- Ease of modeling and data collection,
- Soundness of the theoretical basis and
- Ease of explanation to management.

The following definitions are used in this particular generic scenario:

- **Attack** – A sequential set of actions against an information system to attempt to achieve an adversary's objective.
- **Attack Steps** – Individual actions that by themselves are not sufficient to attain an adversary's objective.
- **Value Measure** – Scale to assess the degree of attainment of an objective, e.g., we may measure an attack's value to the adversary with the probability of success, $p(s)$. The higher the probability of success, the greater the value of the attack to the adversary
- **Scale** – The units and range associated with a value measure, e.g., a value measure of cost might have a scale of dollars ranging from \$1 million to \$10 million and $p(s)$ may have a scale that ranges of 0 to 1.
- **Score/Level** – A specific numerical rating of an alternative on a value measure's scale, e.g., $p(s)$ of 0.95 (we avoid using the term value for scores since value is defined by the value function.).
- **Value** – Value reflects our preferences for each increment of the value measure, i.e., returns to scale. For example, if each value measure increment is of equal value, we have constant returns to scale. Value is normalized, e.g., 0-1 where 0 is the least preferred level and 1 is the most preferred level of the value measure.
- **Single Dimensional Value Function** – A mathematical function that converts an alternative's score on a value measure into units of value.
- **Attack Step Score** – The score on the attack step measure.
- **Attack Score** – A score directly assessed or an aggregated score that is calculated as a function of the attack step scores.
- **Attack Step Value** – The value assigned an attack step score on the adversary's attack step value function.
- **Attack Value** – The value assigned an attack score on the adversary's attack value function.
- **Attack Aggregation Technique** – A mathematical function that combines the scores of attack steps to an attack score or combines attack step values to attack values.
- **Attack-Based Data** – Value measures that pertain to intrinsic descriptions of a particular attack step and do not depend on the adversary. An example would be describing the likelihood of successfully completing an attack based on the difficulty of the attack.

- **Adversary-Based Data** – Value measures that pertain directly to the adversary and are not an intrinsic description of the attack step. An example would be the probability that adversary X successfully completes an attack step. Adversary-based data requires separate data collection on every attack step for every adversary.

TYPES OF VALUE MEASURES

Value measures can be classified in several different ways depending on their alignment to the objective being measured and the type of measure. Measures can be direct or proxy and also either natural or constructed. A direct measure is used to directly assess how well an objective is accomplished, such as measuring the likelihood of successfully completing an attack step using probabilities. A proxy scale is used to measure the attainment of the goal indirectly, such as measuring the complexity of an attack as a proxy for probability of success. A natural measure is generally agreed upon by everyone. Measuring resources in terms of dollars is an example. A constructed measure is used if no natural measure exists, or if it is too hard to collect data for the natural measure. An example would be creating a constructed scale to measure the degree of difficulty of completing an attack step by describing several situations that might be encountered, ranging from low difficulty to high difficulty. Constructed measures can be either numeric without definitions (1 to 5, 0 to 100) or each constructed scale level can be defined. Defined levels are preferred since they provide a consistent scoring rationale. Overall, since alignment with the objective is most important, a direct, natural scale is preferred. Therefore, we will consider a direct, natural measure as the baseline that all other techniques will be judged against as displayed in Figure 1.

Table 1. Types of Value Measures

Type of Scale	Alignment with Objective	
	Direct	Proxy
Natural	Probability of Attack Success	Time for Red Team to Successfully Attack
Constructed	Adversary Attack Value	Attack Complexity

SCORE AND VALUE AGGREGATION

If we are evaluating individual alternatives, aggregation of scores is usually not an issue in multiple objective decision analysis. For each value measure, we develop a single dimensional value function that converts the value measure score into units of value. After the single dimensional value functions have been developed, we need to develop an overall value function that aggregates the individual values into a overall value. We usually use the additive value function:

$$v(x) = \sum_{i=1}^{n} w_i v_i(x_i) \tag{1}$$

where:

$v(x)$ is the value of the alternative

$i = 1$ to n is the number of the value measure

x_i is the score of the alternative on the ith value measure

$v_i(x_i)$ is the single dimensional value of a score of x_i

w_i is the weight of the ith value measure

and $\sum_{i=1}^{n} w_i = 1$ (all weights sum to one)

Several different aggregation techniques have been proposed. One approach is to aggregate and then value (Group 1 below). We aggregate the attack step measure scores into an aggregate attack measure score and then use the single dimensional value function to calculate the measure value. Mathematically,

$$x_i = f(x_{i1}, x_{i2}, ..., x_{is})$$ (2)

where: s is the number of attack steps, then $v_i(x_i)$ is the single dimensional value of aggregated score x_i and $v(x)$ is the value of the attack.

A second approach is to value then aggregate (Group 2 below). Mathematically, this is the following:

x_{is} is the score of the on the sth attack step of the ith value measure

$v_{is}(x_{is})$ is the single dimensional value of a score of x_{is} on the sth attack step of the ith value measure and

$$v(x_i) = f(v(x_{i1}), v(x_{i2}), ..., v(x_{is}))$$ (3)

We will test the aggregation techniques by evaluating seven different scenarios for each aggregation technique. We will next identify scenarios and specific attack aggregation techniques to be evaluated.

ASSUMPTIONS

To help understand how different aggregation techniques work, we have constructed an illustrative example that has an attack with five attack steps. Each attack step has three value measures: probability of detection, probability of success and resources required. We will create several different scenarios and will vary how the attack steps are scored. We will then examine how well the aggregation techniques meet our expectations, describe their advantages and disadvantages and recommend a standard way for attack aggregation as described in Table 2.

Those techniques that used a direct value assessment received the value in Table 2. For aggregation techniques that used probabilities, we chose the probability that returned a value of "0.9" for each attack step. Techniques that used constructed scales used either the top (bottom) measure for the best (worst) case and one step up (down) for the great (bad) steps. Since each technique is different, we used some judgment on what score or value to give to use.

Table 2. Scenario Description

Scenario	Description
Perfect Steps	Every attack step scores perfectly, i.e., has a value of "1"
Worst Steps	Every attack step scores horribly, i.e., has a value of "0"
Bad Steps	Every attack step has value of "0.1"
"One Good Step"	Four attack steps have value of "0" and one has a value of "1"
"One Bad Step"	Four attack steps have value of "1" and one has a value of "0"
Mediocre Steps	Every attack step has value of "0.5"

AGGREGATION TECHNIQUES

As previously noted, aggregation techniques can be divided into two groups. The first group provides a score to each attack step, aggregates the scores, which are then translated into a value. The second group determines the value of an attack step directly and then aggregates the attack step values for an attack value.

GROUP 1. AGGREGATE THEN VALUE

Direct, Natural Scales (A)

This is the baseline technique. We assume we have the probabilities of detection and success and the cost in terms of dollars. Probabilities at the attack step level are combined using probability theory. Cost scores are summed. Once we have an attack score, we evaluate the score using a single dimensional value function identified in Figure 1.

Constructed to Natural Scales (B)

This technique assigns probability and cost data into qualitative levels (bins) for each value measure. Each bin is then converted into a point estimate of the actual probability or cost identified in Figure 2.

The conversion table we used can be found in Table 3.

Figure 1. Data for Natural, Constructed

Aggegation by Probabilities and costs

Perfect Attack

	Attack Step Scores						Assume independent			
	1	2	3	4	5		Attack Score	Measure Value	Weights	Attack Value	input
Liklihood of Detection	0	0	0	0	0		0	1	0.33		cell reference
Liklihood of Success	1	1	1	1	1		1	1	0.33	1	calculation
Resources Required	0	0	0	0	0		0	1	0.33		

Worst Attack

	Attack Step Scores						Assume independent			
	1	2	3	4	5		Attack Score	Measure Value	Weights	Attack Value
Liklihood of Detection	1	1	1	1	1		1	0	0.33	
Liklihood of Success	0	0	0	0	0		0	0	0.33	0
Resources Required	10000000	10000000	10000000	10000000	10000000		50000000	0	0.33	

Great Attack

	Attack Step Scores						Assume independent			
	1	2	3	4	5		Attack Score	Measure Value	Weights	Attack Value
Liklihood of Detection	0.05	0.05	0.05	0.05	0.05		0.23	0.55	0.33	
Liklihood of Success	0.94	0.94	0.94	0.94	0.94		0.73	0.59	0.33	0.57
Resources Required	25000	25000	25000	25000	25000		125000	0.59	0.33	

Bad Attack

	Attack Step Scores						Assume independent			
	1	2	3	4	5		Attack Score	Measure Value	Weights	Attack Value
Liklihood of Detection	0.75	0.75	0.75	0.75	0.75		1.00	0.000391	0.33	
Liklihood of Success	0.16	0.16	0.16	0.16	0.16		0.00	0.000084	0.33	0.02
Resources Required	1000000	1000000	1000000	1000000	1000000		5000000	0.06	0.33	

One Good Step

	Attack Step Scores						Assume independent			
	1	2	3	4	5		Attack Score	Measure Value	Weights	Attack Value
Liklihood of Detection	1	1	0	1	1		1	0.00	0.33	
Liklihood of Success	0	0	1	0	0		0	0.00	0.33	0
Resources Required	10000000	10000000	0	10000000	10000000		40000000	0.00	0.33	

One Bad Step

	Attack Step Scores						Assume independent			
	1	2	3	4	5		Attack Score	Measure Value	Weights	Attack Value
Liklihood of Detection	0.05	0.05	1	0.05	0.05		1.00	0.00	0.33	
Liklihood of Success	0.94	0.94	0.00	0.94	0.94		0.00	0.00	0.33	0.00
Resources Required	25000	25000	10000000	25000	25000		10100000	0.00	0.33	

Mediocre Attack

	Attack Step Scores						Assume independent			
	1	2	3	4	5		Attack Score	Measure Value	Weights	Attack Value
Liklihood of Detection	0.25	0.25	0.25	0.25	0.25		0.763	0.095	0.33	
Liklihood of Success	0.625	0.625	0.625	0.625	0.625		0.095	0.076	0.33	0.09
Resources Required	300000	300000	300000	300000	300000		1500000	0.094	0.33	

Constructed to Multiple Functions (C)

This technique assigns a numeric "weight" to each level (bin) of each value measure as shown in Figure 3. The smallest level is assigned a "1". Each subsequent level is given a number that represents the number of attack steps of the smallest bin that would be required to equal one attack step of the subsequent bins. For example, if it is thought the three attack steps that scored "very low" would equal one attack step that scored "low", then the "very low" level would receive a score of "1" and low would score a "3". The result of the numeric levels is calculated using a Fibonacci sequence[2].

These scores are then aggregated according to the following equation which includes a damping function and an exponential function.

$$v_i(x_i) = e_i\left(\sum_{i=1}^{n}\left(f(x_i)*.75^{i-1}\right)\right) \tag{4}$$

where

x_i = constructed scale level of the ith attack step, where i is ordered from highest to lowest

$f_i(x_i)$ = function that converts the constructed levels to Fibonacci sequence number, 1, 1, 2, 3, 5, 8, etc.

Figure 2. Data for Constructed to Natural

Perfect Attack

	Attack Step Values						Assume independent			
	1	2	3	4	5		Attack Score	Measure Value	Weights	Attack Value	input
Liklihood of Detection	0.01	0.01	0.01	0.01	0.01		0.05	0.90	0.33		cell reference
Liklihood of Success	0.99	0.99	0.99	0.99	0.99		0.95	0.92	0.33	0.94	calculation
Resources Required	0	0	0	0	0		0	1	0.33		

Worst Attack

	Attack Step Scores						Assume independent			
	1	2	3	4	5		Attack Score	Measure Value	Weights	Attack Value
Liklihood of Detection	0.99	0.99	0.99	0.99	0.99		1	0.00	0.33	
Liklihood of Success	0.01	0.01	0.01	0.01	0.01		0.00	0.00	0.33	0.00
Resources Required	10000000	10000000	10000000	10000000	10000000		50000000	0	0.33	

Great Attack

	Attack Step Scores						Assume independent			
	1	2	3	4	5		Attack Score	Measure Value	Weights	Attack Value
Liklihood of Detection	0.25	0.25	0.25	0.25	0.25		0.76	0.09	0.33	
Liklihood of Success	0.90	0.90	0.90	0.90	0.90		0.59	0.47	0.33	0.36
Resources Required	50000	50000	50000	50000	50000		250000	0.53	0.33	

Bad Attack

	Attack Step Scores						Assume independent			
	1	2	3	4	5		Attack Score	Measure Value	Weights	Attack Value
Liklihood of Detection	0.75	0.75	0.75	0.75	0.75		1.00	0.000391	0.33	
Liklihood of Success	0.10	0.10	0.10	0.10	0.10		0.00	0.000008	0.33	0.02
Resources Required	1000000	1000000	1000000	1000000	1000000		5000000	0.06	0.33	

One Good Step

	Attack Step Scores						Assume independent			
	1	2	3	4	5		Attack Score	Measure Value	Weights	Attack Value
Liklihood of Detection	0.99	0.99	0.01	0.99	0.99		0.99999999	0.00	0.33	
Liklihood of Success	0.01	0.01	0.99	0.01	0.01		0.00	0.00	0.33	0.00
Resources Required	10000000	10000000	50000	10000000	10000000		40050000	0.00	0.33	

One Bad Step

	Attack Step Scores						Assume independent			
	1	2	3	4	5		Attack Score	Measure Value	Weights	Attack Value
Liklihood of Detection	0.01	0.01	0.99	0.01	0.01		0.99	0.00	0.33	
Liklihood of Success	0.99	0.99	0.01	0.99	0.99		0.01	0.01	0.33	0.00
Resources Required	50000	50000	10000000	50000	50000		10200000	0.00	0.33	

Mediocre Attack

	Attack Step Scores						Assume independent			
	1	2	3	4	5		Attack Score	Measure Value	Weights	Attack Value
Liklihood of Detection	0.5	0.5	0.5	0.5	0.5		0.969	0.013	0.33	
Liklihood of Success	0.500	0.500	0.500	0.500	0.500		0.031	0.025	0.33	0.04
Resources Required	300000	300000	300000	300000	300000		1500000	0.094	0.33	

Table 3. Conversion Table for Constructed to Natural Scales

	Probability of Detection	Probability
Very Low	Passive attack with no footprint	0.01
Low	Leaves a footprint; no one is looking	0.25
Medium	Leaves a footprint; but looks normal	0.5
High	Leaves an audit trail	0.75
Very High	Sets off an alarm+	0.99

$.75^{i-1}$ is a heuristically derived damping function meant to discount the 2nd through nth score.

The total attack score, x_i, is then converted to a value using an exponential function $e_i(x_i)$ as shown in Figures 4 and 5. Resources Required was determined in the same way as the Constructed to Natural technique.

Figure 3. Data for Constructed to Multiple Functions

	1	0.75	0.5625	0.421875	0.31640625	Aggegation by scores and costs			
Perfect Attack		Attack Step Scores				Assume independent			
	1	2	3	4	5	Attack Score	Measure Value	Weights	Attack Value	input
Liklihood of Detection	1	1	1	1	1	3.1	0.96	0.33		cell reference
Liklihood of Success	1	1	1	1	1	3.1	0.98	0.33	0.98	calculation
Resources Required	0	0	0	0	0	0	1.00	0.33		

Worst Attack		Attack Step Scores				Assume independent			
	1	2	3	4	5	Attack Score	Measure Value	Weights	Attack Value
Liklihood of Detection	16	16	16	16	16	48.8	0.00	0.33	
Liklihood of Success	21	21	21	21	21	64.1	0.00	0.33	0.00
Resources Required	10000000	10000000	10000000	10000000	10000000	50000000	0.00	0.33	

Great Attack		Attack Step Scores				Assume independent			
	1	2	3	4	5	Attack Score	Measure Value	Weights	Attack Value
Liklihood of Detection	2	2	2	2	2	6.1	0.87	0.33	
Liklihood of Success	2	2	2	2	2	6.1	0.93	0.33	0.78
Resources Required	50000	50000	50000	50000	50000	250000	0.53	0.33	

Bad Attack		Attack Step Scores				Assume independent			
	1	2	3	4	5	Attack Score	Measure Value	Weights	Attack Value
Liklihood of Detection	13	13	13	13	13	39.7	0.00	0.33	
Liklihood of Success	13	13	13	13	13	39.7	0.00	0.33	0.02
Resources Required	1000000	1000000	1000000	1000000	1000000	5000000	0.06	0.33	

One Good Step		Attack Step Scores				Assume independent			
	1	2	3	4	5	Attack Score	Measure Value	Weights	Attack Value
Liklihood of Detection	16	16	16	16	1	44.1	0.00	0.33	
Liklihood of Success	21	21	21	21	1	57.7	0.00	0.33	0.00
Resources Required	10000000	10000000	50000	10000000	10000000	40050000	0.00	0.33	

One Bad Step		Attack Step Scores				Assume independent			
	1	2	3	4	5	Attack Score	Measure Value	Weights	Attack Value
Liklihood of Detection	16	1	1	1	1	18.1	0.00	0.33	
Liklihood of Success	21	1	1	1	1	23.1	0.00	0.33	0.00
Resources Required	50000	50000	10000000	50000	50000	10200000	0.00	0.33	

Mediocre Attack		Attack Step Scores				Assume independent			
	1	2	3	4	5	Attack Score	Measure Value	Weights	Attack Value
Liklihood of Detection	5	5	5	5	5	15.3	0.12	0.33	
Liklihood of Success	5	5	5	5	5	15.3	0.58	0.33	0.27
Resources Required	300000	300000	300000	300000	300000	1500000	0.094	0.33	

Figure 4. Constructed to Multiple Functions Value Function for Likelihood of Detection

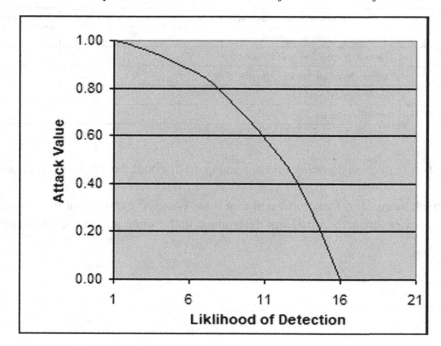

Figure 5. Constructed to Multiple Functions Value Function for Likelihood of Success

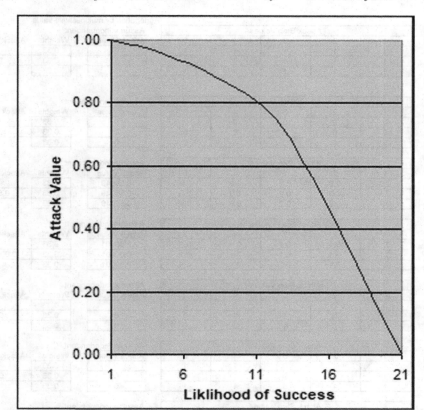

GROUP 2. VALUE THEN AGGREGATE

Multiplicative Value Function (Hard AND) (D)

As shown in Figure 6, this technique uses a multiplicative value function of the form: (4)

Here we use a special case of the multiplicative value function where the scaling constant K approaches infinity. This is known as a "Hard AND" relationship and simplifies to:

$$v(x) = \prod_{i=1}^{n} v(x_i) \tag{5}$$

where
   $v(x)$ is the value of the attack to the adversary
   $v(x_i)$ is the value of the ith attack step

Figure 6. Data for Multiplicative Hard AND

Perfect Attack	Attack Step Values					Aggegation by multiplicative value Assume independent			
	1	2	3	4	5	Attack Value	Weights	Attack Value	input
Liklihood of Detection	1	1	1	1	1	1	0.33		cell reference
Liklihood of Success	1	1	1	1	1	1	0.33	1	calculation
Resources Required	1	1	1	1	1	1	0.33		

Worst Attack	Attack Step Values					Assume independent		
	1	2	3	4	5	Attack Value	Weights	Attack Value
Liklihood of Detection	0	0	0	0	0	0	0.33	
Liklihood of Success	0	0	0	0	0	0	0.33	0
Resources Required	0	0	0	0	0	0	0.33	

Great Attack	Attack Step Values					Assume independent		
	1	2	3	4	5	Attack Value	Weights	Attack Value
Liklihood of Detection	0.9	0.9	0.9	0.9	0.9	0.59049	0.33	
Liklihood of Success	0.9	0.9	0.9	0.9	0.9	0.59049	0.33	0.59
Resources Required	0.9	0.9	0.9	0.9	0.9	0.59049	0.33	

Bad Attack	Attack Step Values					Assume independent		
	1	2	3	4	5	Attack Value	Weights	Attack Value
Liklihood of Detection	0.1	0.1	0.1	0.1	0.1	0.00001	0.33	
Liklihood of Success	0.1	0.1	0.1	0.1	0.1	0.00001	0.33	0.00001
Resources Required	0.1	0.1	0.1	0.1	0.1	0.00001	0.33	

One Good Step	Attack Step Values					Assume independent		
	1	2	3	4	5	Attack Value	Weights	Attack Value
Liklihood of Detection	0	0	1	0	0	0	0.33	
Liklihood of Success	0	0	1	0	0	0	0.33	0
Resources Required	0	0	1	0	0	0	0.33	

One Bad Step	Attack Step Values					Assume independent		
	1	2	3	4	5	Attack Value	Weights	Attack Value
Liklihood of Detection	1	1	0	1	1	0	0.33	
Liklihood of Success	1	1	0	1	1	0	0.33	0
Resources Required	1	1	0	1	1	0	0.33	

Mediocre Attack	Attack Step Values					Assume independent		
	1	2	3	4	5	Attack Value	Weights	Attack Value
Liklihood of Detection	0.5	0.5	0.5	0.5	0.5	0.03	0.33	
Liklihood of Success	0.5	0.5	0.5	0.5	0.5	0.03	0.33	0.03
Resources Required	0.5	0.5	0.5	0.5	0.5	0.03	0.33	

Multiplicative Value Function (Soft AND) (E)

As identified in Figure 7, this technique is another special case of the multiplicative value function shown above where the scaling constant *K* is variable based on the number of attack steps. This equation becomes:

$$v(x) = \frac{1}{2^N - 1}\left(\prod_{i=1}^{N}\left(1 + v(x_i)\right) - 1\right) \tag{6}$$

where

N is the number of attack steps
$v(x)$ is the value of the attack to the adversary
$v(x_i)$ is the value of the ith attack step

Figure 7. Data for Multiplicative Soft AND

Perfect Attack	Attack Step Values					Aggegation by Soft And Assume independent			
	1	2	3	4	5	Attack Value	Weights	Attack Value	input
Liklihood of Detection	1	1	1	1	1	1	0.33		cell reference
Liklihood of Success	1	1	1	1	1	1	0.33	1	calculation
Resources Required	1	1	1	1	1	1	0.33		

Worst Attack	Attack Step Values					Assume independent			
	1	2	3	4	5	Attack Value	Weights	Attack Value	
Liklihood of Detection	0	0	0	0	0	0	0.33		
Liklihood of Success	0	0	0	0	0	0	0.33	0	
Resources Required	0	0	0	0	0	0	0.33		

Great Attack	Attack Step Values					Assume independent			
	1	2	3	4	5	Attack Value	Weights	Attack Value	
Liklihood of Detection	0.9	0.9	0.9	0.9	0.9	0.77	0.33		
Liklihood of Success	0.9	0.9	0.9	0.9	0.9	0.77	0.33	0.77	
Resources Required	0.9	0.9	0.9	0.9	0.9	0.77	0.33		

Bad Attack	Attack Step Values					Assume independent			
	1	2	3	4	5	Attack Value	Weights	Attack Value	
Liklihood of Detection	0.1	0.1	0.1	0.1	0.1	0.02	0.33		
Liklihood of Success	0.1	0.1	0.1	0.1	0.1	0.02	0.33	0.02	
Resources Required	0.1	0.1	0.1	0.1	0.1	0.02	0.33		

One Good Step	Attack Step Values					Assume independent			
	1	2	3	4	5	Attack Value	Weights	Attack Value	
Liklihood of Detection	0	0	1	0	0	0.03	0.33		
Liklihood of Success	0	0	1	0	0	0.03	0.33	0.03	
Resources Required	0	0	1	0	0	0.03	0.33		

One Bad Step	Attack Step Values					Assume independent			
	1	2	3	4	5	Attack Value	Weights	Attack Value	
Liklihood of Detection	1	1	0	1	1	0.48	0.33		
Liklihood of Success	1	1	0	1	1	0.48	0.33	0.48	
Resources Required	1	1	0	1	1	0.48	0.33		

Mediocre Attack	Attack Step Values					Assume independent			
	1	2	3	4	5	Attack Value	Weights	Attack Value	
Liklihood of Detection	0.5	0.5	0.5	0.5	0.5	0.21	0.33		
Liklihood of Success	0.5	0.5	0.5	0.5	0.5	0.21	0.33	0.21	
Resources Required	0.5	0.5	0.5	0.5	0.5	0.21	0.33		

RESULTS

Each aggregation technique was tested using the seven scenarios in Table 1. We created a Microsoft Excel model to test the scenarios. An example of the Direct-Natural Scales technique for the "Perfect Attack" scenario is shown below in Figure 8.

The appendix includes the analysis of the five techniques for the seven scenarios. To explain the results, we need only compare four scenarios since these scenarios bound the problem. Insights from the other three are included below.

In the Figure 9 below, we compare the five aggregation techniques for each value measure for four scenarios: The Perfect Attack, the Great Attack, the Mediocre Attack and the Worst Attack. The Perfect and Worst Attacks all produced identical and desirable results. The interesting data is in the middle with the Great and Mediocre attacks.

Some general insights we learned from the analysis include:

- We consider the baseline (A) to be the "Direct, Natural" scale. Values approaching this scale are thought to be more accurate.

Figure 8. Example Direct-Natural Aggregation in Perfect Attack Scenario

Perfect Attack	Attack Step Scores					Aggegation by Probabilities and costs Assume independent		
	1	2	3	4	5	Attack Score	Measure Value	Weights
Liklihood of Detection	0	0	0	0	0	0	1	0.33
Liklihood of Success	1	1	1	1	1	1	1	0.33
Resources Required	0	0	0	0	0	0	1	0.33

Figure 9. All Aggregation Techniques for Four Bounding Scenarios

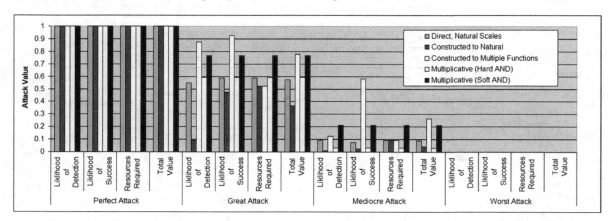

- The Constructed to Natural (B) scale produced significantly lower scores than the baseline. We used a value function and scales from a previous risk assessment. In this case, the closest level of Likelihood of Detection to our scenario goal of 0.9 value was the "Low" measure. This measure had a point estimate of the probability to be 0.75.

- The scales selected for the Constructed to Natural (B) technique (or any constructed technique in general) are very important to the results. Too few levels can greatly distort the attack values and can make differentiation among countermeasures very difficult.

- The Constructed to Multiple Functions (C) scales provided significantly higher scores than the baseline. It appears that the range of the scale used for this technique has a large impact on the resulting attack values.

- The "Hard AND" (D) technique gave results fairly consistent with the baseline. The Mediocre Scores are underestimated for this aggregation technique.

- The "Soft AND" (E) technique produced higher attack values than the baseline (A). It is more forgiving of one bad score and acts in a similar manner to a weighted average. Although not shown on the chart, the "Soft AND" was the only outlier for the "One Bad Step" scenario. All other aggregation techniques valued the attack near 0 while the soft AND gave a value of 0.48. We believe this to be a negative trait – it is too forgiving of the One Bad Step scenario.

- Constructed to Multiple Functions (C) and the Soft AND (E) techniques valued attacks significantly higher than the baseline (A) for the Great and Mediocre attacks.

- Cost data is less sensitive to the aggregation technique selected. Because of this, the focus of the following discussions will be only on the probabilistic values measures.

EVALUATION OF ALTERNATIVE AGGREGATION TECHNIQUES

In order to determine which aggregation technique to recommend, we need to identify the desirable attributes of the aggregation techniques and then evaluate each technique on the attributes. We believe that four good value measures for an aggregation technique would be:

- Closeness to a preferred, but currently intractable approach,
- Ease of modeling and data collection,
- Soundness of the theoretical basis and
- Ease of explanation to management.

1. **Direct, Natural Scales (A)** – This technique is considered the baseline. It is very easy to calculate using probability theory and is easily understood. However, credible probabilistic data for the probability of success, p(s) and likelihood of detection, p(d), value measures do not exist, so it is very hard to implement. This technique also requires adversary-based data, which means that data collection requirements increase n-fold where n is the number of adversaries.

2. **Constructed to Natural Scales (B)** – This technique compares poorly to the baseline. The technique is easier to implement than our baseline because of easier data collection. This technique is easy to explain. However, converting qualitative scales to probabilities cannot be validated.

3. **Constructed to Multiple Functions (C)** – This technique did not score near the baseline. It overstates attack values. The technique has four steps: develop constructed scale, convert constructed scale to numeric scale based on importance of the bins, operate on this scale with a damping function and operate on the damped scale with an exponential function. Each step requires judgment about the function parameters. The technique is not supported by theory. It is not easy to explain the results due to the three functions.

4. **Multiplicative Value Function (Hard AND) (D)** – This technique closely matched the baseline and is easy to implement. There is sound theory behind the technique, and it is easy to explain. As with any constructed scale, the number of levels is very important to accuracy. In practice, it appears to be easier to elicit adversary values for the levels of the measures than it is to elicit probabilities. Data collection requirements are simplified since this data is attack-based.

5. **Multiplicative Value Function (Soft AND) (E)** – This technique did not closely match the baseline. The technique overvalued attack values, though not as bad as the Constructed to Multiple Functions. It is more difficult to implement than the baseline and is not as easy to explain. There is a theoretical basis for the technique, but only if you agree with the technique's weights and assumptions. We have not found this function used in any project in the literature.

Table 4 qualitatively describes the results for each of the attack aggregation techniques and is transformed into value in Table 4. We used the four value measures introduced earlier in this section. The four value measures are weighted equally, and the value functions assume constant returns to scale. Under "Ease of Modeling", an aggregations technique could receive low scores for one of two reasons. First, the technique could have a difficult data collection requirement. The word "data" will appear in parenthesis in the chart. Second, the technique could have a complex mathematical formulation mak-

Table 4. Qualitative Scores of Aggregation Techniques

Technique	Value Measures			
	Close to Baseline	Ease of Modeling	Sound Theory	Ease to Explain
Direct Natural (A)	High	Low (data)	High	High
Constructed to Natural (B)	Medium	Medium	Medium	Medium
Constructed to Multiple Functions (C)	Low	Low (model)	Low	Low
Hard AND (D)	M-H	High	High	Medium
Soft AND (E)	Low	Low (model)	High	Medium

Table 5. Quantitative Assessment of Aggregation Techniques

Technique	Value Measures				Total
	Close to Baseline	Ease of Modeling	Sound Theory	Ease to Explain	
Direct Natural (A)	1	0	1	1	3
Constructed to Natural (B)	.5	.5	.5	.5	2
Constructed to Multiple Functions (C)	0	0	0	0	0
Hard AND (D)	.75	1	1	.5	3.25
Soft AND (E)	0	0	1	.5	1.5

ing the technique harder to model. The word "model" will appear in parenthesis in the chart. A total is shown in Table 5. The total is the sum of the values for each technique.

We have evaluated five attack step aggregation techniques using seven scenarios. We then used our insights from this analysis to evaluate the five aggregation techniques against the four criteria.

Based on this analysis, the following conclusions have been determined:

- Three aggregation techniques (Constructed to Natural (B), Constructed to Multiple Functions (C) and Soft AND (E)) are dominated. Regardless of the weights or the value functions, the Hard AND (D) aggregation technique dominates these three since its Total Value will <u>always</u> be higher.
- The Direct, Natural Scales (A) dominated the Constructed to Multiple Functions (C) and the Soft AND (E).
- The Hard AND (D) technique has a simplified data collection process and performs well compared the baseline aggregation technique (Direct Natural) (A).
- Preference for the Direct, Natural Scales (A) or Hard AND (D) depends on the weights and value functions assigned to the four value measures.
- Cost data is less sensitive to the aggregation technique.

CONCLUSION

Managing risk in order to achieve an appropriate balance between various system costs and mission risk has become one of the main CyberAssurance challenges in the design of complex network systems. Rather than analyze the impact of a small number of design changes, system designers must consider the broad range of cybersecurity design alternatives so they can optimize their design choices based on trades between risk and operational parameters.

The relevant attributes for adaptive security and CyberAssurance for risk-based decision-making will depend on the system(s) and its mission(s), but we expect they will include overall lifecycle costs of the various cybersecurity protections, as well as their impact on performance and usability. Similarly, the nature of the optimization problems will vary from system to system. In general, we expect the system owner will want either to reduce risk as much as possible subject to cost, performance and usability constraints, or to reduce risk below a certain threshold while minimizing some combination of the other attributes. In other cases, where the customer does not have a pre-defined objective, this process could be used to support a multi-attribute utility theory optimization over all the attributes of interest. In all these cases the fact that the risk-based decision-making produces the expression of the entire design space in a single, one-time process enables analysts and risk managers to explore it completely without iterating the entire process.

Future research in this area will need to be applied using this concept to a number of systems to develop a better understanding of the useful parameters and optimization problems. We would also like to examine different methods for solving these optimization problems. In our analysis to date we have implicitly adopted steepest descent techniques. One approach was to identify which family of information assurance functions in our taxonomy had the most impact in terms of risk reduction, increase the strength of protection for the instances in that family and then repeat the process on the remaining families of functions in the taxonomy. Since the exploration method is so coarse and limited, it will almost certainly fail to yield an optimal solution.

For the risk-based decision-making to be widely adopted, it is also important to develop more effective methods for generating inputs to the methodology. In particular, it would be highly desirable to create a reusable repository of scores for attack-step-protection pairs that system engineers and architects could use. Over time it would be advantageous to supplement the SME knowledge in the repository with empirical data regarding the operational characteristics of the various attack steps and the measures of effectiveness with which the various protections defend against the attack steps. Techniques for collecting this empirical data and for updating the scores in the repository would be quite useful.

CyberAssurance for risk-based decision-making is a general, quantitative, risk analysis methodology that efficiently expresses the complete design space, thereby making it possible for system engineers and architects to search the design space quickly to find desirable design alternatives for their systems. By using the notion of attack-step-protection pairs that can be scored independently of one another and of their positions in the system attack trees, the methodology ensures reusability for the most labor-intensive aspects of attack tree-based risk assessment. This makes it possible for system engineers and architects to assess the risk associated with broad portions of the system design space, thus ensuring intelligent trades between security and other critical system attributes. There are other benefits to the process in addition to efficient search of the design space. The methodology supports greater consistency of scoring since the analyst can reuse attack-step-protection pairs across the trees. This reduces the risk of scoring drift, in which new attack steps introduced late in the analysis are accidentally scored differently from a similar attack step that was introduced earlier.

More generally, the CyberAssurance eliminates large components of analyst bias, making it far more likely that they will identify effective but non-intuitive combinations of cybersecurity protections. The ability to identify unexpected, promising design combinations means that the value of risk assessment extends beyond providing a thorough verification of preexisting intuition. Most importantly, the efficiency and flexibility of CyberAssurance helps analysts in their most important challenge: to connect the risk assessment to the specific requests of the decision makers.

Finally, the techniques employed throughout this book suggest very strongly that the CyberAssurance can be integrated into an automated process for design optimization. The prospect that system designers may someday be able to optimize their design in terms of quantitative risk-cost trades is truly exciting. However, there is a great deal of work that must be done to achieve this goal. We must learn what attributes to include in these trades and we must identify possible formulations for the optimization problem and the appropriate situations in which to apply each formulation. It may also be necessary to develop new optimization methods tuned to this class of cyber problems.

REFERENCES

Boranbayev, S., Amrenov, A., Nurusheva, A., Boranbayev, A., & Goranin, N. (2022, March). Methods and Techniques of Information Security Risk Management During Assessment of Information Systems. In *Future of Information and Communication Conference* (pp. 787-797). Springer, Cham. 10.1007/978-3-030-98015-3_53

Hopkin, P. (2018). *Fundamentals of risk management: understanding, evaluating and implementing effective risk management*. Kogan Page Publishers.

Hubbard, D. W. (2020). *The failure of risk management: Why it's broken and how to fix it*. John Wiley & Sons. doi:10.1002/9781119521914

ENDNOTES

1   https://en.wikipedia.org/wiki/Halo_(franchise)
2   https://www.smithsonianmag.com/science-nature/fibonacci-sequ
     ence-stock-market-180974487/

Compilation of References

Abbas, A. E. (2003, March). An entropy approach for utility assignment in decision analysis. In. AIP Conference Proceedings (Vol. 659, pp. 328–338). American Institute of Physics. doi:10.1063/1.1570550

Abeysekara, P., Dong, H., & Qin, A. K. (2019, July). Machine learning-driven trust prediction for mec-based iot services. In *2019 IEEE International Conference on Web Services (ICWS)* (pp. 188-192). IEEE. 10.1109/ICWS.2019.00040

Belton, V., & Stewart, T. J. (2002). Value function methods: Practical basics. In *Multiple Criteria Decision Analysis* (pp. 119–161). Springer. doi:10.1007/978-1-4615-1495-4_5

Boranbayev, S., Amrenov, A., Nurusheva, A., Boranbayev, A., & Goranin, N. (2022, March). Methods and Techniques of Information Security Risk Management During Assessment of Information Systems. In *Future of Information and Communication Conference* (pp. 787-797). Springer, Cham. 10.1007/978-3-030-98015-3_53

Bordis, T., Runge, T., Schultz, D., & Schaefer, I. (2022). Family-based and product-based development of correct-by-construction software product lines. *Journal of Computer Languages*, 101119.

Brooks, T. (2020). An internet control device embedded sensor agent. *International Journal of Internet of Things and Cyber-Assurance*, *1*(3-4), 267–290. doi:10.1504/IJITCA.2020.112534

Brooks, T. T. (Ed.). (2017). *Cyber-assurance for the Internet of Things*. John Wiley & Sons.

Brooks, T. T., & Park, J. (2016). *Cyber-Assurance Through Embedded Security for the Internet of Things*. John Wiley & Sons. *Ltd*, *2*, 101–127.

Cao, K., Liu, Y., Meng, G., & Sun, Q. (2020). An overview on edge computing research. *IEEE Access: Practical Innovations, Open Solutions*, *8*, 85714–85728. doi:10.1109/ACCESS.2020.2991734

Chysi, A., Nikolopoulos, S. D., & Polenakis, I. (2022). Detection and classification of malicious software utilizing Max-Flows between system-call groups. Journal of Computer Virology and Hacking Techniques, 1-27.

Dell'Ovo, M., & Oppio, A. (2018). Combining social and technical instances within design processes: a Value-Focused Thinking approach. In *the 87th Meeting of the European Working Group on Multicriteria Decision Aiding* (pp. 7-7).

Du, Y. M., Ma, Y. H., Wei, Y. F., Guan, X., & Sun, C. P. (2020). Maximum entropy approach to reliability. *Physical Review. E*, *101*(1), 012106. doi:10.1103/PhysRevE.101.012106 PMID:32069657

Farroha, B. S., & Farroha, D. L. (2014, October). *A framework for managing mission needs, compliance, and trust in the DevOps environment. In 2014 IEEE Military Communications Conference*. IEEE.

Greven, A., Keller, G., & Warnecke, G. (Eds.). (2014). *Entropy* (Vol. 47). Princeton University Press.

Hopkin, P. (2018). *Fundamentals of risk management: understanding, evaluating and implementing effective risk management*. Kogan Page Publishers.

Hu, Y. C., Patel, M., Sabella, D., Sprecher, N., & Young, V. (2015). Mobile edge computing—A key technology towards 5G. *ETSI white paper*, *11*(11), 1-16.

Hubbard, D. W. (2020). *The failure of risk management: Why it's broken and how to fix it*. John Wiley & Sons. doi:10.1002/9781119521914

Huskaj, G., Iftimie, I. A., & Wilson, R. L. (2020, June). Designing attack infrastructure for offensive cyberspace operations. In *European Conference on Information Warfare and Security*, ECCWS (pp. 473-482).

Kang, M. H., Moore, A. P., & Moskowitz, I. S. (1997, August). Design and assurance strategy for the NRL pump. In *Proceedings 1997 High-Assurance Engineering Workshop* (pp. 64-71). IEEE. 10.1109/HASE.1997.648040

Keeney, R. L., & McDaniels, T. L. (1992). Value-focused thinking about strategic decisions at BC Hydro. *Interfaces*, *22*(6), 94–109. doi:10.1287/inte.22.6.94

Keeney, R. L., Raiffa, H., & Meyer, R. F. (1993). *Decisions with multiple objectives: preferences and value trade-offs*. Cambridge university press. doi:10.1017/CBO9781139174084

Leitmann, G. (2013). *The calculus of variations and optimal control: an introduction* (Vol. 24). Springer Science & Business Media.

Li, H., Ota, K., & Dong, M. (2018). Learning IoT in edge: Deep learning for the Internet of Things with edge computing. *IEEE Network*, *32*(1), 96–101. doi:10.1109/MNET.2018.1700202

Luenberger, D. G. (1984). *Linear and Nonlinear Programming* (2nd ed.). Addison-Wesley Publishing Company Inc.

Luenberger, D. G., & Ye, Y. (1984). *Linear and nonlinear programming* (Vol. 2). Addison-wesley.

Ma, Q. (2022, February). Design of High-Confidence Embedded Operating System based on Artificial Intelligence and Smart Chips. In *2022 Second International Conference on Artificial Intelligence and Smart Energy (ICAIS) (pp. 58-62)*. IEEE. 10.1109/ICAIS53314.2022.9742917

Matheu-García, S. N., Hernández-Ramos, J. L., Skarmeta, A. F., & Baldini, G. (2019). Risk-based automated assessment and testing for the cybersecurity certification and labelling of IoT devices. *Computer Standards & Interfaces*, *62*, 64–83. doi:10.1016/j.csi.2018.08.003

Necula, G. C. (1997, January). Proof-carrying code. In *Proceedings of the 24th ACM SIGPLAN-SIGACT symposium on Principles of programming languages* (pp. 106-119).

Olson, D. L., & Dorai, V. K. (1992). Implementation of the centroid method of Solymosi and Dombi. *European Journal of Operational Research*, *60*(1), 117–129. doi:10.1016/0377-2217(92)90339-B

Parnell, G. S., Terry Bresnick, M. B. A., Tani, S. N., & Johnson, E. R. (2013). *Handbook of decision analysis*. John Wiley & Sons. doi:10.1002/9781118515853

Pöyhönen, M., & Hämäläinen, R. P. (2001). On the convergence of multiattribute weighting methods. *European Journal of Operational Research*, *129*(3), 569–585. doi:10.1016/S0377-2217(99)00467-1

Rao, S. S. (1979). *Optimization (Theory and Applications)*. Wiley Eastern Limited.

Rao, S. S. (2019). *Engineering optimization: theory and practice*. John Wiley & Sons. doi:10.1002/9781119454816

Runge, T., Potanin, A., Thüm, T., & Schaefer, I. (2022). Traits for Correct-by-Construction Programming. *arXiv preprint arXiv*:2204.05644.

Russinoff, D. M. (2022). *Formal Verification of Floating-Point Hardware Design*. Springer. doi, 10, 978-3.

Seaver, D. A., Von Winterfeldt, D., & Edwards, W. (1978). Eliciting subjective probability distributions on continuous variables. *Organizational Behavior and Human Performance, 21*(3), 379–391. doi:10.1016/0030-5073(78)90061-2

Solymosi, T., & Dombi, J. (1986). A method for determining the weights of criteria: The centralized weights. *European Journal of Operational Research, 26*(1), 35–41. doi:10.1016/0377-2217(86)90157-8

Squartini, T., & Garlaschelli, D. (2017). *Maximum-Entropy Networks: Pattern Detection, Network Reconstruction and Graph Combinatorics*. Springer. doi:10.1007/978-3-319-69438-2

Staff, U. J. (1998). *Joint doctrine for information operations* [Joint publication 3-13]. Department of Defense.

Tran, T. X., Hajisami, A., Pandey, P., & Pompili, D. (2017). Collaborative mobile edge computing in 5G networks: New paradigms, scenarios, and challenges. *IEEE Communications Magazine, 55*(4), 54–61. doi:10.1109/MCOM.2017.1600863

Tsui, F., Karam, O., & Bernal, B. (2022). *Essentials of software engineering*. Jones & Bartlett Learning.

Wall, E. S., Rinaudo, C. H., & Salter, R. C. (2022). Comparing Weighting Strategies for SME-Based Manufacturability Assessment Scoring. In *Recent Trends and Advances in Model Based Systems Engineering* (pp. 485–492). Springer. doi:10.1007/978-3-030-82083-1_41

Wang, X., Wang, J., Xu, Y., Chen, J., Jia, L., Liu, X., & Yang, Y. (2020). Dynamic spectrum anti-jamming communications: Challenges and opportunities. *IEEE Communications Magazine, 58*(2), 79–85. doi:10.1109/MCOM.001.1900530

Wardle, P. (2022). *The Art of Mac Malware: The Guide to Analyzing Malicious Software*. No Starch Press.

Watson, S. R., Buede, D. M., & Buede, D. M. (1987). *Decision synthesis: The principles and practice of decision analysis*. Cambridge University Press.

Weyns, D. (2020). *An Introduction to Self-adaptive Systems: A Contemporary Software Engineering Perspective*. John Wiley & Sons.

Wu, C. H. J., & Irwin, J. D. (2016). *Introduction to computer networks and cybersecurity*. CRC Press. doi:10.1201/9781466572140

Wu, N. (2012). *The maximum entropy method* (Vol. 32). Springer Science & Business Media.

Yang, J. B., & Sen, P. (1996). Preference modelling by estimating local utility functions for multiobjective optimization. *European Journal of Operational Research, 95*(1), 115–138. doi:10.1016/0377-2217(96)00300-1

About the Author

Tyson Brooks is an adjunct professor in the School of Information Studies (iSchool) at Syracuse University. Dr. Brooks has over 25 years of professional experience in the engineering design, architecture, and information security of complex information systems in the U.S. and overseas. Dr. Brooks's expertise includes work in the areas of information assurance, cyber-security, penetration testing, and network-based intrusion analysis and defense in both the public and private sector. Dr. Brooks published his first book on the concept of 'Cyber-Assurance for the Internet of Things' in 2017. He was the past Editor-in-Chief of the International Journal of Internet of Things and Cyber-Assurance (IJITCA) and is an Associate Editor for IEEE Access. Dr. Brooks is also a Senior Member of IEEE and the Association of Computing Machinery (ACM).

Index

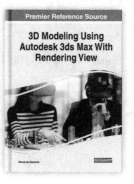

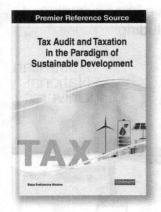

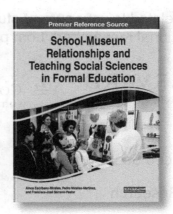
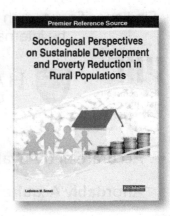

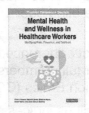

Printed in the United States
by Baker & Taylor Publisher Services

Printed in the United States
by Baker & Taylor Publisher Services